. . . .

BREAKING THE CYCLES OF HATRED

BREAKING THE CYCLES

MARTHA MINOW

INTRODUCED AND WITH COMMENTARIES EDITED BY
NANCY L. ROSENBLUM

PRINCETON UNIVERSITY PRESS

Princeton and Oxford

OF HATRED

Memory,
. . . .
Law,
. . . .
and Repair

Copyright © 2002 by Princeton University Press
Published by Princeton University Press, 41 William Street, Princeton,
New Jersey 08540
In the United Kingdom: Princeton University Press, 3 Market Place,
Woodstock, Oxfordshire OX20 1SY
All Rights Reserved

Library of Congress Cataloging-in-Publication Data

Minow, Martha, 1954–
Breaking the cycles of hatred : memory, law, and repair / by Martha
Minow ; edited by Nancy L. Rosenblum.
p. cm.
Includes bibliographical references and index.
ISBN 0-691-09662-7 (cl. : alk. paper) — ISBN 0-691-09663-5 (pbk. :
alk. paper)
1. Hate crimes.   2. Violence (Law)   3. Reparation.   4. Law
reform.   I. Rosenblum, Nancy L., 1947–   II. Title.

K5301 .M56   2002
364.1—dc21   2002024310

British Library Cataloging-in-Publication Data is available

This book has been composed in Garamond Light and Helvetica

Printed on acid-free paper. ∞

www.pupress.princeton.edu

Printed in the United States of America

10   9   8   7   6   5   4   3   2   1

CONTENTS

. . . .

ACKNOWLEDGMENTS

In the fall of 1999, Martha Minow delivered the Gilbane Fund Lectures at Brown University. A symposium on *Breaking the Cycles of Hatred: Memory, Law and Repair* followed with papers by the authors in this volume and others. Thanks go to the Gilbane Family of Rhode Island, benefactors to Brown University and sponsors of the Gilbane Fund Lectures and to Paul Choquette who served as liaison. Christine Kearney, now on the faculty at the University of Oregon, was program coordinator, and I thank her for her contributions to the success of the event.

Nancy L. Rosenblum

BREAKING THE CYCLES OF HATRED

Memory, Law, and Repair

NANCY L. ROSENBLUM

> You ask me to renew
> A grief so desperate that the very thought
> Of speaking of it tears my heart in two.
>
> But if my words may be a seed that bears
> The fruit of infamy for him I gnaw,
> I shall weep, but tell my story through my tears.
>
> —COUNT UGOLINO IN DANTE,
> *The Inferno*, Canto XXXIII

Every injustice arouses anger, or should. A capacity to understand and feel injustice is the mark of moral maturity; a taste for oppression is the mark of moral deformation. "To have no idea of what it means to be treated unjustly is to have no moral knowledge, no moral life."[1] But of the many faces of injustice, violent hatred stands out. These crimes betray exceptional viciousness and inflict exceptional pain. They evoke especially strong feelings because they exhibit none of the randomness or misfortune of many forms of injury. The intent to terrorize, injure, and degrade is intensely personal. The perpetrator believes the individual deserves to suffer, even though the reason for inflicting suffering is not always tied to the victim's own acts but often to his or her group membership or some ascriptive trait. The deliberate cruelty of the attack is unmistakable. As a result, the injuries suffered on account of one's color or ethnicity, sex or sexual orientation provoke enduring bitterness. The response of victims of hateful violence is a particularly deep resentment—a moral anger. Victims want more than to hold the perpetrators responsible; they want to cause them and their supporters suffering in turn. An unruly longing for revenge is validated by the vindictiveness of the crime. Certain crimes usher in that destructive dynamic: a cycle of hatred.

In *Breaking the Cycles of Hatred: Memory, Law, and Repair*, Martha Minow and the other authors of these essays bring within one compass the universe of hatred and violence—from mass atrocities to local hate crimes to domestic violence.

No subject is grimmer or more morally compelling than crimes of hate. They stand out among acts of injustice. Their viciousness instills horror. They are extraordinary, not ordinary crimes. But this does not mean that they are rare. The darkest, most dehumanizing human actions, from genoicide to child abuse, are recurrent. Hate crimes and group-based violence and domestic cruelty are elements of everyday life for many people. There are innumerable perpetrators and victims. Their experience is captured best in memoirs and fiction; it takes eloquence and literary imagination to make these crimes vivid. But their experience is also available to us in sketchy form in almost daily news reports, if only we pay attention.

Martha Minow delivered the Gilbane Fund Lectures at Brown University in 1999. I introduced each lecture by reading from a *New York Times* story from that week. There was an unceasing string of stories. I had no difficulty finding awful, timely introductions to the lecture themes.

To introduce "Memory and Hate: Are There Lessons from Around the World?," this report from Bazarak, Afghanistan:[2]

> Those who only had their houses burned or crops destroyed often apologize because their story is not bad enough. They are sheepish about complaining.
>
> And so they lead the way to the worse off, the irretrievably broken or unbearably sorrowful—the children of parents who were killed as they watched or the men whose wives were carried off screaming or the old woman whose story no one is sure of, but she has been sobbing for two months now, fingering a red flower embroidered on a pink cloth.
>
> Afghanistan's ruling Taliban militia, along with thousands of Pakistanis lit with the fervor of jihad, went on a destructive spree this summer, killing wantonly, emptying entire towns, machine-gunning livestock, sawing down fruit trees, blasting apart irrigation canals. It was a binge of blood lust and mayhem described in consistent detail by witnesses.

To introduce "Regulating Hatred: Whose Speech, Whose Crimes, Whose Power?" I read from a report about empaneling a jury in Wyoming for the trial of Russell Henderson, the young man charged with torturing Matthew Shepard, a gay University of Wyoming student, and leaving him to die tied to a fence in a winter field.[3]

And to introduce "Between Nations and Between Intimates: Can Law Stop the Violence?" there was the article on parents whose children had been shot at school by a classmate who went on to kill himself. This is a story of violence by and against children. It is also about the pain of survivors. Without a criminal trial, the families had no official forum in which to tell their story, and there was no one to hold directly accountable. The victims' parents brought a civil suit against the killer's parents, their neighbors, thinking that something at home—some family failure, some intimate horror—must have caused the hatred, and looking to hold the parents responsible. "I prayed and prayed and I've forgiven them," one father says. "But I still have medical bills to pay and it was their kids who did this. Forgiveness doesn't mean there aren't consequences."[4]

The wanton Taliban destruction, the torturous murder of Matthew Shepard, and the terrifying school shootings are not isolated events. They are moments in cycles of hatred. Each is part of an identifiable social history or life history of conflict and revenge that does not end with the latest round. We see the cycle of hatred at work at every level of violence. It is a factor in intergroup violence. It stokes bias crimes. Perpetrators of domestic violence and sexual abuse were often victims themselves, who experienced as children the dehumanization they inflict in turn. Crimes of hate have a past; sadly, they have a future, too, as each contributes to the climate of demonization and the desire for revenge. Perpetrators become victims; victims avengers. The cycle extends across generations. It can appear to be almost a force of nature. There is a seemingly implacable logic to anger and vengeance that is barely interrupted by revulsion at violent death, by attempts at forgiveness, or by sheer exhaustion. We can be brought to despair by doomed efforts to find a response adequate to break the cycle; Milton gave voice to this despair in *Paradise Lost* (IV): "Reconciliation is now a fallacious dream."

This volume is distinguished by our effort, set in motion by Martha Minow's essays, to consider the universe of hatred and violence—between racial, ethnic, and religious groups and within families, between intimates and strangers. In many respects, "ethnic cleansing," forced disappearances, hate speech, wife beating, and child abuse are radically dissimilar. Responses to them appear to have little in common. These acts of violence arise in different social and institutional contexts, and the justice sought for mass crimes plainly differs from criminal prosecution of domestic abuse. Each type of crime has generated its own exhaustive literature. Interethnic conflict and intrafamily violence are not commonly viewed together.

Here, we bring a wide range of aggression and suffering together within the framework of cycles of hatred. Our essays employ history, psychology, social science, and law to reflect on three themes. One is the double-edged role of memory: memory fuels cycles of hatred but it is also essential to personal integrity and for bearing witness to injustice. The strengths and limitations of formal legal proceedings against perpetrators of violence, including their adequacy in the eyes of victims, is a second theme. We discuss the relationship between law and repair, and we survey the range of actual and proposed alternative responses—truth commissions and reparations, public apologies, memorials and commemorations, educational programs, the collective efforts of private organizations and voluntary associations, and the beneficent acts of individuals. Our third theme is what characteristics are shared by crimes motivated by hate, and whether responses from one sphere can be useful in others.

Memory, Law, and Repair

In the overview that follows I separate out the theme of memory from the theme of law and repair. This analytic division is useful for the purpose of introduction but it is unfaithful to both the richness of these essays and to the real inseparability of the themes. For memory of hateful violence and responses to it stand in dynamic relation to one another. The influence of one on the other is mutual, and operates in both directions.

Memories are created and fluid, not fixed and given. The choice is rarely between memory and oblivion but among shifting and competing remembrances. The social structures and institutions within which we tell and hear accounts of hatred and violence affect what we recall and record. The grievances that spur us to action and that become resources for expressing and correcting injustice are given name and character in specific social contexts. Public and private settings, among them religious groups, political associations, and courts, are not just arenas in which memory is expressed; they are formative. They play a part in constituting what we recall and how, defining what is a salient fact, what counts as an injury, what comprises legal and historical evidence.

The dynamic interaction between memory and response works in the opposite direction, too. What we remember and feel compelled to relate

affects our judgment of existing structures of public witnessing and recollection, our judgment of the adequacy of public responses to hateful
violence. The experience of injustice and our explanations of it influence
our expectations about what constitutes justice. We try, where possible,
to conform these experiences to established institutional definitions of
injury and crime, to formal notions of criminal responsibility, and to rules
of evidence. When that is impossible, we try to reform legal requirements. We design new collective responses and institutional innovations
to cope with these memories of the experience of injustice.

Experience and memory belong to individuals, and at some level they
are incommunicable. But once hate crimes are brought into public view,
neither remembrance nor understanding is purely personal. Together,
we construct (sometimes conflicting) accounts of injustice and theories
of responsibility. The process is one of constant reciprocal interaction
between memory and law and repair. Thus the truth of Minow's observation in "Memory and Hate," "We each may not have control over what
we come to remember, but we each can play a role in shaping what we
work to recall." The dynamic of memory, law, and repair occurs at every
level of hateful violence and is at the heart of the essays in this volume. I
will introduce them by sorting out three main themes.

MEMORY

One theme is memory. More specifically the moral psychology of remembrance and its role in sustaining or interrupting cycles of hatred.
When is forgetting fatal—an obstacle to personal sanity? What sort of
public remembrances and commemorations are aids to repairing community and comforting survivors? And on the other side, when is remembrance fatal—an obstacle to reconciliation and repair? We may
want to temper memory enough to permit reconciliation between war-
ring groups who must emerge from violence to share a society and a
government. But we are less certain that we want a battered woman to
repress recollections of the fury directed against her—if she does, she
may be unwilling to serve as witness against her aggressor and may be
willingly reunited with her violent partner.

Martha Minow writes in her first essay in chapter 1, "How those who
survive understand and remember what happened can have real consequences for the chances of renewed violence." One of her themes is the
twin perils of memory: the consequences of memory are equally per-
ilous when it leads to vengeance and when it is expected to lead to

saintly forgiveness. Minow points out that memory is collective and public as well as personal and individual, and points out the many ways in which public forms of remembrance—from the testimony produced and preserved in trial records to public education and ceremonial commemoration—can correct error, offer neglected perspectives on events, and move people toward reconciliation.

In "Collective Memory, Collective Action, and Black Activism in the 1960s" Fredrick Harris examines the connection between collective memory and political participation. Harris argues that social theory overlooks the "micro-resources" of mobilization, chief among them narratives of past injustices. He demonstrates the independent influence of collective memories among African Americans bound up with four events: the Scottsboro trial, the *Brown* decision by the U.S. Supreme Court, the Emmett Till murder, and the Montgomery bus boycott. These memories and the retellings they inspire have been crucial resources for both electoral and protest activity by blacks in the South and nationwide.

Ross Cheit and Carey Jaros discuss memory in the context of legal redress for victims of child sexual abuse. In "Beyond Memory: Child Sexual Abuse and the Statute of Limitations," they consider two obstacles to criminal and civil remedies that prevent children from taking action and from serving as reliable witnesses against the perpetrators. One is the possibility of "repressed memory" recovered only long after the event; the other, more common, is cognitive distortions rooted in the victim's shame, fear, and confusion.

The use individuals put memories to—the stories they tell themselves and others about the violence they inflict or endure—is the subject of Austin Sarat's essay "When Memory Speaks: Remembrance and Revenge in *Unforgiven*." Using the film as a template, Sarat shows that memory of a hateful crime can be mythologized and used to stoke dreams of noble causes and heroic revenge. But for those who focus on the grim finality and universality of death, and are thus able to separate death from desert, the memory of violence can be a force for self-restraint. Not all ghosts demand bloody vengeance.

LAW AND REPAIR

Our book's second overarching theme is public responses to violence that work to break the cycles of hate. As Minow observes, contemporary moral and political life is distinguished less by its crimes, ghastly as they are and perpetrated as they are on a massive scale, than by our efforts to respond to them. Great evils past and present, even the most demonic, are nothing new. But "waves of objections and calls for collective responses" *are* new—widespread efforts to unsettle fatalistic views of cycles of hatred and complacent views of the adequacy of existing legal institutions to deal with iniquity. There are official and unofficial efforts to expose the ways in which even fair proceedings thwart victims' search for justice and inhibit the possibilities for personal and collective repair. As Minow poses the question in "Memory and Hate," "Can collective efforts create armatures for pain and structure paths for individuals to move from grief and pain to renewal and hope?"

Many of these essays underscore Minow's conclusion that despite the limitations of criminal trials as a response to hateful violence, inaction is worse. Hate-motivated violence poses distinctive challenges to institutions of justice, and the authors propose legal reforms and innovations, including new legal venues and new remedies for the victims of crimes of hate. There have been, and remain, important gaps in the law when it comes to violence. One development has been the designation of crimes such as sexual enslavement as a war crime, and the empaneling of international and national tribunals to prosecute them. In domestic law the special designation of an act as a "hate crime" is designed to acknowledge the distinctive harms inflicted when unlawful actions are motivated by the desire to injure people on account of their color or ethnic group or sexual orientation. Certain injuries became legally cognizable crimes only recently—marital rape, for example. Judith Lewis Herman reminds us that marital rape, battering, stalking, and sexual harassment are all recent terms made familiar by the women's movement to describe calculated harms to women.

When we think of the cycle of hatred, we think first of intergroup violence, of genocide and crimes against humanity. Minow's first essay, "Memory and Hate: Are There Lessons from Around the World?" focuses on developments over the past fifty years in the theory and practice of international criminal prosecution of perpetrators of mass violence. Punishment is only one, and perhaps not the most important outcome of these tribunals, and Minow emphasizes the additional moral and political benefits of public proceedings: the production of official records, the publicizing of crimes, and the public acknowledgment of their utter wrongfulness. Sensitive to the limitations of formal judicial proceedings, Minow explores the contributions of nonlegal responses to crimes of hateful violence: truth commissions get the most attention in her piece but also reparations and the actions of nongovernmental agencies dedicated to assisting victims and seeking reconciliation.

Two essays are concerned with reparations as a response to cycles of hatred among groups. In "Righting Old Wrongs," Marc Galanter examines the justifications for reparations and the difficulty of settling on appropriate distributions. Reparation to the Maori for the unjust taking of lands in New Zealand took the form of returning territory, for example. This illustrates that "remedial justice inevitably disturbs existing expectations" and imposes real costs. That is one reason why, in many cases, justice has to be rationed, Galanter advises, and why compensation is often token or symbolic. He offers a sophisticated, analytic matrix for assessing remedies for old wrongs with categories for the contours of the wrong, of wrongdoers and their surrogates, of victims and claimants.

Eric K. Yamamoto provides the further caution that, like any form of justice, reparations must be consistent and fair. In "Reluctant Redress," he draws attention to the little-known fact that legislation mandating U.S. government compensation to Japanese Americans did not extend to Japanese Latin Americans, on grounds that they were neither American citizens nor legal residents but rather illegal aliens. Yet these people were kidnapped from their homes, transported to the United States in military ships, imprisoned in internment camps during the war, and often refused the right to return to their homes and families—solely on account of their race. Denied official reparations, these victims were forced to pursue compensation by means of a class action suit against the U.S. government. Yamamoto asks whether the patent *realpolitik* of the government's grudging, unapologetic settlement did as much to perpetuate the cycle of hatred ("empty gestures," "compromise injustice") as to interrupt it.

Another area of legal development concerns laws against domestic hate crimes and their prosecution. These crimes arouse anger, alarm, and resentment; they create fear, silencing and intimidating victims; ultimately, they may cause victims to internalize the message of inferiority, damaging self-esteem. Moreover, hate crimes are more likely to provoke a retaliatory response, a cycle of hatred, than similar actions that do not involve intentional selection of a victim on account of some ascriptive trait or group affiliation.

Minow's second essay, "Regulating Hatred: Whose Speech, Whose Crimes, Whose Power?" focuses on this subject. Crimes against individuals as members of a despised group are bad in themselves, she argues; beyond that, they contribute to the climate of hate that permits mass atrocities. Minow provides a nuanced discussion of hate speech in particular, reflecting on both the harms hate speech produces and the potentially harmful consequences of regulation and selective enforcement.

In "Memory, Hate, and the Criminalization of Bias-Motivated Violence," Frederick M. Lawrence discusses dramatic legal changes in American and British bias crime law. One rationale for the special designation of crimes as hate crimes and of enhanced penalties is the thought that bias-inspired conduct inflicts greater harm on individuals. That said, the definition of hate crime and the designation of protected groups vary according to social context, and in Britain the impetus has been the rapid growth of a multicultural society. Lawrence's essay demonstrates the importance of comparative studies, and how developments in one society can become a model for responses in others.

Judith Lewis Herman in "Peace on Earth Begins at Home: Reflections from the Women's Liberation Movement" and Minow in her third essay, "Between Nations and Between Intimates: Can Law Stop the Violence?" assess legal developments in the area of domestic violence. Among these are restraining orders and judicial rulings that order men to vacate premises and do not constitute an impermissible violation of property rights. They both caution that legal recognition of the oppression of women and children has come slowly, and that even in the United States "Crimes of violence against women are still, for the most part, crimes of impunity." Minow explains: "Society makes it clear that the costs of using violence in the home are low; social controls like police intervention are ineffective; the household is typically secluded from view; many adults think there are circumstances when a man can hit his wife and most adults think young people need 'strong' discipline." Herman emphasizes the relative economic and physical powerlessness of women and children subjected to intimate violence, and prescribes institutional supports for victims of domestic abuse that would enhance their safety, demonstrate social support, and improve the likelihood that they will seek justice.

Cheit and Jaros propose criminal and tort law reform in cases of child sexual abuse. One feature of this form of violence is the secrecy that surrounds the crime, which most often occurs within families and is sustained by threats, keeping victims intensely isolated. Another is the problem of memory and comprehension that plague young victims. Finally, there is the seriousness of the violence, which produces lifelong harms. All militate in favor of exceptions to statutes of limitations in state law that would allow victims to seek justice when they reach adulthood.

In "Justice and the Experience of Injustice," I bring together the range of hateful violence and argue that in every case there is a potential disjuncture between the public requirements of justice and the victims' experience of injustice. From the point of view of legal proceedings and due process for the accused, justice does not always correspond to, indeed is often in conflict with, the victims' sense of what is owed them and what conditions are necessary for repair. The conflict—and the tension it generates—pulls in the opposite direction as well: responding adequately to victims may conflict with wider societal needs for fairness and formal justice. I survey the strengths and limitations of responses to hateful violence from the perspective of victims. The common element of any adequate response, I argue, is to listen to survivors' accounts of injustice. The injured must have an opportunity to make their stories public, even if the justice meted out to perpetrators does not, in the end, fully satisfy them. The disjuncture between the outcome of fair trials and the relief awarded victims supports the search for other ways to recognize, relieve, and commemorate their suffering.

The Universe of Hateful Violence: Common Elements

These essays explore the value of reflecting on intergroup atrocities, hate crimes and hate speech, and domestic abuse as aspects of a whole. Of course, acts of hateful violence often accompany one another in practice. As Minow points out, societies with chronic intergroup violence also experience increased family violence. And violence and humiliation in the home prepare people to debase and harm others. The parallels we draw provide insight into common elements of cycles of hatred and their common effects on society and on victims. Judith Lewis Herman studies the characteristics of trauma suffered by victims of many kinds of hateful violence, including the harms shared by abused women and victims of war crimes. She identifies patterns of personal devastation: an inability to preserve connections with others, anger, losing the desire to live.

Parallels between domestic violence and hate crimes, and between hate crimes and large-scale intergroup violence also encourage us to consider whether hateful violence has common roots, and whether effective ways of combating cycles of hatred and providing solace to victims are transferable from one domain to another. The authors offer various accounts of commonalities among the roots of hateful violence and responses to it. Assessments of the most important shared roots and responses vary, but they are not mutually exclusive.

Several authors focus on the ways in which boundaries inhibit recognition and response to hateful violence: the family as a sacrosanct private sphere, state sovereignty and the norm of nonintervention, the autonomy of religious or cultural communities. All these boundaries contribute to the perpetrators' ability to keep their crimes from public view and to further intimidate victims who suffer in isolation. As Minow puts it in "Between Nations and Between Intimates," "A conception of inviolable boundaries is used to shield both intimate violence and intergroup violence from public scrutiny and intervention."

Boundaries is the subject of Ayelet Shachar's argument that the arbitrary basis of ascriptive groupings is a principal root of cycles of hatred. "The Thin Line between Imposition and Consent: A Critique of Birthright Membership Regimes and their Implications" draws parallels between ascriptive membership in religious or ethnic subcommunities and birthright citizenship. For both, assignments of membership are nonconsensual and based on parentage or birthplace. For both, membership determines individuals' legal status, rights, and opportunities. These morally arbitrary boundaries entrench inequalities within and between groups and create the potential conditions for stigmatization, heightened vulnerability to victimization, and ultimately dehumanization and violence against "outsiders."

Herman focuses on relations of domination and subjugation at the root of both political violence and violence against women. Violence against women is not impulsive or incidental but a necessary and effective way of establishing and maintaining regular dominance. It is part of a system of coercive patriarchal control. Like perpetrators of political violence, Herman argues, batterers believe that they deserve their power, and rarely regret their crimes. To break the cycles of hatred, it is necessary to address the system of coercion, not just isolated acts.

Sarat's reflections on the uses of memory offer another perspective on the roots of cycles of hatred. Monumental history is the enemy of forgiveness and reconciliation. It fuels dreams of revenge. But it is also possible for the finality of death to take precedence. The point is to cultivate personal and cultural resources that demythologize violence.

In "Power, Violence, and Legality: A Reading of Hannah Arendt in an Age of Police Brutality and Humanitarian Intervention," Iris Marion Young draws attention to government's role in normalizing and perpetuating violence. For Arendt, power is a collective act of will that rests primarily on speech and has its basis and stability in consent. Violence is power's antithesis; it is the imposition of will by threat or use of destruction. The conclusion Young draws from this interpretation is that state-sponsored violence—both coercive intervention in other countries on humanitarian grounds and police action at home—may be morally justified in particular cases but is never principled or legally authorized. It is always irregular and discretionary. Even justifiable strategies of "humanitarian intervention" to protect human rights may have the predictable effect of targeting civilians, crippling economies, and loosing police brutality on neighborhoods. Official violence fails to defuse the sources of hostility, and fails to produce legitimate institutions or lasting cooperation.

Minow returns repeatedly to the background conditions that create an atmosphere of support for cycles of hatred: socially approved violence, tacit permission to discriminate, and pervasive violence in mass culture. There is a difference between violent talk and images and actual aggression, of course, but the prevalence of prejudice and incivility can certainly inhibit the effectiveness of public policies to assist vulnerable groups, counter official condemnations of hatred, and subvert widespread support for victims. So can the indirect messages communicated by government's own conduct if police practices are brutal or punishment severe. Our essays reinforce these points.

Focused on memory, law, and repair, our essays do not take up social intervention via public policy to address the underlying social conditions of hate crimes. Economic and social deprivations, by themselves, cannot explain hateful violence. Most people who suffer even the worst deprivation do not hold specific groups responsible for their adversity, and do not retaliate against them even if they do. (Resistance and social revolution are distinguishable from the violence that characterizes cycles of hatred.) Despite common assumptions, evidence relating hate crimes to economic downturns, unemployment rates, or economic competition between groups is sparse and tenuous. The sources of hate crimes and intergroup violence are more complex than the "frustration-aggression-displacement" hypothesis, say, suggests. Like domestic abuse, many forms of vengeance against those blamed for personal suffering are triggered in vulnerable individuals by an unpredictable constellation of social and personal stresses.

Nonetheless, the common roots and responses to cycles of hatred ultimately point to the question of social justice. Reasonable provisions of fair opportunity—and reasonable background conditions of housing and work, child care, health care and nutrition that make opportunities real—can help mitigate attitudes of supremacy and stigmatization on the one side and vulnerability and angry victimization on the other.

These essays can be described overall as contributions to the moral psychology and political theory of violence. The authors begin where moral and political philosophers leave off. The philosophical literature explores concepts like harms to dignity or analyzes justifications for universal rights, and operates mainly at the level of ideal theory. Here, the essays are closer to the ground, and arguments are directly tied to actual events and public responses to them. True, the authors' concerns are aspirational and the essays reflect a spirit of reform, but prescriptions are drawn, as Minow recommends in "Memory and Hate," "in light of what we think are realistic options." The authors take their bearings from social science, psychology, and law. They are attuned to power and its abuses, to vulnerability and its refuges. This ground, we argue, is a starting point for recognizing and breaking cycles of hatred.

Notes

1. Judith N. Shklar, *The Faces of Injustice* (New Haven: Yale University Press, 1990), p. 87.

2. Barry Bearak, "Onslaught by Taliban Leaves Afghans Dead or Homeless," *The New York Times* (October 18, 1999): A1.

3. Michael Janofsky, "A Defense to Avoid Execution," *The New York Times* (October 26, 1999): A18.

4. Lisa Belkin, "Parents Blaming Parents," *New York Times Magazine* (October 31, 1999): 60ff.

1

Breaking the Cycles of Hatred

MARTHA MINOW

Memory and Hate: Are There Lessons from Around the World?*

As we settle into this new century and this new millenium, it is time to take stock. I do not think this era will be remembered particularly for its wars, its mass atrocities, even its genocides. Sadly, these are not so distinctive in the history of humankind, although the emergence of technologies of destruction and mass media does seem to deepen the horror. What I think, and hope, is distinctive of this age is the mounting waves of objections and calls for collective responses to mass violence. Notably, people have turned to the language and instruments of law, casting genocides and regimes of torture as subjects for adjudication, a framework of human rights, reparations, and truth-telling. After the September 11 terrorist attacks in New York and Washington, D.C., calls for international adjudication rivaled public discussions of military responses.

I recently served on an international commission on Kosovo that reported to the United Nations in the fall of 2001. In the course of that work, I met with the ambassadors to the United States from Albania, Macedonia, and Croatia. In the most emphatic terms, they placed the establishment of an independent and operational judiciary in Kosovo as the highest priority—for peace and stability in the region. Yet I know from my informants in Kosovo how remote and challenging this task is. Not only is there a profound shortage of trained individuals; there is barely an agreed-on set of legal rules. And there are such high levels of distrust across the lines of ethnic division that many people think it is

*Gilbane Fund Lecture, Brown University, October 19, 1999. Thanks especially to Nancy Rosenblum, the community at Brown University, Laurie Corzett, and Sandra Badin for assistance, and to Jesse Fisher for assistance with the first lecture. This draws on Martha Minow, *Between Vengeance and Forgiveness: Facing History After Genocide and Mass Violence* (Boston: Beacon Press, 1998).

futile to even bring cases involving Serbs before judges of Kosovar Albanian identity—and vice versa. Petty crime and organized crime are both rampant. Property disputes are profound. To establish an operational court system that can secure the respect of the people is indeed the crucial first step for rebuilding the nation, but to call it difficult is to drastically understate the problem.

We complain a lot in this country about too much of human life becoming the subject of legal disputes. Yet, on the global scale, extending law to deal with collective violence is a vital step toward making a better world. Someone once said that a civilization progresses when what was once viewed as a misfortune comes to be seen as an injustice. I think the world's civilizations progress when horrors that were once seen as beyond human response become targets for international criminal tribunals, reparations, and truth commissions. Don't get me wrong: I'm deeply skeptical about the ability of any of these legal forms. Yet, they represent genuine efforts to do something in response to horror, something that does not repeat violence but instead seeks to condemn it, and end it.

In this essay, I will focus on memory and hatred, and in particular whether there is anything to be learned from the growing use of innovative legal practices in response to mass violence. Genocide, mass rapes, forced disappearances, and that ghastly antiseptic phrase "ethnic cleansing" each signal how animosity toward a group can either ignite or fuel horrific harms. Mass violence—even the seemingly isolated crimes of hatred directed at particular groups—has many ingredients, but invariably one is the dehumanization of a group of people who become the targets of violence and abuse. Cycles of violence sometimes then make perpetrators and their supporters victims of new waves of vengeful responses. How those who survive understand and remember what happened can have real consequences for the chances of renewed violence.

This essay will address criminal trials—conducted internationally and domestically—against perpetrators of mass violence; and about reparations, truth commissions, and nongovernmental advocacy organizations, which are each prominent responses to contemporary mass atrocities. But before delving into these issues, let me emphasize this: the search for a mode of response is profoundly doomed, because nothing after the event can be adequate when

—your son has been killed by a police order to shoot into a crowd
   of children

—your brother who struggled against a repressive government has
disappeared and left only a secret police file
—your niece watches militia members assault and murder her father
—you have been dragged out of your home, interrogated, and raped
by police
—whole peoples have had their life chances taken away by others.

Lawrence Langer, a scholar of the Holocaust, observes, "the logic of law
will never make sense of the illogic of genocide."[1] Of course he is right.
Legal responses are no more adequate than any others.

But inaction is worse. In the absence of a collective response to mass
atrocity, victims lack the basic acknowledgment of what happened that
is essential for mental health and political integrity. In the absence of a
collective response, the dehumanization preceding and accompanying
the violence is left uncondemned and uncorrected. In the absence of
collective responses, individuals are left with what some describe as either too much memory or too much forgetting.

There's an old Russian proverb: "Dwell on the past and you will lose
an eye. Forget the past and you will lose both eyes."[2] Dwelling on the
past, for victims of hatred and abuse, can lead to depression, disassocia-
tion, hopelessness; or the tendency to blame entire groups and the fantasy, or reality, of revenge.

For victims and survivors, failure to deal with the incidents wreaks its
own damage: painful secrets can lead to a freezing of individuals' capacities to love and act. Unaddressed trauma can produce wounded attachments to devastation itself and contribute to what psychologists call the
intergenerational transmission of trauma. Failing to remember hurts bystanders, too, because then they do not face their own choices about
action and inaction nor redress the boundaries between groups that helped
give rise to the atrocities. In the absence of collective responses to violence, perpetrators and their supporters may seem—unacceptably—like
victors or people who got away with it. As French philosopher Jean
Baudrillard put it, "Forgetting the extermination is part of the extermination itself."[3] But with societal response, perpetrators may also become
targets of new intergroup hatreds. Thus, some people will always remember what happened, but if there are no collective efforts to remember, a society risks repeating its atrocities by failing to undo the dehumanization that laid the groundwork for them.

The question, then, is not whether to remember, but how.

Two kinds of responses, in particular, are not sufficient to guide social action: The first is vengeance. A sense of vengeance is understandable, even justifiable, after one has been wronged. Indeed, it is the wellspring of the moral notion that motivates justice. As philosopher Jeffrie Murphy puts it: "A person who does not resent moral injuries done to him . . . is almost entirely a person lacking in self-respect."[4]

Yet vengeance can unleash a response beyond proportion, beyond reason, beyond justice. Laurel and Hardy episodes offer a humorous gloss to the sadly widespread pattern of destructive retaliation. Even a trivial slight triggers a less trivial response, and sets in motion escalating tweaks, punches, and waves of destruction.

Dr. Martin Luther King, Jr., noted that "Hate for hate only intensifies the existence of hate and evil in the universe. If I hit you and you hit me and I hit you back and you hit me back and so go on, you see, that goes on ad infinitum. It just never ends. Somewhere somebody must have a little sense . . . [and] . . . cut off the chain of hate, the chain of evil."[5]

In a remarkably similar vein, Polish Solidarity activist Adam Michnick surprised his colleagues by opposing a purge of communist collaborators from state-run enterprises after the fall of communism. He explained that the logic of revenge is "implacable. First there is a purge of yesterday's adversaries, the partisans of the old regime. Then comes the purge of yesterday's fellow oppositionists, who now oppose the idea of revenge. Finally there is the purge of those who defend them."[6] The thirst for revenge is implacable. It cannot guide responses to mass violence.

Even if revenge could be confined to a response commensurate with the harm, what is to be done when the harm itself defies human scale, when it is grotesque torture, mass killing? No just response can be administered in kind. For by retaliating, you become what you hate.

Transcending the temptation to retaliate is a way of describing the second, inadequate kind of response to broad-scale violence. This alternative is forgiveness. Let me acknowledge that it is admirable. But it is often unachievable, and it cannot be ordered.

Forgiveness involves the one who was wronged in renouncing resentment, stepping out of the wave of repeating rage, and welcoming the wrongdoer into the circle of humanity, reconnection, and even reconciliation. By forgiving the wrongdoer, the victim recognizes their common humanity and breaks the cycle of revenge. One who forgives can avoid the self-destructive effects of holding on to pain, grudges, and victimhood. The act of forgiving can reconnect the offender and the victim, and establish or renew a relationship. It can recognize or prompt contrition. People can forgive while still expecting and demanding punishment, but sometimes forgiveness means forgoing punishment. Official forgiveness usually means amnesty, exemption not only from punishment but also from communal acknowledgment of the harms and the wrongs. Public forgiving also risks public forgetting. Once the public apology is performed, the government—and the community—may well assume that the topic is closed and no more need ever be said about it.

So here are the problems with forgiveness. Many, perhaps most people, find it difficult or impossible to forgive. Perhaps the philosopher Benjamin Spinoza—himself an object of hatred for many in his time—was right when he said that "Hatred is increased by being reciprocated, and can on the other hand be destroyed by love."[7] But loving one's enemies is a very difficult task; it cannot be forced or commanded. I myself find it difficult to forgive the driver who cut me off on the highway this morning. Where the violations are brutal, severe, and intimate, it can be a new assault to expect the victims to forgive. Individuals respond uniquely and differently to horror. Their responses are among the last powers of selfhood they have retained. To demand different ones may be yet another form of degradation and denial of their very being. Fundamentally, forgiveness must remain a choice by individuals; the power to forgive must be inextricable from the power to choose not to do so. It cannot be ordered or pressured. Forgiveness requires the individual's own reach to embrace the wrongdoer. Forgiveness cannot be arrogated from the survivors without inflicting a new victimization. As human rights activist Aryeh Neier warns, when governments or their representatives "usurp the victim's exclusive right to forgive his oppressor,"[8] they fail to respect fully those who have suffered.

If vengeance risks a ceaseless rage that should be tamed, forgiveness requires a kind of transcendence that cannot be achieved on command or by remote control. So, as I have come to see it, the search is for responses to collective violence that etch a path between vengeance and forgiveness.

I have encountered inspiring examples of individuals who have walked that path. Jadranka Cigelj is one. She was raped, repeatedly, after being abducted and confined for months in a gruesome detention camp in Bosnia. After international media exposed the camp, she was released, and essentially crawled her way, starving and devastated, home. She began to talk with other survivors, and decided to gather their stories to submit to the International Criminal Tribunal for the former Yugoslavia. Her prior training as a lawyer no doubt influenced her sense that this would be an appropriate response. She described how she had initially been filled with hatred and a desire for revenge. But she met an eighty-six-year-old woman whose fourteen family members had been murdered, and she had to bury them all with her bare hands. That woman said to Jadranka: "How can you hate those who are so repulsive?" And Jadranka reflected, "I realized that the people I was directing my hatred toward were not worth that; they were only machines for murdering people. . . . [Y]ou realize what is important is to work toward a way to hold these people responsible and punish them. Then one day you wake up and the hatred has left you, and you feel relieved because hatred is exhausting, and you say to yourself, 'I am not like them.'"⁹ Her efforts succeeded in generating the first indictments for rape as a crime of war. The focus on prosecution, punishment, and documentation of victims' stories can offer a way past revenge, for some people, in some times and places. But must individuals be so extraordinary as to forge this path? Or can collective efforts create armatures for pain and structure paths for individuals to move from grief and pain to renewal and hope?

Collective efforts, notably growing in legal idioms during the past fifty years, include criminal prosecutions, reparations, and truth commissions. Each has strengths and weaknesses in forging a path between vengeance and forgiveness. Of course, there are other paths: the creation of artistic memorials; stripping former officials of their pensions and offices; developing educational programs for children and for the entire society; declaring days of commemoration. With criminal prosecutions, reparations, and truth commissions, there is a special emphasis on accountability and truth-telling. It remains to be seen whether alone or together they can also help particular societies build stable democracies or a climate conducive to human rights. But they each offer forms of collective memory, carrying the chance—just the chance—of rebuilding societies rather than stoking hatreds.

Prosecutions

As horrific as was the Great War near the start of the twentieth century, World War II introduced violence and degradation of human beings both on a scale and in a form that defied comprehension. Winston Churchill and Joseph Stalin each urged summary execution of the Axis leaders. Nonetheless, the Allies decided to hold trials and in so doing, establish a body of international legal rules. The rules aspired to recognize human rights with institutions sufficiently strong to enforce them. What emerged was an international military tribunal, empowered to prosecute major war criminals of the Axis countries for crimes against peace, war crimes, and crimes against humanity.

The invention of a tribunal composed of judges from each of the four major Allied powers departed from a prior military court involved in enforcing the laws of war. The category, crimes against humanity, lacked much definition and precedent. The tribunal itself tried to confine its prosecutions of crimes against humanity to those committed in conjunction with a war of aggression, and to norms announced in prior treaties against such wars, but still, the norms and procedures for the Nuremberg and Tokyo trials departed from the past. Indeed, the Nuremberg trials are widely credited with establishing the conclusion that there is no injustice in punishing defendants who knew they were committing a wrong condemned by the international community, even in the absence of an international law specifically prohibiting their behavior. The Nuremberg trials also elevated international law so that it clearly takes precedence over claims of state authority and obligation to obey the law of any one state.

It is a bold vision, but the Nuremberg and Tokyo trials were imperfect means to advance it. Charged at the time as victors' justice—exempting the Soviets and the other Allies from their wartime abuses—the trials also involved highly limited, even selective prosecution. An initial group of only twenty-four defendants stood in for the thousands who caused the deaths of more than 20 million and the unspeakable suffering of many more. The Tokyo trials generated charges of ethnic bias when its sentences seemed more severe than those issued at Nuremberg.

The Cold War put proposals for a permanent international criminal tribunal in the freezer. Nongovernmental organizations emerged as chief advocates for the vision of individual human rights, superior to any state's authority. Some national courts pursued criminal prosecutions and civil liability actions arising from human rights violations. Yet, for many, no response other than international criminal trials could signify the full vision of international human rights enforcement. But no international response followed mass murders in Cambodia, South Africa, Kurdistan, China, the Soviet Union, or elsewhere in the decades after World War II.

Finally, more than forty years after the Nuremberg and Tokyo trials, the United Nations Security Council authorized first the International Criminal Tribunal for the former Yugoslavia and then the International Criminal Tribunal for Rwanda. In both instances, critics viewed these actions as intentionally weak gestures, following more dire failures of international groups to stop the violence they now sought to address. Ad hoc and temporary, the international tribunals nonetheless stirred hopes for accountability and human rights enforcement in many quarters. The UN Security Council faced head-on the issue of what law should govern, and authorized the new tribunals to resort to the domestic law of the affected nation to fill any gaps in international law. Because these tribunals emanate from an international institution rather than the victors' military command, they achieve more legitimacy. At the same time, their operations and success are buffeted by ongoing domestic and regional strife.

Thus, the tribunal addressing the former Yugoslavia operated amid ongoing peace negotiations with potential targets of prosecution, and then in the midst of a war in Kosovo. The indictment of Serb leader Slobodan Milosevic by itself symbolized the ascendance of law as a response to violence and terror. The tribunal for Rwanda addressed the genocidal destruction of some 800,000 people while domestic trials seemed to some to commit new rounds of revenge, with tens of thousands turning out to watch the executions of twenty-two convicted after superficial trials by the Rwandan courts of genocide.

Given restrictions on freedom of the press in the former Yugoslavia and technological devastation in Rwanda, the most likely audiences for both tribunals exist outside the nations most affected by the violence. Despite slow progress, cumbersome procedures, and widespread uncertainty about their effectiveness, the tribunals have impressively generated credible documentation and condemnation of atrocities. Even with inevitable selectivity in prosecution, at best trying a small percentage of those actually involved in collective violence, the tribunals help create official records of the scope of the violence and its participants; afford public acknowledgment of what happened and its utter wrongfulness; and produce some convictions with punishment for individuals—each fulfilling the commitment to hold individuals, rather than whole peoples or nations, responsible for violence. As one Bosnian commented, "It is important that the Serbs know who is a war criminal and who isn't. . . . Otherwise, this world will think it is all of us."[10]

The aspiration to a rule of law, rather than a rule of power, explains in part the movement to establish a permanent International Criminal Court, which 120 nations—but not the United States—endorsed. Despite early active support, the United States declined endorsement chiefly because of fears that our military personnel serving abroad could face criminal charges driven by political motives;[11] the UN Security Council retains too much control over prosecutorial decisions, and ambiguities over the definitions of crimes of aggression and the jurisdiction of national courts remain. But the existence of a permanent court could wrest the prospect of prosecutions from ad hoc politicized deliberations, and provide a focal point for crucial investigative work of the kind that a French team recently undertook in Kosovo, locating the murdered bodies of men who disappeared early in the recent war.

It would be too much to expect that international criminal prosecutions would effect deterrence. Instead, the tribunals and their work offer rituals of accountability, defying impunity and public acknowledgment, defying forced forgetting. International tribunals and news accounts of their unfolding work also remind bystanders to take action to prevent the circumstances in which tyrants mobilize ordinary people to destroy others.

Enforcement by third-party national courts can also have this effect, as the indictment and extradition procedures for former Chilean president Augusto Pinochet suggest.[12] Simply the act of detaining General Pinochet in England, pending an extradition hearing triggered by an indictment by a Spanish prosecutor, thrust Chile under international scrutiny. With indictments pending in Belgium, Germany, France, Switzerland, as well as Spain, the moral condemnation of Pinochet's human rights abuses grew. These European developments at the same time exposed how much the culture of fear and the conspiracy of silence about murders and torture persisted and forestalled the transition to democracy in Chile, much less enforcement of human rights there. When the United States declassified thousands of documents in the summer of 1999, disclosing U.S. knowledge of human rights abuses and a desire to uncover the truth, the failure of a truth-seeking process in Chile since its supposed transition to democracy became even more blatant.

But then, by 1999, the demand for justice within Chile grew. And the Chilean Supreme Court stepped in and boldly declared that the amnesty law secured by Pinochet does not cover the cases of disappearances. This symbolic achievement ended the impunity of the Right Wing while offering some concrete hope of answers for families of the disappeared. Suddenly, many things that seemed impossible have now become possible. Some twenty-five military officers have been arrested, real investigations are now underway in the nation, and the Supreme Court even agreed to allow an interrogation of Pinochet in conjunction with potential domestic prosecutions.[13] Chileans now are beginning to face their past and, as a result, shape their own future.

Reparations

Reparations offer another response, often following long advocacy by survivors and negotiation with representatives of the wrongdoers. Reparations may take the form of monetary payments, or the return of stolen homes, art, or the bones of loved ones. Reparations may also involve explicit apology, the creation of memorials, and other gestures of restorative justice. Since World War II, Germany made payments of some $13.7 billion to assist the fledgling state of Israel alongside payments to individuals.[14] After decades of debate over the internment of Japanese Americans and Japanese citizens in the United States during World War II and the seizure of their properties and businesses, the U.S. government authorized the Civil Liberties Act of 1988. Its grant of $20,000 for each survivor of the camps and its explicit apology strikes some as too little, too late. Nonetheless, these steps, combined with the public movement and public testimonies about the internment, have offered a form of acknowledgment and response without expecting survivors to forgive. The victory for remaining survivors was bittersweet. Perhaps its most remarkable legacy is the subsequent response of some Japanese Americans to open discussions with Native Hawaiians about possible reparations for the land and authority that Japanese immigrants took.

The symbolic gesture and the struggle for it give victims a chance to reclaim their dignity and their history. But at the heart of reparations is the paradoxical search to repair the irreparable. Once paid, compensation may wrongly imply that the harms are over and need not be discussed again. Money can never remedy nonmonetary loss, however, and the fight over money carries the risk of trivializing the harms. Even restitution cannot restore the lifetimes that were lost. Yet sometimes modest requests for reparations can express the dignity of the survivors with scrupulous effort to avoid implying an actual remedy. Many South Africans simply requested tombstones for their lost relatives. One South African woman asked only that the bullets be removed from her vagina where they remained lodged from the time she was shot repeatedly by Apartheid police while hanging wash on a line. Reparations can meet burning needs for vindication without unleashing vengeance.

Perhaps, ironically, reparations without apologies seem inauthentic, and apologies without reparations seem cheap. Apologies are most meaningful when accompanied by material reparations; and reparations are most meaningful when accompanied by acknowledgment of their

inadequacy in the effort to apologize and make amends. Yet taken sep-
arately, and, especially, taken together, apologies and reparations offer
responses to mass atrocity that demand recognition of wrongs done
without obliging survivors to forgive.

Truth Commissions

A notable, third development in response to mass violence is truth
commissions. It is an unfortunate term for those who have read George
Orwell. Nonetheless, commissions of inquiry can expose and document
torture, murders, and other human rights violations that would otherwise
be denied and covered up by repressive regimes and their successors.
The Brazilian report, *Brasil: Nunca Mas*, documented 144 political murders, 125 disappearances, and over 1,800 other incidents of torture following a risky, surreptitious investigation led by religious groups and
journalists. The enormous public reception, making the report a best-
seller, contributed largely to the decision of President José Sarney to sign
the United Nations Convention Against Torture in 1985.

Other inquiries have taken more public forms, collecting testimony
from survivors and issuing public reports tracing the causes of violence.
The most dramatic and impressive example is South Africa's Truth and
Reconciliation Commission (TRC). The negotiated peaceful transition of
power after Apartheid included a promise to create a process for granting amnesty to participants in the past conflicts. The first democratically
elected parliament then created the TRC. It included a committee to receive applications from individuals seeking amnesty. Although many
doubted that anyone would come forward, over 9,000 individuals did
apply for amnesty. The statute made grants of amnesty contingent upon
full disclosure, demonstration of a political rather than a self-serving motive, and means commensurate with that political motive. The applications and cross-examined testimony have answered many questions
about who did what, when, and how on behalf of the Apartheid government and on behalf of the resisting liberation groups. The amnesty process remains the most controversial feature of the TRC. Fewer than 400
of the 9,000 applicants satisfied the conditions for amnesty. Especially
difficult—politically, and as a choice of how to spend precious resources—
remain decisions by the chief prosecutor over whether to indict individuals whose applications were denied.

But perhaps more important to the TRC was its human rights committee, designed to collect testimony from survivors of violence on all sides of the conflicts. Over 22,000 offered statements. Many appeared in public hearings that were broadcast around the nation. Offering unassailable evidence of the human rights violations denied for so long by members of the Apartheid government, this process also gave voice to survivors of violence and offered concrete and symbolic occasions for reconciliation between individuals on different sides of the conflicts. The commissioners also held hearings to examine the roles of entire societal sectors, such as the medical profession, the judiciary, the business community, and the media, in enabling and benefiting from Apartheid.

Yielding a five-volume report as well as memorable national broadcasts of live testimony, the TRC indicated a mode of accountability without retribution, a focus on individual responsibility, and also an assessment of larger social forces. The language of reconciliation offended many who sought retribution, however. The TRC's own recommendations for monetary reparations remain merely paper suggestions. It is economic redistribution that remains the biggest unaddressed issue there, and a reparations strategy could still emerge.

Father Mxolisi Mapanbani told the following story, which became a touchstone for South Africa's Truth and Reconciliation Commission. Once, there were two boys, Tom and Bernard. Tom lived right opposite Bernard. One day, Tom stole Bernard's bicycle and every day Bernard saw Tom cycling to school on it. After a year, Tom went up to Bernard, stretched out his hand and said, "Let us reconcile and put the past behind us." Bernard looked at Tom's hand. "And what about the bicycle?" "No," said Tom. "I'm not talking about the bicycle, I'm talking about reconciliation." The barriers to reconciliation are huge, as depicted in a political cartoon showing the TRC chair, Archbishop Desmond Tutu uttering "oops" as he surveys a map that took him to an abyss between one land mass marked "truth" and another marked "reconciliation."

Still, the power of speaking and testifying was exhibited time and again at the TRC. Lucas Baba Sikwepere, blinded by the Apartheid-era police officer known as the Rambo of the Peninsula, commented after testifying at the TRC: "I feel what has been making me sick all the time is the fact that I couldn't tell my story. But now I—it feels like I got my sight back by coming here and telling you the story."[15] And Cynthia Ngewu, mother of one of the individuals known as the Guguletu Seven, commented: "This thing called reconciliation . . . if I am understanding it correctly . . . if it means this perpetrator, this man who has killed Christian Piet, if it means he becomes human again, this man, so that I, so that all of us, get our humanity back . . . then I agree, then I support it all."[16]

The commission's work was insufficient in and of itself to produce national reconciliation. But it offered avenues for individuals to reach toward it while also correcting the national narrative and memory. Consider the following three stories from the TRC: they are hopeful and disturbing. This tempered assessment of the TRC's contributions must remain open to debate and assessment as the nation proceeds and as people within and beyond South Africa consider what the TRC accomplished.

First, there is the story of Amy Biehl. Amy Biehl was a white American who went to South Africa to work in the townships. She was murdered in a gross incident of group violence committed by young men in the township. Her parents, in shock and grief, went to South Africa to try to understand what happened. They have since devoted their time and resources to assisting people in the township where the murderers grew up, creating schools, art programs, and small industry. Amy's killers were prosecuted and convicted by the local criminal court. They then applied to the TRC for amnesty. The Biehls attended the hearings, and did not object to amnesty. They found for themselves a path if not to forgiveness, then away from vengeance. They turned with remarkable devotion to try to eradicate the conditions of racial hatred and economic privation that produced their daughter's murderers.

Second, General Magnus Malan, army chief and later defense minister for the Apartheid government, faced prosecution for charges of gross human rights violations. Charged with authorizing an assassination squad that mistakenly killed thirteen women and children in 1987, Malan survived a nine-month trial and was found not guilty in 1996. Then, in 1997, Malan volunteered to speak before the TRC. He expressly did not seek amnesty but instead seemed to want the chance to tell his own story. He acknowledged cross-border raids he had authorized; he described how he had set up a covert unit to disrupt Soviet-backed liberation activities. He denied that he had himself approved assassinations or atrocities. He also made clear that he opposed the TRC itself, and viewed it as a witch-hunt. But he said that he came forward to take moral responsibility for the orders he had given and to make his story part of the official record. He said, "I have come here to tell you my story and to face your judgment . . . I shall be content if what I am saying may spur the slightest understanding of former adversaries. I shall rejoice if my efforts can contribute in the minutest sense toward reconciliation and if all soldiers may obtain moral amnesty. . . . It is understanding and forgiveness we really seek, not legal pardons."[17]

Then, there is the far more troubling story of Jeffrey Benzien, who applied for amnesty for actions committed as a security police officer in the 1980s. Initially, he gave vague statements, but, like all amnesty applicants, he faced the possibility of cross-examination by his own victims. Under Ashley Forbes's close questioning, Benzien calmly testified how he had developed a particular method for torturing individuals taken into custody. He demonstrated it through a simulation with a volunteer during the hearing. Called the "wet-bag" technique, the torture method involved forcing the suspect face down on the floor with hands handcuffed behind the back, then Benzien would sit on the individual's back, place a wet cloth bag over the prisoner's head, and twist it around the neck so the individual would start to suffocate. When the body became slack, Benzien would release the bag, and thus stop just short of killing the prisoner in time to continue the interrogation.

A survivor of Benzien's methods, Tony Yengeni, asked "What kind of man uses a method like his one of the wet bag, on other human beings, repeatedly listening to those moans and cries and groans, and taking each of those people very near to their deaths?" Benzien replied that in hindsight, he saw that what he had done was wrong, but at the time he thought he was working to rescue South Africa from a communist movement and to protect his family's freedoms. Some observers thought he reenacted the role of manipulator even during the hearing, when he goaded his questioners into recalling what he alleged as their friendship and conviviality.[18]

At the time of his application, Benzien was still employed as a policeman. Should this man remain free from punishment, still in a position of power? When he was then granted amnesty, many in South Africa and around the world understandably had bitter things to say about the TRC.

No Closure

Contemporary responses to mass atrocities lurch among the rhetorics of law (punishment, compensation, deterrence); history (truth); theology (forgiveness); therapy (healing); art (commemoration and disturbance); and education (learning lessons). None is adequate and yet, by invoking any of these rhetorics, people wager that social responses can alter the emotional experiences of individuals and societies living after mass violence. Perhaps, rather than seeking revenge, people can rebuild.

As public instruments shaping public and private lives, legal institutions affect the production of collective memories for a community or nation. Social and political decisions determine what gives rise to a legal claim. Not only do these decisions express views about what is fair and right for individuals; they also communicate narratives and values across broad audiences. Whose memories deserve the public stage of an open trial, a broadcast truth commission, or a reparations debate? What version of the past can acknowledge the wrongness of what happened without giving comfort to new propaganda about intergroup hatreds?

Research across a wide range of academic disciplines has produced a new consensus about human memory. It turns out that recollections are not retrieved, like intact computer files, but instead are always constructed by combining bits of information selected and arranged in light of prior narratives and current expectations, needs, and beliefs. Thus, the histories we tell and the institutions we make create the narratives and enact the expectations, needs, and beliefs of a time. ⋅

Two seeming paradoxes emerge. Our memories are constructed but no one person can choose how; our memories are not simply retrieved but neither are they free floating, entirely manipulable to present interests.

Failure to remember, though, can impose unacceptable costs. Failure to remember, collectively, triumphs and accomplishments diminishes us. But failure to remember, collectively, injustice and cruelty is an ethical breach. It implies no responsibility and no commitment to prevent inhumanity in the future. Even worse, failures of collective memory stoke fires of resentment and revenge. Michael Ignatieff offered this explanation of the conflicts surrounding the former Yugoslavia:

> [T]he past continues to torment because it is not the past. These places are not living in a serial order of time but in a simultaneous one, in which the past and present are a continuous, agglutinated mass of fantasies, distortions, myths, and lies. Reporters in the Balkan wars often observed that when they were told atrocity stories they were occasionally uncertain whether these stories had occurred yesterday or in 1941, 1841, or 1441.

He concludes that this "is the dreamtime of vengeance. Crimes can never safely be fixed in the historical past; they remain locked in the eternal present, crying out for vengeance."[19]

The twentieth century will not be remembered as unique because of mass atrocities, but it may be remembered for the creation of international human rights tribunals, reparations, and truth and reconciliation commissions. No human institutions are perfect. International criminal trials are marred by political wrangling, selective prosecution, the limits of discoverable and admissible evidence and the dangers of politicized justice; domestic trials may be put on hold indefinitely precisely where terror has been most effective. Reparations risk trivializing atrocities and focusing on money when money can never redeem the past. Truth commissions may be too tepid, too ineffectual, even while gathering stories of too-often silenced survivors. Remaining questions, which will be addressed in later essays, include: What other responses can society bring to survivors and also prevent new rounds of hatred? Can laws usefully prevent or diminish the dehumanization of particular people that contributes to gross human rights harms—or do laws governing hate crimes and hate speech make things worse? Is there anything to be learned by comparing public responses to intergroup violence with responses to intrafamily violence? Have we learned anything about how to react to and remember violence so that the sum total of hatred diminishes, rather than increases?

We each may not have control over what we come to remember, but we each can play a role in shaping what we work to recall. I remember a story about a cynical young man who came to a town determined to discredit the local sage, a man renowned for his wisdom. The youngster decided to summon all the inhabitants and hold a bird in his hand, and say, "Wise man, is the bird dead or is the bird alive?" If the sage responded that the bird was dead, he would open his hand and let the bird fly away. If the sage replied that the bird was alive, then the young man would choke it to death. With all the people in the town assembled, and bird in hand, the young man called out, "Wise man, is the bird dead or is he alive?" The wise man wisely responded, "The fate of that bird is in your hands."

The fate of our fate *is* in our hands. Especially for those of us who feel we are bystanders in a world of atrocities, we have a challenge. We find a flawed, only partly remembered world; we can and must have a hand in what we come to remember so we can transform the future that awaits.

NOTES

1. Lawrence L. Langer, *Admitting the Holocaust* (New York: Oxford University Press, 1995), p. 171.

2. Quoted in Philip Perlmutter, *Legacy of Hate: A Short History of Ethnic, Religious, and Racial Prejudice in America*, rev. ed. (Armonk, NY: M. E. Sharpe, 1999), p. xi.

3. James E. Young, *The Texture of Memory: Holocaust Memorials and Meaning* (New Haven, CT: Yale University Press, 1993), p. 1 (quoting Baudrillard).

4. Jeffrie G. Murphy, "Introduction," in Jeffrie G. Murphy and Jean Hampton, *Forgiveness and Mercy* (New York: Cambridge University Press, 1988), p. 16.

5. "Loving Your Enemies," speech delivered by Dr. Martin Luther King, Jr., at Dexter Avenue Baptist Church, Montgomery Alabama, Nov. 17, 1957.

6. Quoted in Lawrence Weschler, "A Reporter at Large," *New Yorker* (December 10, 1990), p. 127.

7. Benjamin Spinoza, *The Ethics Part III—On the Origin and Nature of the Emotions* in Spinoza, *Ethics*, G.H.R. Parkinson, ed. and trans. (Oxford, UK: Oxford University Press, 2000), p. 197.

8. Quoted in Susan Jacoby, *Wild Justice: The Evolution of Revenge* (New York: harper and Row, 1983), p. 117.

9. Quoted in Gayle Kirshenbaum, "Women of the Year: Jadranka Cigelj and Nusreta Sivac," *Ms. Magazine* (January/February 1996): 67–68.

10. Quoted in Elizabeth Neuffer, "Elusive Justice: It Will Take an International Court to Deter War Criminals," *Boston Globe* (December 29, 1996): Sec. D, pp. 1–2.

11. As one of his last acts in office, President Clinton sought U.S. endorsement; this is one of many policies of the former administration that President Bush has rejected.

12. Thanks to Sebastian Jerez for research on Pinochet.

13. See Sebastian Rotella, "Chilean Military Faces Ghosts of Pinochet Regime," *Los Angeles Times* (October 19, 1999): A1; Clifford Krauss, "Chilean Military Facing Reckoning For Its Dark Past," *New York Times* (October 3, 1999): 1. See also Editorial, "Chile Finds Life After Pinochet," *Chicago Tribune* (October 5, 1999): 14.

14. Abby Ellin, "Media Business," *New York* Times (December 5, 2001): C7. Roy Brooks, Introduction, in Roy L. Brooks, ed., *When Sorry Isn't Enough* (New York: New York University Press, 1999), p. 9.

15. Testimony before Human Rights Committee of the South African Truth and Reconciliation Commission, quoted in Antji Krog, *Country of My Skull* (Johannesburg, South Africa: Random House, 1998), p. 31.

16. Quoted in id., p. 109.

17. Suzanne Daley, "Apartheid-Era Defense Chief Defends Role in Ordering Raids on Neighboring Countries," *New York Times* (May 8, 1997): 16.

18. "Burying South Africa's Past: Of Memory and Forgiveness," *Economist* (November 1, 1997): 21–23.

19. Michael Ignatieff, "The Elusive Goal of War Trials," *Harper's* (March 1996); reprinted in "Articles of Faith, Index on Censorship," *Harper's* (September/October 1997): 15–17.

. . . . . .

Regulating Hatred: Whose Speech, Whose Crimes, Whose Power?*

To talk about hatred is to get very close to terror. I mean to respect this subject by beginning, though, with humor. I do so for several reasons. First, I like it. Second, sharing a joke or a funny line may make us— writer and reader—feel like part of a community. And it is the construction of community, however temporary, that seems to me the best protection against hatred. Finally, psychological experiments suggest that people become better able to solve problems after they have been laughing than after they have been otherwise entertained. One study asked people to perform the odd task of trying to attach a candle to a corkboard wall with only matches and a box of tacks.[1] Apparently, those people who had seen a humorous film prior to attempting the task were more likely to figure out a way to do it than did those who had watched a serious film. Now maybe it's just that they were able to see the humor in the task itself. But if humor can help each of us solve problems—and help each of us feel motivated and able to tackle the difficult issues of intergroup hatred and violence—I will give it a try.

I love cartoons, and here are three of my favorites. One cartoon shows a dog typing on a typewriter: "The quick brown dog jumps over the lazy fox."[2] It is a reversal of the familiar saying, "The quick brown fox jumped over the lazy dog." What makes it funny is the surprise and the invitation to the viewer to recognize how much where we stand and who we are influences what we assume; our perspective influences our stereotypes, and we don't usually even know it.

Let's try another. Here a judge with glasses, a big nose, and a mustache looks down from the bench at a defendant with the identical glasses, big nose and mustache. The judge bangs the gavel and declares, "Surely not guilty. Next case."[3] Here the symbol of fairness and neutrality betrays his bias, and doesn't even realize it. I hope the humor lies in the

* Adapted from Gilbane Fund Lecture #2, October 26, 1999, Brown University. Thanks to Elaine Chiu, Kate Cook, Jesse Fisher, and Douglas Kropp for research help, and to Chai Feldblum, Nan Hunter, Elizabeth Spelman, and Carol Steiker for helpful conversations on the issues addressed here. An earlier version of this essay appears as "Regulating Hatred: Whose Speech, Whose Crimes, Whose Power—An Essay for Kenneth Karst," *University of California at Los Angeles Law Review* 47 (2000): 1253.

reader's recognition of this, rather than amusement at the glasses, big nose, and mustache, which I actually found adorable.

The last cartoon has three frames.[4] The first shows a minister reading a letter that says, "Dear Preacher, I am sick and tired of your holier than thou attitude. Signed, Fed Up." The second frame shows the minister thinking, and then writing back: "Dear Fed Up: I forgive you." In the third frame, the minister says to himself, "Shame on you." Here, the minister repeats the very sin of superiority that his critic points out. Exposing hypocrisy is fun; so is identifying flaws in authority figures who are supposed to exemplify the values they betray. But the minister in this case at least has a moment of self-recognition; the sin is not so much unthinking as reflexive, inviting not a change in conduct but the tongue-in-cheek chance for repentance.

All three cartoons highlight how perspective affects perception. Who we are and where we stand affects what we take for granted, what we find fair, and what we think is tolerant and accepting. Seeing from where we stand is inevitable, given our embodied selves. Shorthand and stereotyped thinking seem hard-wired, given the limited space in the human brain. Identifying with those like ourselves is comforting and perhaps even crucial to our survival, but each inclusion also marks an exclusion, and each generous act toward one of our own risks selfishness or even cruelty toward one who seems to be "other." And whatever power we have risks obscuring criticisms and even the recognition that there are contrary perspectives, and that our own view is just that, a view, rather than truth or reality itself.

So, of course, I picked these cartoons to advance my own view, which is this: attention to perspective is vital to treatments of hatred, whether that hatred erupts in vicious speech or violent acts. Thus, I will urge constant attention to the influence of perspective on beliefs—and to the insights afforded by alternative perspectives—as we consider whether and how government should regulate speech and conduct that, from some perspectives, can be called hateful. Central questions must include: (1) whose speech is hateful, and deserves regulation, (2) whose crimes would and should be regulated, and (3) whose power is implied, exercised, amplified, or diminished in the process of regulating hatred.

Mass ethnic and racialized violence shares with eruptions of single, horrific incidents of hatred one constant precondition. That precondition is the dehumanization of a group—the treatment of people marked by membership as subhuman, dirty, a cancer on the society, incompetent, immoral, unworthy, or excrement calling for immediate disposal. Of course, these attitudes must be held in some way by the individual who uses the verbal slur and the individual who assaults a stranger simply due to her apparent membership in a group. But the wrongdoer's reference group also holds the dehumanizing view, and often, it circulates in the broader society as well. It is not an accident precisely which groups are targeted for hate. In the United States, it is usually persons of color, immigrants, gays, and lesbians; sometimes women, Jews, Catholics, persons with disabilities. Each of these markers signals long histories of degradation and subordination. Someone seething with resentment, fear, and status anxiety will find ready resonance in the broader community if he expresses it along these familiar lines of social division. Hatred is especially aroused by frustration and perceptions of threat; hatred may involve sadism, rage, anger, and envy; and people tend to persecute those who are already defeated or apparently weaker because they are seeking to avenge past humiliations and want to guarantee a way to reclaim their own status or self-esteem.[5]

In this light, acts of hate speech and hate crimes are bad in and of themselves and also because they contribute to the climate that permits mass atrocities. Sometimes, they are tightly tied together, as with the fraternity at Arizona State University that forced Jewish pledges to sign a pledge reading: "My number is 6 million. That's how many Jews were killed and I should have been one of them, sir."[6] Or flyers found at Brown University in 1992 that read: "Once upon a time, Brown was a place where a white man could go to class without having to look at little black faces, or little yellow faces, or little brown faces, except when he went to take his meals. Things have been going downhill since the kitchen help moved into the classroom. Keep white supremacy alive!"[7]

Efforts to regulate hate speech in the face of such incidents reflect the crucial commitment to condemn such subordinating and exclusionary speech. I will consider what in this country has been a basically failed effort centering on college campuses. Those speech codes adopted in public settings have by now all been struck down by courts as violations of the First Amendment,[8] but the debate about such restrictions continues and has continuing significance for private institutions. I will also discuss the development of hate crime legislation that has met some, but less, opposition in this country. A hate crime involves criminal conduct such as vandalism, assaults, and murder where the object or victim is selected because of antipathy for the associated group.[9] Defacement of a place of worship with racial, religious or ethnic slurs expresses hatred in a way that spray-painting the names of school sweethearts does not, although the cleanup costs may be the same in both instances.

In 1998, three members of a fledgling white supremacist group in Texas beat up James Byrd, Jr., a forty-nine-year-old son, brother, and father, who loved church music and was an African-American. A white man, John William King, and his white collaborators chained James Byrd's legs together, and tied his feet to the back of a pickup truck. They dragged James Byrd three miles until he hit a culvert, breaking his body into pieces. When the trial judge offered King the chance to say something to James Byrd's family, King smirked and uttered an obscenity. Although King did not testify at his trial, his many writings expressing Nazi philosophy and his racist and Nazi body tattoos spoke his views. This incident was followed by another heinous crime, when Russell Henderson killed Matthew Shepard, a young gay man, and then with the help of an associate, tied him to a post as a warning to others.

Each of these and similar incidents of hate crimes and hate speech depend on the dehumanization of individuals simply because one feature of their identities draws them into a group that some other people disparage or despise. The incidents also contribute to continuing dehumanization, enacting a victimization that can in a perverse way give new power to the picture of such group members as pathetic or vulnerable, and certainly new power to the sheer significance of such group memberships.

Understanding the perspective of those whose groups are targeted is crucial here. A black woman I know who works at a predominantly white university had the shock of learning about a Ku Klux Klan presence in the university. Her white friends tried to reassure her that there was nothing to fear from such a kooky, marginal group. Her response was to ask, "How can I feel safe when my friends don't respect my sense of danger?"

Even seemingly benign group stereotypes, appearing in jokes, television situation-comedies, and pop music can perniciously animate and advance the degradation of certain groups that, in turn, renders them targets for severe abuse. Teens are the most frequent actors behind hateful graffiti, but they do not make up the language or targets; instead they mirror what is already out there, somewhere in their community: the fear combined with denunciation of gays and lesbians, immigrants, Jews, persons of color.[10] A leading book on hate crimes explains that stereotypes even in seemingly innocuous sitcoms may seem benign but "[t]hey have been used to justify atrocities committed against members of stigmatized groups. Thus, the image serves an important purpose: adult men couldn't be beaten, enslaved, or murdered with impunity, but those considered subhuman or childlike could be enslaved and treated as though they were animals."[11]

Members of mistreated groups may respond in kind; hatred can indeed go both ways. A recent issue of the *New York Times Magazine* includes an article by Andrew Sullivan emphasizing that "people who are demeaned and objectified in society may develop an aversion to their tormentors that is more hateful in its expression than the prejudice they have been subjected to." Sullivan cites FBI crime statistics indicating that Blacks are three times more likely than whites to commit a hate crime.[12] Bracketing at least for now the real risk that these statistics themselves reflect bias in the reporting of crimes to the disadvantage of blacks, there is something important to acknowledge here. It is this very pattern of revenge, retaliation, and escalation that has preoccupied me and others in recent years.[13] Even righteous indignation can lead to unacceptable and unbounded vengeance.

The challenge then is to devise collective social responses that acknowledge wrongs without generating vengeance—social responses that fight back against hatred without becoming hate-filled and hateful.

What are the effects, symbolic and practical, of different kinds of responses to brutal eruptions of hatred—both after violent and offensive incidents and before as preventive steps? Let us pay vigilant attention to the matter of perspective: Whose speech will be deemed hateful, from whose perspective? Whose crimes? And how will the apparatus that emerges with regulation of hatred be perceived by those it is intended to help? What is right and what is wrong in the arguments for, and the arguments against, using law to regulate hateful speech and hate-motivated crimes?

Regulating Hate Speech and Hate Crimes: Judging the Arguments, Pro and Con

Speech and violence motivated by hatred toward others because of aspects of their identity are hardly new. Certainly since ancient times, societies have included speech and violence organized against individuals simply because of their group membership. More recently, in 1982, Richard Delgado wrote an article arguing for a tort action for racial insults, epithets, and name-calling based on the psychological harms and analogies to libel and slander laws.[14] Mari Matusda, in 1993, argued for carefully drafted hate speech regulations to address face-to-face, one-on-one insults that demean on the basis of race or sex, again drawing analogies to existing permissible regulations of expression.[15] Their work helped to inspire and guide initiatives on several college campuses to adopt speech codes. That such regulations restrict expression is not in doubt; the question has been whether such restrictions violate the U.S. Constitution's guarantee of the freedom of expression. Because that guarantee only guards against governmental restrictions, private institutions may do as they wish. Nevertheless, many of these private institutions voluntarily subscribe to a principle of freedom of expression as part of the mission of learning and inquiry. In the meantime, each public university or college that adopted a speech code faced immediate lawsuits, and ultimately each of these suits prevailed.[16]

In a parallel story, efforts led by Catharine MacKinnon and Andrea Dworkin to create a civil action against pornography[17] ultimately yielded successful court challenges.[18] And in another parallel story, cities, states, and now the federal government have adopted so-called "hate crime statutes" that criminalize or provide for increased punishment for crimes committed with a motive of bias against members of recognizable groups.

In each of these contexts, First Amendment defenders made the familiar and powerful absolutist arguments against regulation. They have argued that the freedom of expression must be preserved absolutely, for exceptions made for the speech we hate open the way for more exceptions, and still more, until the freedom itself is undermined. Proponents of regulation, by contrast, emphasized the actual harms inflicted by the expression—harms to individuals and to society.

I actually think both sides in that argument were right. I know, I know; I sound like the rabbi who listened first to one complainant, and said, "You're right," and then listened to his opponent, and said, "You're right." His wife shouted from across the house, "They can't both be right!" at which point the rabbi said, "You're right, too." But there *are* important ways in which both the proponents and opponents of regulations are right.

The proponents are right in recognizing harms, real harms: from venomous speech and from violence directed at people or symbols because of their group associations and from the impact of hateful speech and violence specifically on the domain of freedom of expression itself.[19] Thus, too often, the advocates of the First Amendment ignore or try to minimize the ways in which slurs and bias-based comments both produce psychological damage for individuals and perpetuate the dehumanization of members of particular groups (which in turn can invite further degradation and violence). Freedom of speech that undermines equality neglects the way that equality is itself a central principle of the First Amendment.[20] Freedom of speech itself depends on the assumption of individual human dignity, yet practices of degrading speech that deny or violate that dignity should at least trouble defenders of free speech. Moreover, as Steve Shiffrin summarizes, racist speech

> is an assault on the dignity of people of color; it humiliates and causes emotional distress, sometimes with physical manifestations; it helps spread racial prejudice, stigmatizing people of color not only in the eyes of the societally dominant race but also in the eyes of the victims themselves, inspiring self-hatred, isolation, and impairment of the capacity for interpersonal relationships, and finally, it frequently creates the conditions for violence.[21]

Similar assessments have been made of sexist and homophobic speech. In the wake of biased speech, members of disadvantaged groups often have their own speech chilled.[22] Why participate if only to be demeaned?[23] The response of withdrawal—from classroom discussion, political debate, even from the activity of personal achievement—is understandable in the face of comments demeaning to one's group. Speech absolutists ought at least to worry about the net reduction, and content distortion, of speech's marketplace that hate speech can produce. Arguably, even worse than this kind of "silencing" is what happens to those who nonetheless persist and speak. They may be heard only through the distorting lens of hate speech, with stereotypes about Asians, or Hispanics, or women, or disabled persons, coloring the impression of the speaker's ideas.[24] This fact jeopardizes the confidence that a marketplace of ideas will provide a fair test and sort out the bad ideas. In fact, some bad views about people can persist and even color evidence that would undermine those very views.

Acknowledging such harms may seem threatening to those who believe that protection for freedom of expression and thought is, or should be absolute. Yet it is only honest to acknowledge the harms first, and then decide what to do. Of course, other harms have justified restrictions on speech. Consider how far from absolute protection is our existing law: it permits restrictions for civil actions for defamation and slander; it permits restrictions against fighting words and words that amount to a clear and present danger to national security or physical safety (as in, you can't falsely shout "fire" in a crowded theater).[25] In the university context, of course the law permits a whole variety of speech restrictions, including the classroom practices requiring students to raise their hands, speak one at a time, and speak only when recognized. No one thinks it an unacceptable restriction on freedom of expression for professors to establish the classroom norm that students must speak respectfully about others, even though this means suppressing some things that people want to say. More indirect limitations on speech arise from the fact that no outside guests have a right to speak at a university; they must be invited, and decisions not to invite someone are not construed as violations of freedom of expression.

If we look beyond the United States, several other constitutional democracies restrict hateful speech and group defamation. The English, Canadian, German, and South African constitutional schemes would be instructive if American judges and Americans more generally were less insular and more willing to look, as do judges in those countries, at what other nations do.[26] The proponents of regulations in this country are right insofar as they, too, suggest that it is possible to reconcile the freedoms guaranteed in a constitutional democracy with particular restrictions on the expression of hatred because that expression itself can jeopardize those freedoms.

Further, the case for restricting hate speech and for punishing the opinion dimension of hate crimes can be strengthened by recognizing that the government is itself a source of important speech and ideas. The adoption of hate speech and hate crime laws, in the words of one observer, "telegraph[s] a message that violent bigotry is not just a crime against a single person but a crime against an entire group."[27] Even if actual adoption of such rules had no practical enforcement effect, they would have the powerful symbolic effect of public disapproval of group hatred. As Steve Shiffrin notes, "Much of this debate is about symbols, not about important threats to free speech or about effective attacks on racism." Instead, the debates really manifest cultural struggles over the meaning of America.[28]

In a society where hateful incidents are common, the government's response of silence conveys a powerful message that such views and conduct are within acceptable bounds and should evade the official disapproval of the community. This broader perspective that includes government speech and government silence in the assessment of freedom of expression also reminds us that other governmental policies communicate messages that may themselves contribute to apparently private acts of hatred. So when a state, like California, presides over a public debate in which many blame immigrants for the state's economic difficulties, and then adopts a referendum, like Proposition 187, to exclude immigrants from public benefits and services, it endorses and amplifies the expression of resentment through an assignment of blame to people in a particular group. When that same state also adopts hate crimes legislation, it sets up those who act on the publicly endorsed resentment. In an even more extreme case, Germany adopted an immigration law widely understood as a surrender to the street fighters who have attacked refugees and their homes. Responding to a skinhead rampage of violence against new immigrants, the German Parliament in 1992 passed a law making it difficult for refugees and anyone seeking asylum to enter Germany. Critics claim that the terrorist strategy thus swayed German public policy, in essence holding the nation hostage and allowing the neo-Nazi view to prevail.[29]

Yet it is precisely the hope of preventing the escalation of destructive ideologies that makes the free speech proponents right as well. Erwin Staub, a leading observer of the origins of genocide and group violence, notes that "The tradition of pluralism, freedom, and respect for the individual limit the potential influence of destructive ideologies within the United States."[30] It seems that the scope afforded individual freedoms in the United States siphons off the aggression against minority groups that itself arises from deep-seated senses of fear and economic competition, although Staub himself prescribes more concerted efforts to meet human needs and to build connections across subgroups to decrease the violent potential in the United States.[31]

Broad freedoms of expression also help head off mass intergroup violence within the United States on a different basis. Here the explanation is that restrictions on hate activities, at least within this political culture, seem to increase the feelings of resentment and fury of those holding hateful views—while rallying to their side very different people who are wedded to the abstract principles of freedom of speech and limited government.[32]

Certainly, the free speech absolutists have a good point when they warn against unintended consequences and curtailments of expression that proponents of restrictions may well not want.[33] The lawyers among them engage in the baloney-slicing activity of distinguishing regulation of expression that is not deserving of First Amendment protection (such as obscenity and fighting words) and regulation of expression that does deserve such protection, but I'll leave that kind of analysis for another day.

Instead, let's consider the perspective not of legal advocates but of people subjected to truly hateful speech about their own groups. Wouldn't they often be tempted to speak back, and engage in their own put-downs and verbal assaults? Isn't it then a real risk that administrators and others in positions of authority will notice and seek to restrict such minority speech even more than speech directed against them?[34]

It's difficult in this regard to ignore that the two leading U.S. Supreme Court cases on hate speech came out in opposite ways, and the one approving restrictions applied to a Black defendant while the one rejecting restrictions involved a white one. In a 1992 case called *R.A.V. v. City of St. Paul,*[35] the Court struck down as unconstitutional a hate-crime statute in a case in which several white adolescents burned a cross on the property of an African-American couple.[36] But the very next year, in *Wisconsin v. Mitchell,*[37] the Court upheld a hate crime statute used to impose an enhanced penalty on an African-American youth who seriously led his friends in beating up a white teen after discussing a movie depiction of white Ku Klux Klan violence against a praying African-American child.[38]

Of course, other factors helped to distinguish the two cases, which occurred one year apart. The first case criminalized expressive conduct but only criminalized some fighting words, and thus, the Court concluded, represented an impermissible viewpoint discrimination, while the second case permitted an enhanced penalty where a victim or object is intentionally selected because of the actor's belief or perceptions regarding the victim's membership in an exhaustive list of groups. Nonetheless, it is not beyond imagination that a primarily white Court could better identify with a white victim than a black one. Indeed, Mari Matsuda and Charles Lawrence commented about how the first decision involved the Court in a bizarre reversal: "The cross burners are portrayed as an unpopular minority that the Supreme Court must defend against the power of the state. . . . The reality of ongoing racism and exclusion is erased and bigotry is redefined as majoritarian condemnation of racist views."[39] And, somewhat ironically, the Court in the second case gave no hint that the film watched by the black adolescent happened to condemn the American legal system as complicit with violence against African-Americans.[40] Perhaps the Justices cannot speak of or even cannot see their own possible implication in the patterns of power that might incite a black adolescent to violence against an unknown white person.

Similarly, it is worrisome that anti-pornography restrictions in Canada were used to censor two books by anti-pornography activist Andrea Dworkin.[41] Remember, perspective matters. Agents entrusted to enforce laws restricting hateful and subordinating speech reflect their own perceptions about what precisely is hateful and subordinating—and those perceptions inevitably will be partial to, and potentially even discriminatory against the least powerful or most vulnerable members of the society. The First Amendment absolutists are right to remind us all that restrictions on speech will be administered by people who have their own motives, perceptions, and values—which may well depart from those animating the movements against hate speech, pornography, and hate crimes.[42]

Thus, the case against hate speech and hate crime regulations rightly points out the dangers of selective enforcement with a likely disparate impact on the weakest and most minority members of the society. There may even be reasons to suspect that members of maltreated minority groups may be more likely to engage in escalating violent reaction against those they hate; this hate itself (though not the violence) may be understandable, even justifiable, in a world offering them insufficient social and legal protections. The targeting of hate-motivated crimes thus may have a disparate impact on members of mistreated minority groups.

Opponents of regulation are right to warn of the dangers of building up the powers of the state, which then will be exercised by people who identify with the majority group.[43] And they are right to caution that regulation would itself increase racism and other "isms" as the potential targets of regulation erupt with resentment at what they would call special protections.[44] If many perpetrators of hate crimes are themselves at risk of paranoia or a toxic mix of shame and rage, selecting them for punishment can even increase the violence,[45] although this hardly suggests excusing their behavior.

Here's one more way in which the absolutists are right, although it is not a point they themselves usually make. Freedom of expression and wide latitude for opinions, for associations, and for organizing have been absolutely central to every social movement for change in the United States. Without such freedoms, we would not have had the civil rights movement, the women's rights movement, and the gay rights movement. To the extent that advocates of hate regulation are more fundamentally advocates of equality, they need an ample free speech doctrine to enhance their larger political strategy and aim.

What Is Wrong with Both the Anti-Regulation and Pro-Regulation Views?

Paradoxically, this very point leads me to turn to what's wrong with the views of those who oppose regulations—and then also what's wrong with the pro-regulation views. It thus turns out that they're both wrong—and yes, they can both be wrong.

Among the most elaborated criticisms of hate crimes regulations is a recent book by James B. Jacobs and Kimberly Potter.[46] They argue that hate crimes legislation emerged from identity politics—where people organize for recognition around the categories of race, gender, and sexual orientation for strategic advantage—and that this form of politics sparks a contentious debate as to which prejudices count and which do not. They claim that regulation reflects symbolic politics, rather than having the effect of actually reducing violence, and hate crimes statutes actually exacerbate intergroup conflict with unreliable data and conflicts over how specific incidents should be labeled and treated.

Stripped to its core, this is like the objection to affirmative action or any other effort to remedy group-based harms through a recognition of the group. Yes, there's a difference. In the hate speech and hate crimes contexts, protections are symmetrical: anti-white and anti-male, anti-straight and anti-Christian speech and actions are potentially as actionable as anti-black, anti-Asian, anti-Hispanic, anti-female, anti-Semitic, anti-Muslim words and violence. But hate speech proposals and hate crimes laws do select for special regulation these kinds of group-based divisions rather than targeting greed, or political party affiliation, or countless other potential bases for disagreement and violence. Groups could as easily be defined by reference to these kinds of traits. Hence, laws that confine themselves to racial, sexual, religious, and ethnic groups are underinclusive. The rejoinder to this point is like the defense of anti-discrimination laws: that some group traits are highlighted when they are used as grounds for discrimination in order to remedy discrimination.

Now reasonable people can and do disagree about how best to remedy historic and continuing group-based discriminations. Nonetheless, the only fair and honest starting point is to acknowledge the underlying dilemma. When people have been badly treated because of group membership, ignoring their group membership *and* recognizing it can both hold risks for perpetuating group-based harm. I argue elsewhere that the only way out of this dilemma embraces both kinds of responses: there must be group-conscious legal claims for dealing with past bad treatment on the basis of group membership, and there must be vigorous expansions of the freedoms of individuals to define themselves rather than be categorized as members of groups.[47]

Of course, I may be wrong. But I challenge those who prefer no hate crimes to explain precisely what their strategy is for remedying the actual and persistent degradations and exclusions experienced by many persons of color, women, gays, and lesbians, and disabled people. If the difference in opinion is about the relative importance of these kinds of goals in our polity, then let's make that clear, rather than suggesting that there is something itself discriminatory or volatile in using law to remedy the targeting of members of some groups for hateful speech and actions.

To those who question how there is anything worse in being the target of a hate crime because one is a member of a despised group rather than because of one's status as a friend, co-worker, or lover, I assert as loudly as possible that being the target of any crime is horrible. But the link between group membership and the dehumanization itself injures and produces increased risks of victimization. This warrants vigilant public attention. Yes, the particular list of groups identified in any piece of legislation can be underinclusive. But I find the Canadian solution to the problem of underinclusion in hate-crimes legislation quite promising; Canada's law permits enhanced sentencing upon evidence of "any other similar factor" like bias based on race, national origin, language, sex, and the other familiar catalogue of group categories.[48] To find crimes targeting individuals because of their group membership deserving of enhanced punishment when compared with parallel crimes lacking that feature is not to find some lives more valuable than others.[49] But terror and degradation pinned on individuals because of their group affiliation warrants disapprobation by the community in which they live. That kind of expression of stern condemnation is what the criminal law affords.

Additional defects mar the argument that hate crimes legislation violates the First Amendment protection against governmental restraints on freedom of expression. The claim is that increased criminal sanctions should not apply to those who are thinking about the race or other group membership of a target because their opinions, including hateful ones, are rightful subjects for First Amendment protection. What is quite peculiar about this argument is that it neglects the way in which many if not most crimes have expressive content; nonetheless, we have long been untroubled in deploying state power against people who act violently on their beliefs.

Psychiatrist James Gilligan writes that violent people, in particular, are very oriented "toward expressing their thoughts in the forms of actions rather than words."[50] Mutilating a victim, for example, expresses something that killing alone does not.[51] Shooting a shopkeeper in the midst of a robbery communicates that his safety and even his life are at that moment of less value to the perpetrator than the stolen money or goods.

Being shot at is one violation; being shot at because you are a member of a group selected for degradation or harm is a further, distinct violation.

Fine, the First Amendment advocate says, but the government should not be in the business of ranking expression, and giving some forms more and some forms less punishment. Each murder, each assault, each act of comparable physical violence should receive the same punishment. Otherwise, the government is itself interfering with the thoughts of the actors, and those thoughts deserve First Amendment protection. Well, in response, I can only note that for better or for worse, our tradition of criminal law does indeed look into people's minds. The kind of intention underlying a crime does affect blameworthiness. Premeditated murder is worse than killing in the heat of the moment. Jacobs and Potter argue that greed, jealousy, or simple cold-bloodedness are not connected to political beliefs the way that bigotry is, and therefore it is only when criminal law provides enhanced punishment for bigotry that First Amendment problems arise.[52]

Yet, as my colleague Carol Steiker—an experienced public defender— responds, our criminal law permits reduction of criminal sanction where the wrongdoer was understandably provoked.[53] Historically, these reductions have occurred in the cases of mutual combat and the observation by a husband of his wife committing adultery. From one perspective, these are male-oriented protections, and reformers may want to change the specific grounds for provocation. But the point here is that our law inevitably calls for judgments about different kinds of motives, and even about what kinds of norms held by individual defendants about human relationships should be validated by the state and what kinds should not.[54]

Surely, the government can recognize views degrading particular groups as worthy of condemnation and punishment. If this were not the case, as Cass Sunstein points out, then civil rights laws themselves would be in constitutional jeopardy. For acts of racial and gender discrimination in employment, housing, and education also express views. Sunstein comments: "Perhaps it could be said that the civil rights laws sweep up communicative discharges as an incidental part of an effort to prevent a class of activities defined in terms of conduct rather than expression. But if the justification behind the civil rights laws is in fact sufficiently neutral, the same seems true [of a hate crimes law]."[55] Otherwise, housing, education, and employment decisions would not be subject, lawfully, to review to ensure they are not made on the basis of the racial identity of the applicant.

But those who favor restrictions on hate crimes and hate speech are also wrong to imagine that these would be the most effective or even very effective measures in curbing group hatred. I have already touched on the danger that regulating hatred can itself have unintended consequences and the risk that it can trigger new and increased resentments against the supposed beneficiaries of the protections. Especially in the context of this country's political culture, people charged under hate speech rules become martyrs and even poster children for those worried about governmental power. Censorship and punishment of ideas can turn those ideas into forbidden fruit, especially attractive to youth engaged in rebellion and others searching for symbols of disobedience.

The efforts to use state power to restrict hatred may be so deeply and even inherently ineffective that they end up a form of permission and further terror, demonstrating in their very inefficacy the total vulnerability of those whom they would protect. To have hate crimes legislation on the books with few prosecutions and even fewer convictions can speak volumes to those who regularly face unaddressed harassment and threat. Yet enforcement is notoriously difficult; proof is difficult to gather except where the perpetrators have spoken and written their hatred frequently and accessibly. Investigating people before they commit acts of violence poses much more obvious dangers of violations of freedoms of speech and association. The FBI's own history of suppressing dissenting groups has rightly led to far more self-restraint today. But the result is that even the most visible and threatening hate groups—groups whose Web sites and leaflets animate and support shooters in Littleton, Colorado, Los Angeles, California; Bloomington, Indiana, and elsewhere—remain considerably insulated from investigation.

Even more basically, government rules against hate may be inherently doomed. Judith Butler has explored the "paradoxical production of speech by censorship" that "works in implicit and inadvertent ways."[56] As she notes, "The regulation that *states what it does not want stated* thwarts its own desire, conducting a performative contradiction that throws into question the regulation's capacity to mean and do what it says."[57]

What Do I Think?

The most powerful defect in the push to regulate hate crimes and hate speech, however, is how such regulation detracts from other efforts to address the sources and effects of group hatred. For example, there are limited resources in terms of attention, time, and money to combat the kind of hatred of gays and lesbians that leads some people to assault and even murder individuals simply because they have, or are believed to have, a same-sex orientation. Targeting the societal permission to discriminate against gays and lesbians in the workplace, in housing, and in the benefits associated with family status would address more deeply the practices of dehumanization than would hate crimes legislation and would remove the societal supports for the actions of the most violent homophobes. Gay and lesbian advocacy organizations have rallied around hate crime legislation because, through passage of these laws, they hoped that even people who condemn homosexuality would agree that no one should be tortured or murdered. The memory of Matthew Shepard—tied to a fence, severely beaten, burned, and left to die in Laramie, Wyoming—helped to animate this as a federal strategy, as did the fact that Wyoming subsequently refused to adopt its own hate crimes legislation in response.[58] But preventing pervasive social degradation of particular groups would do more to protect them from harm and improve their life chances than prosecuting a few extremely violent individuals who act upon the pervasive stigma and dehumanization of targeted groups.

In the case of speech codes on college campuses, the focus on restrictions seems to be simply a distraction and a diversion of precious resources away from more effective remedies. Those codes invite challenge, and a wide range of civil libertarians and academic freedom supporters join in support of those who have tested the regulations. Rather than devote energy to the disciplinary code debate, I suggest that we address the following questions: What are the sources of the hate incidents? How can hateful actions be cabined or curtailed? College campuses are now more diverse, with members of more different groups than they had in the past. Many college students encounter people who differ from themselves for the first time in the intense and intimate settings of classrooms and dorms. Yet colleges have not undergone any fundamental changes. Most have not diversified their faculties to resemble the makeup of their student bodies; nor have they renovated curricular offerings. Instead, their role models and course content reiterate longstanding assumptions about who and what are essential and who and what are marginal.

Nonwhite students have for decades spoken powerfully of the burdens they feel when no white students point out racist dimensions of a class discussion or reading. Why must the minority educate the majority, and why is the majority's ignorance so durable?[59] Of course, the very language of "majority" and "minority" is too crude. Prejudices persist beyond specific expressions of hate and across many lines of group affiliation and identity. A Latina told me she was just settling in for a comfortable lunch with other Hispanic students when one made an anti-gay comment that she wanted to oppose but found it hard to voice. Catholic women in a class joined across racial lines to object to assumptions others made about abortion politics. A Korean immigrant led the discussion in one class in opposition to bilingual education; his chief opponent was a Russian immigrant. The palpable differences in security, support, anger, and injury among different students in the same class should remind us to attend to the influence of perspective on such basic questions as the meaning of free speech and the requisites for learning.

Colleges need to address not only the content and omissions in the curriculum, but also how the hidden curriculum—manifested in eating and living arrangements, the management of students' job hunts, and other pervasive features—makes it seem possible and even acceptable to put down or threaten members of particular groups. Here, the practices permitted for dorms and fraternities require vigorous review. Group-based social and living arrangements may provide comfort and security for college students. Yet the connections between white fraternities and hate incidents against nonwhites, women, and gays are too frequent to ignore. Offering an alternative that models the hard work needed for building solidarity, Northeastern University sponsors a fraternity organized around diversity.[60] Imagine how differently students in that fraternity perceive intergroup issues in the classroom and elsewhere.

Yet no one should romanticize the relationship between familiarity and tolerance. Intergroup contact per se does not foster tolerance and mutual understanding, especially against the background of competition and economic insecurity. The hidden curriculum in colleges may actually sustain scapegoating and group-linked hatreds through the competitive sorting dimensions of higher education and the job-seeking process on campuses. Most colleges and universities have yet to fold into the fields of academic study and orientation programs for students analysis of the links between economic competition and upsurges of intergroup conflict, but they should. Competition for grades and jobs, especially in periods of economic uncertainty, fertilizes resentments and the sense of jeopardy that feed into pre-existing group prejudices. Again, I must comment on how the adoption of Proposition 187 in California made blaming immigrants for economic constraints in the state a feature of public policy; how surprising, then, are hate crimes against immigrants? Making

these precise connections between economic tensions and group targeting a subject for study and attention could at least help students name
and distance themselves from the process of loading general fears and
defenses onto particular groups. Similarly, engaging students in the task
of recognizing hate literature and troubling stereotypes or terms of group
derision, whether on the Internet or in classic works of literature and
philosophy, can sharpen their analytic abilities while equipping them to
monitor sources of unconscious and yet pervasive prejudices.

Oddly, the focus on speech codes in colleges and concerns about
ensuring freedom of beliefs seemed at least for a while to shield incidents and injuries that easily fit within standard notions of libel, destruction of property, intentional infliction of emotional distress, and basic
rules against assault.[61] When two white men at a university poured urine
on an African-American woman, when members of a white fraternity
tied up a pledge and dumped him with "KKK" painted on his body on
the campus of an African-American college, when property is destroyed
or defaced, state criminal and tort laws and well-established student disciplinary codes have obvious and straightforward application without
any jeopardy to freedom of expression. Collective outrage and counter-
speech remain crucial and powerful responses to hateful speech on campuses and elsewhere. A Klan march in New York elicited, as one would
hope, a much larger protest opposing the Klan's messages of hatred.

The agenda of regulating hatred, whether through hate speech restrictions or hate crimes legislation, has the unfortunate effect of focusing on
the individual perpetrator rather than the victims or the social forces that
assist and inform the perpetrator. Hate crimes prosecutions zero in on
the one with the gun, not the one with the hate-filled talk radio show,
the anti-women rap music, the neo-Nazi Web site, or the homophobic
preacher. As a result, the attention in the enforcement process and any
surrounding publicity and debate is oriented toward the individual wrongdoer. The more violent the action, the more likely the focus on the individual's psychological state and sources of imbalance. Especially in the
context of criminal law, these are crucial to determinations of guilt and
blameworthiness. But if the goal is to eradicate the dehumanization of
the hated group, attention would more fruitfully turn to both the lives
and circumstances of the victims and to the surrounding social traditions
and practices that made and continue to make their group subject to
dehumanization.

A shift to these concerns also reflects what many people recommend
for responding to misbehavior by children: give the attention to the vic-

tim rather than the wrongdoer because part of the reason for the misbehavior is to gain adult attention. Of course, this does not mean permanently ignoring the wrongdoer nor excusing him from consequences.
But comforting the victim and ensuring that her needs are taken care of
before dealing with the offender expresses the right order of values and
rejects the wrongdoer's framing of the matter. With young children, it
can work to invite a group to brainstorm ideas for responding to those
who mock or degrade others.[62] Engaging observers in this task can generate effective ideas; it can also cultivate the capacity for responding in
students themselves, who ultimately are in the best position to take responsibility for the social norms within the peer group.

What would it take to empower those who are the actual or likely
targets of other people's aggression? One stirring effort in this direction is
represented by the dramatically successful civil lawsuit brought against
Tom and John Metzger and the White Aryan Resistance Organization for
recruiting young skinheads who then killed an Ethiopian immigrant in
Portland, Oregon.[63] The trial exposed how the cable access television
programs, newspapers, hotlines, and personal recruitment by the leaders
of the hate group mobilized and sustained the young perpetrators. The
court ordered Tom and John Metzger to pay $6 million in damages to the
victim's family and also assigned damages to their organization.[64] Although the Metzgers were unrepentant, and threatened to target police,
lawyers, and judges in the future, the suit sent shock waves through hate
organizations, practically bankrupted at least one of these organizations,
and illuminated ways in which technologically sophisticated hate organizations contribute directly and indirectly to violence against vulnerable
groups. The lawsuit's architects at the Southern Poverty Law Center and
the Anti-Defamation League demonstrated how nongovernmental organizations can redirect attention through civil action from punishing the
individual perpetrators of a hate crime to exposing the social roots of
hate violence. This particular civil trial put the public spotlight on the
larger chain of actors and forces behind the young people who commit
the lion's share of criminal property damage and violent assaults attributable to group hatreds.

It also seems vital to recognize adolescents and even younger children
as prime audiences for efforts to prevent verbal and violent expressions
of intergroup hatred. Adolescents are the prime absorbers of pop culture
and the prime perpetrators of hate crimes. Adolescence and early adulthood are the periods in American life when most people develop the
kinds of memories and tastes that will be most enduring in their life-

times.[65] Younger children are even more impressionable. So for elementary school students, I endorse educational programs for responding to hatred, promoting tolerance, and developing critical tools to combat unexamined prejudices. Yet I worry that such programs may be too late for adolescents. I invite you to join me in thinking about what would be effective with teens. Can the pop culture be infiltrated by anti-hate messages? Is it possible to develop humor—jokes and ribbing—that do not depend upon group stereotypes and put-downs—and actually combat them? What would it take for anti-hate to be cool?

One more big area requires sustained attention. Violence and humiliations in the home prepare people for committing violence and humiliating others. How do current responses to violence against women and children stem from or contribute to hate speech, hate crimes, and even mass interethnic violence of the sort we have seen only too vividly in Bosnia, Rwanda, and elsewhere? Even proponents of hate crimes legislation are torn about how to treat gender, because of the difficulties in determining when an assault, rape, or murder of a woman by someone who knows her reflects a hatred of her gender as opposed to something more particular in their relationship. Yet the vulnerability of women to intimate and ferocious violence may both reflect and underlie hatred directed at other group identities. Many extremely violent individuals were severely abused as children (although far from most survivors of child abuse go on to commit violence). James Gilligan argues that "human violence only erupts when there are triggers from the social environment, which act on a personality that has been sensitized to shame."[66] It is crucial, therefore, to address potential connections between intimate and intergroup violence. The bigger issues connecting these harms and legal responses to them involve the relationship between collective memory and collective messages. How can collective responses to hatred break rather than invigorate cycles of revenge?

NOTES

1. See Daniel Goleman, "Humor Found to Aid Problem Solving," *New York Times* (August 4, 1987): C1.

2. Mankoff, *New Yorker* (August 22, 1988): 61.

3. Carsootii, *New Yorker* (November 21, 1988): 55.

4. D. Marlette, Kudzu, *Chicago Tribune* (November 28, 1988): Sec. 5, p. 8.

5. See Neil Frude, "Hatred Between Children," in Ved Masma, ed., *How and Why Children Hate* (London: Jessica Kingsley Publishers, 1993), pp. 72–73 (dis-

cussing Anthony Storr, *Human Aggression:* [New York, Atheneum, 1968], p. 92); Robin Higgins, "Hate in Nursery Rhymes," in *How and Why Children Hate*, supra, at 1.

6. Jack Levin and Jack McDevitt, *Hate Crimes: The Rising Tide of Bigotry and Bloodshed* (New York: Plenun, 1993), p. 129.

7. Id., p. 135. For other incidents, see Jon Weiner, "Words That Wound: Free Speech for Campus Bigots," *The Nation* 250 (February 26, 1990): 272; Steven J. Heyman, "Righting the Balance: An Inquiry into the Foundations and Limits of Freedom of Expression," *Boston University Law Review* 78, no. 6 (1998): 1275, 1376–79.

8. For a summary of these developments, see Kenneth L. Karst, *Law's Promise, Law's Expression: Visions of Power in the Politics of Race, Gender, and Religion* (New Haven, CT: Yale University Press, 1993), pp. 90–103.

9. See Frederick M. Lawrence, *Punishing Hate: Bias Crimes Under American Law* (Cambridge, MA: Harvard University Press, 1999), p. 9. For the competing view, see James B. Jacobs and Kimberly Potter, *Hate Crimes: Criminal Law and Identity Politics* (New York: Oxford University Press 1998).

10. See Robert Leikind, "Hate Graffiti Can't Be Blamed on 'Just Kids,'" *New Haven Register* (October 28, 1993); reprinted in Preliminary Report of the Special Subcommittee on Bias Incidents and Hate Crimes to the Board of Police Commissioners, New Haven, Connecticut, *Bias and Hate Crimes in New Haven: A Cooperative Strategy for Change* (Fall 1994) (appendix).

11. Levin and McDevitt, *Hate Crimes*, supra, at 25.

12. Andrew Sullivan, "What's So Bad About Hate?" *New York Times Magazine* (September 26, 1999): 50.

13. See Martha Minow, *Between Vengeance and Forgiveness: Facing History after Genocide and Mass Violence* (Boston: Beacon Press, 1998); Tina Rosenberg, *The Haunted Land: Facing Europe's Ghosts after Communism* (New York: Random House, 1995).

14. Richard Delgado, "Words That Wound: A Tort Action for Racial Insults, Epithets, and Name-Calling," *Harvard Civil Rights-Civil Liberties Law Review* 17 (1982): 133. See, generally, Samuel Walker, *Hate Speech: The History of an American Controversy* (Lincoln: University of Nebraska Press, 1994).

15. Mari J. Matsuda, "Public Responses to Racist Speech: Considering the Victim's Story," *Michigan Law Review* 87 (1989): 2320, see also Charles R. Lawrence, III, "If He Hollers Let Him Go: Regulating Racist Speech on Campus," *Duke Law Journal* (1990): 431, 449–57; Toni M. Massaro, "Equality and Freedom of Expression: The Hate Speech Dilemma," *William and Mary Law Review* 32 (1991): 211.

16. See *University of Wisconsin Madison Post v. Board of Regents*, 774 F. Supp. 1163 (E.D. Wis. 1991); *Doe v. University of Michigan*, 721 F. Supp. 852 (E.D. Mich. 1989).

17. See Catharine A. MacKinnon, *Feminism Unmodified: Discourses on Life and Law* (Cambridge, MA: Harvard University Press, 1987), pp. 184–85; Cathar-

ine A. MacKinnon, *Only Words* (Cambridge, MA: Harvard University Press, 1993), pp. 22–23; see also Karst, *Law's Promise, Law's Expression*, supra, at 43–50.

18. See *American Booksellers Association v. Hudnut*, 598 F. Supp. 1316 (D. Ind. 1984), affirmed, 771 F.2d 323 (7th Cir. 1985), affirmed, 475 U.S. 1001 (1986). See also Frank I. Michelman, "Conceptions of Democracy in American Constitutional Argument: The Case of Pornography Regulation," *Tennessee Law Review* 56 (1989): 291; Cass R. Sunstein, "Neutrality in Constitutional Law (with Special Reference to Pornography, Abortion, and Surrogacy)," *Columbia Law Review* 92 (1992): 1. See, generally, Paul Brest and Ann Vandenberg, "Politics, Feminism, and the Constitution: The Anti-Pornography Movement in Minneapolis," *Stanford Law Review* 39 (1987): 607.

19. See Frank I. Michelman, "Family Quarrel," *Cardozo Law Review* 17, no. 46 (1996): 1163, 1177; Frank I. Michelman, "Super Liberal: Romance, Community, and the Tradition in William J. Brennan, Jr.'s Constitutional Thought," *Virginia Law Review* 77 (1991): 1261, 1278–79.

20. See Kenneth L. Karst, "Equality as a Central Principle in the First Amendment," *University of Chicago Law Review* 43, no. 20 (1975): 64.

21. Steven H. Shiffrin, *Dissent, Injustice, and the Meanings of America* 77 (Princeton, NJ: Princeton University Press, 1999), p. 77.

22. See Owen M. Fiss, "The Supreme Court and the Problem of Hate Speech," *Capitol University Law Review* 24 (1995): 281, 287–88.

23. See Karst, *Law's Promise, Law's Expression*, supra, at 102; Gilbert Paul Carrasco, "Hate Speech and the First Amendment: On a Collision Course?," *Villanova Law Review* 37 (1993): 723, 727–29; Robert C. Post, "Racist Speech, Democracy, and the First Amendment," *William and Mary Law Review* 32 (1991): 267, 273.

24. See Shiffrin, *Dissent, Injustice, and the Meanings of America*, supra, at 30.

25. See Frank I. Michelman, "Saving Old Glory: On Constitutional Iconography," *Stanford Law Review* 42 (1990): 1337, 1349–50 (1990) (questioning formalist First Amendment analysis).

26. See Kent Greenawalt, *Fighting Words: Individuals, Communities, and Liberties of Speech* (Princeton, NJ: Princeton University Press, 1995), pp. 11–27; David Kretzmer, "Freedom of Speech and Racism," *Cardozo Law Review* 8 (1987): 445; Kenneth Lasson, "Racism in Great Britain: Drawing the Line on Free Speech," *Boston College Third World Law Journal* 7 (1987): 161, 179–81; Mathias Reimann, "Purient Interest and Human Dignity: Pornography and Regulation in West Germany and the United States," *University of Michigan Journal of Law Reform* 21 (1987–1988): 201; Jeffrey Ian Ross, "Hate Crimes in Canada: Growing Pains with New Legislation," in Mark S. Hamm, ed., *Hate Crime: International Perspectives on Causes and Control* (Cincinnati: Anderson Publishing, 1994), pp. 151–72; Martha Shaffer, "Criminal Responses to Hate-Motivated Violence: Is Bill-41 Tough Enough?," *McGill Law Journal* 41 (1995): 199; Justice Richard J. Goldstone, "The South African Bill of Rights," *Texas International Law Journal*

32 (Summer 1997): 451, 467–68 ("The right [to freedom of expression] does not extend to—(a) propaganda for war; (b) incitement of imminent violence, or (c) advocacy of hatred that is based on race, ethnicity, gender or religion, and that constitutes incitement to cause harm," citing South African Constitution Section 16 [1993]); Edward J. Eberle, "Public Discourse in Contemporary Germany," *Case Western Reserve Law Review* 47 (1997): 797.

27. Brendon Lemon, "The State of Hate," *The Advocate* (April 13, 1999): 28.

28. Shiffrin, *Dissent, Injustice, and the Meanings of America*, supra, at 31.

29. Mark S. Hamm, "Conceptualizing Hate Crime in a Global Context," in Mark S. Hamm, ed., *Hate Crime* supra, at 173, 182–189.

30. Erwin Staub, *The Roots of Evil: The Origins of Genocide and Other Group Violence* (Cambridge: Cambridge University Press, 1989), p. 242.

31. Id., at 243.

32. See Levin and McDevitt, *Hate Crimes*, supra, at 48, 55–63. See also Kenneth L. Karst, "Boundaries and Reasons: Freedom of Expression and the Subordination of Groups," *University of Illinois Law Review* (1990): 95, 148–49.

33. See Post, "Racist Speech," supra, at 325–27; Nadine Strossen, "Regulating Racist Speech on Campus: A Modest Proposal?," *Duke Law Journal* (1990): 484, 521–22.

34. During the questions following a presentation I made in 1989 about hate speech regulations, Professor Regina Austin commented that if the regulations aim for a climate of civility on campuses, the likely targets for punishment will be people in minority groups, people who may most need avenues to protest and resist dominant modes of expression. Speech codes authorizing punishment of students for offensive and injurious statements in classrooms, public speeches, and demonstrations bode ill for unpopular views without getting at the sources of hate.

35. 505 U.S. 377 (1992).

36. The St. Paul Legislation read: "Whoever places on public or private property a symbol, object, appellation, characterization or graffiti, including, but not limited to, a burning cross or Nazi swastika, which one knows or has reasonable grounds to know arouses anger, alarm or resentment in others on the basis of race, color, creed, religion or gender commits disorderly conduct and shall be guilty of a misdemeanor." *R.A.V.*, 505 U.S. at 380 (quoting St. Paul, Minnesota Legislative Code Section 292.02 [1990]).

37. 508 U.S. 476 (1993).

38. Compare *R.A.V. v. City of St. Paul*, 505 U.S. 377, 396 (1992) with *Wisconsin v. Mitchell*, 508 U.S. 476 (1993). The Wisconsin law, based on a model statute drafted by the Anti-Defamation League and copied now in most states, provides for increasing the penalty for crimes against people or property if the victim or object has been intentionally selected "in whole or in part because of the actor's belief or perception regarding the [victim's] race, religion, color, disability, sexual orientation, national origin or ancestry. . . . whether or not the actor's belief or

perception was correct." Wisconsin Statute Annotated Section 939.645 (St. Paul, MN: West, 1996).

39. Mari J. Matusda and Charles R. Lawrence, III, "Epilogue," in Mari J. Matsuda, Charles R. Lawrence III, Richard Delgado, and Kimberle Williams Crenshaw, eds., *Words that Wound: Critical Race Theory, Assaultive Speech and the First Amendment* (Boulder, CO: Westview Press, 1993), p. 135.

40. Judith Butler connects this point to ideas about gender and sexuality in Judith Butler, *Excitable Speech* (New York: Routledge, 1997), pp. 60–62. In the film, *Mississippi Burning* (Metro-Goldwyn-Mayer, 1988), the courts are complicit with the Klan; only when a lone Justice Department official acts against the law and brutalizes those he interrogates does something like justice emerge. Butler argues that in this way, the film depicts the courts as feminized and the lone official injects a needed dose of masculinity. Butler, at 61.

41. See Jeffrey Toobin, "X-Rated," *New Yorker* (October 3, 1994): 70, 74.

42. See, generally, Jeannine Bell, "Policing Hatred: Police Bias Units and the Construction of Hate Crimes," *Michigan Journal of Race and Law* 2 (1997): 421, 443, 457.

43. See Kathleen M. Sullivan, "Resurrecting Free Speech," *Fordham Law Review* 63 (1995): 971, 983–84; Kathleen M. Sullivan, "The Supreme Court, 1991 Term—Foreword: The Justices of Rules and Standards," *Harvard Law Review* 106 (1992): 22, 44; Kathleen M. Sullivan, "The First Amendment Wars," *New Republic* (September 28, 1992): 35.

44. For regulations opposed by those they seek to protect, see Shiffrin, *Dissent, Injustice, and the Meanings of America*, supra, at 85.

45. James Gilligan, *Violence: Our Deadly Epidemic and Its Causes* (New York: Grosset/Putnam, 1996) pp. 111–12, 156, 287.

46. Jacobs and Potter, *Hate Crimes: Criminal Law and Identity Politics*, supra.

47. Martha Minow, *Not Only For Myself: Identity, Politics, and the Law* (New Press, 1997).

48. See Bill C-14, codified in Canadian Criminal Code as section 718.2: "A Court that imposes a sentence shall also take into consideration the following principles:

(a) sentence should be increased or reduced to account for any relevant aggravating or mitigating circumstances relating to the offence or the offender, and without limiting the generality of the foregoing,

  (i) evidence that the offense was motivated by bias, prejudice, or hate based on race, national or ethnic origin, language, colour, religion, sex, age, mental or physical disability, sexual orientation, or any other similar factor. . . ."

Shaffer, *Criminal Responses to Hate-Motivated Violence*, supra, at 248, note 175 (quoting R.S.C., ch. C-46, Section 718.2 [1985] [Can.]). Of course, Canada also treats hate speech differently. See Mayo Moran, "Talking About Hate Speech: A

Rhetorical Analysis of American and Canadian Approaches to the Regulation of Hate Speech," *Wisconsin Law Review* (1994): 1425.

49. See Richard Cohen, "The Trouble With Hate-Crime Laws," *Washington Post* (October 19, 1999): A19 (op-ed).

50. James Gilligan, *Violence: Our Deadly Epidemic and its Causes* (New York: Grosset/Putnam, 1996), p. 62. See id., at 75: "Behavior can be just as symbolic as words; . . . like words, bodily behavior communicates meanings, often of astonishing specificity, about matters of life-and-death importance, which can be understood quite clearly, consistently, and reliably by those to whom the behavioral signs and signals are directed."

51. Id., at 85.

52. Jacobs and Potter, *Hate Crimes*, supra, at 127.

53. See Carol S. Steiker, "Punishing Hateful Motives: Old Wine in a New Bottle Revives Calls for Prohibition," *Michigan Law Review* 97 (1999): 1857, 1862–64. Steiker relies in part on the related work by Victoria Nourse, "Passion's Progress: Modern Law Reform and the Provocation Defense," *Yale Law Journal* 106 (1997): 1331.

54. See Steiker, "Punishing Hateful Motives," supra.

55. Cass Sunstein, "Words, Conduct, Caste," *University of Chicago Law Review* 60 (1993): 795, 828.

56. Judith Butler, *Excitable Speech* (New York: Routledge, 1997), p. 130.

57. Id.

58. See Steve Lopez, "To Be Young and Gay in Wyoming," *Time* (October 26, 1998): 38; "Gay Student Found Beaten, Tied to Fence: Wyoming Victim in Critical Condition, Four Suspects Arrested," *Dallas Morning News* (October 10, 1998): 3A, available at 1998 WL 13109150.

59. See Kimberle Crenshaw, "Foreword: Toward a Race-Conscious Pedagogy in Legal Education," *National Black Law Journal* 11 (1989): 1, 3–6.

60. Levin and McDevitt, *Hate Crimes*, supra, at 129.

61. See Heyman, "Righting the Balance," supra, at 1378–79.

62. "If I were a teacher and saw students mocking classmates with severe disabilities, I'd get those [classmates] who had observed it to brainstorm for responding. Ultimately, students are the best people to take responsibility for those kinds of social norms, and often they have the best ideas for how to work with the individuals involved." Dr. Charles Peck, professor of special education, Washington State University at Vancouver, quoted in *Teaching Tolerance, Responding to Hate at School: A Guide for Teachers, Counselors, and Administrators* (Montgomery, AL: Southern Poverty Law Center, 1999), p. 8.

63. See Levin and McDevitt, *Hate Crimes*, supra, at 99–103.

64. Id.

65. See Howard Schuman and Cheryl Rieger, "Collective Memory and Collective Memories," in Martin A. Conway et al., eds., *Theoretical Perspectives on Au-*

tobiographical Memory (Boston: Kluwer Academic Publishers, 1992), pp. 322–36.

66. Gilligan, *Violence*, supra, at 223.

.   .   .   .   .

Between Nations and Between Intimates: Can Law Stop the Violence?*

Yogi Berra is supposed to have said, "When you come to a fork in the road, take it." And "You can observe a lot by watching." And one more: "If people don't want to come out to the ball park, nobody's going to stop them."

That last one you really have to think about. Nobody's going to stop the people who don't want to come. Nobody's going to stop the apathy. I hope, and believe, that in the last thirty years actually a lot of *somebodies* have tried to stop the apathy surrounding violence in two settings: violence in the home and violence between identifiable ethnic, religious, and national groups.

Struggles against domestic violence actually can be traced, in this country at least, to the first wave of the women's movement. The women who led the Temperance Movement wanted to stop men from spending their paychecks on liquor and then coming home, broke, drunk, to beat their wives and children.[1] More recently, a lone experiment in St. Paul, Minnesota, in 1974, to create a temporary home to shelter women from violence in their own homes, inspired the thousands of shelters in place today while launching a movement for criminal law enforcement and judicially issued civil orders of protection against violence in the home. The animating vision was safety: people should be safe from physical assaults, forcible rape, and coercion by their intimate family members. The reformers have aimed to enable separation. The goal has been to make a safe place for victims (which means, chiefly, women) to go and to use the power of the law either to incapacitate the violators or to order them to stay away. Many states followed up with rules requiring police to arrest people found to be using violence against their spouses

* Gilbane Fund Lecture #3, Brown University, November 2, 1999. Special thanks to Nancy Rosenblum, James Herzog, Mark O'Connell, Pamela Steiner, Iris Young, Judith Herman, and David Estlund for their helpful comments. An earlier version of this essay appears as Martha Minow, "Between Intimates and Between Nations: Can Law Stop the Violence?," *Case Western Reserve Law Review* 50 (2000): 851. Susan Sturm and Betsy Harries inspired this work.

or intimate partners, and other rules requiring prosecutors to prosecute such cases—each seeking to make the criminal sanction effective.

With intergroup violence around the world, the goal has been to halt the violence and the strategy has been to advance intervention by non-governmental groups and international teams. The Middle East, Northern Ireland, Bosnia and Kosovo, Somalia and East Timor, are only the most recent settings to elicit combinations of investigatory reports, humanitarian aid, third-party negotiators, military peacekeepers, and even military intervention.

A conception of inviolable boundaries used to shield both the intimate violence and the intergroup violence from public scrutiny and intervention. For husbands and wives, it was the boundary of the home; the private sphere, shielding violence in the home, lay beyond the reach of the law, whether as criminal or tort.[2] For conflicting ethnic and religious groups, it was the boundary of the state; no one outside could be heard on matters occurring within without triggering claims that the nation's own sovereignty was at stake. The triumph of individual rights, at least as rhetoric, broke through these boundaries over the past several decades. In this country, now, it is a distinctively minority and losing view to treat the home as beyond public scrutiny, and violence behind the veil of privacy. Internationally, as manifested by Amnesty International reports, NATO management of Kosovo, Secretary-General Kofi Anan's address to the United Nations declaring an end to the old conception of state sovereignty,[3] and international responses to the elevation in 2000 of a Nazi sympathizer to the governing coalition in Austria, the rights and dignity of each individual trump state borders.

Because of this basic similarity, I began to wonder what might be learned by exchanging insights about how best to respond to violence in both kinds of settings. I have only just started this research. I will sketch here potential lines of thought and inquiry in hopes of sparking further interest in the matter.

Comparing Intrafamily and Intergroup Violence

First, let me note that many others are drawing the comparison and connection. A town hall meeting organized by the East Harlem Coalition Against Domestic Violence a few years ago set as its topic: "If change is possible in South Africa, is it possible for battered women in New York State?"[4]

One of the most memorable calls I received after I published my book, *Between Vengeance and Forgiveness*,[5] was from a woman named Judy Bethke who runs social service programs for abused children in Dorchester, a very poor section of Boston. She told me she had been asked to consult with people in Northern Ireland about the trauma children there experienced under the Troubles. I toured her facility and consulted with her, and I was shocked to see the locked ward with two six-year-olds on suicide watch, and far more devastation stemming from child abuse than I'd ever seen before. Bethke told me that when some of her Northern Ireland contacts also toured her facility, they commented that perhaps they were lucky that in their part of the world, the violence had not permeated all the way inside the family—but recent reports of domestic violence there shrink this silver lining.

Trauma is indeed a uniting theme in any comparison of violence in intimate and intergroup settings. Judith Herman wrote a highly influential book, titled, *Trauma and Recovery*, that connects the experiences of Holocaust victims, U.S. soldiers in Vietnam, battered women, child abuse victims, and incest survivors. She documents how victims of trauma in each of these circumstances come to give up their connections with others and even their moral principles in the face of terror, and how they often lose the desire to live. Those who survive often have trouble controlling their anger. They relive traumatic events. They often have difficulties sustaining relationships, beliefs, and a sense of meaning.[6]

The shared features of trauma justify comparing violence against women by their intimate partners and violence against neighbors by their neighbors. The two contexts also share the traditional assumption of firm borders and boundaries, shielded against public scrutiny, and the ascendancy of individual human rights over the past thirty years that challenge those traditional assumptions. Once each individual is understood to be a rights bearer of equal dignity, the rationales of state sovereignty and privacy can no longer shield violations of individual rights from view. Instead, such shields begin to look like governmental complicity with the perpetrators of violence.

So far so good. But a funny thing happened on the way to the comparison. I began to notice a striking difference in the typical legal remedy pursued in the two contexts of domestic violence and intergroup violence. For domestic violence, the usual remedy of choice is separation: get the woman to a shelter, or make sure she gets a civil protection order with an order for the abuser to vacate the premises and stay away from her and the children, or get the police to arrest the violator immediately and to prosecute, even if the woman has second thoughts.[7] For intergroup violence, the usual remedy is reconciliation, at least sufficient enough to permit peaceful coexistence. The analogy to separation would be partition of the territory—an option that is widely viewed as a poor solution.

Now, obviously, the circumstances differ considerably. With interethnic conflict, there are likely two groups with claims to the same or neighboring territory and no good options for relocating one of the groups. And interethnic conflict seemed to stop at the doorway of private homes—at least until Sarajevo and Rwanda showed us family members killing family members. Sometimes, the source of the intergroup violence can be traced to demagogic leaders or to factions that receive the blame while the mass of individuals themselves are then encouraged to work out a way to live together.

By contrast, with violence between intimate adults, closed doors signal danger and safety itself has seemed to require separation. Central questions, rightly or wrongly, have addressed why women stay in battering relationships, and what it takes to either help her to leave or to get him removed.[8] Landmark decisions have even ruled that a court order directing the man to vacate the premises does not violate his property rights, even if the lease or deed is in his name.[9] Often, the woman is caring for children and therefore has a greater need for the home; also, tacitly, the options of vacate orders and even battered women's shelters acknowledge that women may not be safe from other kinds of violence and economic disaster if they simply get out of their homes. The assumption is that the battered individual is much less powerful, economically and physically, and therefore law must not only separate her from the abuser, but also stand in for her in decisions about whether to arrest and prosecute him.

This actually presents a profound dilemma. Should victims' choices be respected enough to determine whether to arrest and prosecute an abuser, or is paternalism warranted, given the danger that victims may recant and oppose the arrest or prosecution of the abuser out of fear of future violence?[10] The paternalist approach risks recreating the pattern of forced helplessness that makes so many women victims of violence. But respecting the choice of women whose choices are so constrained by the realities of intimate violence risks further coercion, danger, and fear for the women and any children in the home. Certainly, the picture of the helpless victim contributes to the difficulties faced by battery victims who do not fit that image because they fight back and even kill the aggressor.

The responses to child abuse in this country provide a middle ground between legal responses to battering between adults on the one side and intergroup conflict on the other. Over the past twenty years, we have been extremely torn in this country about whether to remove from the home children who have been abused—and to make this removal permanent, requiring a new permanent placement—or instead to try to preserve the family, infuse it with services and supports, and make coexistence, if not reconciliation, possible.

Advocates of family preservation successfully secured passage of the federal Adoption Assistance and Child Welfare Act of 1980, which emphasizes that the most desirable place for children is with their own families and which requires states receiving federal funds to make "reasonable efforts" to prevent unnecessary out-of-home placements and to make reasonable efforts to return a child to the family of origin.[11] Its supporters stress that the racial and class biases of governmentally employed social workers lead to extreme misuse of the removal option. Societal circumstances of poverty and stressful conditions contribute to problems within the home and parents should not be blamed for them; the most likely alternative placement—foster care—does not offer children stability, love, a permanent home, or even safety from abuse. Families of color and immigrant families are in jeopardy—one out of five mothers in some communities are labeled outlaws[12]—if state power to remove children is unchecked.[13] The nation's longstanding history of breaking up African-American families and removing Indian children from their communities should caution against ready use of governmental power to separate children from their families today, warn those who favor family preservation.

In addition, removal of the child to foster care or even an adoptive home produces an irremediable loss of foundational relationships, a loss that can impose lifelong trauma. An unfixable sense of loss and rejection may also be coupled with fantasies about the absent parent that may even lead the child to idealize his rage and violence. Someone must take care of children until they can take care of themselves. Some advocates for family preservation maintain that those who gave birth to them are more likely to care what happens to them than anyone else. Others emphasize that social programs such as home visiting for newborns and their families, day care, Head Start, and family support programs can give children real life chances without removing them from their families of origin.[14] When governments instead remove children from their parents and extended families, they are putting full responsibility on parents for patterns that, at least in part, are affected by—or capable of remediation by—social practices.

Advocates of removal argue, in contrast, that giving parents second, third, and fourth chances wrongly minimizes the effects of abuse and neglect on children and also wrongly turns the children into secondary rather than primary subjects of concern.[15] They stress that the focus on family preservation led child welfare agencies, lawyers, and judges to try to preserve families at all costs, even when families seemed hopelessly dysfunctional and when children had suffered extreme forms of abuse. Therefore, they successfully sought the 1997 federal Adoption and Safe Families Act to specify that reasonable efforts were *not* required in such cases.[16]

Removal advocates further claim that rehabilitation efforts do not work, at least in instances of severe child abuse.[17] The high levels of substance abuse by violent and neglecting parents should—excuse the expression—*sober up* the do-gooders about the difficulties in getting the parents to change. Recidivism rates in substance abuse and failure rates in treatment programs should be enough to show that most of the using parents will continue to use, and continue to put their children at risk.

Most basically, each new chance given to parents postpones the moment when the child will need a permanent placement. Not only does this make it harder for children to move and adjust, it also means the children will be older, more scarred, and frankly less attractive to potentially permanent adoptive homes, rather than temporary foster homes. Adoption by strangers would be better than extended foster care even with kin if, in the words of one commentator, "the strangers can promote [the children's] best lifetime developmental opportunities for success and self-sufficiency."[18] Some experts recommend removing the children as infants at the first sign of parental substance abuse—and then placing the infants with adoptive parents who exist in far larger numbers than prospective adoptive parents willing to take older and potentially troubled children. Above all, experts agree, children's safety and well-being should be the focus.[19] But they disagree about what arrangements following abuse best serve the child.

I will not be able to resolve this argument over family preservation and child removal, by myself, here and now.[20] But the fact that child abuse has produced this intense disagreement over appropriate legal responses helps to highlight the contrasting responses to domestic violence between adults and to intergroup violence. Joining the family preservation and intergroup reconciliation modes are two quite different claims. First, relationships themselves are vital; breaking them off itself produces trauma while work on reconciliation can be healing and constructive.

Second, and in quite a different key, there are no good alternatives. Where exactly can the children go where they will have a better chance for love, care, and freedom from abuse? In most states, a child removed to foster care then faces the risks of several more changes in placement—and the same or greater chances of abuse in the foster home as the chances that exist among biological families. This should give pause to any judge or social worker who takes seriously the injunction, "First do no harm."[21] With interethnic conflict, commonly, there are no other places for people to go either; who exactly should have to leave Jerusalem? The ethnic Albanian Kosovars did not belong in Albania, nor did the Albanians want them. I don't think that anyone thinks it a good result that the Serbs largely fled Kosovo (or faced some terrible acts of revenge) as the ethnic Albanians returned. And yet some Serbs still engage in vicious violence against the ethnic Albanians while each claim Kosovo as their own.

The analogy between the removal of a child and the removal of an ethnic group from a scene of conflict is not perfect. But two elements join the strategy of removing a child from the home of abusive parents and the strategy of seeking safe separation for adults in abusive relationships. Safety is the highest priority; and fundamental pessimism is the rational stance toward the possibility of changing the behavior of those who are violent.

For children, those seeking removal view the relationships themselves as less valuable than giving the children a new start; those children may say that they want to stay with an abusive parent but that is because they know nothing else. Similarly, with intimate abuse between adults, the overpowering assumption in this country is that the relationships themselves are not worth salvaging. The tendency of many abused women to try to reconcile with their abusers is seen as a problem, not a strength. These women should be encouraged to assume more self-reliance even though their own judgments about whether or not to support the arrest and prosecution of the abuser should not determine the law enforcement response.

Now some women in abusive relationships have clearly asked for help in stopping the violence, but do not want to end the relationship. Some advocates have urged forms of reconciliation between the partners while always putting safety first. The goal is not false forgiveness, which damages the individual and the society, but the creation of right relation-ships.[22] Something analogous is at work in the international efforts of nongovernmental organizations to promote peaceful coexistence and prevention of intergroup violence by helping young people from societies historically fraught with conflict to exchange perspectives about the past and commit to a different kind of future through processes of mediation, truth-telling, and reconciliation.[23]

At least the following can be learned by comparing responses to domestic violence and intergroup violence: (1) we respond in light of what we think are realistic options; (2) safety from violence at times may seem achievable only by separating those at risk from those who are violent; (3) the value of preserving or renewing relationships may be taken more seriously for abused children than for abused between adults, and more for groups rather than between individuals; and (4) law offers no solutions to violence.

On the last point, it is important to underscore that the use of criminal law enforcement is especially difficult to pursue in each of these contexts, however much it may be touted by some as the best means to ensure safety and accountability. The development of civil remedies for adults in intimate relationships really stemmed from the recognition that most people in those relationships find it difficult to turn to the criminal justice system to respond to assaults and other forms of violence. For a long time, the police and prosecutors would not take the complaints seriously. In addition, to this day, many family members are disinclined to pursue a remedy through the criminal system.[24] The civil protection order seems like a good middle ground; a complainant can go to a judge, usually in the absence of the opposing party, to get a temporary restraining order. Therefore she need not be intimidated by the abuser; nor need she choose between some form of legal response and still having a partner who is not in jail but instead is earning a living and can pay his share of the housing costs and child support. A violation of the civil order could, of course, trigger jail time. Advocates hope that this threat is sufficient to secure compliance in many cases, or that the jail time can be tailored to still permit the offender to earn a living. Or, in the eyes of one analyst, the criminal sanctions can be ordered more quickly for violating the civil protection order than in a full-scale criminal prosecution for assault.[25] Yet others note how defenseless the woman alone with her civil protection order remains when the offender shows up with a gun or a knife. Indeed, recent studies indicate that the very steps she takes toward separating from a violent partner can escalate the violence by jeopardizing his sense of control, and it is precisely when she initiates some kind of external involvement that she needs to be able to fall back on the full-scale powers of the criminal law enforcement system.[26]

Developing better understandings of the sources and dynamics of violence seems crucial to generating effective responses. We don't yet have effective responses—or sufficient understandings to guide them.

Connecting Intrafamily and Intergroup Violence

One way to deepen understanding of both intimate and intergroup violence is to confront the connections between them. Doing so invites competing theories: one draws on psychoanalysis and related theories; a second considers violence through the lens of gender; and a third examines societal approval of violence. I will sketch each, again with the hopes of identifying avenues of effective response and prevention.

INTERCONNECTIONS BETWEEN INTERGROUP AND INTIMATE VIOLENCE

Societies with chronic conditions of war and intergroup conflict also witness increases in family violence. This may reflect how people bring societal stress into the home, tempers flare, and people displace onto those in their intimate sphere their frustrations over loss of control elsewhere. Or it may reflect a more basic contagion theory of violence: people surrounded by violence pick it up and pass it on. Data linking intimate violence against women to high rates of neighborhood violence in this country support both theories.[27]

Also striking is the prominence of individuals who themselves had been abused as children in the ranks of perpetrators of grotesque violence. An intensive study of Eugene De Kock, one of the most terrifying figures in Apartheid–South African violence, reveals that he himself had been abused as a child.[28] The man who confessed to beating Matthew Shepard to death experienced sexual abuse as a child; his lawyer outlined a defense explaining that the murder "was driven by a drug-fueled rage born of childhood nightmares of sexual abuse and by the openly gay college student's pass at him."[29] Charles Manson, who masterminded eight grotesque murders, was himself as a child bounced between foster homes and correctional facilities where he was routinely beaten.[30] Psychiatrist James Gilligan, who for years headed Bridgewater State Hospital for the criminally insane in Massachusetts, observed that in the course of his work with the most violent men in maximum security settings, "not a day goes by that I do not hear reports—often confirmed by independent sources—of how these men were victimized during childhood . . . on a scale so extreme, so bizarre, and so frequent that one cannot fail to see that the men who occupy the extreme end of the continuum of violent behavior in adulthood occupied an equally extreme end of the continuum of violent child abuse earlier in life."[31] Adolf Hitler was tyrannized as a child by an alcoholic stepfather.[32]

Even to note such links is to risk suggesting what my colleague Alan Dershowitz derisively dubs the "abuse excuse." I certainly resist this idea; moral and legal responsibility is not dissolved simply by facts about a perpetrator's own past suffering. Most child abuse survivors do not go on to murder others; nor do most child abuse survivors go on to abuse their own children, so something far more complex is underway than simple learned and repetitive behavior. Yet trying to understand the roots of violence is a critical step to preventing it.

PSYCHOLOGICAL THEORIES

Finding out that a perpetrator of violence was himself victimized as a child can at first seem perplexing; how could anyone who experienced abuse and its horrors go on to commit it? Psychoanalytic theorists offer several explanations. The child may come to identify with the aggressor in an effort to regain mastery and overcome the shame of being a victim. Some may identify with the aggressor in the mistaken view that through aggression they can reclaim the love or connection breached in the childhood experience. The very mistaken association between aggression and what was lost may lead to compulsive, repetitive violence because the hope of mastery and connection is, of course, never secured through momentary acts of violence.

The childhood abuse may have engendered such a sense of humiliation that further experiences with humiliation produce either rage or a sense of deadness that seems to be overcome only by committing acts of violence that at least give a brief sense of being alive.[33] The survivor of child abuse may so lose a capacity to feel and relate to the world that it becomes easy to dehumanize others.[34] Often, such people feel dehumanized themselves; they may describe themselves as acting like machines, disembodied and disconnected from the world and from themselves. Or a sense of fear about an engulfing or exploding world may lead to a need for control, expressed by engulfing or exploding.[35] Adults who were sexually or physically abused as children often had the profound experience of forced silence about and disconnection from intense feelings and pain—and then become unable to recognize the truth in any other relationship.[36] None of these notions adequately explains why many who survive childhood abuse never go on to commit violence against others.[37] Do they process the experiences differently, have feelings of inhibition rather than aggression? Or do they find capacities to feel and to analyze that assist them in controlling aggression? The psychoanalytic framework needs development but does assist in mapping a logic of violence from the perpetrator's perspective.

GENDER LENS

A gender lens similarly offers explanations for violence that seem compelling but fall short of explaining why many—if not most—men do *not* assault their partners. The gender analysis also has not helped sufficiently to explain why women often physically abuse their children.[38] But the gender analysis resonates for many people and supports the political movement to name and respond to intimate violence. The gender analysis locates domestic violence as a feature of a patriarchal society. Such a society makes control and ownership, including control and ownership of women and children, the aspirations for men. Young boys learn to identify with the power of men over women and children in such a society and to expect the gratification that comes from such power. Girls learn by watching adults that a woman is to be subservient, caring, attentive, and nurturing.[39] In a world that assigns radically different roles by gender, and monitors them through internalized notions of honor and shame, adult men are allowed to humiliate women.[40] This analysis has assisted students of male violence in African-American communities to identify the special burdens for men who are denied the attributes and honor of maleness everywhere but in the home; violence against wives and lovers offers one small avenue for male prerogatives that the women may themselves even understand as part of the cost of societal racism that produces frustration, helplessness, and hopelessness.

A recent book, titled *The Dark Side of Man*, draws on scholarship about primates, the biology of the human organism, and study of the brain to conclude that all men are physiologically prepared for aggression.[41] Even their use of rape in wars, argues author Michael Ghiglieri, can be traced to biological imperatives.[42] Oddly, though, Ghiglieri prescribes education of children in self-discipline, fairness, and cooperation,[43] despite the portrait of biological necessity he paints. Perhaps biology plus socialization causes violence. Yet it is striking that in most of human history, *men* have waged most wars against other men. The recent use of rape as a systematic strategy in Bosnia-Herzgovina seems a deliberate effort to demoralize the Muslim men.[44] Perhaps the most arresting fact about changes in warfare over this century is the shifting ratio of civilian to military casualties. At the start of the century, 85–90 percent of wartime casualties were military, itself still chiefly composed of men; by the 1990s, 80 percent of the casualties were civilians—and disproportionately, women and children.[45] Whether this should be understood as yet another elaborate play of patriarchal societies against one another or some new sort of gender equality, it is a terrifying fact.

THE THEORY THAT SOCIETY APPROVES OF VIOLENCE

The societal approval approach to violence starts with the prevalence of violence (some would claim its increasing presence). "People hit family members because they can," argue Richard Gelles and Murray Strauss.[46] The knowledge—conscious or unconscious—that bosses, neighbors, police, and prosecutors would trigger procedures and punishments constrains people from striking fellow workers and strangers. But hitting in the home triggers either little response, or advice that the family members should "kiss and make up."[47] Society makes it clear that the costs of perpetuating violence in the home are low; social controls like police intervention are ineffective; the household is typically secluded from view; many adults think there are circumstances when a man can hit his wife and most adults think young people need "strong" discipline.

Societal approaches at times emphasize the pervasiveness of violence in mass media and mass culture. The government's own uses of violence—in response to crime, disorder, homeless people, and international affairs—also contribute to a pervasive message that violence is acceptable, necessary, and even admirable.[48] In the midst of a training video on responses to intimate violence, Linda Mills comments on how the 1991 U.S. action against Iraq—killing thousands of civilians—mirrors the place of violence as a suppressed yet ever-present dimension of daily American life.[49] Two therapists recently described how perpetrators of intimate violence embrace a "colonizer's view" of power, enacted through stratification and control rather than mutually enhancing relationships.[50] Perhaps there is something of the societal view in Alexandr Solzhenitsyn's comment, "Violence does not and cannot exist by itself; it is invariably intertwined with the lie," and in Rap Brown's assertion, "Violence is as American as cherry pie."[51]

Breaking *Out* of Violent Cycles

Although I have been critical of the limitations of the psychoanalytic, gender, and societal views of violence, they each afford useful insights. They also adopt contrasting methods and offer distinctive explanations. They may support alternative responses to violence. We need not assume that they require incompatible responses to violence nor that only one is correct or persuasive. Taken together, they suggest that triggers from the social environment, including patterns of gender inequality and male dominance, incite violence in individuals who have been sensitized to shame.[52] In one more particular respect, the three theories are remarkably consonant.

Psychoanalytic, gender, and societal theories each emphasize how violent behavior models violent responses. According to psychoanalytic theorists, state-ordered punishment repeats shame and aggression that, in turn, animate the violent offender.[53] Male styles of power over others in the image of the patriarchal state replicate and underscore the gendered patterns of behavior condemned by the gender lens. Societal approval of violence—itself teaching the acceptability of violence—is perhaps nowhere more graphic than in the case when the state itself embraces violence, as in imposing the death penalty and in training police to assault, shoot, and even brutalize suspects.

Each of these approaches therefore implies that the best societal response must somehow break out of the cycle of violence rather than repeating and perpetuating it. For law, this of course poses a serious dilemma. The state's use of force, constrained and directed by law, is still force; the state's monopoly on lawful violence is no less violent for being lawful. If law responds to violence with punishment for offenders, is it then not enacting, modeling, and perpetuating violence?

This question raises quite practical concerns for those who administer the law. A few years ago, I led a discussion for a group of judges about a short story by Alice Munro titled "Royal Beatings."[54] The story reveals a repeated family dynamic. The stepdaughter triggers the anger of the stepmother and both of them know the cycle that will follow: the stepmother calls the father to discipline his daughter. After giving her a look filled "with hatred and pleasure,"[55] he lashes her with his belt and then his hands, and the beating continues long after she shrieks and cries. Yet the daughter knows she is playing a victim role and watches the subsequent acts unfold with the confidence of a scriptwriter. Later the stepmother comes, as always, to comfort her with a tray of food to eat in bed.[56] As the judges and I discussed this repeated pattern and acknowledged that all three participants apparently knew, each time, what had happened and what would happen, one judge commented, "You know, when a family like this comes to court, I never know whether the court is breaking the pattern or simply becoming another participant in it."

Dr. Martin Luther King, Jr., brilliantly argued, and demonstrated, that "Nonviolence is the answer to the crucial political and moral questions of [his] time; the need for man to overcome oppression and violence without resorting to oppression and violence."[57] How can this kind of insight, this moral jujitsu, guide the state itself?

I do not have a full answer to this question. But I have an intriguing example. In 1990, the superintendent of police in New Haven, Connecticut, decided that a radical change in approach was needed to deal with violence in the community. With the support of other city leaders, the police department declared that it would abandon the military model and instead embrace a form of community policing committed to maintaining order "legally, humanely, respectfully, and equitably."[58] It adopted a new slogan: "Police others as you would police you."[59]

Then the department really showed it meant action. It moved out all the teachers from its police academy and hired a woman named K. D. Codish to direct the academy and all training for the department. As she states her message, "It was no longer enough to be big, strong, male and tough. Instead, reading, writing, talking, listening, solving problems, caring about people, being part of the community, being 'nice' and acting respectfully to felons as well as to elected officials were now what the job was to entail, and therefore, what should be taught at the academy. Soon it would be more important to know the telephone number of the local drug treatment clinic than the statute number of the drug violation."[60] Still crucially recognizing and implementing boundaries to ensure people's safety, the police should also be sources of help to those at risk of behaving with violence toward others or themselves.

Codish shifted the academy to a university model with opening sessions on anti-discrimination policies, nonviolence and alternative dispute resolution, community mediation, children's responses to parental arrests, violence against women, mental illness, and homelessness. The academy now requires all attendees to participate in classes held at community sites, such as homeless shelters, where the officers-in-training share meals with people from and about whom they are to learn.

A crucial element of the training program directs the students to conduct field and library research and then work in collaboration with artists to develop artistic presentations of their findings in forms that can be shared with the public. A sculpture installation on families struggling with mental illness, a visual art exhibit on child abuse, and a video exploring a day in the life of a homeless person are recent examples.[61]

Given the recasting of the training and roles for police, the department has also shifted its recruitment strategies and hiring criteria. Codish explains that maturity, life experience, communication skills, and abilities to deal with stress are better predictors of good performance than physical stature, strength, or a love of adventure.[62]

Community policing is working well in New Haven and other cities are using New Haven as a model.[63] Certainly, arrests and criminal prosecutions with convictions and jail time still are part of the law enforcement practice. More needs to be learned about what really goes on there, and elsewhere, in the name of community policing. But this kind of creative reconstruction suggests directions for uses of state power that do not model the violence it is intended to prevent.

This essay attempts to initiate inquiry into whether legal and communal responses to violence can and should depart from violence—and if so how—as well as other thoughts about the comparisons of and connections between intimate and intergroup violence. In Kosovo after the crisis, for example, simply getting a standard civil police system in place became an enormous challenge. Currently, the few Serbs who remain require individualized guard protection to survive risks of vigilante revenge. In addition, the Albanian Kosovars run the hospitals and will not permit treatment for Serbs. Perhaps the international peacekeeping force could focus on making medical care available to everyone, regardless of ethnicity, and thereby model the combination of security and protection that breaks cycles of violence.[64] Yet it remains difficult even to find the authority, legitimacy, and political will to accomplish this goal.

I cannot resist two more Yogi Berra-isms. The first, I know, I am taking out of context. Perhaps his most famous comment about baseball is "How can you think and hit at the same time?" This is often imported into academic circles to chide those of us who do a lot of thinking and not so much doing. But I think it is also a pretty nifty reminder of mindfulness as a potential guard against the brutal kind of hitting.

And then, there is Yogi's apt comment, reserved for just this kind of moment, at the end of my essay, but not the end of our work in finding solutions to intrafamily and intergroup violence: "It ain't over till it's over."

NOTES

1. See Elizabeth Pleck, *Domestic Tyranny: The Making of American Social Policy Against Family Violence from Colonial Times to the Present* (New York: Oxford University Press, 1987), pp. 99–107.

2. See, generally, Nadine Taub and Elizabeth M. Schneider, "Perspectives on Women's Subordination and the Role of Law," in David Kairys, ed., *The Politics of Law: A Progressive Critique*, 3rd ed. (New York: Basic Books, 1998), pp. 122–23; Katherine M. Schelong, "Domestic Violence and the State: Responses to and Rationales for Spousal Battering, Marital Rape and Stalking," *Marquette Law Review* 78 (1994): 79, 114 (criticizing the justification of protecting the privacy of the marital relationship for nonintervention in cases of domestic violence).

3. Peter Ford, "Few Sacred Borders to New UN," *Christian Science Monitor* (September 19, 1999): 1.

4. Quoted in Joyce Klempere, "Programs for Battered Women: What Works?," *Albany Law Review* 58 (1995): 1171.

5. Martha Minow, *Between Vengeance and Forgiveness: Facing History after Genocide and Mass Violence* (Boston: Beacon Press, 1998).

6. Judith Lewis Herman, *Trauma and Recovery* (New York: Basic Books 1992), pp. 72–73, 92–93, 121, 137, 229.

7. See infra text at note 10 for further discussion of the dilemmas over mandatory arrest and no-drop prosecution rules.

8. When should her retaliation be excusable is another much debated and litigated subject. See Elizabeth M. Schneider, "Feminism and the False Dichotomy of Victimization and Agency," *New York University Law Review* 83 (1993): (questioning the use of a battered woman defense that relies on expert testimony about battered woman syndrome to demonstrate that the defendants should not be held responsible for their actions on account of their condition of victimization); see also Iris Marion Young, "The Generality of Law and the Specifics of Cases: A Comment on Elizabeth Schneider," *University of Pittsburgh Law Review* 57 (1996): 549 (arguing that whether to use the battered woman defense should be decided based upon the specifics of each individual case). Given my work on vengeance and forgiveness, I would argue that victims of intimate abuse surely deserve some compassion and understanding when they have impulses or take actions of vengeance, but it would be better for society to prevent such actions. It is not that victims should be asked to forgive or forget, but they should be assisted to find a path between vengeance and forgiveness.

9. See *Cote v. Cote*, 599 A.2d 869 (Md. Ct. Spec. App. 1992) (holding that a protection order requiring respondent to vacate marital home does not constitute a taking); *State ex rel. Williams v. Marsh*, 626 S.W.2d 223 (Mo. 1982) (upholding constitutionality of ex parte temporary protection order which evicted the complainant from the family home); *Boyle v. Boyle*, 12 Pa. D. & C. 3rd 767 (Pa. Ct. Comm. Pleas. 1979) (no due process violation in the eviction of the batterer).

10. Thoughtful discussions appear in Cheryl Hanna, "No Right to Choose: Mandated Victim Participation in Domestic Violence Prosecutions," *Harvard Law Review* 109 (1996): 1849, and Joan L. Neisser, "Lessons for the United States: A Greek Cypriot Model for Domestic Violence Law," *Michigan Journal of Gender and Law* 4 (1996): 171.

11. For a discussion of the law from a social work perspective, see Christopher G. Petr, *Social Work with Children and Their Families: Pragmatic Foundations* (New York: Oxford University Press, 1998), pp. 137–56.

12. See Barbara Bennett Woodhose, "Poor Mothers, Poor Babies: Law, Medicine, and Crack," in S. Randall Humm et al., eds., *Child, Parent and State: Law and Policy Reader* (Philadelphia: Temple University Press, 1994), pp. 111, 117.

13. Peggy Cooper Davis runs a project funded by the Open Society Foundation that pursues many of these issues and emphasizes the threat to cultural preservation from child welfare practices. The most successful family preservation program is Homebuilders in Tacoma, Washington, which suggests that intensive services infused in the homes of highly vulnerable families can keep them together even though most similar families would separate without the intervention. See David Hamburg, *Today's Children: Creating a Future for a Generation in Crisis* (New York: Times Books: 1992), p. 83.

14. See Irving B. Harris, *Children in Jeopardy: Can We Break the Cycle of Poverty?* (New Haven, CT: Yale Child Study Center, 1996) (addressing the need for social programs for poor children ages zero to three and teenagers in order to break the cycle of poverty).

15. See Elizabeth Bartholet, *Nobody's Children: Abuse and Neglect, Foster Drift, and the Adoption Alternative* (Boston: Beacon Books, 1999) (arguing for the use of adoption to protect battered children in the same way battered women are protected).

16. See id., at 42. Under this law, agencies are no longer required to make reasonable efforts to preserve families in all cases and instead are required to plan for a permanent home, which can be an adoptive home. The law also requires the filing of petitions to terminate parental rights in cases in which a child has been in foster care for certain periods of time or has been subject to especially egregious abuse. See id., at 158. Yet public and private funding for family preservation continues to grow. Id., at 43.

17. Id., at 109–10 (summarizing studies of rehabilitation efforts geared towards child abusers).

18. Richard P. Barth, "Abusive and Neglecting Parents and the Care of Their Children," in Mary Ann Mason, Arlene Skolnick, and Stephen D. Sugarman, eds., *All Our Families: New Policies for a New Century* (New York: Oxford University Press, 1998), p. 231.

19. See Richard Gelles, *The Book of David: How Preserving Families Can Cost Children's Lives* (New York: Basic Books, 1996) (arguing that the primary goal of social policy should be child safety, and not family preservation).

20. Elsewhere, I have suggested that a complete approach toward family violence would require dealing with family dynamics and societal attitudes as well as the violent behavior of individuals. Minow, "Words and the Door to the Land of Change," *Vanderbilt Law Review* 43 (1990): 1665, 1671–72.

21. One study indicates that the rate of substantiated abuse and neglect in New York City foster family care was more than 1-1/2 times that of children in the general population. See Michael B. Mushlin, "Unsafe Havens: Cases for Constitutional Protection of Foster Children from Abuse and Neglect," in S. Randall Humm et al., eds., *Child, Parent and State*, supra, at 186, 189 (citing Vera Institute of Justice, *Foster Home Child Protection* [February 1981], pp. 63–64 [unpublished report]).

22. Jeanne Safer, *Forgiving and Not Forgiving: A New Approach to Resolving Intimate Betrayal* (New York: Avon Books, 1999). See also Linda Mills, *The Heart of Intimate Abuse: New Interventions in Child Welfare, Criminal Justice, and Health Settings* (New York: Springer Publishing Co., 1998).

23. See Eugene Weiner, *The Handbook of Interethnic Coexistence* (New York: Continuum, 1998).

24. Seymour Moskowitz, "Saving Granny from the Wolf: Elder Abuse and Neglect—the Legal Framework," *Connecticut Law Review* 31, (1998): 77, 100.

25. David M. Zlotnick, "Empowering the Battered Woman: The Use of Criminal Contempt Sanctions to Enforce Civil Protection Orders," *Ohio State Law Journal* 56 (1995): 1153, 1214 (arguing that criminal contempt is a good enforcement tool but not a panacea; contempt enforcement permits faster adjudication than criminal prosecution; it is more likely to result in jail time, and it is a procedure that empowers women).

26. Martha R. Mahoney, "Legal Images of Battered Women: Redefining the Issue of Separation," *Michigan Law Review* 90 (1991): 1, 5–6 (noting that a woman is most in danger when she is first in contact with authorities).

27. See Jane Ann Grisso, "Violent Injuries Among Women in an Urban Area," *New England Journal of Medicine* 341 (December 16, 1999): 1899.

28. The recruitment of disturbed individuals by oppressive governments to do their dirty work may be widespread. Slobodan Milosevic apparently recruited criminals and murderers to administer his policy of ethnic cleansing. See Charles M. Senott, "Deadly Paramilitary Units Carry Out Will of Milosevic," *Boston Globe* (March 30, 1999): A1; Chris Hedges, "Fatal Fight Over Spoils by Insiders in Belgrade," *New York Times* (November 9, 1997): A14.

29. Patrick O'Driscoll, "Lawyer: Panic Drove Defendant; Groups Decry Defense in Shepard Case," *USA Today* (October 26, 1999): 6A.

30. Kenneth Wooden, *Weeping in the Playtime of Others: America's Incarcerated Children* (New York: McGraw Hill, 1976), pp. 47–57 (detailing Charles Manson case history).

31. James Gilligan, *Violence: Our Deadly Epidemic and Its Causes* (New York: G.P. Putnam, 1996), p. 45.

32. Robert Coles, "The Death of a Child: Review of *What Lisa Knew* by Joyce Johnson," *New York Times Book Review* (April 8, 1990): 1.

33. Gilligan, *Violence*, at 45–88.

34. Gilligan, *Violence*, supra, at 52. He suggests that the violators lack the ability to perceive their victims as human beings with feelings, "But how can one know that others have feelings, or be moved by the feelings of others, if one does not experience feelings oneself?" Id., at 52. I am grateful for Pumla Gobodo-Madikezela's comments at the panel discussion of the South African Truth and Reconciliation Commission, J.F.K. School of Government, Harvard University, October 18, 1999, on this topic.

35. See R. D. Laing, *The Divided Self* (Baltimore: Penguin, 1969), p. 83. Laing was himself describing people commonly identified as schizophrenic. Gilligan argues that murderers kill because they see no choice: it is either he or me. The triviality of a precipitating event can actually trigger a heightened sense of shame and on some level awareness of an incapacity to use nonviolent means to ward off the feelings of low self-esteem. Such people lack emotional capacities that normally inhibit violent impulses stimulated by shame. Gilligan, *Violence*, supra, at 11.

36. Jean Baker Miller and Irene Pierce Stiver, *The Healing Connection: How Women Form Relationships in Therapy and in Life* (Boston: Beacon Press, 1997), p. 82.

37. Some of these victims, though, may be violent against themselves in various ways.

38. See bell hooks, "Violence in Intimate Relationships," in *Talking Back: Thinking Feminist/Thinking Black* (Boston: South End Press, 1989), pp. 84–91 (applying a feminist perspective to violence in intimate relationships).

39. Id., at 162 (describing the difficulty in breaking free of this training).

40. Gilligan, *Violence*, supra, at 265. Though the theory becomes complicated when a young man kills his father; a young man may need to avenge the honor of his mother and in this way work out a form of patriarchal logic. Id., at 263–65.

41. Michael P. Ghiglieri, *The Dark Side of Man: Tracing the Origins of Male Violence* (Reading, MA: Perseus Books, 1999).

42. Id., at 92 (claiming that rape during times of war is based upon the soldier's sex drive and urge to procreate).

43. Id., at 256 (explaining strategies to reduce violence).

44. Mary Kaldor *New and Old Wars: Organized Violence in the Global Era* (Stanford, CA: Stanford University Press, 1999), p. 56.

45. Id., at 100.

46. Richard J. Gelles and Murray A. Strauss, *Intimate Violence* (Newbury Park, CA: Sage Publications, 1988), p. 20.

47. Id., at 22.

48. I have made similar assertions in the past. See Minow, "Words and the Door to the Land of Change," supra, at 1665, 1672 ("Law is itself violent in its forms and methods. Official power effectuates itself in physical force, threatened or carried out.").

49. *The Space in Between: A Portrait of Intimate Abuse* (film by Linda Mills; funded by U.S. Dept. of Health and Human Services, 1997).

50. Miller and Stiver, *The Healing Connection*, supra, at 57.

51. Quote from 1967 press conference, cited in *Bartlett's Familiar Quotations*, 16th ed. (Boston: Little, Brown and Company, 1992), p. 772.

52. See Gilligan, *Violence*, supra, at 223.

53. John Braithwaite has advanced a conception of "reintegrative shaming," a method of punishing while embracing the wrongdoer as still a vital and valued member of the community. See John Braithwaite, *Crime, Shame and Reintegration* (Cambridge, UK: Cambridge University Press, 1989). This work has helped to inspire instructive experiments in restorative justice. Yet these efforts, and the "reintegrative shaming" notion, require the presence of a sufficiently coherent and engaged community to have the capacity to reintegrate a wrongdoer. In many circumstances of contemporary violence, this is precisely what is lacking.

54. This was part of the "Doing Justice" program at Brandeis University. Launched by Saul Touster, the program conducted sessions with judges and other professionals and used fiction to explore general themes of professional accountability, moral choice, and public and private roles. The story by Alice Munro appears in R. V. Cassill, *The Norton Anthology of Short Fiction*, 2d ed. (New York: Norton, 1981), p. 473.

55. Id., at 486.

56. Id., at 488–89.

57. Martin Luther King, Jr., Nobel Prize Acceptance Speech (delivered in Oslo, Norway, December 10, 1964), in James M. Washington, ed., *A Testament of Hope: The Essential Writings of Martin Luther King, Jr.* (San Francisco: Harper & Row, 1986), p. 224.

58. Thanks to Susan Sturm and Elaine Chiu for teaching me about this. See *New Haven Police Academy, Preventing Broken Windows* (1999–2000), p. 2 (on file with the *Case Western Reserve Law Review*).

59. Id., at 7.

60. K. D. Codish, *The New Haven Police Academy: Putting One Sacred Cow Out to Pasture* (1998), p. 1 (on file with the *Case Western Reserve Law Review*).

61. New Haven Police Academy Term Projects 1998, "Different Drummers: People with Mental Illness" (1998).

62. Id., at 3.

63. See Jack Cavanaugh, "Public Safety: Walking a Beat Returns to Stamford," *New York Times*, (December 21, 1997): Sec. 14, p. 1. The New Haven police also work closely with the Yale Child Study Center to understand the roots of violence. See Andrew Julien, "Students, Dodd Speak on Violence," *Hartford Courant* (May 11, 1993): B13.

64. Thanks to Michael Ignatieff, James Herzog, and Mark O'Connell for discussions related to this point.

2

Justice and the Experience of Injustice*

NANCY L. ROSENBLUM

> But examine the passions and feelings of mankind. Bring the
> doctrine of reconciliation to the touchstone of nature, and then
> tell me, whether you can hereafter love, honour, and faithfully
> serve the power that hath carried fire and sword into your land?
> . . . But if you say you can still pass the violations over, then I
> ask, Hath your house been burnt? Hath your property been
> destroyed before your face? Are your wife and children destitute
> of a bed to lie on, or bread to live on? Have you lost a parent or
> a child by their hands, and yourself the ruined and wretched
> survivor? If you have not, then are you not a judge of those
> who have. . . . I mean not to exhibit horror for the purpose of
> provoking revenge, but to awaken us from fatal and unmanly
> slumbers, that we may pursue determinately some fixed object.
>
> —THOMAS PAINE, *Common Sense*[1]

No natural law guarantees that time heals all wounds. The cycle of hatred is a destructive dynamic set in motion by the memory of past harms.
To be sure, collective memories sometimes demoralize victims of injustice and dampen the desire for revenge. If past experiences are mainly
ones of vulnerability and defeat, memories may inhibit action and
weaken resolve—Tom Paine's "fatal and unmanly slumbers." But even
"lost causes," recalled in a certain spirit, can strengthen solidarity and
arouse people to retaliate. Memories of domination, violence, and humiliation, and stories of a shared fate, are cultivated and sustained by
groups. They are inflamed and manipulated by ambitious leaders with
an interest in mobilizing victims and those who identify with them to

* I owe thanks to my friend and critic Susan M. Okin for her challenging comments, to Avi
Soifer for his thoughtful suggestions, and to Ionnis Evrigens for his able research
assistance.

seek revenge. Paine used memories of injustice to incite revolution: if you have suffered injury and still "can shake hands with the murderers," he wrote in *Common Sense*, "then are you unworthy the name of husband, father, friend, or lover, and whatever your rank or title in life, you have the heart of a coward, and the spirit of a sycophant."

Once aroused, the passion for revenge is ineradicable. It is a source of personal and political instability. It is not rule-bound or orderly. Wild revenge is just that. And in addition to personal revenge, social and religious codes dictate obligations of vengeance that are experienced as categorical. Avengers feel perfectly justified in wreaking destruction— they feel liberated to become persecutors in turn. They owe debts to the dead. When it comes to vengeance, generality and proportionality have no place, and cruelty is acceptable. The victims' own perception of affliction, the strength of their passion, their own sense of who is responsible, and the available means of destruction are the only limits.[2] Personal retaliation and organized vengeance are incompatible with measured justice.

Wild revenge cannot be tamed but it can be outlawed and suppressed. We create legal institutions to prosecute criminals using fixed and impersonal rules. Punishment is justified in large part by retribution, but it is meted out according to known standards and proportionality. Where systems of justice are absent or when the application of laws and remedies is biased or undependable, personal revenge and organized vengeance will out.

The most important public recourse in the face of hateful violence, then, is criminal law and punishment, and prosecution is the best response, indeed the defining response, from the point of view of justice. But formal judicial proceedings are often inadequate from the standpoint of victims, which is why individuals, groups, and whole communities look outside the law for relief. The limitations of formal justice are most vivid when there are many "dirty hands." When the perpetrators are not a few identifiable individuals but permeate a society, and when crimes take place on a massive scale, we are faced with the phenomenon suggested by titles like *Hitler's Willing Executioners*.[3] If prosecution is possible at all, it takes place in a remote international forum, against a few select individuals, applying international or third party law that may have neither the efficacy nor the legitimacy of domestic legal systems.

In fact, the limitations of formal legal proceedings hold for the full range of hateful violence across the full spectrum of legal venues. Some failings are remediable; others are inherent in the best system of justice. I focus here on one common, overarching limitation: the inadequacy of legal proceedings to fully take into account the self-understanding of victims and to address their experience of injustice. Legal institutions sometimes fail to fully deal with those harmed in ways the law recognizes. Certainly they fail those who suffer indirectly in ways the law fails to acknowledge at all, and many victims find themselves without standing in our systems of justice.

So we should not imagine that formal justice, cool and cognitive, quenches survivors' desire for revenge. Or that victims and their sympathizers find a fair trial and reasonable punishment an adequate response to the harm they have suffered. Blind justice is no substitute for the wide-eyed satisfaction, perhaps the sheer physiological release, of inflicting pain in turn. Revenge is uniquely satisfying. "Somehow injustice and justice are not psychologically complimentary or symmetrical . . ."[4]

Except for the rare saintly soul or those who settle into grim resignation, bitterness remains despite the administration of formal justice. It may even be exacerbated if the victims' wounds and costs—to their safety and sanity and dignity—are unacknowledged and unaddressed by public agencies. More so if victims' own accounts of their injuries are actively disdained. A wholesale public failure to acknowledge the experience of injustice can perpetuate cycles of hatred.

Attending to the voices of the aggrieved is not a simple thing, however, conceptually or in practice. I made the point in my introductory essay, and repeat it here, that the institutions and social contexts within which we tell and hear stories of hatred and violence affect what we recall and record. The grievances that spur us to action and that become resources for expressing and correcting injustice are given shape in institutional settings that largely determine what we tell, indeed whether we tell anything at all.

For one thing, reporting accounts of hateful violence is fraught with fear, sometimes paralyzing fear. A common goal of perpetrators of hateful violence is to terrorize and isolate their victims and inhibit them from speaking out. Secure and stable institutions that offer safe places and reduce risk are a condition for moving from raw memory, to motivating grievances, to taking steps to seek prosecution and reparation. Clearly, it is difficult or impossible to elicit testimony from witnesses in criminal cases unless they have real protection from intimidation.

Just as important, institutional frameworks dictate the available conceptual apparatus for naming harms and blaming wrongdoers. They create the legal fictions and evidentiary burdens, the day-to-day vocabulary of causality and attribution of responsibility. Rules of evidence and legal norms of accountability dictate which memories are considered worthy of public acknowledgment and which are considered inadmissible, discounted as subjective and unreliable. One scholar of the Nuremberg trials explains:

> Testimonies are often labeled as "subjective" or "biased" in the legal proceedings. . . . The lawyers of war criminals have asked the most impertinent questions of people trying to find words for a shattered memory that did not fit into any language. . . . The fault is not theirs, but lies with a certain method of argument on the part of the lawyers. . . . They demand precise statements of facts, and in this way deny that in the concrete process of remembering, facts are enmeshed within the stories of a lifetime. . . . A lawyer's case is after all merely another kind of story.[5]

As this suggests, victims' experience of injury and their accusations against those they hold responsible come up against definitions of harm and accountability established by legal institutions. We try, where possible, to accommodate these experiences to the rules of evidence and criminal responsibility of ordinary justice, and when that is impossible we try to reform legal proceedings. The experience of injustice is a spur to changes within existing legal institutions and to institutional innovation. Beyond that, it is a spur to invent alternative collective responses more attentive to the voices of the aggrieved.

Increasingly, disrupting cycles of hatred is a goal of both formal and informal responses to hate and violence. The element shared by every adequate response is attention to the survivors' accounts of injustice. The injured must have an opportunity to make their stories public, even if the justice meted out to perpetrators does not, in the end, fully satisfy them. At the same time, however, responding to victims may conflict with wider societal needs for due process and formal justice.

Which is why there is no single or best response to hateful violence. Different public actions to break the cycle of hatred reflect different values and provide different benefits. One, albeit the paramount one, is seeing that justice is done by means of fair criminal prosecutions. Another is addressing the experience of injustice. This is an independent requirement that is often best met by other means. The fact that we endorse, reform, extend, and strengthen the formal apparatus of justice in dealing with crimes of hateful violence does not absolve us of the additional responsibility of attending to the voices of the aggrieved.

Memory and repair depend on "our willingness and our capacity to act on behalf of the victims."[6]

Procedural and Substantive Justice: What About the Voice of the Aggrieved?

Philosophers usefully distinguish procedural from substantive justice. To say that something is procedurally just is to say that the formalities defining a process have been correctly adhered to.[7] In the context of courts, where formal justice is most at home, procedural justice entails adhering to existing rules for taking legal decisions and fulfilling the promise that like cases will be treated alike. Due process says little about the actual content of the laws being upheld by these proceedings, however. By itself, procedural fairness says little about what society, through its system of laws, means by "giving each his due." It does not reveal a people's fundamental interests as specified by its conception of justice.

In particular, procedural justice tells us little about what counts as a legally cognizable injury. We recognize the possibility of disjuncture between the outcomes of trials scrupulously conducted according to fair rules on the one hand and substantive justice on the other. Procedural justice and substantive justice do not guarantee one another. Procedurally correct oppression is sadly familiar.

Substantive justice is about the actual definition of harms awarded legal recognition and about the connection between punishment and desert. We know that certain harms do not have corresponding legal remedies. We have all suffered (and probably inflicted) broken promises, personal betrayals, or grave insults. We sometimes try to fit these into legal categories of breach of contract, fraud, or libel in order to get public vindication and redress, but this is not always possible. Without adequate recourse, we feel doubly injured. This is not to say that all harms can or should be recognized by law and made amenable to legal remedy. I mention these familiar instances to evoke a sense of the powerful feelings of injustice aroused when much graver injuries are beyond the reach of civil and criminal law.

Devastating harms may not be recognized at all, and victims may not have legal standing to seek punishment or reparation. There have been, and remain, important gaps in the law when it comes to violence and crimes of hate. Certain injuries became legally cognizable crimes only recently—marital rape, for example, or "stalking," or sexual enslavement as a war crime. The special designation of a crime as a "hate crime" is meant to acknowledge the distinctive harms inflicted when ordinary harms are motivated by the desire to injure people on account of their color or ethnic group or sexual orientation.

Even if injuries are legally cognizable, a disjuncture exists between the sorts of satisfaction promised by formal and substantive justice. The reasons for demanding fairness are independent of our reasons for defining something as a harm requiring punishment. The formalism of trials is designed to provide impersonal procedural justice, and the chief purpose of due process in criminal law is to protect the accused from government exercising its power arbitrarily. The rights of the accused have central place, as they should. Protection against politically motivated prosecution is vital. So fairness is an incomparable good, but not the only one. Famously, truth is not the principal objective of formal juridical proceedings. Nor is recognition of the pain of victims the principal object of due process, much less providing them relief. Again, punishment in criminal cases is proportional and justified as deterrence or general social retribution; the objective is not reparation, still less the subjective gratification of victims, and least of all reconciliation and repair.

Another way of framing this point is to say that procedural and substantive justice have not only different purposes but also different audiences. Formal justice is not addressed to victims. The dimensions of fairness, due process, and formal justice matter for the broader society (and for the defendant). The legitimacy and integrity of the legal process is the overarching consideration, not least because of the need to ensure that the public response to legal proceedings is not a new sense of harm and a new cycle of redress. We expand legal venues, and appeal more and more often to domestic and international tribunals because of the incomparable, independent value of fairness, due process, and formal justice.

Of course, due process does serve important functions specific to crimes of hateful violence. Trials generate credible documentation of crimes. The collection and recording of actions and the naming of perpetrators creates a public record. Legal processes provide access to official records, assisting the work of historians and journalists in exposing and explaining harms. The process may also provide relief to victims: there is the personal and collective catharsis of telling their story, even if it is truncated and skewed by legal formalism. Above all, trials demonstrate a public commitment to acknowledging and punishing the wrong. However limited and selective, prosecution is a vivid, material insistence on holding individuals publicly responsible.

Nonetheless, an important limitation of legal formalism is its meaning for victims of hateful violence. Fair procedures that satisfy neutral observers may fail to satisfy the injured and those who sympathize with them. Justice may actually frustrate survivors and inflame their sense of having been wronged. My point is that one element of the division between formal and substantive justice is the specific disjuncture between justice and the experience of injustice.

It may not be necessary for legal justice, formal and substantive, to exactly coincide with the victims' sense of injustice, however. Nor is it necessary for the outcomes of formal proceedings to meet their expectations about the proper dimensions of public outrage and their hopes for punishment or reparation. We may depend on judicial proceedings to satisfy the demand for due process and justice. But legal proceedings, which are not designed (and cannot be expected) to explore the history, memory, and vengeful passion of injustice, are not the best way to respond to victims. We can employ other mechanisms to provide recognition of the full dimension of their suffering and loss, and to offer additional or alternative measures of substantive relief. Other institutions can supplement or substitute for the limitations of law, and other public responses can contribute to reparation and repair.

In the next section I survey recent reforms in legal responses to intergroup violence, hate crimes, and domestic violence—the designation of new crimes and the creation of new legal venues. These legal developments are commendable from the point of view of justice, but do not necessarily translate into improvements from the standpoint of the experience of injustice. I go on in subsequent sections to consider alternatives— both official nonlegal remedies and constructive private responses to violent hate that are designed to attend to the voices of the aggrieved. My hope is to provide a short catalogue of and commentary on responses to the experience of injustice.

Expanding Justice: Naming New Crimes and
   Creating New Courts

I begin with *international criminal prosecution,* an increasingly accepted response to intergroup violence. The years since the international military tribunal at Nuremberg and the Tokyo war crimes trial have brought new legal institutions and authorities, from special international tribunals with limited and retroactive jurisdictions to a permanent International Criminal Court endorsed by 120 nations in 1998 (currently unratified by the United States).[8] International prosecution of war crimes and human rights violations has developed slowly and remains limited in scope, however. The ambiguities brought to light during the Nuremberg and Tokyo trials continue to plague these efforts. The chief ones are selective prosecution, usually of a few high-ranking officials, which opens prosecutors to the charge of scapegoating and political motivation; uncertainty about which law to apply; vulnerability to the accusation that trials are the work of foreign victors—war and revenge by other means (consider the Tokyo trials prosecuted by allied victors guilty, in Japanese eyes, of the war crime of the nuclear attacks on Hiroshima and Nagasaki); and charges of cultural imperialism.

Despite these real impediments, three background conditions have enabled the steady expansion of legal proceedings against perpetrators of ghastly intergroup violence.[9] They are important here because they offer insight into why progress that is undisputed from the standpoint of justice does not necessarily mean corresponding progress from the standpoint of the victims of injustice.

The principal development is the articulation of human rights in the Universal Declaration of Human Rights of 1948, in conventions on genocide and apartheid, and in the 1966 international covenants on civil and political, economic and cultural rights.[10] For jurisdictional reasons, the Nuremberg trials formally prosecuted conspiracy to wage aggressive war, but the enduring moral and political message of these proceedings was the idea of the Holocaust as a "crime against humanity." The charge against the first woman indicted by the International Court at the Hague (for Bosnian Serb actions against Bosnian Muslims and Croats) included counts of "extermination," "persecution," "deportation," and "inhumane acts."[11] One crucial advance made by the Universal Declaration and other declarations of principles, by treaties, and by covenants is the relevance of human rights outside the context of violations committed during war time to include violations committed during what is, from the international perspective, "peacetime."

Political philosophy is chiefly concerned with the justification of human rights claims. Philosophers ask whether human rights standards are "neutral" or nonpartisan, reasonable to accept regardless of one's cultural views? Or are they "ineliminably religious"[12] or ideological—belonging to a family of views about social justice and political legitimacy that are variously called liberal or "Western"?[13] For example, a severe liberal account identifies human rights with the rights of citizens in liberal democracies and argues that nonliberal societies "are always properly subject to some form of sanction" because they fail to treat people as "truly free and equal."[14]

Expansive catalogues of human rights invite these challenges. They contain wide-ranging declarations regarding slavery; racial, ethnic, and religious discrimination; freedom of movement, asylum, and nationality; religious liberty; legal due process and political rights like freedom of expression; economic claims ranging from "basic needs," to an adequate standard of living, to an array of rights to social welfare (like the right to work).[15] These lists reveal profound tensions: between self-determination rights of peoples and rights of individuals, for example. Latent too is disagreement about responsibility for meeting social and economic rights claims: Do they impose affirmative duties on governments to provide for their citizens' welfare? Should human rights be declared for things many governments cannot deliver in the foreseeable future?

Additional criticism has it that even a moral minimum of the worst harms is biased in the sense that it favors the "modernizing, cosmopolitan side of disagreement" about rights. We know, however, that by itself enforcement of human rights does not operate to make societies more liberal overall.[16] More importantly, we know that the controversies about basic human rights arise within as well as between societies, so the idea of human rights cannot be fairly described as an alien imposition by the external forces of cosmopolitanism. Local acceptance is not a prerequisite for the enforcement or moral effectiveness of human rights in any case. Charles Beitz argues that "a value could count as a genuine human right even if it were not explicitly accepted in every culture, just in case members of each culture could reasonably accept it as consistent with their culture's moral conventions."[17] The Universal Declaration of Human Rights, Mary Ann Glendon explains, was meant "to provide a common standard that can be brought to life in different cultures in a legitimate variety of ways."[18]

Undeniably, philosophers, theologians, and political officials can demonstrate the existence of ecumenical agreement among the world's cultures on a core of "basic rights."[19] "Overlapping consensus" does not eliminate disagreement about the religious or moral foundations of these rights, however. It simply points to a universally acknowledged and justifiable class of "basic" or human rights proper—"urgent rights" recognized as reasonable by what John Rawls calls "decent" societies.[20]

Even "basic rights" is an evolving category. Experiences during the period following World War II inspired recognition of rights of nationality, movement, and asylum. Recently, attention has turned to the enumeration of crimes against women, which is endemic worldwide. Rape and sexual slavery during war have been added to the list of recognized war crimes (though mainly in circumstances where they were officially organized and condoned, as in the case of the Japanese military's "comfort women"), along with borderless crimes like the trafficking of women.

As many have noted, for the most part human rights are aspirational. They comprise a sort of reserve moral currency used for judgment and condemnation. One way of winning broad acceptance for human rights has been to give them the form of declarations of principles rather than binding treaties and conventions that impose enforceable duties. These declarations aim at prevention as much as prosecution and punishment.

Nonetheless, for sufferers of horrible crimes of violent hate the objective is not aspirational but immediate assistance, and articulation of human rights—coupled with publicity about violations of those rights—have been crucial. From the standpoint of victims, recognition of suffering and real aid are often more important than justice or political intervention. By providing a universally comprehensible language for naming injuries, it gives voice to the aggrieved. Appeal to human rights is a way of pressing urgent claims urgently. It demands justice but only secondarily; first of all it calls for material assistance in stopping and coping with the immediate consequences of injustice. Human rights are invoked by victims and their sympathizers to broadcast suffering and to excite in all hearers a sense of responsibility for stopping the violence. They make unwillingness to act to protect victims a violation of moral duty on the part not only of governments and international organizations but nongovernmental associations and private individuals as well. They give victims firm moral ground from which to accuse not only the perpetrators of violence but every agent that fails to respond.

The availability of human rights as a language for victims is an indispensable reinforcement of the second condition for giving rights effect: the determination by governments and organizations that state boundaries should not be allowed to shelter serious violations with impunity. They "are a class of rights that . . . restrict the justifying reasons for war and its conduct, and they specify limits to a regime's internal autonomy."[21] The accepted norms of independence, respect for other peoples and for state sovereignty, and the duty of nonintervention are potentially outweighed by duties of assistance. Condemnation and intervention, including forceful intervention, are justifiable. Human rights propel governments to be witting and willing trespassers across boundaries. More so as the character of war has changed. Since 1945 most wars have been fought inside internal borders, and one estimate is that civilians account for 90 percent of war deaths during this period.[22] The same justifications endorse intervention against acts of violent hate committed outside the context of war.

In fact, human rights enforcement does not always take juridical form or involve coercion. International tribunals are part of a growing repertoire of intervention to stop, punish, and impede human rights violations. Particularly in the years since World War II, we have seen the invention of various forms of official intervention in response to violence, among them: commissions of investigation, coordinated humanitarian aid, third-party negotiators, and international peacekeepers. (Few recent events are more troubling than the withdrawal of United Nations peacekeepers from Rwanda in 1994, stranding the people they were there to protect and leaving no resistance to the Hutu slaughter of 800,000 Tutsi.[23]) Noncoercive measures undoubtedly outnumber coercive ones. Governments' human rights records are used as criteria of eligibility for international assistance programs, financial guarantees, and international trade by other states, international agencies, and nongovernmental organizations. A variety of economic and military sanctions and withholdings from violators have become common practice. Relief efforts are as vital in response to the disasters of hateful violence as they are in response to natural disasters. And even relief has complicated, unintended consequences: when soldiers steal food meant for civilians, their capacity for hostilities is reinforced; when wells are purified and people gather there, they become easy targets for bombing. This led one observer of aid to propose the "Do no harm movement."[24]

These juridical and nonjuridical responses to human rights violations have developed in tandem and are mutually reinforcing. They both depend on the third condition of justice: publicity. Perpetrators naturally try to conceal their work and justice is impossible without knowledge of what is going on in remote places where victims are isolated from view. The need for publicity increases the practical importance and moral imprimatur of organizations like Amnesty International and Human Rights Watch. Their business is exposure. They are dedicated to uncovering abuses and mobilizing public support in opposition. Reporting and recordkeeping by nongovernmental organizations, peacekeepers, commissions of inquiry, and the press lay the groundwork for legal prosecution. For their part, trials are often a vehicle of massive publicity and public education; one scholar argues that collective memory of the Holocaust is weakest in Austria, Poland, Italy, and the Netherlands—societies that did not conduct postwar trials of collaborators.[25]

As important as they are, legal proceedings in response to human rights violations have as their goal justice and not assistance to the aggrieved. This point emerges clearly in discussions of "universal jurisdiction." This important contemporary legal development refers to the prosecution of international criminal law in national courts; the trial of Adolf Eichmann in Jerusalem is a well-known example; a more recent illustration is the indictment by British courts of former Chilean leader Augusto Pinochet. Universal jurisdiction is based solely on the nature of the crime and covers only the most violent acts, such as slavery, war crimes, crimes against peace and humanity, genocide, and torture. Because of the gravity of the harms and the moral outrage at impunity, prosecution is warranted even where the state has no traditional jurisdictional links to either the victims or the perpetrators of the crimes. Mary Robinson, UN high commissioner for Human Rights, explains that universal jurisdiction is a "search for ways to end impunity in the case of gross violations of human rights." The goal is to identify and punish perpetrators. International prosecutions alone "will never be sufficient to achieve justice," and territorial states often fail to investigate and prosecute.[26] Universal jurisdiction takes exception to measures that put violators beyond the reach of the law, such as sovereign immunity and amnesty. Principles of universal jurisdiction are intended to encourage states to prosecute these crimes, even if their own national laws do not specifically provide for it, and to encourage the incorporation of international obligations into national law. Principles speak to "legislators seeking to ensure that national laws conform to international law, to judges called upon to interpret and apply international law and to consider whether national law conforms to their state's international obligations, to government officials of all kinds exercising their powers under both national and international law. . . ."[28]

In all these legal venues, the goal is justice and the audience for prosecution and punishment is the "world community." Attention is not focused on victims or on repair. So predicting the impact of these tribunals is particularly precarious business insofar as the objective is not only holding the perpetrators legally accountable but also transforming how people see the past, breaking the cycle of hatred. Judicial proceedings generate raw material for historians, and they are often historically significant themselves, but they do not produce full or even adequate historical accounts of events. As dramatic attempts to create collective narratives, trials can be distorting. For political reasons, the prosecutors at the Tokyo trials deliberately excluded Emperor Hirohito from indictment, for example. The prosecution of Vichy leaders after the war was designed in part to reflect the Gaullist story that the French nation had been united in opposition to German occupation.[28] In the case of the trial of members of the Argentine junta, the legal focus was on deprivation of the rights of the "disappeared" and not, as some had hoped, on the "dirty war" as the suppression of a just social struggle. As triggers of national catharsis, the prosecution of violent crimes can fail. The Argentine trials apparently did little to counter the widespread memory of the rule of the military junta as one of admirable orderliness and lack of crime. This limits the significance, certainly the emotional repair, of legal proceedings for victims.

Moreover, procedurally correct and morally justifiable proceedings typically have the deliberate drama of show trials. As such, their purpose may conflict directly with the objectives of victims. They are intended to highlight and punish *selective deeds*, often in the explicit hope of cutting short a flood of people coming forward with their own experiences of atrocity and accusations. Whether the spirit in which these limits are set is practical or cynical, it shuts out the voices of the aggrieved.

This is not to diminish the constructive work done by international tribunals like the ones created for the former Yugoslavia and Rwanda, by third-party national courts indicting human rights violators, by domestic courts prosecuting "their own," or the potential importance of universal jurisdiction. It is simply to point to the fact that justice and response to the experience of injustice are to a considerable extent independent of one another.

The same postwar period that brought developments in both the theory and practice of international criminal prosecution has seen rapid evolution in the law and prosecution of *hate crimes*. Violence against persons and property are one form of hate crime; censorship, speech codes covering public places (the British Football Offences Act, for example), and other requirements of civility are also covered by criminal and civil laws aimed at curbing bias. *Hate crime* designates a specific category of criminal act, in which ordinary vandalism or assault, threats and harassment, rape, or murder is compounded by the selection of the victim as a member of a despised group.

Unlike human rights, the designation of acts as hate or bias crimes is highly dependent on social context, and the demands for justice vary from society to society and within jurisdictions in a single society. The categories of protected groups depend on historical patterns of prejudice, discrimination, and domination. In the United States, race is the paradigmatic category, though violence and vandalism based on religion and ethnic origin occur frequently enough. Hate crimes based on sexual orientation are depressingly common, too. The protected class can be expanded further, to include disability, for example. Demands for hate crime laws and prosecution vary depending on background conditions—not only the strength of public commitment to civil rights and liberties but beyond that the strength of the belief that publicly condemned forms of conduct must be expressly enforced by specific legislation.

In the United States, legislators at every level of government have proposed a spate of legal measures. In 1990 the federal Hate Crime Statistics Act authorized data collection by law enforcement agencies. There are recurrent attempts to establish federal civil rights cases out of specific felonies usually treated as state crimes in state courts, and the movement to federalize crimes due to animus against the victim's race or gender has strong supporters. For their part, many state and municipal governments have outlawed hate speech or enacted hate crime statutes. Besides creating new categories of crime, these laws typically provide for mandatory minimum sentences for hate crimes or for increased penalties for offenses in which the perpetrators select victims based on their ascriptive membership in a particular despised group.

The constitutions of many countries permit outlawing hate crimes and hate speech, uphold group defamation statutes, and so on. By contrast, the U.S. Supreme Court has struck down as unconstitutional both specific hate speech regulations and hate crime laws such as the Violence Against Women Act. The traditional liberal alliance between advocates of civil rights and advocates of civil liberties breaks down over hate crime and hate speech legislation. Wariness about these legal developments has its origins in the very reasons that inspired these measures in the first place: the notion that the *motivation* for certain acts alters both their social impact and their significance for victims.

One rationale for naming a separate crime and for enhanced penalties is precisely the thought that bias-inspired conduct inflicts greater harm and distinctive harms. More than ordinary crimes, the argument goes, hate crimes arouse anger, alarm, and resentment. They create fear, silencing and intimidating victims. Ultimately, they may cause victims to internalize the message of inferiority, damaging self-esteem. Another rationale for enhanced punishment is that hate crimes aggravate the societal harms relative to similar actions minus the intentional selection of a victim, precisely because hate crimes are more likely to provoke a retaliatory response. More controversially, supporters argue that bias crime has a harmful impact on all people who identify themselves as members of the target group.

So designating specific crimes as "hate crimes" entails official acknowledgment that these are crimes against an individual qua member of a group—if not against the group as a whole. Prosecution of the perpetrator of hateful violence looks to restore victims to their full status as equal persons and citizens, a crucial rehabilitation. Minow observes in "Memory and Hate" that what every form of hate crime shares as its precondition is the dehumanization of the victim. For advocates of bias law, addressing the experience of injustice demands more than punishment of the crime; it requires public affirmation, reaffirmation really, of the victims' human and civic worth. For proponents, in short, the most important rationale for hate crime legislation is that it addresses not only the demand for justice but also the experience of injustice. It is a demonstration of public commitment to equality and civility. It is largely symbolic in that it reinforces already pronounced public values about the wrongness of the doctrine of racial superiority, say. It enlists government in going beyond public condemnation of violent crimes to the designation of bias acts as criminal and to enhanced punishment. Indeed, the government's willingness to go further by creating new categories of crimes, enhanced punishment, and agreement to silence hateful speech becomes a touchstone of public respect for the vulnerable group.

Some of the same difficulties that plague international criminal tribunals operate in the prosecution of hate crimes as well. There is the problem of selective enforcement of bias laws. Sporadic prosecution may be viewed by victims as an added insult to injury. This is compounded by claims that enforcement is biased; legal scholars have noted that hate speech laws may be used with particular severity to censor gay pornography, for example. Finally, there are unintended practical consequences: hate speech laws may frustrate relatively safe outlets for expressing prejudice and fuel resentment, escalating violence.

I conclude this overview of the limitations of even the most responsive definitions of new crimes and the creation of new venues from the perspective of victims with a very brief consideration of responses to *domestic violence*. Here too, there have been substantial developments in definitions of violence among intimates as legally cognizable harms and in efforts to bring the legal system to bear more effectively against them. Marital rape is one example of the application of public crimes to the previously sacrosanct realm of private family life. Battering, stalking, and sexual harassment are all new terms made familiar by the women's movement to describe calculated harms to women. Gaps in the law remain. For example, in some venues civil relief for domestic abuse is available only to those who are victims of family members or who cohabit with their abusers; the legal class of victims does not extend to "partners."[29]

The difficulty of using law to address violence between intimates is complicated in multicultural societies where the internal practices of minority communities are socially taught and condoned by many group members. These practices may not be recognized by perpetrators as crimes at all and victims may have no official avenues of relief. In 1996, in the face of much opposition rooted in sympathy for traditional practices and the immunity of family life from official intervention, the U.S. Congress passed a federal law against female genital circumcision, for example.[30] The problem is more widespread and intractable in countries where the state either does not have a uniform civil law or does not enforce it but allows the personal law of particular religious or ethnic subcommunities to govern members. These personal laws attribute an inherited legal status to women, typically disadvantage women and limit their life prospects, and encode conditions that make them vulnerable to abuse and impotent to effect change.

Even when domestic violence and abuse laws are conscientiously and fairly applied, the limitations of formal legal proceedings are evident. The reluctance of victims to press charges or to appear as witnesses in criminal proceedings is one of those limitations. Shame and intimidation, habits of denial and appeasement, passivity rooted in abject loss of self-respect all inhibit recourse to the legal system and cooperation with authorities. The isolation common to women and children subject to brutal domination and their inability to imagine a safe alternative exacerbate their unwillingness to engage the criminal justice system. Every jurisdiction in the United States provides civil protection orders in cases of physical harm or involuntary sexual relations, but the uncertainty and time limitations of protection orders and orders to vacate property are notorious.[31] These are damaging limitations; in many instances, lodging complaints and obtaining a temporary restraining order to require the abuser to leave the home have the opposite effect. Instead of increasing women and children's safety, it provokes violent retaliation.

There are obvious similarities between the limitations of law in dealing with international and intergroup violence on the one hand and domestic violence on the other. Among them are the reluctance of powerless victims to become adversarial, the incapacity of the system to protect them from escalated anger and aggression, and material and psychological obstacles in the way of successful prosecution. When it comes to violence among intimates, there are also distinctive difficulties—tenuousness and delicacy—in applying general policy in case-by-case decisions.

It is worth noting the economic reasons why victims of intimate violence are reluctant to seek legal redress, and why it has costly consequences if they do. Apart from the court costs in petitioning for civil relief, there are the predictable financial consequences of charging (or just alienating) violent partners. Child support, lost earnings, loss of the partner's income, medical costs, and legal fees are some of the financial burdens facing women who take action against their abusers.

Institutional innovations have not overcome these difficulties, but they are helpful. In "Peace on Earth Begins at Home" (chapter 8), Judith Herman argues that the most important are mandatory arrest policies and staffing courts with victim/witness advocates. Offering the opportunity to make a victim's impact statement at the sentencing stage of a trial is another. Herman also commends the 1984 Victims of Crime Act, which provides compensation for medical and mental health treatments from a fund accumulated from fines imposed on convicted offenders—an "indirect form of social restitution." Finally, we know that the availability of legal redress for domestic abuse must be accompanied by education of public officials—judges and police especially—to overcome traditional ambivalence about intervention in "domestic disputes," reluctance to impose harsh penalties in hope of reconciliation, and even sympathy for male perpetrators. As a matter of law, municipalities and officials are not liable to civil suits for failing in their duty of protection; the *DeShaney* case, among others, ruled that absent a "special relationship" to an individual, failure to respond or investigate is not punishable. Government is not liable for inaction by police or court officials or social service agencies; government has no constitutional obligation to protect citizens from the actions of private individuals.[32]

This overview suggests that legal proceedings are an irreplaceable avenue to justice but an imperfect avenue to a full accounting of the experience of injustice and to addressing the needs of victims. They are also imperfect when it comes to reconciliation and repair. Given the limitations of legal prosecution, even with ongoing efforts at reform, are there other ways to respond to the voices of the aggrieved?

Nonjudicial Responses to Injustice: Truth Commissions, Reparations, Apologies, and Public Memorials

Formal justice does not exhaust measures to break the cycles of hatred, and in this section and the next I consider the way in which other responses compensate for the limitations of criminal and civil law, beginning with nonjudicial measures governments use to address victims' grievances. They are aimed less at justice than at confronting the experience of injustice and breaking the cycles of hatred.

Truth and Reconciliation Commissions are sometimes described as substitutes for formal criminal proceedings where those are politically impossible. But they are better understood as alternatives or supplements that offer quite different goods. Archbishop Desmond Tutu makes it clear that the South African TRC explicitly rejects the "Nuremberg trial paradigm" by advocating reconciliation over punishment.[33]

What promise does this institutional innovation hold out? For one thing, it provides a public forum for the psychologically and morally necessary act of telling what happened in a way that does more to respect the memory of victims than trials, which are constrained by strict proceduralism. Survivors' stories are not truncated or skewed by the exacting requirements of legal formalities and standards of evidence. Cool impartiality is not the ideal. Witnessing and accusing take a personal turn. The point is to expose and accuse—to broadcast the details of the perpetrators' actions and the victims' anguish. The mandate of the Chilean truth commission was "to contribute to the overall clarification of the truth about the worst violations of recent years"—to break the silence.[34]

Truth commissions also help establish a cumulative factual record of the sort that no single trial or set of trials could match. Scholars have noted the passionate preoccupation with lists—names, numbers, incidents of murder, disappearance, and torture. Because the South African TRC granted amnesty only to individuals who confessed their crimes, at least in some instances it effectively overcame denial and documented government-sponsored brutality. The Commission did not preclude the right of victims to press criminal charges or seek restitution, and the TRC offered amnesty to perpetrators only if their disclosures were complete and accurate.

For Archbishop Tutu, the TRC provides a stage for "magnanimity." It encourages people to waive their rights to a criminal proceeding and profess a willingness to forgive their oppressors. He also argues that letting go of revenge can be healing. The Archbishop's expectations are high: nothing less than rehabilitation of victims and aggressors.

More modest objectives attach to these commissions too. If truth commissions promise a grant of amnesty to participants, they create possibilities for reconciliation in individual instances—keeping in mind that reconciliation need not entail personal forgiveness. They may also help to reintegrate the accused into postwar society, a principal objective. At a minimum, the public framing of conflict and confrontation brings antagonists into a safe site and models a civil, nonviolent universe. It reminds every party to the cycle of hatred of their inseparable political and economic connection to one another.

Reparation is another avenue for addressing cycles of hatred, either as a supplement to criminal and civil proceedings or as an alternative. Apart from personal vengeance, it is the most literal form of substantive redress—the terms "reparation" and "compensatory justice" invoke "making whole." Reparations is backward looking. The idea is to provide a remedy that restores the injured to their previous condition—either because the condition before the wrong occurred was substantively just or simply because the change is a patent injury.

Moral and political philosophers illuminate some of the difficulties with the notion of compensatory justice and reparations in cases of hateful violence. The main objections are to notions of group rights and group wrongs that seem to challenge legal categories of individual grievance and individual responsibility. The normal model of compensation involves actual, identifiable injured individuals, a discrete and measurable harm, and actual, identifiable aggressors who are responsible for compensating their victims. In cases of political reparations, each of these elements is ambiguous: the relevant harm may be hard to define and not confined to a discrete event, the class of victims may be diffuse, restoration to the status quo ante may be impossible, and the aggressors may not be identifiable or, if they are, they may be unable to make restitution. Compounding matters, the line between official and private violence may be blurred—lynchings in the South, for example, were performed by "private citizens," mobs, or vigilantes, but government officials were passive, if not complicitous, and the state failed in its duty of protection.[35]

Another difficulty is determining the recipients of compensation. U.S. reparations were limited to Japanese internees themselves and to the heirs of those who died after the 1988 Congressional promulgation; other descendants were excluded from the settlement.[36] When injustices are farther in the past and when they consist of societywide, historical harms rather than discrete acts within living memory, as in the case of slavery in the United States, who is owed indemnity? Supporters point out that it is not necessary to argue that each and every African American suffered grave harm or the exact degree of harm; a moral approximation will do. This approximation marked German compensation that went to living Jewish survivors of the concentration camps but also to the state of Israel and to Jewish philanthropic organizations. Compensation also extended to those who were not camp survivors—those who endured forced labor and lost professional opportunities, livelihoods, and property. This adjustment in the normal model of compensatory justice allows for reasonable approximation along the lines of class action suits.[37] Still, some undeniable injuries do not seem amenable to reparation. Jacob Levy points out that second-class status or degrading "misrecognition" are not the sort of concrete wrongs to which compensation naturally applies.[38]

The question is not only whether there is or should be a "statute of limitations" on past injustices, however grave, but whether we should expect that an act of public acknowledgment and compensation would settle current grievances and significantly erase current hates and social divisions. Reparation for slavery has become a subject of discussion in public forums, though it is not on any official political agenda, kept alive by organizations dedicated to the idea. Yet almost a century and a half has passed since the abolition of slavery in the United States. This is one reason why a policy of reparations is not practicable, and why advocates of compensation to African Americans may be on stronger ground when they link compensation to ongoing harms of racial injustice—the failure to fully vindicate their rights—and why "reparation" is a spur to broader discussions of distributive justice.

Ascribing collective guilt and determining who must pay is as vexing as figuring out who is owed. Reparation challenges our commitment to the idea of personal culpability. There is a familiar conceptual way around this difficulty, however. In many contexts, we have recourse to the perfectly ordinary notion of the corporation as a person in the eyes of the law and, by extension, of the state as a public corporation with enduring life. Corporate responsibility is a common legal notion; the present U.S. government assumes the debts of earlier ones. In cases of reparation, we attribute governmental or civic responsibility for past harms.[39] It is not necessary to say that each and every white American is complicitous in or benefits from racial injustice, say. The notion of corporate *civic responsibility* charges reparations to the public treasury; the fact that all taxpayers are contributors does not impute collective guilt.

In part because of the need for flexibility in designing remedies, we see increasing resort to legislative rather than judicial settlements. Payment to the victims or surviving spouse and children of Japanese Americans interned during the war was the result of a congressional resolution, and reparations were appropriated out of general tax revenues. Another example is reparations payments to African-American victims of race riots in the United States; in 1994 the Florida Legislature attributed public responsibility to the city for failing to protect black citizens and for deputizing white vigilantes, and provided compensation to survivors of lynching and mob violence in 1923. In 2000 the Tulsa Race Riot Commission recommended reparations to survivors and descendants of the bloody riot in Tulsa in 1921 in which thousands of whites stormed black neighborhoods, destroying homes and businesses and killing forty. At press time, the matter was before the Oklahoma Legislature. In practice, we see, compensation is token or symbolic, as in the $20,000 granted to each survivor of the mass imprisonment in Japanese internment camps in the United States during World War II, or, more literally the restoration of Jim Thorpe's 1912 Olympic medals.

A recent development in this area is reparations claims against private companies that profited from these crimes. In negotiated settlements, Holocaust victims received compensation not only from German, French, and Austrian governments but also from Swiss banks. A California law that took effect in 2001 requires insurance companies to research their past business practices and to report whether they sold policies insuring slave owners against the loss of their slave property, and to whom. This is presumably a prelude to private lawsuits seeking damages.[40] Other insurance companies are now voluntarily reviewing archives and considering the shape of potential claims.

What can be said for reparations from the standpoint of victims? More than ordinary criminal proceedings, they speak to the experience of injustice. In particular, they provide public recognition of collective responsibility, official and unofficial, by governments and by social actors. In recent years, official reparations to victims of Germany in World War II were supplemented by settlements from German and Swiss companies, Volkswagen among them. There is the return of art confiscated from Jews and others by private collectors and public museums. The publicity these instances of reparation received exerted moral pressure on Japanese courts to agree to hear suits for damages brought by the

Chinese, suits that had previously been summarily dismissed. The Japanese government had argued that the terms of the 1951 San Francisco Treaty ending the war settled Japanese debts. But ongoing international investigations of atrocities committed by the Imperial Army, including sexual slavery imposed on over a hundred thousand women in countries controlled by the Japanese army, keep the subject alive. And civil courts provide another avenue of redress. There have also been out-of-court settlements by at least one Japanese company that acknowledged the slavelike conditions of Chinese laborers.[41] Once civil redress is tried in a few instances, we become aware of how widespread corporate responsibility in mass violence has been and how little this remedy has been exploited.

Reparations address victims directly; they send a message to individuals acknowledging their loss and reaffirming their dignity, particularly when they are accompanied by official acts of apology. From the standpoint of repair, perhaps the most important official action, taken in addition to reparations or standing alone, is apology. Overcoming legal obstacles to reparations and providing access to civil trials for damages are important, but public recognition of responsibility and apology has an even more profound impact. The Canadian government's apology for injustices against Canadian First Nations is one example. And when apology is denied, the silence looms large. Asian women forced into prostitution by the Japanese army rejected compensation by private foundations set up with private donations for the purpose; the victims demanded an official apology.[42] Nor did the 1995 Japanese Parliament's statement of remorse for conduct during the war suffice; it was not an official apology. Similarly, President François Mitterand established a National Remembrance Day recognizing anti-Semitic persecution in France, but did not offer an official apology, insisting that the Vichy government had not represented France.[43] President Clinton offered regrets for the deaths of unarmed Korean refugees who were shot by Americans after fleeing the advance of the North Korean Army in the early days of the Korean War. For those working for forty years for a review of the events and compensation, the president's condolences and promise that the United States would erect a monument in Seoul in honor of the civilians who died during the war fell short: "We want a more sincere apology, not a vague statement of regret, from the U.S. government."[44]

Public apologies do distinctive work. Like reparation, they are meant to help undo an offense and restore harmony. Apology puts injury and responsibility on the record. Beyond that, apologies are linked to honor and face. An apology can grant victims face—it admits that they deserved better treatment. "Interpersonal apologies are largely messages about the apologizer's feelings, meant to inform the other and give confidence in the future of the relationship, but international apologies are . . . more communications to the world than to the offended party: their point is to restore the other's face."[45] Moreover, the act of apology has reciprocal benefits. The honor of victims demands an apology; the honor of the wrongdoer demands that one be given.

An apology is more than an expression of regret—the wish that one had not done an act; it is an admission of wrong.[46] And unlike other forms of repair, there is an expectation of reciprocity that holds out the hope of reconciliation. Apology is normally followed by an expression of forgiveness. So it matters symbolically who is chosen to proffer the apology. Responsibility for explicit forgiveness is more ambiguous.

I conclude this overview of official, nonlegal responses to hateful violence with *public commemoration* in the form of monuments, architecture, postage stamps, coins, ritual events, public holidays, museum exhibitions, art and education projects, theatricals and so on. Governments erect civic icons intended as objects of veneration and monuments meant to serve as reminders and warnings, like the many dedicated to the memory of Holocaust victims by the postwar generation in Germany.

Legislating what people should remember is no guarantee of the content of memory, of course. Nor should it be: we are sensitive to tutelary efforts by governments to produce a privileged national narrative intended to shape as well as reflect public consciousness. We know that every important element of public commemoration is challenged by competing perspectives on the meaning of the past and the moral status of historical actors. We need only think of the erection and subsequent destruction of monuments to Stalin, for example, and other symbols of now-discredited regimes and heroes. Or the political and legal battles that rage over flying the battle flag of the Confederacy in public places in the South—and over the varied meanings of the flag (defense of slavery and white supremacy, Southern defense of the Constitution and states' rights, treason, and so on). The pluralism that underlies cycles of hatred ensures that narratives will be contested. History is always "what the people—a people, some people, these people, those people—believe about the past."[47] A burgeoning literature describes the controversies as well as the real public goods memorials produce.[48] The same is true of other public accountings; rewriting textbooks is a key example.[49]

Measures intent on comprehending and memorializing the past are

potentially conflicted. For that reason they are most likely to be beneficial if we concede at the outset that the goal is not a final and comprehensive history or cultural meaning but the memory of specific injustices
and collective moral responsibility for responding to victims. Then, they
are irreplaceable. Jurgen Habermas writes:

> Is there any way to bear the liability for the context in which such
> crimes originated . . . other than through remembrance, practiced in
> solidarity, of what cannot be made good, other than through a reflex-
> ive, scrutinizing attitude toward one's identity-forming traditions?[50]

Voluntarism: Private Responses to Victims of Injustice

Moving from formal legal proceedings to other forms of official recognition and repair does not exhaust responses to injustice. The spectrum
extends beyond criminal and civil law and public policies to the voluntary actions of private men and women, acting on their own or as members of organized groups. Efforts at repair must be public in the sense of
being publicized and made known but they need not be governmental.
Marc Galanter reminds us that invitations to memory and attempts at
repair are the result of enormous effort by "moral entrepreneurs, organizers who devote themselves to investigating, publicizing, and campaigning about old wrongs."[51]

The significance of memory for people personally and individually
should underlie every discussion focusing on addressing the needs of
victims. The trauma of violence, especially when it is personalized and
designed to be humiliating, has distinctive characteristics: recurring terror, difficulty controlling anger, difficulty sustaining relationships, loss of
the desire to live.[52] These point to some of the psychological obstacles to
reconciliation and repair. They also point up the complex needs survivors have for assistance in remembering safely and recovering the capacity for agency if they are to break out of the cycle of hatred. "Comforting the victim and ensuring that her needs are taken care of before
dealing with the offender expresses the right order of values and rejects
the wrongdoer's frame on the matter," Minow advises in "Regulating Hatred," (chapter 1).

Voluntary actions differ fundamentally from official ones. For one
thing, they depend on a degree of felt affinity between victims and sympathizers. Affinity need not be a matter of identification (shared religion
or ethnicity, say); it can be based on a sense of civic or moral commu-

nity. One of the aspirations of human rights doctrine is to cultivate this sense of affinity, and the moral caring that should accompany it.

Attending to victims requires moral affinity, but not severe altruism. All too often, hateful violence is part of everyday life. In *The Faces of Injustice* (see note 4), Judith Shklar coined the phrase "passively unjust citizens" to refer to those who do not intervene to prevent or stop injustice when they can. Neighbors who do not report wife beating or child abuse to authorities, for example, or those who do not speak up when they overhear vicious hate speech, who fail to rebuke the hateful and to stand up for the hated. Individuals do not want to get involved; minding one's own business is a powerful norm. Or they fatalistically believe that "it cannot be helped." Or they interpret violent actions as impulsive not regular and systematic. Or they have no sympathy for the victims; rationalizations for why women are battered or sexually abused are commonplace.

Passive injustice is an extension to all citizens of Cicero's prescriptions in De Officiis (@23): "Of injustice there are two types: men may inflict injury; or else, when it is being inflicted upon others, they may fail to deflect it, even though they could. . . . the man who does not defend someone, or obstruct the injustice when he can, is at fault just as if he had abandoned his parents or his friends or his country." Shklar argues that in a constitutional democracy, intervening to prevent injustice is a civic responsibility.[53] Even in democracies, the difficulty and danger of intervening to resist some forms of hate crimes may be prohibitive. More so in regimes lacking ordinary securities. Still more so when hate crimes take the form of large-scale violence waged by powerful groups. Under some circumstances, failure of individuals to intervene is understandable, even prudent; acting to stop injustice, heroic. However, this does not justify amnesia, which as Minow observes in "Memory and Hate" "hurts bystanders too because then they do not face their own choices about action and inaction."

Another face of passive injustice is more applicable here than intervening to resist crimes in progress: indifference to victims after the fact. Here, we are all obligated to offer sympathy and relief to victims of hate. Nongovernmental agencies and voluntary associations of all kinds and the personal actions of individuals go a long way toward reaching out to victims, making them and not the perpetrator the center of attention and concern.

Following a firebombing of a minority family's house in West Haven, Connecticut, petitions were circulated, asking the victimized family to remain, demonstrations were held protesting the hate crime, and police found and prosecuted the perpetrators. A Billings, Montana, community responded to a 1993 skinhead attack on a Jewish home by pasting drawings of a menorah printed by the *Billings Gazette* on their windows and staging a Martin Luther King Day march.[54] In chapter 8, Judith Herman describes an array of strategies pursued by voluntary associations to aid victims of domestic violence—from small support groups to creating safe havens—that allow victims to acknowledge their situation, to overcome shame, and to develop a sufficient sense of safety to enable them to take steps to protect themselves. Effective responses to victims' experience are not only humane; they can also reduce the fear of retaliation that prevents many victims from cooperating in the investigation and prosecution of crimes. In this way, voluntary aid to victims enables justice at the same time as it speaks directly to the experience of injustice.

In short, private actions, organized and unorganized, are terribly important for two reasons. First, they remind us that responsibility for breaking the cycles of hatred does not rest solely with government. It falls on ordinary citizens. And many of us take on that responsibility. Battered women's shelters, for example, originate in the work of private organizations but receive public support. It requires resources and sustained attention over time to make offers of comfort and assistance effective. To provide not only safety but also sustained concern.

Beyond that, voluntary responses to hate crimes do not require us to judge the ˌvictims' perceptions of injustice before offering support. Formal legal proceedings, even truth commissions and memorials, are based on some baseline agreement on the account of injustice and the sense of the proportionality between determination of injury and subjective perception. They determine what the parties deserve according to a system of rules. Here, taking the victim's view seriously does not require judgment. Deferring to subjective sentiment does not have legally or politically dubious consequences. It does not demand complete agreement with the victims' account of blame and guilt and/or with their notion of the punishment perpetrators deserve. Sympathy flows more freely. Indirect victims, who fall outside the reach of the law and are not included in official acts of reparation and commemoration, can be embraced. Those consumed by bitterness can be assisted in looking ahead as well as looking back. For some of what is missed in ordinary responses to injustice is the harm suffered when victims lack the resources to look forward and can only look back. That is one of the darkest consequences of injustice. If one objective of responses to the experience of injustice is to temper the desire for aggressive retaliation, another is to overcome passivity and despair. Demoralization is a common result of victimization. In the face of these terrible personal injuries, we recognize limits to the possibilities of both private sympathy and assistance as well as public repair. Therapy, love, a dose of resignation, and an iota of optimism are vital. But they fall outside the domain of political and legal practices; at least, they fall outside the parameters of this essay.

Of course, victims are agents too. We respond personally and individually to the experience of injustice. Forgetfulness is not required to break cycles of hatred. Memories do not necessarily dictate another vengeful round in the cycle of hatred. What matters is the personal use individuals put their memories to—the stories they tell themselves and others. Not everyone's ghosts demand bloody vengeance. The grim realities of violence, the willingness to focus on the finality and universality of death, can act as a brake on vengefulness. So the course victims take, psychologically as well as actively, is significant. A certain amount of resignation is necessary to break cycles of hatred.

Breaking the cycles of hatred is not the same as meting out positive substantive justice. It also entails responding to the experience of injustice. In the end, no punishment, reparation, acknowledgment, or commemoration will entirely meet victims' needs or fully erase their grievances. But efforts to address victims' sense of injustice directly and personally are vital. They may have positive, transforming effects—reconciliation, for example. The main thrust, however, is more modest: the moral injunction to do what is necessary to rupture the repetitive cycle of hate, of fear and vengeance. To do what is necessary to see that acts of violent hate do not become provocations to violent revenge.

Notes

1. I want to thank my research assistant, Harvard graduate student Ionnis Evrigenis, for bringing this quotation and much else to my attention.

2. In *The Multiculturalism of Fear* (New York: Oxford University Press, 2000), p. 63, Jacob Levy discusses the incentives to commit, provoke, or threaten violence and injustice in the present and to overstate wrongs against one's own group in the past.

3. Daniel Jonah Goldhagen, *Hitler's Willing Executioners: Ordinary Germans and the Holocaust* (New York: Knopf, 1996).

4. Judith Shklar *The Faces of Injustice* (New Haven, CT: Yale University Press, 1990), at 101.

5. Selmay Leydesdorff, cited by Mark J. Osiel "Never Again: Legal Remembrance of Administrative Massacre" *University of Pennsylvania Law Review* 144, no. 2 (1995): 464–704, at 540, note 296.

6. Shklar, *The Faces of Injustice*, at 2.

7. Brian Barry, *Political Argument* (Berkeley: University of California Press, 1990), at 97. See Barry on the two principal justifications for fairness: the distributive argument and the aggregative argument at 105ff.

8. Although there are some crimes, like forced pregnancy, that are covered by the treaty but not explicit in U.S. law, each nation retains the right to try its own nationals under its own laws.

9. I leave aside the enabling condition of the end of the cold war; it has had the effect of altering the parties to disputes concerning the meaning and enforceability of rights from the U.S./U.S.S.R. and allies to a more fluid array of parties, often context dependent.

10. I leave aside here the long prehistory of contemporary human rights doctrine, codified and uncodified: *ius gentium*, natural law doctrines, and others. For a detailed account of the drafting of the Universal Declaration of Human Rights, see Mary Ann Glendon, *A World Made New: Eleanor Roosevelt and the Universal Declaration of Human Rights* (New York: Random House, 2001).

11. Biljana Plavsic is the defendant; Marlise Simons, "Ex-Serb Chief Denies Guilt at Bosnia War Crimes Trial," *New York Times* (January 12, 2001): 8.

12. Michael J. Perry, *The Idea of Human Rights* (New York: Oxford University Press, 1998).

13. For a recent discussion, see Charles R. Beitz, "Human Rights as a Partisan Concern," unpublished paper.

14. Rawls disputes this position and argues for tolerance, *The Law of Peoples* (Cambridge, MA: Harvard University Press, 1999), at 60, though he develops the law of peoples from within political liberalism and sees it as an extension of a liberal conception of justice for a domestic regime to a society of peoples, at 9. They are also, he argues, reasonable from a decent nonliberal point of view.

15. On government responsibility for preventable starvation, for example, see Amartya Sen, *Poverty and Famines* (Oxford, UK: Clarendon Press, 1981). On the attempt to include the right to participate in government and form political parties in the Universal Declaration, see Glendon, *A World Made New*, at 184.

16. Timothy Garton Ash suggests a correlation (but no causal direction) between "the degree of facing up to the past, however clumsily, and the state of progress from dictatorship to democracy," cited in Osiel "Never Again," at 504.

17. Beitz, "Human Rights as a Partisan Concern," at 12. Still, there is disagreement over whether proximity to events gives neighboring people or states, which are more likely to have to deal with the consequences of human rights enforcement, greater weight to positions in favor of or against humanitarian intervention or criminal prosecution.

18. Glendon, *A World Made New*, at xviii.

19. See Glendon, *A World Made New*, on the UNESCO document by philosophers and rebuttals to the charge of cultural bias or colonialism, and on the number of states and nongovernmental organizations involved in writing the Universal Declaration.

20. Rawls, *The Law of Peoples*, on "urgent rights," at 79. Rawls's categories of regimes include outlaw societies, societies burdened by unfavorable conditions, and benevolent absolutisms, at 4.

21. Rawls, at 79.

22. Ian Fisher, "Can International Relief Do More Good Than Harm?" *New York Times Magazine* (February 11, 2000): 72–76, at 75.

23. Samantha Power, review of *A People Betrayed*, *New York Times Book Review* (February 11, 2001): 33.

24. Fisher, "Can International Relief Do More Harm Than Good?" at 76.

25. Cited in Osiel, "Never Again," at 639.

26. Foreword, *The Princeton Principles on Universal Jurisdiction* (Princeton, NJ: Program in Law and Public Affairs, Princeton University, 2001), at 15, 16.

27. Introduction, *Princeton Principles*, p. 26.

28. Osiel, "Never Again," at 543, 537.

29. Robert A. D'Amico II, "Notes: Civil Remedies and the Domestic Abuse Victim: Does Current Rhode Island Law Provide Sufficient Relief?" *Suffolk University Law Review* 25 (1991): 389.

30. On this issue, see Susan Moller Okin, "Is Multiculturalism Bad for Women?" *Boston Review* (October/November 1997): 22.

31. The decisive case is *State ex. Re. Williams v. Marsh*, 626 S.W.2d 223 (1982).

32. *DeShaney v. Winnebago County Department of Social Services*, 489 U.S. 189 (1989).

33. Desmond Tutu, *No Future Without Forgiveness* (New York: Doubleday, 1999).

34. Cited in Osiel, "Never Again," at 671, note 757.

35. Levy, *The Multiculturalism of Fear*, at 45.

36. See the essay by Eric K. Yamomoto, "Reluctant Redress," in this volume.

37. On altering and going beyond this model in ordinary civil law, especially notions of how to distribute damages, see Cass Sunstein, "The Limits of Compensatory Justice," in John W. Chapman, ed., *Nomos XXXIII* (New York: New York University Press, 1991), pp. 281–310.

38. Levy *The Multiculturalism of Fear*, at 244.

39. For this and the following discussion, I am indebted to Robert K. Fullinwider, "The Case for Reparations," *Philosophy and Public Policy* 20, no. 2/3 (Summer 2000): 1–8.

40. Tamar Lewin, "Calls for Slavery Restitution Getting Louder," *New York Times* (June 4, 2001): A15.

41. Howard French, "Japanese Veteran Testifies in War Atrocity Lawsuit," *New York Times* (December 21, 2000): A3.

42. Osiel, "Never Again," at 677–78.

43. Barry O'Neill, *Honor, Symbols, and War* (Ann Arbor: University of Michigan Press, 1999), p. 189.

44. Elizabeth Becker, "Army Admits G.I.'s in Korea Killed Civilians at No Gun Ri," *New York Times* (January 12, 2001): A1.

45. O'Neill, p. 192.

46. O'Neill, *Honor, Symbols, and War*, at 177, 183.

47. Robin Winks cited in Sanford Levinson, *Written in Stone: Public Monuments in Changing Societies* (Durham, NC: Duke University Press, 1998), at 64.

48. See Sanford Levinson, *Written in Stone.*

49. See, for example, Frances Fitzgerald, *America*, rev. ed. (Boston: Little Brown, 1979). One constructive function of commemorative art and history projects done locally is expressive; for some people, creative production is the most vivid and cathartic representation of their experience. These projects have a further public result, at least potentially: they bring conflicting views into public spaces and discourse in less threatening forms and forums than courts or official proceedings. They are a way of representing, if not working through, memory and repair.

50. Cited in Osiel, "Never Again," at 611.

51. Marc Galanter, "Righting Old Wrongs," in this volume.

52. Judith Herman, *Trauma and Recovery*, cited in Minow, "Between Nations and Between Intimates," chap. 1.

53. Shklar, *The Faces of Injustice*, at 40ff.

54. See the discussion in Nancy L. Rosenblum, *Membership and Morals: The Personal Uses of Pluralism in America* (Princeton, NJ: Princeton University Press, 1998), pp. 279ff.

3

Righting Old Wrongs*

MARC GALANTER

> This is how one pictures the angel of history. His face is turned
> toward the past. Where we perceive a chain of events, he sees
> one single catastrophe which keeps piling wreckage upon
> wreckage and hurls it in front of his feet. The angel would like
> to stay, awaken the dead, and make whole what has been
> smashed. But a storm is blowing from Paradise; it has got
> caught in his wings with such violence that the angel can no
> longer close them. This storm irresistibly propels him into the
> future to which his back is turned, while the pile of debris
> before him grows skyward. This storm is what we call progress.
>
> —WALTER BENJAMIN (1940): 257–58

The Burgeoning of Efforts to Right Old Wrongs

An urge to reform the past seems to be in the air. I cannot claim to
have a representative sample of such undertakings, but my unsystematic
canvass reveals a rising tide of interest in reforming the past. Indeed, it is
a characteristic feature of our times.

In 1972, 167 black soldiers who had been dishonorably discharged in
the 1906 Brownsville Affair were exonerated; only one of the discharged
soldiers was alive at the time of the exoneration.[1] In 1974, a class action
lawsuit compensated the participants in the infamous 1930s Tuskegee
syphilis study in which black subjects were not informed that they were

* This essay descends from a paper presented to the Conference on Memory and Morals:
Sephardim and the Quincentenary, held at the University of Miami, October 3–5, 1991.
Along the way it benefited from the able and imaginative assistance of Jesse Wing (J.D.,
University of Wisconsin, 1991) and from the stimulating responses of Upendra Baxi, Marvin
Frankel, Maivan Clech Lam, Judith Lichtenberg, David Luban, Beverly Moran, Boaventura
DeSousa Santos, and members of faculty seminars at Osgoode Hall, Berkeley, Harvard, and
Duke.

suffering from syphilis.[2] In 1980 the Sioux received compensation for the 1877 taking of the Black Hills, which were set aside in 1868 for their "absolute and undisturbed use and occupation." That same year Congress enacted the Maine Indian Claims Settlement Act, giving Passamaquoddy and Penobscot Indians $81.5 million as compensation for being cheated out of their lands in 1794.[3] In 1986, the State of Georgia pardoned Leo Frank (lynched in 1915) because of his unjust conviction in the 1913 murder of Mary Phagan.[4] Congress enacted the Civil Liberties Act of 1988, making formal apology to Japanese Americans interned during World War II and providing compensatory payments of $20,000 for about 60,000 surviving internees. (Four years earlier a Federal District Court in California had vacated the 1942 conviction of Fred Korematsu, in effect, reversing the case that upheld the validity of wartime internment of Japanese Americans.) In 1989 the State of Wisconsin apologized to the Sac and Fox for the 1832 Bad Axe Massacre.[5] The next year Congress enacted the Native American Grave Protection and Reparation Act, mandating return by governments of bones and cultural items to tribes.[6]

These examples, which might easily be multiplied, are all from the past thirty years. Earlier instances are not entirely lacking. In 1922, 285 years after Anne Hutchinson's 1637 banishment from Massachusetts because of her religious beliefs, a statue of her was erected in the State House in Boston.[7] In 1959, a statue of Mary Dyer, hanged on the Boston Common in 1660 for her Quaker beliefs, was placed in front of the State House.[8] Even earlier, in 1886, the State of Connecticut made an official apology (and granted a pension) to Prudence Crandall, who had been persecuted by official action when she started a school for black girls in the 1830s. These earlier instances foreshadow a striking feature of the list of contemporary American instances—the extent to which it centers around repudiation of hatred, prejudice, and violence inflicted on racial, ethnic, or religious grounds. The contemporary list adds the theme of group entitlements to that of victimized individuals.

The proliferation of efforts to reform the past is not a peculiarly American phenomenon. Claims for apology or recognition or compensation growing out of old wrongs are part of the common currency of political and cultural life. In recent years, the Vatican pardoned Galileo (1984); Canada apologized to its Japanese and Italian citizens for their 1940s internment (1988, 1990);[9] East Germany apologized to Jews for the Holocaust (1990); West German companies began paying World War II slave laborers (1990); Japan apologized to Korea for brutal colonial rule (1991);

and a series of accords culminated in the revocation of the 1492 Edict of Expulsion of the Jews from Spain on its five hundredth anniversary in 1992. Since then measures to return property and uncover and/or punish the crimes of earlier regimes have become familiar parts of the social landscape.

Apart from claims that have been granted in significant measure, there are also numerous claims that are pending, including some that have been around for many years (like Greece's claim for the return of the Elgin Marbles). Others are relatively new on the scene, like the claim for reparations for American slavery, which stands out for its scale and political salience, and also because it raises so abundantly the perplexities of righting old wrongs.[10] What does it mean to do justice in the face of such old and large wrongs? What can be done? What should be done? What are we obligated to do? Are there hidden costs or unexpected benefits that flow from such enterprises?

Ordinary Justice and Old Wrongs

I want to approach these questions by considering current and emergent practices of righting old wrongs as they spin off from our ordinary practices of remedy in cases of fresh wrongs. I emphasize that I do not regard these ordinary practices as constituting a regime suffused by exemplary justice disturbed by occasional eruptions of injustice.[11] Instead, they are part of a world in which injustice—undeserved human suffering, unrewarded virtue, and unpunished evil—is pervasive and institutionalized. These legal practices, our technology of remedial justice, are weak and flawed instruments of justice, but they are the best we have.

In addition to underfunding, poor design and management, corruption, bureaucratic torpor and all the other infirmities that beset public institutions, there are inherent constraints on the extent to which legal institutions can realize our ideals of justice. These inexpungeable limitations of human justice include at least three that are relevant to our inquiry:

1. Because it is accomplished piecemeal over time, remedial justice inevitably disturbs existing expectations: "Every social change, every new law, every forced alternation of public rules is unjust to someone. . . . To redress one injustice is to create another."[12] It is hoped, a lesser one.
2. Providing remedial justice consumes resources. As a consequence, the resulting distribution of benefits or entitlements cannot be

aligned with the underlying, substantive merits as suggested by the principles of compensation or punishment that animate the process. And since these costs are substantial, there is never enough remedial justice to answer all claims; justice has to be rationed, creating new disparities and deprivations.

3. Remedies for injustice are typically administered by institutions. But these institutions embody a dilemma. As such a justice institution becomes differentiated, complex and maze-like in order to operate with increasing autonomy and precision, the justice institution itself becomes a source of new imbalances. Some users become adept in dealing with it; those with other advantages (like wealth, organization, or knowledge) find that these advantages can be translated into advantages in the legal arena. There arise new differences in access and competence—thus law itself may amplify the imbalances it set out to correct.[13] Even though these institutions are designed to secure justice, they are embedded in, permeable by, and responsive to features of social life, that reflect disparities of power, wealth, and knowledge.[14] The dilemma is that elimination of these linkages would isolate these institutions so that they would be less responsive to the changing needs and values of the society.

For all their imperfections, the law's familiar remedial practices offer us a place to start. We may ask whether they are useful in assessing and responding to claims arising out of old (and often very large) wrongs.[15] I am not urging that models drawn from private justice and current remedies are the most appropriate for old wrongs—or that they are the only kinds of redress that might be applied. But they are a repository of questions about doing justice that help us to think about justice on a large temporal scale.

For the most part, the ideas of vindication and compensation of old wrongs track legal notions of property, tort, contract, and criminal law. But in one important respect they depart from ordinary legal arrangements: they elevate the themes of memory, witness, and redemption over the closure and finality that are a major component of the law.

Our ordinary practices of justice are based on the notion that injustice and remedy should be closely associated in time. Indeed, the commonplace commands our ready assent: "Justice delayed is justice denied." True justice, this adage reminds us, is virtually instantaneous. For with the passage of time, evidence deteriorates, witnesses scatter and forget, making it ever more difficult to recreate an accurate account of events. And changing circumstances make adequate remedy more difficult as the victim's deprivations accumulate. So promptness is viewed as a major element of the quality of justice and we devote resources to expediting cases.

Yet the ordinary administration of justice tolerates some passage of time. Claims are often not made immediately, especially where the claimant is weak or ignorant. We are committed to due process; we are counseled to let justice take its course and cautioned against a precipitous "rush to judgment." In the interest of having institutions that can administer justice on a routine and regular basis, we are solicitous of the convenience of judges, lawyers, and witnesses. (In the United States, a period of a year or two is considered normal for a case in our courts—appeals may stretch this by several more years.) Sometimes we try to make up to the victim for the delay by awarding interest or back pay. But the ordinary administration of justice assumes that some delay is unavoidable and lets the cost of it fall on the claimant/justice-seeker.[16] But suppose the claim and requested remedy are separated from the original violation not by months or years, but by decades or centuries? In the ordinary administration of justice, we have statutes of limitations that cut off old claims and rules of prescription that extinguish old rights. Difficulties of ascertaining the truth about ancient events reinforce a strong policy of securing current entitlements by closing issues, leaving things at rest (found in the doctrines of adverse possession, prescription, res judicata, collateral estoppel). The law formulates an authoritative, unchallengeable world of entitlements by writing over all prior claims. It is this impulse to accept present distributions and get on with things rather than revisiting old claims that is challenged by the project of righting old wrongs.

These claims regarding old wrongs raise a series of perplexities. Is it only the technical feasibility of remedy that declines with the passage of time, or does the deservingness of victims decline as well?[17] Does the notion of what is an appropriate remedy change as the time scale is lengthened? Addressing these brings us to basic questions about how much justice is possible, how much we want, and how much we can afford.

If we consider all the wrongs and injustices that have and can and will happen, would each of them deserve to be remedied in a world in which remedies are not costless? Remedies cost in time, expense, attention, and lost opportunities, so all injustices cannot be remedied. How do we choose those deserving of remedy?[18] Is the passage of time a good basis for abandoning some candidates for remedy?

A Matrix of Old Wrongs

Rather than take up these questions in the abstract, I propose to construct a matrix for analyzing these questions, drawing on some of the cases of old wrongs that have appeared on the public agenda in recent years.

THE CONTOURS OF THE WRONG

Wrongs differ along many dimensions, including the following:

1. Was the injustice compressed into a well-defined time period—like the expulsion or the dismissal of the Brownsville soldiers? Or was it a continuing social practice like slavery or the exclusion of black players from organized baseball?
2. Was the injustice a single discrete event (stripping Jim Thorpe of his Olympic medals), a series of events, or a long, cumulative social process (e.g., the subordination and oppression of the untouchables in India, the oppression of women in many societies)?
3. Was it the doing of a specific agency or did it reflect a diffuse social process? Was there sponsorship or approval by government or other authorities that represented the whole society? (Or even several societies, as with the slave trade.)
4. Was the wrong the manifestation of a deliberate policy like the Holocaust or slaveholding regimes? Or was it an inadvertent result of carelessness, like the Johnstown flood?
5. What was the moral status of the act when it was done? Was it a violation of familiar norms? Was there an acknowledgment that it was wrong? Or was it done under a claim of rightness that seemed self-evident?

Obviously there are many intermediate points on each of these scales.

WRONGDOERS

In some cases the wrongdoers are still around (e.g., the International Olympic Committee that took away Jim Thorpe's honors). But in examining older and more diffuse wrongs, the question is whether there are identifiable and credible surrogates for the perpetrators. In the case of the internment of Japanese Americans, the target was not the officials responsible, but the government that promulgated the unjust policy. But who are the contemporary representatives of the wrongdoers in the case of American slavery? Suppose we could identify a class of wrongdoers in the past (slave traders, slaveholders, officials who enforced the system, etc.). Who are their contemporary representatives? One possibility is all of their descendants. But presumably biological descent is not the relevant test. Injustice is often registered in the gene pool: among the descendants of American slaveholders are many American blacks. Only those descendants who inherited the social identities of the wrongdoers? How about descendants of whites who were not slaveholders? Or of those whites who came to America after slavery was abolished?

Presumably, we might regard those ancestors as themselves participants in the caste order of invidious exclusion of blacks and beneficiaries of that order (advancing more easily since blacks were excluded from desirable occupations). Are beneficiaries of unjust practices as liable to remedy them as active perpetrators? (Is failure to make such a distinction itself a new act of injustice?) What this discussion clarifies is that the relevant continuities are social rather than genetic. It is the inheritance of advantage or disadvantage (including advantaged/disadvantaged social identities) that should count, not the inheritance of protoplasm. How is such liability affected by the existence of other perpetrators—for example, African tribes that captured slaves and sold them to Europeans? Is the liability of those tribes dissipated by later colonization and failure to prosper? Is liability here "joint and several" so that the current representative of any wrongdoer should be responsible for the whole of this vast wrong? Would there be a right to have the burden shared by other wrongdoers (i.e., by their present representatives), analogous to the right of contribution enjoyed by parties liable for ordinary wrongs? How about relative culpability? In the Expulsion story, what about the even harsher treatment that Jews from Spain received after having resettled in Portugal?

VICTIMS/CLAIMANTS

A similar set of ramifying complexities are encountered in identifying the victims. In some instances, there are living individual victims of the original injustice—Japanese Americans who were interned forty-five years earlier; black baseball players who never made it to the major leagues; the surviving veterans of the Brownsville Affair, who had been discharged sixty-six years earlier.

But the effects of injustices are not confined to the immediate injury or to the persons of the victims: unjust discharge or taking of property may impair their future opportunities and constrict the life chances of their children. As these effects ramify over time they are particularly difficult to specify since there are so many intervening variables to confound the causal link between the original injustice and the deprivations of living individuals.

When the immediate victims are dead, can we find identifiable and credible surrogates for the victims? In a general way, we think of their descendants. Sometimes there are distinct, specific descendants—for example, the great-grandson of the black Civil War soldier slain serving in an all-black regiment, but not paid the $14 monthly received by white soldiers. The great-grandson seeks $237 (the difference in pay) plus interest—estimated as $345,000 at 6 percent compounded.[19] Presumably, whatever entitlement this great-grandson has is shared by all of the soldier's biological descendants. Are they more deserving than blacks in general? And is biological descent a sufficient test? Presumably, the only ones qualified are those who have maintained an identification with the original victims. This would exclude the many descendants of American slaves who have lived as white for generations (and the male descendants of oppressed women). Are remedies only for those descendants who themselves suffer from disabilities traceable to the original victimization?[20] But that may include others than descendants—for example, blacks who have come to the United States from Africa in this generation suffer from current discrimination—they may find it difficult to get a job, housing, or a taxi. Is the victim group defined in terms of current invidious treatment or the cumulative effects of the original injustice?

The problems of representation are exemplified in disputes about the recovery from museums of Native American remains and artifacts. In 1990, Congress enacted the Native American Grave Protection and Reparation Act, which requires that institutions identify lineal descendants or tribes in cases where any remains, burial goods, or sacred or culturally important artifacts appeared to be affiliated with that individual or tribal group.

Just how close a nexus is required between original victims and present claimants? And how is that to be established? Although they may share some larger social identity, all Native Americans are not surrogates for one another. There may be questions about which of the competing present claimants is an appropriate representative of the original vic-

tims;[21] or there may be a question of whether a claimant group is sufficiently continuous in identity with the original group. Thus the governor
of Illinois refused to turn over skeletons from a 900-year-old burial
mound to current tribes because the Mississippian tribes ceased to exist
hundreds of years ago. The claimants contended that "All tribes have a
common ancestry and history and . . . the display disrespects their religious beliefs."[22]

Identities are not fixed and natural, but socially constructed. Identities
like "Native American" or "Hispanic" are not biological categories, nor
are they natural facts like geological formations or rainfall, impervious to
fiat and uninfluenced by understanding. But neither are they the artificial
products of policy, like courts, legislatures, or corporations, that can be
readily dismantled or altered by human design. Like language usages,
they have an intermediate character, combining natural givenness with
some malleability. Social identities are not innate qualities that inhere in
or emanate from the group or individual; instead, they are asserted to,
imposed by, and negotiated with various other components of the society.[23] As this shows, claims are put forward in terms of identities that may
have emerged subsequent to the historical injustice in question. That is,
new "composite" identities like "Native American" or "Hispanic" may be
created in the claiming process. Since identities can be projected backward as well as forward, contemporary accounts of old wrongs may not
only turn on standards unknown at the time, but involve identities that
had not yet emerged.

Are we content with a claimant who is the material or cultural legatee
of the victim or do we require that the claimant is being victimized pres-
ently as a result of that earlier victimization? If we are looking for injury
now as well as injury then, we come to the question of ascertaining the
causal connection between the original violation and any present injury.
As time goes on, there are more intervening events that can diffuse,
deflect, or mitigate the effects of the original injustice, so that the extent
to which present conditions can be attributed to the original violation
diminishes.

Finally, suppose we find more than one set of qualified victims? Suppose there are layers of violations and victims? That is, victim A seeks
restoration of the situation at time T1 when he possessed some good;
victim B seeks restoration of the situation at time T2 when he was in
possession of that same good. This situation is pointedly present in contemporary Hungary, where a commitment to compensate people who

were deprived of their property by the communist regime led to questions about earlier layers of expropriation. The following hypothetical case was raised in Parliamentary debate: "A Jewish shopkeeper lost his store in 1939, when Hungary's quasifascist Government began to curtail Jewish property rights. The store was then owned by a German, who in turn lost it shortly after World War II, when many ethnic Germans, held collectively accountable for the Nazi occupation in 1944, were driven from Hungary. The next owner, an ethnic Hungarian, lost the shop in the late 1940s, when the Communist Government embarked on successive nationalization campaigns."[24] The layered quality of wrongs and claims figures prominently in the claims for the restoration of lost nations. Such claims seek to restore the status quo ante a conquest, massacre, or expulsion.[25] They seek restoration of an earlier status quo rather than, as in the case of the Japanese internees, a resolution or reconciliation that does not involve undoing or reversing the original dislocation/ displacement.

Layers remind us that claims to remedy the past are not necessarily compatible; not all can be granted. Nor are they necessarily deserving. In response to passage in 1996 of a controversial U.S. law permitting sanctions against those who trade with Cuba, two Canadian MPs proposed a bill to enable descendants of Tories to claim compensation for lands seized from their ancestors during the American revolution.[26] This tongue-in-cheek claim is a prototype for the endless number of historic grievances that match the formal requirements of a "righting old wrongs" claim, but that have so far not attracted organized and sustained support.

FORUM

For the most part the forum in which these claims are put forward are governmental rather than private,[27] political rather than judicial.[28] The making of such a claim frequently acknowledges the remedies and standards of the "majority"—the group that prevailed, the historical winners (often the "wrongdoer"). That is, the wrongdoer is being asked to live up to its standards—to standards that affirm its best view of itself. So in a curious way claims about old wrongs can be an act of affiliation, joining. Such claims can say, "Since our lot is with you, we ask that you apply your avowed standards to your own actions."[29] This relinquishes or downplays any claim to independent jurisdiction, unlike nationalist claims for separation, where the standards invoked are those of the "international community" or a third party.

STANDARDS

A claim must be deserving according to contemporary standards. Claims that fail this test, even though based on solid legal entitlements of the earlier time, attract little support. Few would support the claims of colonial powers to repossess colonies wrested from them. Or the property claims of slaveholders. Some rewritings of entitlements are based on a broad agreement that they are a move toward higher standards that justify disappointing what were once considered "reasonable" expectations.

By what standard is the determination of wrong or injustice to be made? Some instances of righting old wrongs involve acts that were clearly regarded as wrong at the earlier time. Take, for example, the murderer apprehended many years later after leading an exemplary life. Has the passage of time weakened the claim to punish him? Frequently we think not. But in many of these cases, what is now regarded as wrong was at the time done under a claim that it was right—sometimes a secure claim confirmed by central social institutions, other times a more debatable and controverted claim. The new judgment on old acts may turn on a reassessment of the facts (as in the Japanese internment case) or it may involve a reversal in the moral valance of the original act, so that what was viewed as good is now seen as bad (e.g., the exclusion of blacks from major league baseball). Or consider the turnabout that is involved in the restoration of Native American skeletons. In the nineteenth century these were collected as scientific specimens; now they are restored as "ancestral remains." Behavior that was once commendable scientific collection is now viewed as desecration and graverobbing.

Often doing justice involves emergence or clarification of a new standard. Acts may be evaluated by criteria that were not accepted or authoritative when the acts took place. Thus, the advent of religious tolerance led to Anne Hutchinson and Mary Dyer being redefined as heroic victims of persecution rather than obnoxious heretics. Those who condemned them, something that seemed entirely acceptable at the time, were themselves condemned for intolerance. When we raise (i.e., change) standards, we face a dilemma of choosing between ex post facto imposition and affirming the unreformed past.[30]

In most cases we do the latter. Consider the Johnstown Flood, in which a poorly designed dam constructed at a private vacation resort burst and flooded the city, at a cost of over 2,200 lives. Our contemporary notions of care and accountability are clearly violated, although efforts at the time to obtain a civil remedy were unavailing.[31] The "visitation of providence" of a century ago would be perceived as an injustice today.

PROPOSED REMEDY

Typically, campaigns to right old wrongs are mounted with a specific remedy in mind. Various sorts of remedies may be thought to be feasible or appropriate. In many instances what is sought is historical vindication: some form of acknowledgment of the wrong (or recognition of the underlying entitlement that it erased) and apology for the injustice. This can take various forms:

Doing the right thing belatedly (e.g., inducting black players into the Baseball Hall of Fame). This leaves unremedied the loss suffered in the interval. It also diminishes in effect after the lifespan of the victim.

Setting the record straight (e.g., the posthumous pardon of Leo Frank, the various campaigns for revision of history books).[32]

Apology: Formal ceremonies of apology may be employed to acknowledge the wrong, as in the State of Wisconsin's apology to the Cherokee for the 1832 Bad Axe Massacre. Apologies have to be seen as sincere and adequate. In 1984 the President of South Korea, seeking an apology for the brutal Japanese occupation of his country, was told by Emperor Hirohito of Japan that it was "regrettable that there was an unfortunate past between us," a formulation spurned as inadequate. In 1990, his son, Emperor Akihito, expressed his "deepest regret" for the sufferings that Japan had brought about in Korea.

Vindication may take a palpable form of public commemoration—a public holiday (e.g., the Martin Luther King birthday holiday) or, more commonly, naming of streets and schools, historical markers on highways or in national parks,[33] erection of statues. Thus statues of religious dissenters Anne Hutchinson and Mary Dyer were erected at the Massachusetts State House. We see many instances of the decommemoration of villains by removal of statues of Stalin, Lenin—as a mark of respect for their victims. Where those who are heroes to some are villains (or at least representatives of villainy) to others, the politics of memorials and symbols can be heated, as with Confederate monuments and flags throughout the American South.[34]

All of these redistribute blame and honor, but involve no material transfer to victims. But in other instances there are important material as well as symbolic transfers.

One frequent pattern is the claim for the return of the property object in dispute (land, ancestral remains), typically without compensation for the intervening time. (Most nationalist claims are of this kind—give us back sovereignty, forget about the interval.)

Token payment: Another frequent pattern involves distribution to victims of a non-equivalent but more than trivial sum as partial compensation for material losses (thus the $20,000 payments to Japanese-American internees). Such material transfers may act as a seal of seriousness, significantly enhancing the apology. As a Japanese-American spokesman said, "The checks are simply a token" warranting the sincerity of the admission of wrongdoing.

Programmatic reconstruction: Occasionally there are attempts to devise a program of beneficial treatment for what are now perceived as victim groups. The most elaborate example of this is India's policy of compensatory discrimination, which affords preferential treatment to the untouchable and tribal peoples.[35] Affirmative action programs in the United States contain unacknowledged reparative elements.

Full reparations: There are rare cases in which proposals are advanced to provide a remedy that fully compensates the victim, "makes whole" the injury, including all intervening and cumulative losses. This raises prodigious questions of calculating compound interest, evaluating nonmaterial claims, and assessing possible offsets for mitigating benefits.[36]

Symbolic remedies preclude the tough questions of identifying victims and wrongdoers for distribution of tangible benefits. They also avoid measuring injuries and wrongs. So symbolic remedies not only provoke less conflict between claimants and others, but also among claimants and among the others. This is less so to the extent that the honor implicated by the symbols is a zero-sum thing, so that something is taken away from those labeled wrongdoers that is not offset by the credit they receive for generosity, fairmindedness, and the like.

When righting an old wrong involves some material transfer, the question arises whether the remedy should be distributive or collective. Should payments be given to individual recipients or to an institution, association, or government as their representative? To the extent that remedies are distributive, should they be individualized (proportionate to the injury or suffering undergone by each individual recipient) or should distribution be formulaic (with all members of the victim group given a fixed amount, as in the Japanese-American internment case)? An intermediate solution, sometimes used in disaster settlements and in class action litigation, creates several layers of beneficiaries, but makes no attempt to match compensation to individual loss or suffering within these broad classes.

The Significance of Righting Old Wrongs

WHY NOW?

If, as I believe, there is more righting old wrongs than there used to be, the question arises, why? The industrialized world is more affluent; we can afford to salve out consciences without reducing our level of amenity. But why do our consciences point in this direction? The answer is surely complex, but let me mention three features of the current scene that strike me as importantly implicated in the popularity of reforming the past.

First, there is the general extension of the frontiers of empathy in late twentieth-century society. Although the pattern of response toward suffering is very mixed,[37] there has been a general softening of manners and enlargement of empathy, marked by the decline in suffering as entertainment and the virtual elimination from public discourse of pejorative expressions about ascriptive groups.[38]

Second, people are more critical. There has been a decline of confidence in established authorities, in government and business and religion[39]—a willingness to concede that they may have done wrong.

Third, critical views are combined with optimism about institutions, including institutions of remedy. The success of science and technology in eliminating many perils and unpleasantnesses has generated expectations that more of life's unfairnesses and undeserved troubles could be remedied.[40] The decline in resignation and the spread of a sense that matters can be made right is dramatized by the succession of "civil rights" campaigns. This optimism about justice, buoyed by a sense of progress, combines with high expectations of institutional performance to inspire projects to redeem the past.

This optimism about the possibilities of corrective justice may conceal a strain of pessimism about comprehensive distributive justice. It is a swing away from the "enlightenment project" of universalistic planning for a just future. (As David Luban says, we seem to find more resonance in our oppressed ancestors than in our happy grandchildren.)[41] Distributive justice is forward looking, but cool, reflective, detached; corrective justice is warm but retrospective, emphasizing continuity and identity—not only the damaged identity of the victim, but the identity of the wrongdoer stained by the injustice. The righting old wrongs project is a conservative utopia. It holds out the hope that if we can right old wrongs we can arrive at a harmonious resting place. But stopping the flow of history is as illusory as fixing up the past. The best we can do is allow ourselves to be sensitized by contemplation of the past to the traces of past wrongs that infect the present according to our own standards.

WHY THIS? SELECTIVITY AND THE VEHICLES OF MEMORY

As claims to reform the past become a familiar part of public discourse, we can discern some patterns of selectivity. Some of the injustices of the past attract an interest in redress; others do not. Among the claims put forward, we find a heavy emphasis on instances of invidious treatment of ascriptive or descent groups. The injuries of class, on the other hand, do not inspire campaigns to reform the past. Our contemporary standards lead us to harsh condemnation of the absence (or inadequacy) of the remedial action in incidents like the Johnstown Flood, the Triangle Shirtwaist Fire, and the Hawk's Nest Tunnel Disaster, whose victims have gone unvindicated and uncompensated (or egregiously undercompensated).[42] Such incidents sometimes inspire writers and historians to set the record straight, but none has inspired a campaign to apply contemporary standards in a new remedial process. Wrongs that affected victims on the basis of class, residence, age, gender, sexual preference, or political group rarely give rise to movements to right old wrongs. On the other hand, wrongs that entail kin-like ascriptive groupings, such as family, caste, tribe, ethnicity, nation, and religion, seem to get carried into the present more vigorously, charged with a sense of injustice and a thrust for redemption.

Why does memory work so differently, so that old "class" injuries lead to resignation, but in descent groups we find a desire to vindicate past wrongs? The latter groups inspire moral entrepreneurs, organizers who devote themselves to investigating, publicizing and campaigning about old wrongs. But that only restates the question: why is it that such entrepreneurs can recruit supporters? Of the various identities that each of us carry, these primordial identities are easier to mobilize. They seem to be carriers of memory that can be organized around feelings of injustice and the possibility of redemption.[43]

Most "righting old wrongs" claims are put forward on behalf of minorities who are asserting their versions of the past against the hegemonic stories of the majority. They call on the majority for acknowledgment and for forebearance from taking advantage of its dominance. In many cases a period of noblesse oblige by the majority is followed by resentment from majorities that demand "parity" with minorities. Compact and dominant majorities, too, may be aggrieved and seek restoration of the past (Hindus in India, proponents of school prayer in the United States, anti-immigrant and nationalist movements in Europe). Once we proceed down the "righting old wrongs" path and confirm that government is the impresario of the drama of group honor and standing, the vistas of victimization open before moral entrepreneurs among majorities as well as among minorities.

THE CLAIMS OF HISTORY

The fashion for righting old wrongs tells us something about ourselves and the way we view our relation to history. To devote ourselves to these claims represents an impulse to confront and undo the injustice of history, to retrospectively and retroactively move the line separating misfortune and injustice so that all human depredations are seen as remedial injustice. It attempts to make history yield up a morally satisfying result that it did not the first time around.[44] It is as if we feel called to supply in our small way the providential character that we would like history to display.

But history contains an endless supply of injustices. We want to feel that we are sensitive to the claims that arise from them without committing ourselves entirely to the enterprise of retro-justification. Which old wrongs will secure remedies is a question about the future, not the past. In part, it is a question of which claims will be articulated and organized. This requires not only entrepreneurs, but supporters. But which claims will be granted depends on the response of the larger society, in many cases cast as the wrongdoer. A positive response is more likely to be forthcoming when the claim can be addressed by symbolic recognition or token payments rather than requiring major allocations of resources that arouse resistance from other groups. So the process can secure symbolic vindication for victim groups that are otherwise flourishing while it gives the majority a welcome sense of absolution (for example, the Sephardic Jews and Spain).[45] But where the symbolic claims are fused with material claims for massive re-allocation of resources, as in the campaign for reparations for American slavery, the outlook seems less hopeful. Could the majority secure absolution and closure at what they consider an affordable price?[46] Prospects are even dimmer in situations where remedy would impose a stigma of criminality on powerful groups (e.g., Latin American generals). So in many societies we find a powerful counterimpulse to let bygones be bygones, close the book, make a fresh start. This counterimpulse often draws on ideological bases similar to those of the movement for reparations (e.g., the claim for a "color-blind" fresh start in race relations in the United States invokes the same "equality principle" that animates the reparations claim).

The controversies about affirmative action programs in India and in the United States suggest the difficulties of using historic wrongs as a basis for distributing reparative entitlements and especially the perplexities of allocating responsibility to pay for these. If there is to be preferential treatment for a distinct set of historically victimized groups, who is to bear the cost? Whose resources and life chances should be diminished in the short run to increase those of the beneficiaries?[47] In some cases, the costs are spread widely among the taxpayers, for example, or among consumers of "diluted" public services. But in other cases major costs are imposed on specific individuals. Differences in public acceptance seem to turn on this distinction: publics in India and in the United States have been broadly supportive of preferential programs where the "cost" of inclusion is diffused broadly. Resentment has been focused on programs where the life chances of specific others are perceived to be diminished in a palpable way. Such remedial exactions may be seen as the conscription of an arbitrarily selected group of citizens to discharge an obligation from which equally culpable debtors are excused.

If our efforts to remedy old wrongs are inevitably selective, incomplete, and flawed—and much the same can be said about righting fresh wrongs—should they be abandoned? In toting up the costs and benefits, we should be careful not to ignore the human value in these sometimes quixotic, often ineffectual, always incomplete efforts to secure justice. As flawed as these efforts are, unreflecting acquiescence in past injustice is worse. A patched and leaky vase may be less desirable than an unbroken vase, but it is better than a pile of shards. When it comes to justice, we don't have the choice of the unbroken vase. A patched and blemished world is the only one we can attain. The effort to do justice may inspire or teach or multiply or just keep us from giving up on the possibility. It is imperative for us, as a commentator on Levinas puts it, "to recognize the absence of justice where justice is postponed or deformed, without succumbing . . . to a belief in its non-existence."[48]

Notes

1. A group of 167 black soldiers were summarily discharged when they failed to identify those responsible for an armed raid on the city of Brownsville, Texas. On the affair, see Lane 1971; Weaver 1970. On the exoneration in 1972, see Jackson 1988.

2. Starting in 1932, the U.S. Public Health Service studied some 400 syphilitic men in Macon County, Alabama, without telling them that they had syphilis, that it was treatable, and that the tests administered to them were not treatment. When a reporter broke the story in 1972, there were Senate Committee hearings that led to "a complete revamping of HEW regulations on human experimentation" (Jones 1981: 214). No official apology or compensation was enacted legislatively. In December 1974, a class action suit was settled for approximately $10 million, giving $37,500 to each of the "living syphilitics" who were still alive and lesser amounts to other classes of victims (Jones 1981: 216–17).

3. Brodeur 1985.

4. A campaign by Jewish organizations to secure a pardon that would repudiate the anti-Semitic lynching culminated in a pardon that did not address the question of Frank's innocence but pardoned him because of "blatant due process violations" and because "the lynching aborted the legal process, thus foreclosing further attempts to prove Frank's innocence. It resulted from the State of Georgia's failure to protect Frank." (Dinnerstein 1987; Frey and Thompson-Frey 1988; Phagan 1987).

5. In October 1989, the Wisconsin Assembly passed a resolution, apologizing for the killing of hundreds of unarmed Indians perpetrated by U.S. soldiers, state militia, and armed settlers (Haas 1989). A ceremony of apology and reconciliation was held at the site in May, 1990 (Ball 1990; Nepper 1990).

6. Federal and state regulation is analyzed in Price 1991.

7. "Ask the Globe," *Boston Globe* (September 16, 1992): 82.

8. Koetke 1985.

9. When the issue of apology and reparations for the wartime internment and confiscation of property of Japanese Canadians was broached in the early 1980s, Prime Minister Pierre Trudeau rejected it because "I don't believe in attempting

to rewrite history in this way." He told Parliament: "I find it more important to be just in our time, for instance by giving jobs with the money to the people who are unemployed now rather than try to use money to compensate people whose ancestors in some way have been deprived." In 1988 Prime Minister Brian Mulroney formally apologized. Prime Minister Trudeau was apprehensive about an infinite regression of competing claims. There was a claim by Italians for their wartime internment; and claims by Ukrainian Canadians for internment during the First World War.

10. In 1990, Representative John Conyers introduced a bill to create a commission to study the effect of slavery on American blacks and to recommend remedies. (At the time, Conyers observed that reparations "may prove too complicated, and we may be too late.") A less cautious view is presented in Robinson 2000. The roots of this recurring claim go back much further. It became visible in the "contemporary" political scene at a Conference on Black Economic Development held at Wayne State University in April 1969, which produced a Black Manifesto dramatically presented at Riverside Church in New York a week later with a demand for the congregation's share of reparations to be paid by the white religious community. See Lecky and Wright 1969; Schuchter 1970.

11. Cf. Shklar 1990: 19.

12. Shklar 1990: 120, 121.

13. Galanter 1974.

14. Cf. Abel 1973.

15. And, we may ask, can we learn something from the problems of addressing those wrongs that might help us to modify everyday practices?

16. Ordinary justice embodies another familiar maxim, "Better late than never," which is a temporal version of "Half a loaf is better than none." It is a counsel of compromise that reminds us that effectuation of a principle comes only at the price of its partial abandonment. Cf. On the paradox of compromise, see Luban 1985.

17. Or does wrongdoers' deservingness of punishment decline with the passage of time? Consider the eighty-year-old war criminal who has been living peacefully as a good citizen for forty years. Should the past come to haunt him now? Or the murderer who escaped and led an exemplary life?

18. Society does not choose in a comprehensive, ordered way. The choices are posed by moral entrepreneurs who provide us with options in a figurative marketplace for justice.

19. United Press International, April 11, 1990.

20. In addition to those who carry the social identity of the original victim, there may be those (like Jewish *conversos* in Spain) who maintained an attenuated identity as descendants of the original victims, although it is less than full identification with the victim group.

21. Thus the Smithsonian awarded a collection of skeletons to a native Hawaiian group and refused to consider the claim of another group that "lacked suffi-

cient documentation to consider a truly competing claim that would be subject to review by the repatriation committee" (Andrews 1991).

22. Ayers 1991. The governor's successor announced plans to close the exhibit of 234 skeletons at a museum but refused to order the reburial of the skeletons and the building of a replica of the burial mound. "[T]he main negotiator for the Indians . . . called the compromise fair. But he said he was not sure if it met all religious requirements. Details of burial requirements vary from tribe to tribe, he said, and exactly how the Dickson Mound skeletons would be entombed has not been worked out" (*New York Times*, 1991a).

23. See Galanter 1984, chap. 10.

24. Bohlen 1991a: A-1.

25. Take, for example, the Baltic states. Similar claims may be made to establish a sovereignty that was never previously exercised, as in the case of Quebec, Palestine, or Pakistan.

26. Schneider 1996; Dale 1996.

27. But cf. Baseball Hall of Fame, International Olympic Committee. In the latter case, IOC responded to congressional resolution. See also the Bell (1987), particularly chap. 5 (pp. 123–39), titled "The Racial Barrier to Reparations," chronicling a fictional private foundation's reparations for blacks.

28. But cf. the role of judiciary as a catalyst and administrator in Native American land claims.

29. Disputes in which one of the parties is also the "judge" (like parent/child, boss/worker, etc.) are actually a very frequent configuration in the world of dispute resolution. Galanter 1986: 163.

30. If we resolve that from time T forward, we will prevent or correct X, then those who suffered from X before time T may complain that they are worse off than those who came later. We tell the pre-T victims they were "born too soon" (and the post-T violators that they were "born too late"). To avoid such invidious distinctions, we may make our new rule retroactive. But then people who innocently relied on the old rule will complain that they are being penalized while their similarly situated predecessors were not.

An example is provided by the practice of New York state legislators to use state employees in their political campaigns. In time, this practice, which was once acceptable, became regarded as unethical. A respected state senator was accused of having engaged in this practice in the past. In a letter to the *New York Times*, a retired legislator pointed out that "Senator Ohrenstein is being charged for actions that took place before the present view of what is right and wrong. The standards have been tightened and all to the good. But Fred Ohrenstein should not be hung in the marketplace as a symbol or even a deterrent" (Stanley H. Lowell, Letter to the Editor, *New York Times*, October 8, 1987, p. 26). Eventually, most of the charges in the 564-count indictment were dismissed by the Court of Appeals, which ruled that the legislature had a right to regulate its own affairs; the remaining counts were dropped in the interests of justice" in 1991 (Sullivan 1991).

31. McCollough 1968: 258. "Not a nickel was ever collected through damage suits from the South Fork Fishing and Hunting Club or from any of its members." But Johnstown illustrates the difficulty of identifying the social descendants of such a victim group. Are the current citizens of Johnstown (or those living in the low-lying parts of the city) the appropriate surrogates? Or the descendants of those who lived there in 1889?

32. Vindication may be substantive or it may be confined to condemnation of earlier procedure. On the basis of a report finding that there was a "real possibility of miscarriage of justice," the governor of Massachusetts issued a carefully worded proclamation on the fiftieth anniversary of the execution of Sacco and Vanzetti, designed to remove "any stigma and disgrace" from their names, declaring, in part, that their "trial and execution . . . should serve to remind all civilized people of the constant need to guard against our susceptibility to prejudice, our intolerance of unorthodox ideas, and our failure to defend the rights of persons who are looked upon as strangers in our midst."

33. *New York Times* 1991a details the conflict over the proposed renaming of the Custer Battlefield National Monument to the Little Bighorn Battlefield National Monument. To proponents, this was the correction of an anomaly; to opponents it was an exercise in politically motivated historical revisionism.

34. These controversies are sensitively traced in Levinson 1998. (An instance at a remove from identity politics is the dispute about the removal of a statue of Senator Joseph McCarthy from the Outagamie County [Wisconsin] Courthouse to the County Historical Museum.)

35. Galanter 1984.

36. The notion of full compensation is itself morally ambiguous. The notion that justice is satisfied by the exaction from the wrongdoer of something equivalent to the loss inflicted by the undeserved injury of the victim (an eye for an eye, measure for measure, paid back, getting even) is flawed by the following paradox. Suppose our remedial process inflicts on Y a loss equal to the undeserved loss that Y inflicted on the innocent X. Y is losing because he deserved to lose, while X lost in spite of the fact that he did not deserve to. In some sense Y is ahead in this exchange, for his well-deserved loss is equated with the undeserved loss of X. By this equation, X is devalued—his loss without fault (victimization) is made morally equivalent to Y's loss with fault. That is, Y gets the same "penalty" for doing something bad that X got without doing anything bad. To assert the equal value of X requires that the punishment/loss of Y be enhanced so that Y's relatively greater loss reflects his greater culpability. Cf. Miller 1990: 301–2. But this is obviated when there is a transfer to the victim that makes him "whole." Thus civil compensation overcomes the paradox of equivalence that plagues the criminal law. However, factors like delay and insurance and compro-

mise because of transaction costs, often decouple the compensation from the judgment about wrongdoing. Law becomes "de-moralized." This is the basic argument for punitive damages (see Galanter and Luban 1993), which reflect a recognition of this paradox of equivalence in cases where there are gross or aggravated moral failings by Y.

37. For example, we begrudge anything to the poor while there have been major efforts to include the disabled. And cf. the recent movement to recognition of animal rights.

38. The enlargement of empathy does not mean more individualized, face-to-face dealings with such others; it has happened at the same time that more of our dealings with others are through media transmission, impersonal markets, and associations that span immense distances.

39. Lipset and Schneider 1987.

40. Friedman 1985.

41. Walter Benjamin, *Illuminations* (New York: Schocken Books, 1968). I am grateful to David Luban for directing me to this phrase.

42. On the inadequate remedies in these and other disasters, see Galanter 1990.

43. Is this is a permanent feature of these identities or a reflection of the way identities are organized at this moment in history—and here in America? To Americans, at least, class and residence seem to be accidental features, not intrinsic to the self. No one supposes that contemporary children deserve to be compensated for the victimization imposed by child labor a century ago. But, being a woman, or gay, or disabled—these are not transitional conditions, but are seen as intrinsic and permanent identities. They inspire campaigns for justice, but they do not mobilize claims for wrongs done to predecessors.

44. Ironically, it implies an extended responsibility to avoid acting toward others as an external force, but rather to recognize the humanity of the other and take responsibility for him. This occurs against the background of a long historical movement away from face-to-face relationships where we have to take the other into account in impersonal specialized relationships, through markets and administrative structures.

45. Interestingly, Spain's willingness to revisit the remote and symbolic question of the Expulsion contrasts with its decision after the restoration of democratic government to destroy the files of Franco's secret police and make a fresh start.

46. Cf. appeal of Charles Krauthammer 1990 that "[i]t is time for a historic compromise: monetary reparations to blacks for centuries of oppression in return for the total abolition of all programs of racial preference. A one-time cash payment in return for a new era of irrevocable color blindness."

47. In the long run, successful affirmative action may be an investment in human capital that provides net benefits for nonbeneficiaries as well as for beneficiaries. But in a society where standing vis-à-vis others is part of what people possess, such programs involve some taking.

48. Sugarman 1978: 220–21.

References

Abel, Richard (1973). "A Comparative Theory of Dispute Institutions in Society." *Law & Society Review* 8:217–347.

Andrews, Robert M. (1991). "Smithsonian Returns Ancestral Remains." *Wisconsin State Journal* (August 10, 1991): 4A.

Ayers, Donald B. (1991). "Activist: Governor Could Be Extradited if Burial Museum Stays Open." *United Press International* (March 15, 1991) (available on Nexis).

Ball, Ian (1990). "Paleface Apology for Bad Axe Massacre." *Daily Telegraph* (May 7, 1990): 1.

Bell, Derrick (1987). *And We Are Not Saved.* New York: Basic Books, Inc.

Benjamin, Walter (1969 [1940]). "Theses on the Philosophy of History." In Hannah Arendt, ed., *Illuminations*, Harry Zohn, trans. New York: Schocken Books.

Bohlen, Celestine (1991a). "Hungarians Debate How Far Back to Go to Right Old Wrongs." *New York Times* (April 15, 1991): A1.

Bohlen, Celestine (1991b). "Victims of Hungary's Past Press for an Accounting, but With Little Success" *New York Times* (August 4, 1991): Sec. 1, p. 3.

Brodeur, Paul (1985). *Outrageous Misconduct: The Asbestos Industry on Trial.* New York: Antheon Books.

Dale, Stephen (1996). "Canada-U.S.: Helms-Burton Look-Alike Attracts Interest." *Inter Press Service* (September 18, 1996) (available on Nexis).

Dinnerstein, Leonard (1987). *The Leo Frank Case.* Athens: University of Georgia Press.

Fitzgerald, Frances (1980 [1979]). *America Revised: History Textbooks in the Twentieth Century.* New York: Vintage Books (Boston: Atlantic-Little Brown).

Frey, Robert Seitz, and Nancy Thompson-Frey (1988). *The Silent and the Damned: The Murder of Mary Phagan and the Lynching of Leo Frank.* Lanham, MD: Madison Books.

Friedman, Lawrence M. (1985). *Total Justice.* New York: Russell Sage Foundation.

Galanter, Marc (1974). "Why the Haves Come Out Ahead: Speculations on the Limits of Legal Change." *Law & Society Review* 9:95–160.

———. (1984). *Competing Equalities: Law and the Backward Classes in India.* Berkeley: University of California Press.

———. (1986). "Adjudication, Litigation and Related Phenomena." In L. Lipson and S. Wheeler, eds., *Law and Social Science.* New York: Russell Sage Foundation.

———. (1990). "Bhopals, Past and Present: Changing Responses to Industrial Disaster." *Windsor Yearbook of Access to Justice* 10:151–70.

Galanter, Marc, and David Luban (1993). "Poetic Justice: Punitive Damages and Legal Pluralism." *American University Law Review* 42 (1983): 1463.

Haas, Joanne (1989). "AIDS, Assault Bills Clear Assembly." United Press International (October 10, 1989, BC cycle).

Jackson, Derrick (1988). "Whites Have Much To Learn About Forgiveness." *Newsday* (May 13, 1998): 98.

Jones, James (1981). *Bad Blood: The Tuskegee Syphilis Experiment.* New York: Free Press.

Koetke, Michelle R. (1985). "Mary Dyer's Difference." *Christian Science Monitor* (June 20, 1985): 35.

Krauthammer, Charles (1990). "Reparations for Black Americans." *Time* (December 31, 1990): 18.

Lane, Ann J. (1971). *The Brownsville Affair: National Crisis and Black Reaction.* Port Washington, NY: Kennikat Press.

Lecky, Robert S. and H. Elliott Wright (1969). *Black Manifesto: Religion, Racism, and Reparations.* New York: Sheed and Ward.

Levinson, Sanford (1998). *Written in Stone: Public Monuments in Changing Societies* (Durham, NC: Duke University Press).

Lipset, Seymour Martin and William Schneider (1987 [1983]). *The Confidence Gap: Business, Labor and Government in the Public Mind.* rev. ed. Baltimore: Johns Hopkins University Press.

Luban, David (1985). "Bargaining and Compromise: Recent Work on Negotiation and Informal Justice." *Philosophy and Public Affairs*, 14, no. 4 (Autumn): 397–416.

McCollough, David G. (1968). *The Johnstown Flood.* New York: Simon & Schuster.

Miller, William Ian (1990). *Bloodtaking and Peacemaking: Feud, Law and Society in Saga Iceland.* Chicago: University of Chicago Press.

Nepper, Mark (1990). "Apology Accepted: State Expressed Sorrow for 1832 Indian Massacre." *Wisconsin State Journal* (May 6, 1990): Sec. 1, p. 1.

New York Times (1991a). "Conflict Emerges Over Custer Park." (October 13, 1991): 37.

———. (1991b). "Governor of Illinois Plans to Close a Display of 234 Indian Skeletons." (November 29, 1991): A9.

Phagan, Mary (1987). *The Murder of Little Mary Phagan.* Far Hills, NJ: New Horizon Press.

Price, H. Marcus, III (1991). *Disputing the Dead: U.S. Law on Aboriginal Remains and Grave Goods.* Columbia: University of Missouri Press.

Robinson, Randall (2000). *The Debt: What America Owes to Blacks.* New York: Dutton.

Schneider, Howard (1996). "Canada Spawns a Helms-Burton Spoof; Lawmakers Seek Restitution for Those Whose Kin Fled U.S. Revolution." *Washington Post* (July 25, 1996): A24.

Schuchter, Arnold (1970). *Reparations: The Black Manifesto and Its Challenge to White America.* Philadelphia: J. B. Lippencott Co.

Sher, George (1980). "Ancient Wrongs and Modern Rights." *Philosophy and Public Affairs* 10:3–17.

Shklar, Judith N. (1990). *The Faces of Injustice*. New Haven, CT: Yale University Press.

Singh, Chhatrapati (1990). "The Concept of Time in Law." *Journal of the Indian Law Institute* 32:328–49.

Smith, Claire (1991). "Belated Tribute to Baseball's Negro Leagues." *New York Times* (August 13, 1991): A1.

Sugarman, Richard (1978). "Commentary on Levinas' 'To Love the Torah More Than God.'" *Judaism* 28:218–23.

Sullivan, Ronald (1991). "New York Judge Dismisses Charges Against Legislator." *New York Times* (September 5, 1991): A20.

United Press International (1990). "Reparation Sought for Member of All-Black Civil War Unit" (April 11, BC cycle).

Weaver, John D. (1970). *The Brownsville Raid*. New York: W.W. Norton & Co.

4

Reluctant Redress: The U.S. Kidnapping and Internment of Japanese Latin Americans[1]

ERIC K. YAMAMOTO[2]

Introduction

In July 1999, President Clinton signed an appropriations bill authorizing several billion dollars in aid for rebuilding Kosovo and keeping the peace. A news article cited the horrors there—the ethnic cleansing and the weeks of nonstop U.S./NATO bombing; it offered details of past and likely future U.S. involvement.

The article ended with change of subject, a curious "by-the-way" tag-along—that the appropriations bill also authorized U.S. reparations money for Japanese Latin Americans. This tag-along reference caught my eye for four reasons. First, I worked on redress for American citizens of Japanese ancestry interned during World War II on account of their race without charges, trial or, as has now been revealed, any evidence of necessity.[3] Second, I had spoken with several of the 2,000 former citizens of Latin American countries who had been kidnapped from their homes in Peru (mainly) and imprisoned in U.S. internment camps during World War II and held as hostages, solely because they were of Japanese ancestry; and I had heard their stories of destroyed lives and continuing bitterness. Third, the Japanese Latin American story is not about the United States going abroad as "peacekeeper" or "human rights protector" or "reconciliation facilitator." It is about the United States as human rights violator, here on American soil—"in here" not "out there." And it is about a fresh U.S. "reparatory process" characterized mostly by denial, foot dragging and unkept promises—hence the title of my essay "Reluctant Redress."

And fourth, the news blurb caught my eye because the larger Japanese

Latin American story—with its cloak-and-dagger intrigue, governmental abuses of power, human suffering, grass-roots organizing, court suits, legislative and bureaucratic machinations—is rich with insights, in small scale, about how our present-day government handles (and mishandles) reparations for historical injustice. More particularly, it reveals the government's apparent realpolitik, short-term approach to group justice— and group healing—with little apparent appreciation for how to break the cycles of bitterness and recrimination so aptly described by Martha Minow in her Gilbane lectures[4] and her recent book *Between Vengeance and Foregiveness*.[5] Indeed, the question here, for the United States as a society, is whether present-day government and public responses to the Japanese Latin Americans have broken, or perpetuated, that cycle.

Japanese Latin Americans: Kidnapping and Internment

Let's explore that question first by examining the U.S. seizure and internment of Japanese Latin Americans (JLAs) during World War II, by listening to one of many previously untold stories.

The day his youngest child was born, Kenzo Watanabe sat perplexed in a Peruvian jail. Mr. Watanabe, a Peruvian citizen of Japanese descent, knew he had done nothing wrong. But he was then forced, as were 2,000 others at varying times, to board a U.S. military ship without his family and endure a twenty-day trip to the United States. At a New Orleans detention center, he was greeted with sprays of DDT in mass shower stalls. From there the United States sent Mr. Watanabe to an internment camp in Texas and held him hostage for trading with Japan— even though he was not a Japanese national. There he stayed, locked behind barbed wire and armed guards. His business gone; home lost; family well-being unknown.

At the end of World War II, Mr. Watanabe was a man without a home or a country. He was tainted. The Peruvian government blocked his return. The United States prevented his family from joining him because bureaucrats said he, and other JLAs, gained "illegal entry" into the United States (he was labeled an "illegal alien," and the irony of this will soon emerge). He struggled to survive. After ten years, Mr. Watanabe obtained permission to visit Peru, to reunite with family and greet the child he'd never seen. His wife, much beleaguered though, died on his return.

Mr. Watanabe's story and those of other JLAs have only recently come to light. How should the United States respond?

Redress

PARTIAL REPARATIONS

Congress passed the Civil Liberties Act of 1988 providing $20,000 for each Japanese American (meaning citizen and legal resident foreigner) survivor of the U.S. World War II internment camps. Congressional fact-finding and court cases in the early 1980s laid the foundation for reparations. They established that the mass imprisonment of 120,000 innocent Japanese Americans resulted from wartime hysteria, political expediency, and U.S. racism—there had been no legitimate military reason. President George Bush sent a letter of U.S. apology to each former internee along with a reparations check.

The Civil Liberties Act, however, excluded Japanese Latin Americans like Kenzo Watanabe. The Act, by its terms, applied only to U.S. citizens and "legally present" noncitizens—so-called "legal resident aliens." The U.S. Office of Redress, which pointed to JLAs' "illegal alien" status, denied JLA reparations.

This exclusion, it turns out, was no accident. It was an intentional byproduct of the political effort to deflect attention away from international wrongdoing by the United States. As one observer noted:

> Original drafts of the Civil Liberties Act provided redress to Japanese Latin Americans. But the bill was rewritten to focus more heavily on violations of [U.S.] citizens' rights under the Constitution, rather than on [international] moral wrongdoing by the U.S. government. In the process, the bill's drafters added the "citizen and permanent resident alien" clause, excluding Japanese Latin Americans.

This legal shift away from a broad focus on "moral wrongdoing" by the United States to a tight focus on "citizens' rights," coupled with the government's refusal to accord citizenship status to all but a few JLAs, deprived JLAs of redress. Equally important, it also affected the moral core of the United States' reparatory effort. Here's why.

MOCHIZUKI CLASS ACTION

In 1996, five JLAs, led by Carmen Mochizuki, filed a class action suit against the government. The suit asserted that the interned JLAs were wrongly designated as "illegal aliens" and improperly denied redress under the Civil Liberties Act—they lacked legal papers for entry into the

United States because the United States kidnapped them and brought them here.

Federal Judge Loren Smith, however, indicated that he planned to dismiss the suit. But before doing so, he suggested "settlement because of the moral issues involved." The government offered (after considerable inside skirmishing), and many of the Mochizuki class members accepted (after heated debate and continuing dissension), a compromise settlement: $5,000 for each JLA interned and the standard-form presidential letter of apology. But the JLAs would receive reparations only if money remained after Japanese Americans citizens were paid (they were told not to worry, money was available). And the United States would not expressly apologize for, or explain, the JLA abductions and subsequent internment.

Here's what else the settlement (and therefore the reparations process) failed to address. The United States was not at war with the Latin American countries. Nor was Japan. The JLAs were completely innocent of wrongdoing. Most were model citizens. They were kidnapped, torn from their families, imprisoned in another country, and held hostage by the United States—because of their race. Upon their eventual release from United States internment prisons, the U.S. branded them "illegal aliens," they were disparaged racially as "Japs," and they were treated socially as unwanted foreigners. For a long time, the United States not only refused to deal with these consequences, it simply denied that it had orchestrated the debacle.

Perhaps most significant, nowhere in the settlement process did the United States expressly accept responsibility for wrongdoing or acknowledge the racialized aspects of the controversy. Nor did it acknowledge what is now seen by many as a clear human rights violation.[6]

Reflections

The JLAs' human story—their suffering and struggles to lift themselves up—is poignantly recounted in Seiichi Higashide's *Adios to Tears*. It describes shattered lives—the difficulties in sustaining relationships, beliefs, and a sense of meaning—and attempts to work and reconnect families.

So how should we view the JLA settlement and U.S. reparations? Certainly, we should start by noting important distinctions. These were not death camps. There was no ethnic cleansing, as in Kosovo. And the raw numbers were comparatively small. Yet, there is no denying the human suffering resulting directly from the government's kidnapping, transportation, and incarceration on account of race and place. And although officials from Latin American countries collaborated, the United States was front and center as the orchestrator. So let's look deeper.

How did the JLAs and government spokespersons react to the U.S. reparations package? Were the presidential apology and $5,000 reparations simply a legal settlement—the resolution of a dispute? Or did they reflect "justice done"—genuine, if partial, efforts to heal wounds of Japanese Latin Americans, real if belated strides toward restructuring U.S. institutions and national security practices?

Listen to some JLA reactions. For them, this was the "ending of a chapter," the "healing of the wounds." Hear also President Clinton: "Th[e *Mochizuki*] settlement addresses the injustice endured by Japanese Latin Americans who were interned (in the United States)." And Acting Assistant Attorney General for Civil Rights Bill Lann Lee: "The government did the right thing in settling the case," and "[a]cknowledging the wrong and bringing closure to the uncertainties of litigation . . . bring[s] to an end an inglorious chapter in our nation's history."[7]

But listen more deeply, to Carmen Mochizuki, the named plaintiff in the class action suit. She was eight years old when she was abducted from her native Peru and brought to Texas: "I am disappointed we did not receive the same amount of redress [$20,000] that was given to the Japanese Americans." Says Isamu Shibayama: "I'm bitter. . . . Why should we be [again] discriminated against. . . . [W]e all went through the same thing." Shibayama "opted out" of the *Mochizuki* settlement because he "felt it offered too little and did not come with a sincere apology." He has since filed a separate lawsuit seeking full redress.

For similar reasons, a daughter of a JLA internee shook her head at the settlement. "[My deceased father] would be shocked and heart-broken" to hear that the government denied full compensation to JLAs. "Despite everything, he had such faith in America's ability to repair the damage it had done."[8]

Several months after the settlement, the wound was salted. The Office of Redress informed the Mochizuki plaintiffs that it had run out of funds to make even limited reparations payments to the JLAs (with a few exceptions). The reparations bottom line: a nonspecific presidential letter of apology; no reparations payments for many.[9] Says attorney Robin Toma, "Many people feel that [the settlement process] is a bitter pill to swallow. . . . What it has meant to many internees is another symbol of inferior treatment. Of being discriminated against yet again."[10]

So was the legal settlement in the face of grass-roots publicity and high-level lobbying simply *realpolitik*—politically expedient even as it was too little, too late, too insincere to feel like justice, to heal the wounds? Or maybe, it was the best that could be done politically and legally.

But, if so, and if the Civil Liberties Act itself shifted focus away from moral wrongdoing by the United States, what does this U.S. reparatory effort mean in terms of the country's moral authority on recent human rights controversies in Beijing, Tibet, Kosovo, East Timor, Sierra Leone, and Chechnya? And what are the implications for how we think about the goals, processes, and effects of ongoing reparations movements in the United States, targeting the United States. For instance, what about reparations for African Americans for the continuing harms of slavery, Jim Crow violence and segregation, and present-day systemic discrimination? And for Native Hawaiians still struggling to rebuild culture, self-governance, and selfhood largely destroyed by the now-conceded wrongful U.S.-aided overthrow of the sovereign Hawaiian nation a hundred years ago? For Native Americans? Puerto Ricans?[11]

As mentioned at the outset, the 1999 congressional appropriations bill for rebuilding Kosovo included a rider for paying reparations to the JLAs. Was this happenstance—both appropriations in the same bill? Or was there a deeper connection between further funding of the United States and NATO human rights intervention in Kosovo and justice for JLAs in the United States? Whatever the connection, it constitutes for many JLAs "bittersweet victory," "incomplete justice," "empty gestures," and "compromise injustice."[12] Yet for others, and government officials, the limited settlement reflects a sense of "healing the wounds," "closing a chapter," "bringing an end to the uncertainties of litigation," "doing the right thing."

Amid these disparate responses, the question remains: Have we, here in the United States, done justice? In terms of the "practice of justice," have our words and acts engendered: (1) *recognition*—acknowledgment of the harms (psychological and material) and critical social and legal analyses of the institutional structures fostering the disabling government actions; (2) *responsibility*—individual and institutional actors' acceptance of responsibility for the harms and for redressing the damage to people, groups, and community fabric; (3) *reconstruction*—concrete acts to reconstruct selfhood of those harmed, to rebuild communal life and to reform institutional structures; and (4) *reparation*—"repairing"[13] the tears in the social fabric that hurt all members of society and thereby mending broken relationships.[14]

Assessed in this light of inquiry into "justice practice," and looking at reluctant redress for Japanese Latin Americans, we can ask the United States as our country and only then others: Are we breaking our cycles of pain, denial, and violence?

Notes

1. Copyright © Eric K. Yamamoto 1999.

2. My appreciation to Michelle Kim for her invaluable work on this project.

3. Eric K. Yamamoto, "Friend, Foe, or Something Else: The Social Meaning of Redress," *Denver Journal of Law & Social Policy* 23 (1992): 223.

4. For example, Martha Minow, "Memory and Hate: Are There Lessons for the World?" (see chapter 1).

5. Martha Minow, *Between Vengeance and Forgiveness* (Boston: Beacon Press, 1999).

6. Natsu T. Saito, "Justice Held Hostage: U.S. Disregard for International Law in the World War II Internment of Japanese Peruvians—A Case Study," *Boston College Third World Law Journal* 19 (1998): 275.

7. Jim Lobe, "Rights: U.S. Settles With WWII Japanese Latin Americans," *Inter Press Service* (June 16, 1998); Caroline Aoyagi, "Bittersweet Victory for Japanese Latin Americans," *Pacific Citizen* (June 19–July 2, 1998): 1.

8. Dara Akiko Tom, "Japanese-Descended Latins Also Interned," *Seattle Times* (August 10, 1998): A7; Glenn Chapman, "Japanese Latin Americans Sue Over World War Kidnapping, Internment," *Agence France-Presse* (February 19, 1999); Naomi Sodetani, "Japanese Latin American Internees Get Apology," *Hawaii Herald* (June 19, 1998): A9.

9. Joe Suzuki, a former JLA internee, and current attorney for the National Coalition for Redress and Reparations, filed a class action suit four months after the *Mochizuki* settlement. Suzuki charged the United States with failing to invest the reparations money appropriated by Congress, as required by statute, and asserted that investment would have generated enough money to compensate all JLAs. Takeshi Nakayama, "U.S. Sued for Causing Redress Fund Shortfall," *Rafu Shimpo* (October 15, 1998): 12. In October 1999, the federal court in San Francisco dismissed the suit. "Judge Says He Can't Fix Reparations Mistake," *Honolulu Advertiser* (November 13, 1999): A7.

10. Caroline Aoyagi, "Bittersweet Victory for Japanese Latin Americans," *Pacific Citizen* (June 19–July 2, 1998): 3.

11. Eric K. Yamamoto, "Racial Reparations: Japanese American Redress and African American Claims," *Boston College Law Review 40* (1998): 477.

12. The government's failure to recognize the harms inflicted and its resistance to full reparations spawned a dispute between some Japanese Latin Americans and some Japanese Americans. Shortly after the *Mochizuki* settlement, the Japa-

nese American Citizens League (JACL) supported the settlement in a press release: "The JACL recognizes that there are JLAs who feel the terms of the *Mochizuki* settlement are inadequate . . . While the JACL believes that such sentiments are well founded and legitimate, the JACL is committed to full implementation of the *Mochizuki* settlement." See Takeshi Nakayama, "U.S. Sued for Causing Redress Fund Shortfall," *Rafu Shimpo* (October 15, 1998): 12. Response to the JACL position was swift and acidic. "Why do we Japanese from Latin America get one-quarter what our American brothers got?" said Tomas Hayashi, a former JLA internee. See "Japanese in Peru Only Partly Appeased by Reparations Offer," *Rafu Shimpo* (June 17, 1998): 1.

13. Elizabeth Spelman, *Repair* (Boston: Beacon Press, 2002) (peeling the layered meanings of "repair" and offering powerful understandings of the potential for repairing broken social relationships).

14. See Eric K. Yamamoto, *Interracial Justice: Conflict and Reconciliation in Post-Civil Rights America* (New York: New York University Press, 1999), pp. 174–93 (setting forth a framework for inquiry into "justice practice" characterized by the four "Rs": Recognition, Responsibility, Reconstruction, and Reparation).

Memory, Hate, and the Criminalization of Bias-Motivated Violence: Lessons from Great Britain

FREDERICK M. LAWRENCE*

Martha Minow reminds us that bias crimes exist within a context and within a culture.[1] Similarly, a polity's bias crime law reveals context and provides insights into the society's self-understanding. The past several years have witnessed developments in the treatment of bias-motivated violence under British law that are extraordinary both in their depth and their sheer velocity. This paper sketches the background of British bias crime law, along with the case for understanding recent developments as an instance of dramatic legal change. I also offer some tentative observations as to the reasons for these changes, and the implications of these observations for using bias crime law as a window into a society's self-perception as a multicultural society.

Before doing so, this paper first outlines a framework for understanding bias crimes, using the American context as a point of departure, and addresses several of the challenges that Professor Minow has set for those who argue in support of bias crime legislation. I will not take up the challenges raised concerning the regulation of hate speech with which I generally agree. As I have argued elsewhere, I believe that bias crimes can and indeed must be distinguished from hate speech. The latter, however despicable, is entitled to constitutional protection; the former, however "expressive," is deserving of enhanced punishment.[2] I will, however, take up two interrelated challenges that Professor Minow presents. They are the overarching foundational challenges that any bias

*© 2001 by Frederick M. Lawrence. This paper, based on a talk given at the Gilbane Symposium at Brown University, November 19, 1999, is part of larger project concerning bias-motivated violence in Great Britain. That project has been supported in part by a grant from the Ford Foundation. My thanks to Rosanne Felicello and Kenneth Westhassel for their assistance in the preparation of this paper.

crime regime, and perhaps all aspects of criminal law enforcement, must face. First, criminal punishment must elevate society even as it punishes wrongdoers. "The challenge," as Professor Minow says, "is to devise collective social responses that acknowledge wrongs without generating vengeance, social responses that fight back against hatred without becoming hate filled and hateful."[3] Second, criminal punishment has an essential educative and expressive function. Perhaps put more accurately, criminal punishment plays a role in the development and expression of societal values, a wide-ranging process that involves public and private realms, and moves well beyond legal systems to embrace education, civic and social organizations, and private social relations. As Professor Minow puts it with characteristic elegance, humor, and succintness: "What would it take for anti-hate to be cool?"[4] The experiences of the United Kingdom may have much to teach us in this regard.

The Nature of Bias Crimes[5]

Bias crimes are the criminal manifestation of prejudice. They may be distinguished from parallel crimes—crimes that are similar in all manner but for the absence of bias motivation—in terms of the mental state of the actor as well as the nature of the harm caused. A parallel crime may be motivated by any one of a number of factors, whereas bias crimes are motivated by a specific, personal, and group-based reason: the victim's real or perceived membership in a particular group. Different bias crime laws cover different Groups.[6] In the United States, every bias crime law covers race and ethnicity in some form. Many also include religion, some sexual orientation, gender, or other characteristics.

Bias crimes attack victims not only physically but at the very core of their identity, causing a heightened sense of vulnerability beyond that normally found in crime victims. Perhaps most dramatically, victims of bias crimes directed against racial minorities experience the attack as a form of violence that manifests racial stigmatization and its resulting harms.[7] The stigmatized individual may experience clinical symptoms[8] and social symptoms.[9] The bias-motivated violence carries with it the clear message that the target and his group are of marginal value.[10] Stigmatization of bias crime victims is not limited to racially motivated bias crimes nor to minority group victims. Group-motivated crimes generally cause heightened psychological harm to victims over and above that caused by parallel crimes.[11]

The impact of bias crimes reaches beyond the harm done to the immediate victim or victims of the criminal behavior. There is a more wide-spread impact on the "target community" that shares the Group characteristic of the victim. Members of the target community do more than sympathize or even empathize with the individual bias crime victim.[12] Members of the target community of a bias crime perceive that crime as if it were an attack on themselves directly. A cross-burning or a swastika-scrawling will not just call up similar feelings on the part of other Blacks and Jews respectively. Rather, members of these target communities may experience reactions of actual threat and attack from this very event.[13]

Finally, the impact of bias crimes may spread well beyond the immediate victims and the target community to the general society. Such crimes violate not only society's general concern for the security of its members and their property, but also the shared value of equality among its citizens and racial, religious, or other Group harmony in a multicultural society.[14]

This societal harm is, of course, highly contextual. We could imagine a society in which racial motivation for a crime would implicate no greater social value than those violated by a criminal act motivated solely by the perpetrator's dislike of the victim's eye color. This notion of contextuality, in turn, helps us understand which categories should and should not be included in a bias crime law. The characteristics that ought to be included in a bias crime law are those characteristics that implicate societal fissure lines, divisions that run deep in the social history of a culture. In the United States the strongest case is for race. Racial discrimination, the greatest American dilemma, has its roots in slavery, the greatest American tragedy.[15] Strong cases can also be made for the other classic bias crime categories—color, ethnicity, religion, and national origin. The very act of determining which Groups will be included in a bias crime law is a legislative and thus social determination of social fissure lines.

Bias Crimes in the United Kingdom

Bias-motivated violence is a problem of longstanding in the United Kingdom. Only relatively recently, however, has British law formally recognized this problem.

Violence directed against the "other" in Britain may be traced back to the early stages of the millennium. After the coronation of Richard I in 1189, Jews were massacred in London and in York. Indeed, in 1290, Jews were expelled from England altogether.[16] People of color—from Africa, Asia, and the Middle East—have lived in Britain, primarily in England, since at least the sixteenth century. Their experience too was one of separation from the main community, violence, and, in 1596, efforts of mass deportation.[17]

It was only in the twentieth century that a large number of members of ethnic minorities began to live in Great Britain. During World War I, the decades that followed, and particularly in the years immediately following World War II, people from colonies or former colonies came to Britain. In the earlier years of the century, Britons saw both periods of racial violence—such as the race riots in Liverpool, Cardiff, and Glasgow in 1919—and periods of almost complete separation due to what was knows as the "colour bar."

Total separation became harder to maintain as the numbers of members of racial, ethnic, or religious groups coming to Britain increased following World War II, especially those coming from Southwest Asia. Racial violence was a persistent problem, characterized by a series of racist riots in London and other urban areas where minority populations had begun to settle. The most notorious of these riots occurred in 1958, in Nottingham, and in the west London neighborhoods of Notting Hill and other parts of north Kensington. In the years that followed, racist violence continued throughout Britain, but racial violence itself did not occupy a position of any prominence on the political or legal landscape.[18]

The British legal system did not begin to address the problem of racial violence until the mid-1960s and, even then, there was no recognition of bias crimes as a particular social phenomenon. Rather, the focus of legislative efforts was on *incitement* of racial violence. The violence itself, it was presumed, could be addressed by existing general criminal legislation.

The first substantive criminal civil rights sanctions under British law were found in the prohibition of incitement to racial hatred in the Race Relations Act 1965.[19] This provision made it a crime to publish or distribute written matter or to use words in a public place or at a public meeting that are "threatening, abusive or insulting" if done "with intent to stir up hatred against any section of the public in Great Britain distinguished by colour, race, ethnic or national origins."[20]

The racial incitement law was revised to its current state as part of the Public Order Act 1986.[21] "Racial hatred" is defined as "hatred against a group of persons in Great Britain defined by reference to colour, race, nationality (including citizenship) or ethnic or national origins."[22] The Public Order Act 1986 proscribes the use of words—oral or written—or behavior that is "threatening, abusive, or insulting" and is either intended "to stir up racial hatred, or having regard to all the circumstances racial

hatred is likely to be stirred up thereby."[23] The Act also criminalizes possession of racially inflammatory material with intent to display, publish,
distribute, or broadcast if the actor either intends to stir up racial hatred,
or under the circumstances, is likely to do so.[24]

Two issues bear special mention with respect to the crime of racial
incitement. First, even with the relative easing of the Crown's burden
under the Public Order Act 1986, there has been a reluctance on the part
of prosecuting authorities in Britain to bring cases for incitement of racial
hatred. Attorneys General[25] have avoided bringing cases with a strong
probability of losing for fear that unsuccessful cases of racial incitement
may damage race relations rather than help.[26] Law enforcement officials
have also expressed a more concrete source of frustration in enforcing
this law: distributors of hateful pamphlets and fliers, even in a pre–
e-mail world, are virtually impossible to identify.[27]

Second, the provisions of the 1986 law, as was true of its 1976 and
1965 predecessors, do not target bias crimes per se, but rather incitement
of racial violence. Perhaps the closest thing to a bias crime law that
existed in Great Britain prior to 1998 was to be found in the Football
(Offences) Act 1991.[28] This statute proscribes such behavior as throwing
objects toward the players or spectators and going onto the playing field.
In addition, the law criminalizes the "chanting of an indecent or racialist
nature."[29] "Racialist" chanting is defined as "threatening, abusive or insulting to a person by reason of his colour, race, nationality (including
citizenship) or ethnic or national origins."[30]

The Joint Committee Against Racialism's 1981 report on racial violence
to the Home Secretary may, in fact, have marked the starting point of
British bias crime law.[31] Thereafter, the Home Secretary ordered the first
official study of racially motivated violence, which was followed by various efforts to measure and to address the problem, leading, by the
mid-1990s, to a much-heightened awareness of the issue.[32] Continued
study by the Home Office demonstrated disturbing evidence of the per-
sistence of the problem, but also encouraging evidence of increased understanding of its causes and dimensions.[33]

Nonetheless, other than the incitement laws, there was no specific
legislation banning racially motivated violence. This omission was not
due to oversight. As late as 1994, a private members' bill was introduced
in Parliament. The Racial Hatred and Violence Bill would have expanded
the reach of the Public Order Act 1986 to include racial violence itself.[34]
The bill failed for lack of government support. The Government at the
time preferred to treat bias crimes generally, using existing laws that

dealt with provisions of the Public Order Act 1986 that proscribed verbal assaults.[35]

The Labour Government that came to power in 1997 raised the issue of racial violence in its program and manifesto. This culminated in the Crime and Disorder Act 1998 provisions concerning racially motivated crimes, the United Kingdom's first bias crime law.[36]

The 1998 Act created a "penalty enhancement statute"[37] that increases the severity of a penal sanction for crimes that are "racially aggravated." Under the law, a crime is racially aggravated when:

> . . . the offender demonstrates towards the victim of the offence hostility based on the victim's membership (or presumed membership) of a racial group; or the offense is motivated (wholly or partly) by hostility towards members of a racial group based on their membership of that group.[38]

"Racial group" is defined identically with the racial incitement laws, namely "race, color, nationality (including citizenship) or ethnic or national origins."[39] Certain enumerated crimes, when racially aggravated, receive enhanced terms of punishment under the law.[40] For all other crimes, racial aggravation must be taken into account by the sentencing judge as a factor that increases the seriousness of the offense.[41]

The Broader Framework from Which to View Bias Crimes— Lessons from Great Britain

Early scholarly reaction to the racial violence provisions of the Crime and Disorder Act 1998 has been mixed to critical.[42] It is still too early to gauge the enforcement of this provision, nor is this the purpose of this paper.[43] We may, however, begin to offer preliminary observations about what this change in the law signals about British society. This will also provide a context in which to return to Professor Minow's challenges to the defenders of bias crime laws.

The change in the law has occurred at an extraordinary time in the development of bias law in the United Kingdom. On February 22, 1999, the "Macpherson Report," the findings and recommendations of the commission looking into the police investigation of the murder of Stephen Lawrence, was issued. Lawrence, a Black teenager, was murdered in 1993, purportedly by five white youths. No one was ever convicted of the crime. The Macpherson Report highlighted "institutionalized racism" in the British law enforcement system.[44] Moreover, Britain is at a "turning point" in its self-understanding as a multicultural society.[45] Issues of race and ethnicity have become part of the public dialogue in the United Kingdom as never before.[46]

Not surprisingly, this heightened profile of the multi-ethnic nature of the British polity has been reflected in the criminal law. As theorists such as Emile Durkheim and, more recently, Joel Feinberg, have articulated, punishment represents societal condemnation of certain behavior.[47] Social cohesion thus emerges from the act of punishment. Through its choices concerning punishment, a society reveals, in part, the content of its values.

Criminal punishment, unique among official sanctions imposed by an authority, carries with it social disapproval, resentment, and indignation. As summarized by the Royal Commission on Capital Punishment, "[T]he ultimate justification for any punishment is, not that it is a deterrent, but that it is the emphatic denunciation by the community of a crime."[48]

What happens when a legislature enacts a bias crime law and it is signed into law? This act of law-making constitutes a societal condemnation of racism, religious intolerance, and other forms of Group bigotry that are covered by that law and, of perhaps greater significance here, a formal awareness of the role of these Groups in society. What happens if bias crimes are not expressly punished in a criminal justice system, or, if expressly punished, not punished more harshly than parallel crimes? Here, too, there is a message expressed by the legislation. The message is that Group harmony and equality are not among the highest values held by the community. Perhaps more accurately, the message suggests a lack of formal awareness of the status and role of ethnic, racial, or other Groups in the society. Simply put, it is impossible for the punishment choices made by the society *not* to express societal values.

The racial violence provisions of the Crime and Disorder Act 1998 are a powerful reflection of the evolving attitudes in Britain of the multi-ethnic dimensions of the society. In a monochromatic society—in reality or as perceived by its legal system—we would expect a bias-motivated assault to be punished identically to a parallel assault; the Group bias motivation of the crime is rendered largely irrelevant in such a society and thus not part of that which is condemned. In a multi-ethnic society, however, we would expect bias-motivated crimes to receive some special treatment by the criminal law, to reflect the harm caused by the motivation underlying the crime.

Defenders of bias crime laws, in the United Kingdom or the United

States, must grapple with the kinds of arguments presented by Professor Minow in her lectures. In the balance of this paper, I shall take up two— what I will call the "disparate enforcement" problem and the "big picture" problem.

The disparate enforcement problem is based on the concern that those charged with enforcing bias crimes laws might not share the intention of the legislature and either underenforce the laws or, worse, selectively enforce the law precisely against those whom the laws were most meant to help.[49] Some have suggested that this is the explanation for the U.S. Supreme Court's overturning the conviction of a white youth for burning a cross on the lawn of a black family in *R.A.V. v. City of St. Paul,*[50] and one year later upholding the conviction of a black youth for instigating the bias-motivated beating of a white youth in *Wisconsin v. Mitchell.*[51] (Less cynical and arguably more sophisticated explanations have been offered for these two holdings.)[52]

Disparate enforcement, however, is an argument that proves too much. Not surprisingly, a society infected with racism or other forms of bigotry will produce a criminal justice system that has discriminatory aspects. This observation has been advanced as an argument against capital punishment, although the U.S. Supreme Court has declined to strike down the practice on this basis.[53] Even accepting the power of the disparate enforcement argument as a critique of a racially disparate implementation of the death penalty, we may still ask whether this should be an argument against implementation of a criminal justice system altogether.[54] How ironic to begin the assertion of the disparate enforcement argument with an area of the criminal law expressly designed to address violent manifestations of Group-based violence. Surely there have been instances, in the United Kingdom and the United States, of bias crime cases being brought against members of ethnic minorities. But two important points should be made. First, many if not most (even if not all) of these cases, are perfectly legitimate bias crime cases. Consider the *Mitchell* case itself. On October 7, 1989, Todd Mitchell, a nineteen-year-old Black man, directed and encouraged a number of young Black men and boys to attack a fourteen-year-old White boy, Gregory Riddick. Mitchell selected Riddick solely on the basis of his race. He and his cohort had been watching the movie *Mississippi Burning,* and were particularly affected by the scene in which a Black boy who is praying is beaten by a White man. Mitchell selected Riddick and instigated the severe beating with such language as "Do you all feel hyped-up to move on some White people?"[55] Far from being a good example of the concerns raised by the disparate enforcement problem, *Mitchell* is a good example of a legitimate bias crime prosecution.

Second, bias crime laws have been used effectively in cases of racist, homophobic, or other bias-motivated crimes directed against minority Group members. Further study is needed to determine the true dimensions of the disparate enforcement problem with respect to bias crimes.[56] But until and unless there are compelling data in this regard, there is no reason that in this, of all areas of the criminal law, the disparate enforcement problem should cause us to withdraw the criminal sanction that has been attached to bias-motivated crimes.

Professor Minow is right to caution us concerning the "big picture" problem, the risk of focusing too narrowly on bias *crimes* and thereby failing to observe the true breadth and depth of bigotry in our society in all its many and varied manifestations. Group bigotry is a serious and multitiered social illness, and it would be facile in the extreme to expect bias crime laws to cure this condition completely or even to address all of its aspects. Professor Minow warns that bias crime laws will keep us from seeing the full dimensions of racism and other forms of bigotry[57] and may distract us from noncriminal cures, such as civil antidiscrimination laws and education programs.[58] I share her description of the social pathology, but not her prescribed course of treatment. As I have written elsewhere:

> The punishment of hate will not end racial hatred in society. That great goal requires the work not only of the criminal justice system but of all aspects of civil life, public and private. Criminal punishment is indeed a crude tool and a blunt instrument. . . . But our inability to solve the entire problem should not dissuade us from dealing with parts of the problem. If we are to be "staunch defender[s] of the right to be the same or different," we cannot desist from this task.[59]

Bias crime laws need not cause us to oversimplify the nature of bigotry nor to rely on criminal sanctions exclusively. The educative or expressive aspects of the criminal law may in fact help focus us on just how serious and complex a social problem bigotry is, and just how far-ranging true solutions must be. No one would suggest that criminal laws concerning domestic violence or acquaintance rape are sufficient to address all aspects of sexism and gender inequality in society. But no one should deny the significant role—however limited—that the criminal law can play in this regard. Put differently, the absence of criminal sanctions for such crimes would send a devastating message with regard to the overall social response to the problem.

So, as Professor Minow asks, can we find a way to make "anti-hate cool"? Have the British? It is far less socially acceptable today than it once was to express anti-Black or anti-Asian or anti-immigrant views in the United Kingdom.[60] The racial violence provisions of the Crime and Disorder Act 1998 have played some role—both as cause and effect—in the growing expression of ethnic and other Group tolerance and condemnation of bigotry. Efforts to make expressions of hatred not only "socially unacceptable" but also "un-cool" are perhaps best exemplified by such programs as the Anti-Defamation League's "Team Harmony" program in Boston in which thousands of youths from diverse backgrounds are led by, among others, entertainment stars and famous professional athletes, in a celebration of tolerance and diversity. The participation of police and prosecutors in such programs may suggest that law enforcement has an important role, whatever its dimension, in helping to make anti-hate cool.

.   .   .   .   .

The treatment of bias crimes under United Kingdom law offers a significant window into the self-perception of British society. The role of Groups in the United Kingdom today is at a critical stage of evolution. The Parekh Report speaks of Britain at the "crossroads," faced with the "recognition that England, Scotland, and Wales are multi-ethnic, multifaith, multicultural, multicommunity societies."[61] In such a nation, violence motivated by Group bias will continue to receive special attention from both the law enforcement community, and the various communities that together comprise the society.

Notes

1. See Martha Minow, "Regulating Hatred: Whose Speech, Whose Crimes, Whose Powers?" (chap. 1 this volume).

2. See Frederick M. Lawrence, *Punishing Hate: Bias Crimes Under American Law* (Cambridge, MA: Harvard University Press, 1999), esp. pp. 80–109 (hereafter "Lawrence, *Punishing Hate*"); Frederick M. Lawrence, "Resolving the Hate Crimes/Hate Speech Paradox: Punishing Bias Crimes and Protecting Racist Speech," 68 *Notre Dame Law Review* 673 (1993).

3. Minow, "Regulating Hatred" (chap. 1 this volume).

4. Id.

5. For a more detailed discussion of the nature of bias crimes, their cause, and their resulting harm, see Lawrence, *Punishing Hate*, at 29–44.

6. I have discussed elsewhere the legal and social implications of a legislative determination of the scope of bias crimes. See id. at 11–20. This paper uses "Group" as the generic term for the categories encompassed by any particular bias crime statute.

7. See, e.g., Gordon W. Allport, *The Nature of Prejudice* (Cambridge, MA: Addison-Wesley Pub. Co., 1954), pp. 148–49; Erving Goffman, *Stigma: Notes on the Management of Spoiled Identity* (Englewood Cliffs, NJ: Prentice-Hall, 1963), pp. 7–17, 130–35; Robert M. Page, *Stigma* (London and Boston: Routledge & Kegan Paul, 1984); Harold W. Stevenson and Edward C. Stewart, "A Developmental Study of Racial Awareness in Young Children," 9 *Child Development*, 399 (1958).

8. See, e.g., E. Harburg, J. C. Erfurt, L. S. Hauenstein, D. Chape, W. J. Schull, and M. A. Schork, "Socio-Ecological Stress, Suppressed Hostility, Skin Color, and Black-White Male Blood Pressure: Detroit," 35 *Psychosomatic Medicine*, 276, 292–94 (1973); Kenneth Clark, *Dark Ghetto: Dilemmas of Social Power* (New York: Harper & Row, 1965), pp. 82–90.

9. See, e.g., Irwin Katz, *Stigma: A Social Psychological Analysis* (Hillsdale, NJ: Lawrence Erlbaum Associates, Inc., 1981); Harry H. L. Kitano, *Race Relations* (Englewood Cliffs, NJ: Prentice-Hall, 1974), pp. 125–26; A. Kiev, "Psychiatric Disorders in Minority Groups," in P. Watson, ed., *Psychology and Race* (Chicago: Aldine, 1973), esp. pp. 416, 420–24.

10. Allport, *Nature of Prejudice*, at 56–59 (discussing the degrees of prejudicial action from "antilocution," to discrimination, to violence).

11. Lawrence, *Punishing Hate*, at 39–41.

12. See, e.g., Martha Minow, *Making All the Difference: Inclusion, Exclusion, and American Law* (Ithaca: Cornell University Press, 1990), p. 221 (stating the importance of empathy in combating discrimination in the United States).

13. See, e.g., Robert Elias, *The Politics of Victimization: Victims, Victimology, and Human Rights* (New York: Oxford University Press, 1986), p. 116; Andrew Karmen, *Crime Victims: An Introduction to Victimology* 2d ed. (Pacific Grove, CA: Brooks/Cole, 1990), pp. 262–63; Jack Levin and Jack McDevitt, *Hate Crimes: The Rising Tide of Bigotry and Bloodshed* (New York: Plenum Press, 1993), pp. 205, 220–21, 234.

14. See Lawrence, *Punishing Hate*, at 43–44.

15. See, e.g., Andrew Hacker, *Two Nations, Black and White, Separate, Hostile, Unequal* (New York: Scribner's; Toronto: Maxwell Macmillan Canada; New York: Maxwell Macmillan International, 1992), pp. 4–6; Jennifer L. Hochschild, *Facing Up to the American Dream: Race, Class and the Soul of the Nation* (Princeton, NJ: Princeton University Press, 1995).

16. Colin Nicolson, *Strangers to England: Immigration to England 1100–1945* (London: Wayland, 1974).

17. Peter Fryer, *Black People in the British Empire* (London: Pluto, 1988); Peter Fryer, *Staying Power: The History of Black People in Britain* (London: Pluto, 1984).

18. See Benjamin Bowling, *Violent Racism: Victimisation, Policing and Social Context* (London: Oxford University Press, 1998).

19. Race Relations Act 1965 (1965 ch. 73) §6.

20. Id. §6(1).

21. Public Order Act 1986, 1986 ch. 64 §§17–29. The law of racial incitement had previously been revised as part of the Race Relations Act 1976. 1976 ch. 74 §70. The most significant change from the prior law concerned mens rea. Whereas the 1965 Act required that the offending act be done "with intent to stir up hatred," 1965 ch. 73 §6(1), the 1976 Act required only that "having regard to all the circumstances, hatred is likely to be stirred up against any racial group in Great Britain by the matter or words in question." 1976 ch. 74 §70(2).

22. Id. §17. This language tracks the language used in the Race Relations Act 1976, 1976 ch. 74 §§70(2), 70(6).

23. 1986 ch. 64, §18 (use of words or behavior, or display or written material), §19 (publishing or distributing written material), §20 (public performance or play), §21 (distributing, showing, or playing a recording), §22 (broadcasting).

24. 1986 ch. 64 §23.

25. The approval of the Attorney General is required for charges to be brought under the racial incitement laws. 1986 ch. 64 §27(1). This requirement carries through a provision from the prior racial incitement laws. Race Relations Act 1976, 1976 ch. 74 §70(5); Race Relations Act 1965, 1965 ch. 73 §6(3).

26. See Joshua Rozenberg, *The Case for the Crown* (Wellingborough: Equation, 1987), pp. 138–39.

27. The observation in the text is based on the author's interviews with members of the Crown Prosecution Service charged with enforcing racial violence laws and members of the Metropolitan Police Service ("Scotland Yard") Racial and Violent Crime Task Force.

28. Football (Offences) Act 1991, 1991 ch. 19.

29. Id. §3(1).

30. Id. §3(2).

31. Joint Committee Against Racialism, *Racial Violence in Britain* (1981).

32. See, e.g., *Racial Attacks and Harassment*, House of Commons, Home Affairs Committee 3rd Report, Session 1993–94. See Benjamin Bowling, "Racial Harassment and the Process of Victimisation," *British Journal of Criminology* 33, no. 2 (1993) at 234. See also Bowling, *Violent Racism.*

33. See Rae Sibbet, *The Perpetrators of Racial Harassment and Racial Violence*, Home Office Research Study # 176 (London: Home Office, 1997).

34. See untitled note, *Criminal Law Review*, at 313–14.

35. See Public Order Act 1986, 1986 ch. 64 §4(1).

36. Crime and Disorder Act 1998, 1998 ch. 37 §§28–32, 82 (England and Wales); §§33, 96 (Scotland).

37. For some purposes, it is useful to distinguish between "pure bias crimes" and "penalty enhancement" laws. Penalty enhancement laws explicitly rely upon some other criminal provision, such as assault, and increase the sentence if the crime is committed with bias motivation. Penalty enhancement crimes may mandate an enhancement of the sentence or may provide discretion to the sentencing judge to increase the penalty if she deems it appropriate to do so. Pure bias crime laws, by contrast, create a freestanding prohibition of some bias-motivated conduct. See Lawrence, *Punishing Hate*, at 92–94.

38. 1998 ch. 37 §28(1). See §33(2) (the provision for Scotland uses similar but not identical language to the same effect).

39. Id. §§28(4), 33(6).

40. Id. §§29–32.

41. Id. §§82, 96.

42. See, e.g., Maleiha Malik, "'Racist Crime': Racially Aggravated Offences in the Crime and Disorder Act 1998 Part II," 62 *Modern Law Review* 409 (1999) (provisions of 1998 law represent important but not sufficient response to racial violence); Fernne Brennan, "Racially Motivated Crime: The Response of the Criminal Justice System," *Criminal Law Review* 17 (1999) (criminal law does not play significant role in responding to racist behavior in racial violence).

43. In a paper tentatively titled "Bias Crime in a Multicultural Society," I will argue that the early experience with the racial violence provisions of the Crime and Disorder Act 1998 has been mixed, including both important application to instances of bias-motivated violence and mis-application to cases in which bias played only a peripheral role in the criminal act.

44. See *The Stephen Lawrence Inquiry: Report of an Inquiry by Sir William Macpherson of Cluny* (London: The Stationery Office, 1999). See also Brian Cathcart, *The Case of Stephen Lawrence* (London: Viking, 1999).

45. See, generally, "Commission on the Future of Multi-Ethnic Britain," in *The Future of Multi-Ethnic Britain* (The "Parekh Report") (London: Profile, 2000), particularly at 1–11.

46. See Andrew Marr, *The Day Britain Died* (London: Profile Books, 2000); Yasmin Alibhai-Brown, *Who Do We Think We Are?* (London: Penguin Books, 2000); Mike Phillips and Trevor Phillips, *Windrush: The Irresistible Rise of Multiracial Britain* (London: HarperCollins, 1998).

47. See, e.g., Emile Durkheim, *The Division of Labor in Society*, W. D. Hall, trans. (New York: Free Press, 1984), pp. 62–63; Robert Reiner, "Crime, Law and Deviance: The Durkheim Legacy," in Steve Fenton, ed., *Durkheim and Modern Sociology* (Cambridge and New York: Cambridge University Press, 1984), pp. 172–82; Joel Feinberg, "The Expressive Function in Punishment," in Joel Feinberg, *Doing and Deserving* (Princeton, NJ: Princeton University Press, 1970), pp. 103–4.

48. Royal Commission on Capital Punishment, Minutes of Evidence, Ninth

Day, December 1, 1949, Memorandum submitted by the Rt. Hon. Lord Justice Denning (1950).

49. Minow, "Regulating Hatred," supra note 1.

50. *R.A.V. v. City of St. Paul*, 505 U.S. 377 (1992).

51. *Wisconsin v. Mitchell*, 508 U.S. 476 (1993).

52. My own views on this question are set out in *Punishing Hate*, at 80–109.

53. *McClesky v. Kemp*, 481 U.S. 279 (1987).

54. Id. at 314–19 (expressing the opinion that a challenge to capital punishment based on disparate enforcement "taken to its logical conclusion, throws into serious question the principles that underlie our entire criminal justice system").

55. *Wisconsin v. Mitchell*, 485 N.W. 2d 807, 809 (Wisc. 1992).

56. A study of the implementation of the racial violence provisions of the Crime and Disorder Act 1998 by the Institute for Criminology at the University of Cambridge has been commissioned by the Home Office and is expected to be released in the near future. I am currently working on an evaluation of the disparate enforcement problem in the American bias crime context for the *Journal of Law and Contemporary Problems* to be published in 2002.

57. Minow, "Regulating Hatred," supra note 1. ("The agenda of regulating hatred whether through hate speech restrictions or hate crimes legislation has the unfortunate effect of focus on the individual perpetrator but not the victims nor the social forces that assist and inform the perpetrator. Hate crimes prosecutions zero in on the one with the gun, not the one with the hate-filled talk radio show, the anti-women rap music, the neo-Nazi Web site, or the homophobic preacher.")

58. Id.

59. Lawrence, *Punishing Hate*, at 175, quoting Allport, *The Nature of Prejudice*, at 518.

60. See, e.g., Phillips and Phillips, *Windrush*.

61. *The Future of Multi-Ethnic Britain*, supra note 45, at 2.

6

Collective Memory, Collective Action, and Black Activism in the 1960s

FREDRICK C. HARRIS

The essays by Minow in this volume touch on a variety of themes that explore the consequences of memory and hate. Collective violence, trauma, forced forgetting, the call for reparations, efforts to curtail hate speech, truth commissions, and the like are all, in some way, linked to the role that collective memory plays in the political life of social groups. Without some sustained memory of past injustices and victories over past harms, social groups would not be able to map the courses of action to consider in their organized opposition against hate. Noting the positive and negative consequences of a society confronting its past, Minow observes in "Memory and Hate" that the "failure to remember, collectively, triumphs and accomplishments diminishes us. But failure to remember, collectively, injustice and cruelty is an ethical breach." This essay explores the evolution of collective memories by considering how the social construction of past events by social groups can serve as a catalyst for collective action. It does so through an illustration of how events related to the struggle for racial justice—both triumphant and tragic events—served as a catalyst for black political activism during the modern civil rights movement in the United States.

The influence of collective memory on the political action of social groups has received scant attention from scholars of collective action. Though research in public opinion formation demonstrates how significant historical events shape political attitudes, theoretical perspectives on collective action have not provided guidance on how the collective memory of social groups might influence the ability of individuals to engage in cooperative action. This omission in theories of collective action is surprising. As scholars in a variety of disciplines have demonstrated, historical events often have long-term consequences, shaping the way individuals interpret the political world. The memory of the Vietnam

War and the Watergate scandal, for instance, continues to linger in America's political consciousness, influencing public opinion on government corruption and attitudes toward military intervention in international conflicts (Beamish, Molotch, & Flacks 1995; Sturken 1997; Stuckey 1992; Schudson 1992).

The work of social theorist Maurice Halbwachs (1951), one of the first scholars to develop a theory of collective memory, suggests that collective memory constitutes the choice of preferences that naturally evolve from social groups. "While the collective memory endures and draws strength from its base in a coherent body of people," Halbwachs noted, "it is individuals as group members who remember" (Halbwachs 1951: 48). These group-oriented memories are "part of a totality of thoughts common to a group, the group of people with whom we have a relationship at the moment, or with whom we have had a relation on preceding day or days" (Halbwachs 1992: 52).

In contrast to individual memory, in which an individual's past is experienced by that person alone, collective memory contains "recollections that are instantiated beyond the individual by and for the collective" (Zelizer 1995: 214). Just as public opinion reflects the consolidation of individual preferences into a collective whole, collective memory functions in a similar vein, comprising the "sum total of personal recollections of various individual members" who experience or have knowledge of specific events (Zerubavel 1996: 293–94).

Since collective memory reflects the choice of preferences that evolve from social groups, the link between collective memory and collective action seems intuitive. Because collective memory is formed through "a shared past that is retained by members of a group" (Schuman & Scott 1989), it may assist group cooperation by strengthening bonds of solidarity and reducing the material cost of inducing members to cooperate with others. Consequently, for those who express commitments to a group, collective memory can provide social incentives for collective action, strengthening support for a cause. Additionally, memories of past events that reflect the preferences of social groups may also serve as a lens to interpret new information that may influence the life chances of a social group. Like voters who look retrospectively at candidates' past economic and political performance to make decisions before casting their ballot (Fiorina 1981), collective memory may have similar effects on individual decision-making by providing group members with historically nuanced perspectives that may enhance their possibility of joining collective action efforts.

In her first essay, titled "Memory and Hate," Martha Minow observes the retrospective force of memory on politics: to remember both past oppression and prior struggles against oppression may affect a group's political action in the future. Noting that "recollections are not retrieved, like computer files, but instead are always constructed by combining bits of information selected and arranged in light of prior narratives and current expectations, needs, and beliefs," Minow suggests how events can be appropriated by politicized social groups and then secured as collective memory over time, only to be retrieved when those memories can serve some political purpose in the here and now.

However, for oppressed groups, the positive influence of collective memory on collective action might not be a given. Depending on what is remembered, and the context of mobilization, the collective memory of marginal groups may either facilitate group solidarity or discourage it. Past events symbolizing the cost of challenging structures of oppression may weaken the possibility of cooperation among oppressed groups, while events symbolizing victory may signal that successful cooperation is viable. Indeed, collective memories, like all preferences of groups that live under systems of domination, are often hidden in "off-stage" settings, social spaces where marginal groups freely articulate their views about the dominant class and its institutions (Scott 1990; Couto 1993; Kelley 1994).

James Scott (1990) calls the narratives of marginal groups in autonomous settings "hidden transcripts." These transcripts are especially voiced when the possibility for overt resistance against domination is formidable. When structures of domination weaken and the possibility for collective action gains strength, the hidden transcript becomes public, allowing oppressed groups to freely express their grievances (Scott 1990: 108–35). However, Scott and other scholars have left unanswered whether the shared memories of past injustices may actually deter collective resistance, even when opportunities for resistance grow. As a reflection of the hidden transcript, the collective memory of events that symbolize the material and physical cost of being a member of an oppressed group could have mixed effects on the ability of the oppressed to collectively challenge their domination, even when opportunities for collective action are favorable. Memories of past events may either stimulate collective action by reminding members of oppressed groups of their grievances or might hinder the ability of group members to cooperate if they interpret events as potentially costly to them.

The history of slavery, state-sanctioned segregation, racial violence, and other forms of racial domination created—over several generations—shared memories of momentous events that were seen as altering the life chances of African Americans (Couto 1993; Fabre & O'Meally 1994; Dawson 1994; Cohen 1999). Whether gained directly through individual experiences or indirectly through the voices of familial experiences, the formation of collective memories in black communities contributes to a sense of "linked fate" in African-American political life (Dawson 1994). This perspective on African-American political behavior posits that individual blacks will evaluate the conditions of blacks as a group when determining their own political preferences. Although the collective memory of African Americans is implied rather than directly tested in the linked-fate model, the model, nonetheless, points to the importance of collective memory as a way to offer insights into contemporary political action in black communities. As Dawson explains: "The collective memory of the African-American community continued to transmit from generation to generation a sense that race was the defining interest in individuals' lives and that the well-being of blacks individually and as a group could be secured only by continued political and social agitation" (Dawson 1994: 51).

On the other hand, as Cathy Cohen (1999) points out, some shared memories of the past might actually inhibit collective action in black communities. In her analysis of the slow response of black leadership and institutions to the AIDS crisis in black communities, the collective memory of the exploitation of blacks through the mainstream medical establishment created barriers to community institutions' mobilizing against the crisis. As Cohen observes, blacks "do not have to reach far back into their collective memory to recall the racist blame placed on them as the originators of diseases such as tuberculosis and syphilis," adding that "even more ingrained in the minds of black Americans is the medical exploitation of black sharecroppers during the Tuskegee Syphilis Study" (1999: 50).

To illustrate the complex relationship between collective memory and collective action among oppressed or historically oppressed groups, this essay explores how the shared memories of significant historical events that affected the life chances of African Americans influenced black activism during the modern civil rights movement. It allows us to consider the influence of particular memories on black activism during a period of heightened political mobilization in black communities and, in the context of the South, a period in which participation exposed actors to considerable risks.

How did events of the past—both positive and negative—influence black activism during the 1960s? Did knowledge of tragedies and successes inspire or deter activism? Did the memory of positive events have a greater impact on black activism than events that signaled to actors the dangers of activism? To answer these questions, this essay further considers the theoretical links between collective memory and collective action through social movement perspectives on micromobilization. This perspective argues that micro-level processes, such as feelings of political empowerment and the interpretation of grievances by actors, are combined with macro-level resources, such as institutional and organizational capacities, in the formation of collective action. The essay then summarizes estimates of how particular shared memories of events associated with the movement before the 1960s continued to influence black activism during the 1960s. Narratives of eyewitnesses are used to supplement estimates from survey findings. The essay concludes with a discussion of theoretical implications and suggestions for future research.

Collective Memory, Micromobilization, and Collective Action

The evolving micromobilization perspective on social movements provides a framework to explore the participatory effects of collective memory on black activism during the 1960s. Micro-level resources reflect the "variety of contexts in which face-to-face interaction is the social setting from which meanings critical to the interpretation of collective identities, grievances, and opportunities are created, interpreted, and transformed" (Mueller 1992: 10). While resource mobilization theory describes the "tangible" or macro-level resources for collective action, such as indigenous leadership, communication, social networks, meeting places, and financial support, the micromobilization perspective considers fewer visible factors in the process of collective action, such as group solidarity, feelings of political empowerment, and a group's political culture.

Implicit in his critique of the limits of the macro-dynamics of social movement theory, historian George Lipsitz (1988) recognizes the micro-dynamics of collective memory as a resource for collective action. He argues that collective memory provides actors with a retrospective lens through which to articulate and evaluate grievances, noting that "even when oppositional groups confront an unfavorable outside opportunity structure, or when their own institutions are bureaucratic, sectarian, or weak, they still retain the capacity to fashion a counterhegemonic struggle by drawing on the collective memory of the past as a critique of the present" (241–22).

This perspective of collective memory is also implicit in what Robert Bellah and his colleagues describe as "communities of memory" (Bellah et al. 1985). Communities of memory are composed of social groups that do not forget their past, a past that is kept alive by the telling and retelling of narratives that convey "examples of the men and women who have embodied and exemplified the meaning of the community" (Bellah et al. 1985: 153). Not only do communities of memory sustain memories of triumph over adversity through the telling of stories, but these communities also pass on narratives that are "painful stories of shared suffering that sometimes create deeper identities" than narratives that illustrate triumph (Bellah et al. 1985: 153).

Several scholars of the modern civil rights movement have commented on how shared memories of the past inspired African Americans to become active in the movement (Lipsitz 1988; Couto 1993; Payne 1995). In his analysis of movement activism in the Mississippi Delta, Charles Payne (1995) notes that activists were more likely to emerge from families where elders shared stories of injustices and defiance, than from families where elders did not speak of past experiences. Family narratives of resistance instilled a sense of defiance across generations by "keeping the story before" the next generation who engaged in overt resistance as opportunities for activism emerged (218).[1] Similarly, Richard Couto's analysis of civil rights leadership in local communities also demonstrates how collective memory influenced movement participation. In climates of fear and oppression, elders shared their experiences of police brutality, economic exploitation by whites, and political corruption by political elites in "off-stage" settings. Recounting narratives of exploitation helped to sustain opposition in communities where the opportunities for collective action were severely limited (Couto 1993: 68–69). When political opportunities emerged, community elders publically shared memories of past injustices in the "free spaces" of community institutions, where "people are able to learn a new self-respect, a deeper and more assertive group identity, public skills, and values of cooperation and civic virtue" (Evans & Boyte 1986: 17).

Again, the theory of micromobilization provides a framework to explore the effects of collective memory on black political activism during the civil rights movement. Like other micro-level resources for collective action, collective memory may have stimulated movement participation by providing a lens through which actors could articulate grievances, cement loyalties, establish goals, and reflect on the possibility for successful cooperation. On the other hand, knowledge of events that may have symbolized the risk of transgressing the racial status quo may have depressed black political action, especially in the South where the risks of overt resistance were greater. The knowledge of tragic events may have reinforced the sense of fear and apathy in Southern blacks that several scholars reported during and immediately after the movement (Matthews & Prothro 1966; U.S. Commission on Civil Rights 1968; Solomon & Van Evera 1973).

An analysis of four events—two that symbolized risk and two that symbolized triumph—demonstrates that specific collective memories of African Americans positively influenced black activism during the 1960s. Using a rare survey of African Americans that was conducted by the Louis Harris Polling group in 1966,[2] the analysis estimated the effects of four events on black activism: the persecution of the "Scottsboro Boys" during the 1930s,[3] the landmark 1954 *Brown* decision, the 1955 murder of Emmett Till,[4] and the 1955–1956 Montgomery Bus Boycott. Although there were considerable variations across regions, with Southern blacks substantially less likely to recall events than blacks outside the South, all events, except the Scottsboro trials, were positively related to black activism, even when controlling for demographic and organizational factors that affect participation.[5]

The results suggest that a decade after the initial stage of the modern civil rights movement, blacks were not only influenced by the possibilities of political opportunities wrought by the *Brown* decision and the Montgomery Bus Boycott, they were also influenced by tragic events like Till's murder, even though the murder may have reminded them of the risks associated with challenging Jim Crow. The bus boycott and the *Brown* decision symbolized the possibilities of successful cooperation, serving as a signal to insurgents that the American political system was open to change. The finding that the Scottsboro trials, which occurred roughly thirty years before the survey was taken, had no influence on black activism in the 1960s suggests that some historical events may lose their force as a resource for collective action, even if a substantial portion of community of memory has knowledge of the event.

Two possibilities point to why the Scottsboro trials diminished as a politically significant event by the time of the civil rights movement. First, the tragic lives the men led after their release or escape from prison and the obscurity of the others made it difficult for movement activists to re-appropriate the event as a symbol of racial injustice. For many, the Scottsboro incident had become a failure rather than a victory in the fight for racial justice (Goodman 1994).

Second, processes that would sustain the political meaning over time had probably weakened by the 1950s. Since radically leftist organizations initially appropriated the event as a symbol of class struggles and the National Association for the Advancement of Colored People (NAACP) withdrew its support of the cases early on (Carter 1969; Goodman 1994: 32–38, 82–84), the formal and informal institutions and networks of radical politics that thrived in the 1930s were destroyed by the Cold War politics of the 1950s. As historian Penny M. Von Eschen (1997) explains that era's implication for the direction of black activism, "severing the international and domestic politics in the early Cold War and the silencing of antiimperialist and anticapitalist politics had profound implications for the politics of the black American community and for American society" (186). Thus, repression during the Cold War years and the decidedly anticommunist turn in black political life had eclipsed the meaning of the Scottsboro trials, making it difficult for civil rights activists to reappropriate the event decades later (Horne 1986; Marable 1984: 13–39).

The one event that had the strongest impact above all others from the survey estimates is the murder of Emmett Till, an event that should have inspired a sense of fear in actors, especially among Southern activists in black communities. Narratives of blacks who remember Till's murder allow us to further consider how events that symbolized risk may have inspired black activism during the movement as much as events that symbolized expanding political opportunities.

Asked what she remembered about Till's murder, labor activist Ola Kennedy of Gary, Indiana, could reply three decades later that the fourteen-year-old's death had more of an impact on her activism than the Montgomery Bus Boycott, an event that many considered as the catalyst behind the modern civil rights movement:

I felt sad, mad. . . . The hurt and the shock of it went so deep that I think that it moved me more to wanting to be committed to the struggle to change the unjust situation more so than Rosa Parks' refusal to move [to the back of the bus] because [Till's death] had really happened before. . . . The Emmett Till death really started the fire that really made us know that we had to make changes. (Quoted in Hudson-Weems 1994: 309)

Silas Thomas, a retired meat packer from Memphis, Tennessee, recalls how Till's murder inspired covert activism among blacks in rural Mississippi, a region of the South where whites were most resistant to racial change and where overt activism against racial domination exposed activists to considerable risk.

They tell me the people, especially blacks, down there [in Mississippi] wouldn't work. They couldn't get no cotton picked, no work done there. . . . [Till] didn't do nothing but whistle at a white woman. But they paid for it; they lost their crops 'cause black people wouldn't work for 'em. . . . They came to waking up after that, the murder. That's what started the ball to rolling. That Till case started it. (Quoted in Hudson-Weems 1994: 326)

Joyce Ladner, a former member of the Student Non-Violent Coordinating Committee (SNCC), observes how the impact of Till's death on black protest in Mississippi may have been influenced by the *combined* impact of opportunities presented by the *Brown* decision and the raw emotions that were generated by Till's murder:

I remember Emmett Till. I was eleven or twelve then. . . . A very important thing is that it followed the Supreme Court decision in 1954. . . . So when the spark came in Mississippi to sit in the public library, for example, people who participated had been incensed by the Till incident and were just waiting for the spark to come. The Till incident was the catalyst. (Quoted in Hudson-Weems 1994: 311–12)

Ojida Penn, a music professor from Montgomery, Alabama, who was an adolescent at the time of Till's murder, remembers how the murder nurtured his commitment to racial justice *after* being surprised that such a tragedy could occur in light of the *Brown* decision:

I was twelve then and remember thinking that these white people are really evil. . . . This was after the *Brown vs. Board of Education,* which was a signal that things were all right, and you sort of let your guard down thinking that integration was just around the corner. . . . But when Emmett Till was killed, that made me consider where we were. Till sort of shocked me out of that momentary complacency into which I had lapsed. (Quoted in Hudson-Weems 1994: 318)

Both narratives and estimates from the survey findings suggest that for African Americans in the mid-1960s, particularly those in the South, the memory of Till's death inspired political activism as much as events that symbolized expanding opportunities for collective action. Both the murder and the not guilty verdict of the two white men who were charged with Till's murder sparked protest rallies in a number of cities, including Baltimore, Chicago, Cleveland, Detroit, Los Angeles, and New York (Wexler 1993: 61). It was the social construction of Till's murder by movement activists that moved the event from the possibility of obscurity into a force for social change. Indeed, the way that the event is remembered today—not as a kidnaping and murder but as a lynching—attests to the power that the process of appropriation has on the evolution of collective memories. Till's murder did not involve the type of mob violence that traditionally characterized lynchings, but the kidnaping and murder were appropriated by civil rights activists as such, assisting movement actors in their crusade for civil rights.

What also facilitated the appropriation of Till's murder is the long-lasting visual images of his death, which may also account for why the survey results show that Till's death had a stronger residual impact on black activism than the *Brown* decision and the Montgomery Bus Boycott. Mamie Till Bradley's demand that her son's body be returned to Chicago and displayed so that "the whole nation (can) see what they done to my boy" and the role of the NAACP and the black press played in constructing the murder as a civil rights cause led to the incorporation of the event into the memory repertoire of black communities.

Estimates of the number of people who viewed Till's body at a South Side Chicago church range from ten thousand to six hundred thousand (Feldstein 1994: 271). African Americans around the nation who did not personally witness what had happened to Till had their memory of the murder cemented through photographs of his remains published in *Jet*, a popular weekly magazine that has wide circulation in black communities across the country. Other artifacts facilitating the memory processes in black communities were a self-published pamphlet by a Memphis-based black photographer, Ernest Withers. Priced at one dollar, the pamphlet contained photographs of Till and the murder trial, which sold thousands of copies in black communities across the nation (Withers 2000).

Incorporating the theory of collective memory into our understanding of the dynamics of collective action can tell us much about the politics of memory. Collective memory can shed light on the formation of political solidarities and how those solidarities are sustained over time. It also demonstrates how memories of past injustices can provide an interpretative framework for the articulation of grievances and political opportunities. The combination of narratives and more systematic approaches to uncovering the meaning of shared memories offers a way for scholars to assess variations in group-based political action. Indeed, unraveling the links between collective memory and collective action has consequences for understanding how an array of marginal groups across time and space—Jews who experienced the Holocaust, Koreans who witnessed Japan's imperialism, or opponents of authoritarian and totalitarian regimes in a variety of societies—employ collective memories as resources for collective action.

Additionally, as the narratives point to and the estimates from the survey analysis suggest, the dynamics of collective memory enhance our understanding of the modern civil rights movement. Scholarship on the movement—especially scholarship that emphasizes the macro-dynamics of movements—should reconsider the impact that Till's murder, and other atrocities like it, had on stimulating black insurgency. As other scholars have discovered through oral history (Hudson-Weems 1994), scholarship on the movement has considerably underestimated the impact that Till's death had on the formation of black insurgency. It might be that events such as the Till murder, an event that symbolized black grievances, *interacted* with other events that signaled to insurgents that political opportunities were expanding.

Although this study employs data from the 1960s to explore the effects of collective memory on black political activism, the findings raise questions about the continuing influence of collective memory on contemporary African-American political life. The shared memories of events like the murder of Emmett Till, for instance, may partially explain how Supreme Court nominee Clarence Thomas, who described his nomination process as a "high-tech lynching," solidified black support on behalf of his nomination, despite the nominee's politically conservative views on civil rights.

In the same vein, the notable black support for O. J. Simpson during his murder trial may have reflected not only blacks' negative experiences with the nation's criminal justice system, but also their collective memories of injustices that mirrored the tragedy of events such as the Scottsboro trials. More recent memories of tragedies may even have greater political consequences in contemporary black life. Consider, for instance, the voter registration efforts by the National Association for the Advancement of Colored People (NAACP) during the 2000 fall presidential election. Targeting twelve states where black voters could make a difference in the outcome of the election, the association ran radio and newspaper ads that connected black voter participation to the brutal murder of James Byrd Jr., an African American who was dragged to his death behind a pickup truck in Texas in 1998. Featuring the daughter of Byrd, the ad criticized Republican presidential candidate George W. Bush for opposing hate-crime legislation in Texas. As the ad stated, "When Gov. George Bush refused to support hate-crime legislation, it was like my father was killed all over again. Call George Bush and tell him to support hate-crime legislation. We won't be dragged away from our future." Several analysts credited the ad for contributing to the higher-than-average increases in black voter participation that November.

Explorations into the links between collective memory and collective action not only expand our understanding of black political life, but it will also expand our understanding of the complex dynamics of the politics of memory.

Notes

1. Payne (1995) notes in particular the enormous impact of collective memory on one family's activism—the Greene family of Greenwood, Mississippi. He notes: "Like the children in many Southern Black families, the Greene children were told repeatedly that they were just as good as everyone else, but it went further than that. Certain stories were also repeated. According to Alma Greene Henderson, 'My mama always kept the story before me' about a man who was burned at the stake in nearby Moorhead during the 1920s and also repeated another story, apparently from the same period, involving a black woman whose family was brutalized" (218).

2. The 1966 Harris-*Newsweek* survey interviewed 1,059 black adults more than eighteen years of age who were drawn from a national random sample. The interviews, consisting of more than 200 questions, were conducted face to face and by black interviewers. About 100 respondents, who were a part of an elite sample of black leaders, are eliminated from the sample for this analysis. The demographic and political characteristics of the elite sample warrants its exclusion. In addition to the elite respondents not being coded by region, the respondents in the sample have a considerably higher number of respondents with more than a high school education (58 percent have more than a high school education) and who report membership in civil rights groups (47 percent reported being active in at least one civil rights organization) than the nonelite sample. The population samples for the Harris-*Newsweek* surveys were generated from sixty population clusters throughout the United States. During the period of the survey, the Census Bureau did not collect block-by-block breakdowns of black populations. The Harris-*Newsweek* surveys used counties and major urban divisions to create sixty clusters based on high black populations. Block-by-block estimates were created for each division and county in the sixty clusters. Black

households were randomly selected from block estimates. Although this sampling technique probably undersurveyed blacks in geographic locations with few whites, the Harris-*Newsweek* surveys were among the first to gather large national samples of black Americans. Most surveys of blacks during this period sampled one city or several cities, biasing the reporting of black political behavior toward the urban, mostly Northern populations. For more on the sampling technique of the Harris-*Newsweek* surveys, see Brink & Harris 1964: 12–15. Although there is a comparable white survey from the 1966 study, it did not ask white respondents about their knowledge of past or present civil rights events or about any historical events. This omission does not allow us to test collective memory's effects on whites' participation in the South or outside the South. However, this omission is not crucial to this analysis, since many scholars have already demonstrated that the collective memory of marginal groups are distinct from the collective memory (and world views) of dominant groups (Couto 1993; Scott 1990; Kelly 1994).

3. The Scottsboro trials involved a string of court cases, beginning in 1931, that falsely accused nine black men of raping two white women on a freight train near Scottsboro, Alabama.

4. Emmett Till was a fourteen-year-old boy from Chicago who was murdered by two white men while visiting relatives in Money, Mississippi, in 1955. He was murdered for allegedly whistling at a white woman.

5. For further details of the survey results, see Fredrick C. Harris, "They Kept the Story Before Them: Collective Memory, Micromobilization, and Black Political Activism in the 1960s." Typescript, Department of Political Science, University of Rochester.

Sources

Beamish, Thomas D., Harvey Molotch, and Richard Flacks. 1995. "Who Supports the Troops?: Vietnam, the Gulf War, and the Making of Collective Memory." *Social Problems* 42:344–60.

Bellah, Robert, William Sullivan, and Steven Tipton. 1985. *Habits of the Heart*. Berkeley: University of California Press.

Brink, William, and Louis Harris. 1964. *The Negro Revolution in America*. New York: Simon and Schuster.

Carter, Dan. 1969. *Scottsboro: A Tragedy of the American South*. Baton Rouge: Louisiana State University.

Cohen, Cathy J. 1999. *The Boundaries of Blackness: AIDS and the Breakdown of Black Politics*. Chicago: University of Chicago Press.

Conway, M. Margaret. 1985. *Political Participation in the United States*. Washington, DC: CQ Press.

Couto, Richard A. 1993. "Narrative, Free Space, and Political Leadership in Social Movements." *Journal of Politics* 55:57–79.

Dawson, Michael C. 1994. *Behind the Mule: Race and Class in African-American Politics*. Chicago: University of Chicago Press.

Evans, Sara, and Harry C. Boyte. 1986. *Free Spaces: The Sources of Democratic Change in America*. New York: Harper & Row.

Fabre, Geneviève, and Robert G. O'Meally. 1994. *History and Memory in African-American Culture*. New York: Oxford University Press.

Feldstein, Ruth. 1994. "'I Wanted the Whole World to See': Race, Gender, and the Construction of Motherhood in the Death of Emmett Till." In Joanne Meyerowitz, ed., *Not June Cleaver: Women and Gender in Postwar America, 1945–1960*. Philadelphia: Temple University Press, pp. 263–303.

Fiorina, Morris P. 1981. *Retrospective Voting in American National Elections*. New Haven, CT: Yale University Press.

Goodman, James E. 1994. *Stories of Scottsboro*. New York: Pantheon Books.

Halbwachs, Maurice. 1980 [1951]. *The Collective Memory*. New York: Harper & Row.

———. 1992. *On Collective Memory*. Edited and translated by Lewis A. Coser. Chicago: University of Chicago Press.

Harris, Fredrick C. 1999a. *Something Within: Religion in African-American Political Activism*. New York: Oxford University Press.

———. 1999b. "Will the Circle Be Unbroken?: The Erosion and Transformation of African-American Civic Life." In Robert K. Fullinwider, ed., *Civil Society, Democracy, and Civic Renewal*. New York: Rowman & Littlefield.

Horne, Gerald. 1986. *Black and Red: W.E.B. Du Bois and the Afro-American Response to the Cold War, 1944–1963*. Albany: State University of New York Press.

Hudson-Weems, Clenora. 1994. *Emmett Till: The Sacrificial Lamb of the Civil Rights Movement*. Troy, MI: Bedford Publishers, Inc.

Irwin-Zarecka, Iwona. 1994. *Frames of Remembrance: The Dynamics of Collective Memory*. New Brunswick, NJ: Transaction Publishers.

Kelley, Robin D. G. 1994. *Race Rebels: Culture, Politics, and the Black Working Class*. New York: Free Press.

Lipsitz, George. 1988. *A Life of Struggle: Ivory Perry and the Culture of Opposition*. Philadelphia. Temple University Press.

Mannheim, Karl. 1952 [1928]. "The Problem of Generations." In Karl Mannheim, ed., *Essays of the Sociology of Knowledge*. London: Routledge & Kegan Paul, pp. 276–322.

Marable, Manning, 1984. *Race, Reform and Rebellion: The Second Reconstruction in Black America*. Jackson: University Press of Mississippi, 1984.

Matthews Donald R., and James W. Prothro. 1966. *Negroes and the New Southern Politics*. New York: Harcourt, Brace and World.

McAdam, Doug. 1982. *Political Process and the Development of Black Insurgency: 1930–1970*. Chicago: University of Chicago Press.

Morris, Aldon D. 1984. *The Origins of the Civil Rights Movement: Black Communities Organizing for Change.* New York: Free Press.

———. 1992. "Political Consciousness and Collective Action." In Aldon D. Morris and Carol McClurg Mueller, eds., *Frontiers in Social Movement Theory.* New Haven, CT: Yale University Press, pp. 351–73.

Morris, Aldon, Shirley J. Hatchett, and Ronald E. Brown. 1989. "The Civil Rights Movement and Black Political Socialization." In Roberta S. Sigel, ed., *Political Learning In Adulthood.* Chicago:University of Chicago Press.

Mueller, Carol McClurg. 1992. "Building Social Movement Theory." In Morris and Mueller, eds., *Frontiers in Social Movement Theory,* pp. 3–25.

Payne. Charles S. 1995. *I've Got the Light of Freedom: The Organizing Tradition and the Mississippi Freedom Struggle.* Berkeley: University of California Press.

Schudson, Michael. 1992. *Watergate in American Memory: How We Remember, Forget, and Reconstruct the Past.* New York: Basic Books.

Schuman, Howard, and Jacqueline Scott. 1989. "Generations and Collective Memories." *American Sociological Review* 54:359–81.

Scott, Jacqueline, and Lilian Zac. 1993. "Collective Memories in Britain and the United States." *Public Opinion Quarterly* 57:315–31.

Scott, James. 1990. *Domination and the Arts of Resistence.* New Haven, CT: Yale University Press.

Solomon, Lester, and Stephen Van Evera. 1973. "Fear, Apathy, and Discrimination: A Test of Three Explanations of Political Participation." *American Political Science Review* 67:1288–306.

Stuckey, Mary E. 1992. "Remembering the Future: Rhetorical Echoes of World War II and Vietnam in George Bush's Public Speech on the Gulf War." *Communication Studies* 43:246–56.

Sturken, Marita. 1997. *Tangled Memories: The Vietnam War, the AIDS Epidemic, and the Politics of Remembering.* Berkeley: University of California Press.

Tarrow, Sidney. 1992. "Mentalities, Political Cultures, and Collective Action Frames." In Morris and Mueller, eds., *Frontiers in Social Movement Theory,* pp. 174–202.

U.S. Commission on Civil Rights. 1968. *Political Participation.* Washington, DC: U.S. Government Printing Office.

Verba, Sidney, and Norman H. Nie. 1972. *Participation in America.* New York: Harper & Row.

Verba, Sidney, Kay Lehman Schlozman, and Henry Brady. 1995. *Voice and Equality: Civic Voluntarism in American Politics.* Cambridge, MA: Harvard University Press.

Von Eschen, Penny M. 1997. *Race Against Empire: Black Americans and Anticolonialism, 1937–1957.* Ithaca, NY: Cornell University Press.

Wexler, Sanford. 1993. *The Civil Rights Movement: An Eyewitness History.* New York: Facts on File.

Withers, Ernest C. 2000. *Pictures Tell the Story: Reflections in History.* Norfolk, VA: Chrysler Museum of Art.

Zelizer, Barbie. 1995. "Reading the Past Against the Grain: The Shape of Memory Studies." *Review and Criticism* June: 214–39.

Zerubavel, Eviatar. 1996. "Social Memories: Steps to a Sociology of the Past." *Qualitative Sociology* 19:283–99.

7

Beyond Memory: Child Sexual Abuse and the Statute of Limitations

ROSS E. CHEIT AND CAREY JAROS

The sexual abuse of children in the United States has been widely recognized and condemned in the last twenty years. The problem has been transformed from something rarely acknowledged or discussed into something publicly acknowledged and abhorred. Child molestation is often described as "the most heinous crime other than murder." But unlike murder, the legal responses to child sexual abuse have been ambivalent and inadequate. Prosecutions are rare (Gray, 1993) and a substantial percentage of those convicted of this "heinous" crime receive probation instead of prison (Cheit & Goldschmidt, 1997).

Martha Minow describes the legal responses to violence against children as a "middle case" between interfamilial adult violence, where legal separation is a useful solution, and intergroup violence, where separation may be impossible and coexistence is the primary goal. But the center is turbulent, not stable. As Minow explains: "We have been extremely torn in this country about whether to remove from the home children who have been abused" (Minow, 1999b: 7). The reasons to remove abused children are obvious; then again, there are two strong arguments against removal in the name of child protection: (1) the strength and importance of family preservation and (2) the pragmatic lack of better alternatives for children removed from their homes, or otherwise left parentless through legal remedies.

There is a legal approach that holds out the possibility of providing meaningful redress for child sexual abuse while avoiding the dilemmas posed by issues of child placement and custody. This approach relies on the simple fact that children become adults, and that as adults they are much better positioned to make decisions about possible legal claims that are, for a variety of reasons discussed in this chapter, virtually impossible to make as children. How well does the law accommodate *adults* seeking criminal or civil justice over childhood sexual abuse? Under the existing law in many states, the decision as to whether to pursue legal remedies in adulthood for child sexual abuse is precluded entirely by the statute of limitations. Many states have adopted "delayed discovery" provisions to address these concerns in civil proceedings; the majority of states have not taken such action (Williams, 2000). The criminal law is even more disparate. Most jurisdictions make no special accommodation for child sexual abuse beyond minority-tolling provisions—which allow criminal complaints for events in childhood to be filed shortly after the complainant becomes an adult—but a handful have eliminated the statute of limitations entirely (American Prosecutors Research Institute, 1994).

This chapter examines the traditional justifications for statutes of limitation. The analysis begins with criminal law, where concerns about defendants' rights are paramount. The inquiry then focuses on accommodations that have been made in the civil law to recognize the implications of the trauma involved in child sexual abuse. The overall argument is premised on several features that distinguish child sexual abuse from other civil and criminal wrongs. While we conclude that those features justify various legal reforms, it is important to note that legal remedies have significant disadvantages and will undoubtedly continue to be considered unsuitable by many, perhaps most, potential complainants. As Minow (1999a: 2) observed, the search for responses to various forms of trauma "is profoundly doomed, because nothing after the event can be adequate." In that context, legal actions initiated by adults sexually abused as children are one of many "inadequate" legal responses. Only by reforming statutes of limitations, however, will many of those abused as children be afforded a meaningful chance to decide for themselves whether the advantages of legal action outweigh the disadvantages.

There are three features of child sexual abuse that distinguish it from most other crimes and torts. First, child sexual abuse occurs much more often inside families than outside. If a family member perpetrates the abuse, it is much less likely that anyone will come forward to report it. Those most likely to know about the abuse are in the family whose integrity is at risk if the abuse is reported. This also minimizes the practical effect of legal remedies that rely on legal guardianship; that approach assumes that parents will bring legal actions, when appropriate, on behalf of their children. In the case of incest, however, such laws literally place the state's trust in the hands of the perpetrator.

The second unusual feature of child sexual abuse is that the trauma involved renders some victims unable to recall the abuse until later in life. Dozens of peer-reviewed studies have documented this phenomenon, although estimates of the prevalence among victims of sexual abuse range widely (see, e.g., Brown et al., 1999; Scheflin & Brown, 1997; Turner, 1996). Without appropriate adjustments in the statute of limitations, many of these victims are denied any meaningful possibility of pursuing justice through the criminal or civil courts. These cases, involving "repressed" or "recovered" memories, have recently dominated the public discourse over legal remedies for child sexual abuse. Some states have recognized this phenomenon, adapting the statute of limitations to begin when the abuse is first remembered. The debate over such provisions has become extremely divisive in recent years. Worse, it has diverted attention from larger issues.

The obsession with repression obscures the fact that while most victims of child sexual abuse "remembered all along," many still never had a meaningful chance to decide whether to pursue a legal remedy. The reason involves the third unusual feature of child sexual abuse: cognitive distortions and secrecy. Often lost in the bitter arguments about whether and when one first remembered the abuse is the more fundamental question of how the perpetrator eluded detection in the first place. As John Conte (1986: 8) has observed, sexual abuse "cannot take place if adults who care about children know about the abuse." Secrecy must be maintained through threats or subtler means. Most perpetrators rely on "cognitive distortions . . . to rationalize or minimize" the abuse (id.). Distorting the perceptions of the child enables the perpetrator to repeat the behavior, often for years. For the sexually abused child, the results of secrecy and physical invasion are often shame, fear, and/or confusion. Those reactions limit the child's ability to comprehend the inappropriateness of the abuse, let alone understand the consequences of disclosing it to others. As Richard Hoffman (1999: 5) put it, "the sexual violation of a child is a violation of the child's history, not merely the child's psyche."

These three unusual features of child sexual abuse—familial isolation, memory impairment, and cognitive distortions—cry out for accommodations in the statute of limitations. The rest of this chapter analyzes how well various approaches to the statute of limitations in civil and criminal law address the special problems of child sexual abuse. This is not a survey of how each state handles the issue, but rather an analysis of the general arguments facing all jurisdictions. Through this analysis we address the most common objections to legal reforms and conclude with recommendations that seek to balance the competing values discussed below.

Criminal Law

In criminal law, statutes of limitation are generally analyzed in terms of defendants' rights. Concepts of fairness, repose, and due process explain why the state is prohibited from going forward with criminal charges long after the commission of a crime. For most major felonies, statutes of limitation are between three and seven years. But murder has always been treated differently. In almost every state, there is no statute of limitations for murder. The logic is based on the seriousness of the crime rather than anything specific about the evidence in murder cases. Some would argue that the severity of the crime justifies the same result for child sexual abuse. Ironically, those objecting to extending or eliminating the statute of limitations generally agree that it is—at least they do when discussing the issue of false accusations. Peter Freyd, for example, speaks of "being accused of the worst crime you can have short of murder" (Fried, 1994: 152). Of course, the possibility of being falsely accused of murder has never been seen as a reason to limit the time in which murder charges must be brought.

There is compelling evidence that victims of child sexual abuse can find relief and healing through the prosecution of "old" crimes.[1] As Lamb (1996: 169) explains: "Punishment can communicate something important to the victim. Although it does not erase the crime nor the injury, it pronounces social opinion about her relative responsibility, proclaims that what happened to her was wrong, validates her rights . . ." By searing the crime into the legal record, and thus, into our collective memory, this pronouncement of social opinion benefits society, too. As Minow argues, "Some people will always remember what happened, but if there are no collective efforts at memory, a society risks repeating its atrocities and fails to undo the dehumanization that laid the ground for them" (1999a: 6).

There is clear value—both to victims, and to society as a whole—in providing for prosecution of child sexual abuse cases beyond what is allowed by current statutes of limitations. In order to determine whether reform or elimination of these statutes makes sense, however, we must weigh the arguments for reform against the concerns of potential defendants. The three biggest concerns voiced by opponents of reforming criminal statutes of limitation are, first, defendants' right to repose; second, the limitations of old evidence; and third, the danger in unfair delay. Some would add a fourth concern: the reliability of recollections generated through inappropriate therapeutic intervention. But that is an evidentiary question appropriately addressed at trial.[2]

THE RIGHT TO REPOSE—IS THERE ONE?

Many of those opposed to relaxing criminal statutes of limitation argue that potential defendants have a constitutional right to repose, and that allowing victims to press charges years after the abuse violates this right. For example, Ernsdorff and Loftus (1993: 174) maintain that those cases that do not go forward under the current statute of limitations—in other words, most instances of child sexual abuse—*must* go unredressed "unless we want to jettison the Constitution." Their argument seems to be that *any* prosecution long after the commission of a crime is unconstitutional.

But this is not an accurate representation of American constitutional history; nor is it our common law heritage. In common law, "Any crime could be prosecuted at any time no matter how much time has passed" (Jones, 1981: 398). The original Model Penal Code codified that approach for murder and recognized the compelling logic for other crimes. The Commentary to the Code observed that in many jurisdictions "treason and crimes of comparable gravity often have no time limit" (American Law Institute, 1956: 87). The federal criminal code takes a similar approach, exempting murder and all other capital offenses from any limitation on prosecution (18 U.S. Code section 3282). Canadian federal law provides no statute of limitations for any "indictable crimes," including child sexual abuse (Canadian Criminal Code, Chapter C-46). An informal survey of U.S. state statutes reveals that kidnapping and arson are the crimes most often without a statute of limitations, each in about a dozen states; forgery and misuse of public funds are exempt from the statute of limitations in a handful of states.

Most state statutes of limitation are a hodgepodge of time limitations, adopted at different times without regard to consistency or any overall philosophy. Gerald Uelman analyzed all of the statutes of limitation in the California criminal code—concluding that some of the statutory time limits are unjustifiably long, particularly when the possible criminal sentence is *less* than the time one is at jeopardy for prosecution (e.g., misuse of public funds, even involuntary manslaughter). This analysis eliminates any repose claim for child sexual abuse since, as Uelman (1983: 52) argues, a statute of limitations *shorter* than the maximum penalty "cannot be justified by the repose factor." Once it is decided that a crime should be considered a capital offense, "prosecution of those crimes should not be barred by a statute of limitations" (id.: 61).

The argument for placing child molestation in the same category as murder stems partly from recognition that the effects of child abuse can reach powerfully into adulthood, and that child sexual abuse can cause lifelong harm. As the Supreme Court of Canada argued in its landmark civil decision, "The patent inequity of allowing [perpetrators] to go on with their life without liability, while the victim continues to suffer the consequences, clearly mitigates against any guarantee of repose" (*K.M. v. M.H.*, 1992). An outspoken critic of recovered memory, Martin Gardner, inadvertently provides perhaps the most powerful argument *against* limiting prosecution of child sexual abuse. Claiming that few victims suffer memory impairment, Gardner (1993: 371) declares that for most people the abuse "festers as a lifelong source of shame and anger." By this argument, the "old" wrong is best understood as a continuing wrong, bolstering the justification for contemporary redress. As "recovery is never complete" for the victim (Herman, 1992: 211), there is a proportionality argument, not to mention one of poetic justice, for making repose for perpetrators similarly elusive.

Those opposed to righting old wrongs through extension or elimination of time limits tend to invoke metaphors like "let sleeping dogs lie" (Ernsdorff & Loftus, 1993). This might be how perpetrators look at yesterday's abuse, but it does *not* reflect the experience of many victims. Living with "the open wound of [an] unresolved crime" can be tormenting (*Wall Street Journal*, 1993: A14), as some were quick to point out when 1960s radical Katherine Ann Power was sentenced for her "old" crimes. Unresolved murders are more like festering wounds than they are like sleeping dogs, and child sexual abuse is similar in many respects.

THE LIMITATIONS OF OLD EVIDENCE

It is frequently pointed out that "old" claims pose special evidentiary risks: that "evidence has been lost, memories have faded, and witnesses have disappeared" (*Prudential-LMI Ins. v. Superior Court*, 1990: 684). But the quality of evidence does not always deteriorate with age. There can be surprisingly strong evidence many years after the fact. Personal diaries can provide undeniable evidence of sexual abuse.[3] Photographic evidence can also preserve a crime over time. Moreover, scientific advances in DNA analysis mean that there is better evidence for some old crimes than existed at the time. New York Governor George E. Pataki recently called for an end to the state's five-year statute of limitations for rape and other violent sexual crimes, arguing that without such reforms the police will be able to identify the perpetrators of these crimes with certainty but will be unable to prosecute them (Hu, 2000).

Given that strong and convincing evidence *can* exist decades later, there is no good reason for automatically preventing these cases from going forward. Paul Robinson (2000: A23) notes: "It is the prosecution that must prove the offense beyond a reasonable doubt; thus it is the prosecution that suffers most from deterioration of evidence." Allowing cases to go forward merely allows the state (or the plaintiff) to face the burden of proof. And existing studies suggest that prosecutors are cautious, not overanxious, when deciding whether to take sexual abuse cases (see, generally, Gray, 1993). Given the difficulties in meeting the burden of proof in criminal cases, prosecutors are even less likely to go forward with sexual abuse cases years after the fact—unless the evidence is overwhelming. Based on an examination of the handful of recent criminal prosecutions involving old sexual abuse cases in Rhode Island and Massachusetts, it is clear that prosecutors go forward only with *multiple* sources of corroboration—even though that is not a stated requirement in the law. In the *Quattrocchi* case, the first criminal prosecution in Rhode Island based on recovered-memory testimony, the trial "may well have turned on the testimony by two other young women who accused Quattrocchi of making improper advances when they were children"[4] (Saltzman, 1994). The prosecution of former Catholic priest James Porter in Fall River, Massachusetts—which was initially resisted by the district attorney—involved twenty-eight named victims, three taped confessions, and the testimony of many more victims (*New York Times*, 1993). There was also evidence from multiple victims in the case of Father Joseph Fredette, who was convicted in Worcester, Massachusetts, of sexually assaulting a young teenage boy twenty years earlier (*Providence Journal Bulletin*, 1995; see also Arnold, 1992). More recently, two former Boy Scout leaders in Rhode Island were charged with sexual abuse perpetrated in the late 1970s as a result of testimony from four separate victims (Salit, 1995: 10).

THE DANGER OF UNFAIR DELAY

There are obvious disadvantages for any defendant charged with an old crime (or tort). Generally, the older the charge, the more difficult it is to recreate the facts and locate relevant evidence. Those disadvantages, however, can be as detrimental, if not more, to the state, which has to prove guilt "beyond a reasonable doubt." Trial procedures "give defendants full opportunity to highlight the weaknesses of old evidence" (Robinson, 2000). Moreover, the "old evidence" problem has not been deemed significant enough to outweigh the potential interest in prosecuting old murder cases. Still, such disadvantages should not be accepted lightly. Nor should they be incurred at all if delay is truly "unreasonable." Unfortunately, the "unreasonable delay" argument often amounts to nothing more than blaming the victim for taking time to meaningfully understand his or her injury. The question is whether there is a way to separate the legitimate reasons for delay (e.g., coming to comprehend the sexual abuse) from illegitimate ones ("sitting" on a claim, for example, waiting for whatever strategic advantage might come through delay). This concern is addressed in the criminal law, which prohibits the state from undue delay in prosecution. Delays attributable to cautious investigation or ended by the discovery of new evidence have generally been found to be acceptable under the Due Process Clause. But delays aimed at gaining a tactical advantage, or even ones caused by negligence, are not likely to pass constitutional muster (*Commonwealth v. Sher*, 1999). Nor should they.

Civil Law

Martha Minow argues, in the context of domestic violence, that "the development of civil actions for adults in intimate relations really stemmed from recognition that most people in those relationships find it difficult to turn to the criminal justice system. . . . For a long time, the police and prosecutors would not take the complaints seriously. . . ." (Minow, 1999b: 15) Similarly, the criminal system is often an inadequate forum for victims of child sexual abuse.

Despite the obvious parallels between the civil and criminal justice systems, considerably more reform has taken place in revising civil statutes for claims involving child sexual abuse. Minority-tolling provisions and two forms of the delayed-discovery doctrine—comprehension and memory-based—have been adopted in various jurisdictions to adjust to the statute of limitations to meet the special characteristics that make child sexual abuse different than other torts. While these modifications provide child sexual abuse victims with more opportunities to seek legal redress than were available under traditional statutes of limitation, there is still significant room for improvement.

MINORITY-TOLLING PROVISIONS

Almost all states have decided that the civil statute of limitations for child sexual abuse should be postponed until after the victim attains the age of majority. In many states, the grace period is two or three years; in a few states it is only one. Minority-tolling provisions, which have been adopted without much controversy or notice, reject the argument that it is fundamentally unfair to adjudicate such matters years after the fact, even though doing so places an unusual burden on the defendant, and even though evidence can deteriorate over time. This value judgment is important to remember in response to concerns about the effects of extending statutory time limits further into adulthood. Extensions into adulthood only add to the delay already sanctioned by minority-tolling provisions.

DELAYED "DISCOVERY"

Perception does not always coincide with injury. That is why the "discovery" doctrine operates to delay accrual of the statute of limitations until one "discovers or should have discovered" all of the necessary elements defined by the law (Prosser, 1971: 144–45). Many states have taken some sort of action, legislative or judicial, in response to social and political changes concerning sexual abuse in the 1970s and 1980s. Unfortunately, changes involving "delayed discovery" have been widely misdescribed. Some have suggested that these provisions represent a radical departure from our legal tradition (Gardner, 1992: 667–68). In fact, these provisions stem from well-established doctrines in common law. Others have portrayed these provisions as exclusively memory-based (see, e.g., McNamara, 1995; Loftus, 1993: 520). In actuality, more states have exceptions based on comprehension than ones based on repressed or recovered memory.

Comprehension-based exceptions Those who sexually abuse children employ various methods aimed specifically at distorting the child's ability to understand the significance and context of the physical acts. Such methods "serve to rationalize or minimize what the adult does" and they "make it possible for the adult to engage repeatedly in behavior that hurts others" (Conte, 1986: 20; see also Loftus, 1993: 525). Not only do perpetrators convince themselves that they are doing nothing wrong, they often do likewise with their victims (see, e.g., *Hammer v. Hammer*, 1987: 25). Preying upon the child's *failure to understand* the events, the successful perpetrator avoids the most likely way that such cases might ever become public—through some kind of report by the victim. Ironically, Loftus and her co-authors, arguing against evidence of widespread traumatic amnesia, provide a cogent argument why exceptions based on *comprehension* make sense. Commenting on Williams's famous 1994 study, documenting cases of traumatic amnesia, they argue that:

> Perhaps some of the younger children who were examined, interviewed, or treated for sexual assault did not understand the meaning of their experience. It would be reasonable to assume that a parent might try to keep this knowledge from a young child to facilitate treatment or minimize damage to the child. If so, then some of these children never "knew" that they were traumatized and thus had nothing to repress (Loftus, Garry, & Feldman, 1994: 1178).

Those opposed to exceptions based on comprehension have not faced two important arguments. First, those who remembered all along are often described as having persistent and intrusive memories—the kind that would seem to be at least as accurate, if not more accurate, than other kinds of memories. Second, the logic that supports extending the statute of limitations in these cases is the same logic used in cases of alleged therapeutic malpractice—a cause of action *favored* by those most critical of recovered-memory cases (Pendergrast, 1995: 530). Consider the therapist who convinces an adult patient to have sexual relations as part of "therapy," or who "successfully" suggests a history of child sexual abuse to a patient who was never abused. When should the statute of limitations begin for possible claims of malpractice: when the patient is cognizant of the "acts themselves" or when the patient comes to understand, probably well after leaving the therapist, that these acts constituted a violation of trust? Obviously, the first approach starts the clock before the patient is likely to *understand* the injury. Faced with this obvious injustice, the Massachusetts high court applied the discovery doctrine so that the statutory clock starts when the patient discovers "that his psychological injuries *resulted from* this wrongful conduct" (*Riley v. Presnell*, 1991: 247, emphasis added; see also, *Shamloo v. Lifespring, Inc.*, 1989). "Lulling" the plaintiff into inaction by psychological means was considered a sufficient argument to create a factual question as to when the plaintiff "discovered" the injury. Surely, then, the argument should apply with at least equal force to children "lulled" into sexual abuse, whose comprehension of the events is clouded by what Minow describes as "the profound experience of forced silence about and disconnection from intense feelings and pain . . ." (Minow, 1999b: 15).

Memory-based exceptions   The second application of the discovery doctrine—perhaps the most compelling, and certainly the most controversial—involves victims who remember the abuse for the first time as adults. These cases are compelling because, without an exception, such claimants clearly lack any opportunity to seek legal redress under traditional statutes of limitation. However controversial, the phenomenon of traumatic amnesia is also widely recognized. For example, Turner (1996: 5–15, 43) reviews eight recent studies examining the incidence of traumatic amnesia in adults reporting histories of child sexual abuse. The studies indicate that 18–59 percent report a time when they were completely amnesiac of the abuse. Seven of those studies are based on self-reports. The other study, Williams (1994), compares self-reports from adults with the medical records from their childhoods; the sample population of adult women had all been hospitalized for sexual assault as children. The study is often cited for the finding that 38 percent of those who had been abused did not recall the abuse at the time of the survey. (An additional 16 percent reported that there was a time when they did not recall the abuse.) Critics of this study urge care in applying these findings, pointing out several contextual variables that might limit their broader relevance (e.g., the "index abuse" was mostly a one-time event, not something repeated) (Loftus, Garry, & Feldman, 1994: 1178–80). But even the critics concede that "extreme claims such as 'if you were raped, you'd remember' are disproven by these findings" (id.: 1177).

The arguments offered by Loftus and other critics contain implicit value judgments that should be stated explicitly and defended. To claim that lost memories were "always accessible" is to place the blame on the victim for not "accessing" them earlier.[5] Since children do not have the cognitive (or legal) capacity to consent, what is the *moral* justification for describing remembering or forgetting in a way that blames the abused child for not acting like an adult?

Proposals for Reform

Statutes of limitation for child sexual abuse, civil and criminal, leave much to be desired in many jurisdictions. Unfortunately, the obsession with repression obscures the primary shortcomings of the law, which have nothing to do with memory. The psychological hurdles to understanding sexual abuse sufficiently to rise above the forces of shame and guilt are clearly more widespread than the problems of memory impairment. Most victims face the former and many are prevented by statutes of limitations from exercising a meaningful choice after they actually comprehend what happened in childhood. In states that do not allow for *any* recovered-memory claims—even those with corroboration—the results seem strangely detached from the purpose of the law.[6] Three possible reforms deserve more consideration: extending the minority-tolling provisions; using disclosure as the trigger that starts the statute of limitations; and eliminating the statute of limitations entirely. Notably, none of these proposals are conditioned on the contentious and seemingly irresolvable questions about trauma and memory.

EXTEND THE MINORITY-TOLLING PROVISIONS

Minority-tolling provisions provide a partial solution to the special problems involved in redressing child sexual abuse. If they are designed well, they provide victims with an opportunity to assess their legal options as autonomous adults without reference to irrelevant and impossible questions about the workings of the memory. Through the use of a firm cut-off date, these statutes avoid difficult determinations concerning who is eligible to bring suit, when, and why. But these statutes generally expire too soon. Many, probably most, victims will not have sufficient psychological distance from the abuse to make a meaningful, autonomous decision in the years immediately after turning eighteen.

One obvious solution is to extend these statutes to recognize the special considerations involved in child sexual abuse. Illinois extended the statute of limitations to age thirty. In other words, the victim has twelve years from the age of majority (eighteen) to make this decision. Of course, there is no magic to the number twelve. Connecticut has taken the most liberal approach of the five states using fixed-time periods, allowing seventeen years from attaining majority (Conn. Gen. Stat. § 52-577d, 1999). A long fixed-time period shifts the focus from whether and when one first remembered or forgot, to the underlying issues at fact. Questions about the *reliability* of human memory still play a role, then, but no differently than in virtually any case in which evidence is provided by humans.

DISCLOSURE AS A TRIGGER

Minority-tolling provisions will always leave out some potential victims. Certainty and repose are assured at the price of some victims never having a meaningful chance to decide. One way to address that problem is to use disclosure as the trigger; that is, start the clock once the victim discloses the abuse as an adult. This might be linked to notifying authorities such as the police, which is the trigger contained in California's new criminal law for child sexual abuse (Cal. Penal Code section 803[g]). This approach does not turn on questions about when one first *remembered* the abuse. Some will object to any extension of the statute of limitations, arguing that meritless filings will increase. But if someone is determined to bring a meritless claim, there are ample opportunities to do so under virtually any statute of limitations. Moreover, the burden of having to defend against claims, even those deemed meritless by the defendant, is part of the American judicial system. On the other hand, the burden of *proving* the case is always on the plaintiff (or the state in criminal cases). The statute of limitations simply determines *when* someone is allowed to assume that burden. Care should be taken not to confuse these issues.

ELIMINATE THE STATUTE OF LIMITATIONS

A strong case can be made for eliminating the statute of limitations entirely. The primary objection to this approach involves fairness to defendants. But that objection is more theoretical than it is factual. The opportunity to file criminal charges simply permits the state to carry the formidable burden of proof "beyond a reasonable doubt." Indeed, the experience in states that have eliminated the statute suggests what common sense would predict: only the strongest cases will be carried forward by prosecutors. The public interest in bringing such cases is overwhelming, as they involve substantial injustices and a meaningful potential for preventing future abuse. On the civil side, the argument for eliminating the statute of limitations is not as powerful because civil litigation vindicates private, not public, interests. On the other hand, as Martha Minow points out, the development of civil actions for adults subject to violence in intimate relations "really stemmed from recognition that most people in those relationships find it difficult to turn to the criminal justice system" (Minow, 1999b: 14). Moreover, the civil claimant still must carry the burden of proof, and the plaintiff must find a lawyer willing to take the case. As with "old" prosecutions, it is likely that plaintiff's lawyers will only take "old" cases that have strong factual foundations, including corroborative evidence.

CONCLUSION

The law has long contained a fundamental contradiction concerning child sexual abuse. On the one hand, the law abhors such actions because children are especially vulnerable; on the other hand, it often ignores the implications of their vulnerability by imposing statutes of limitation that are unsympathetic to actual victims. Unfortunately, the debate over whether adults who were sexually abused as children should be able to press civil or criminal charges has been dominated by a narrow and increasingly arcane debate about trauma and the suppression of memory. That debate overlooks the vast majority of adults who were sexually abused as children. It also provides an unduly limited framework for discussing forgetting (Freyd, 1996: 16–27). Most adult victims have "always remembered" such abuse, although knowing that with a certainty is impossible given the phenomenon of episodic memory. But many of those people still face serious obstacles to coming to terms with the abuse and reaching the point where a meaningful decision about legal redress is possible. For this vast but overlooked population, there are powerful reasons for reforming statutes of limitation along the lines suggested above. Doing anything less is equivalent to granting civil and criminal immunity to those countless child molesters who succeed in keeping their misdeeds secret long enough.

Notes

1. Victims of two notorious pedophiles in Smith Falls, Ontario, issued a public statement thanking police for pursuing the "old" case, indicating that the process had "given us back our personhood" (Abraham, 1993: A5), and victims of former Catholic priest James Porter made similar statements, rejoicing that they obtained "freedom from the past" (Corriea & Borg, 1993: A6).

2. Yapko (1994: 31) warns that care must be taken to distinguish "(1) those cases in which someone knows and has known all along that he or she was abused from (2) those cases in which someone independently remembers repressed memories from (3) those cases in which a therapist facilitates recall of

repressed memories from (4) those cases in which a therapist *suggests* memories of abuse." The final category is Yapko's sole concern. Obviously, those cases can only be identified through case-by-case decision-making. Unfortunately, many who share Yapko's concern about improper suggestion fail to heed his caution about reserving judgment until cases are examined on their facts.

3. Pedophiles are often compulsive about recording their experiences and the resulting evidence can be devastating. James O'Boyle, a police officer in East Rockhill Township, Pennsylvania, recorded his sexual encounters with at least fifteen boys over twenty years in his date books (Fried, 1987: 128). A diary found in the Reverend Gary Timmons's apartment in 1995, after he was arrested for molesting boys at a Catholic school in the 1970s, contained notes "describing his sexual encounters with underage California boys" (*San Francisco Chronicle*, 1995: A17). In a similar case, assorted documentary evidence found in a police officer's locker prompted charges that the officer had molested a Rhode Island woman more than twenty years before, when she was between four and six years old (Hulick, 1996a).

4. The defendant's conviction was recently overturned by the Rhode Island Supreme Court, and he can only be retried *without* the testimony of the other women. *State v. Quattrocchi* (681 A.2d 879, R.I. 1996). Curiously, the False Memory Syndrome Foundation trumpeted the court case as a "victory" without mentioning the testimony of the two others, including the defendant's own goddaughter (Cheit, 1999: 307).

5. Since these kinds of memories have often been recognized as "cued" (that is, triggered by, say, a particular sight or smell), it would be interesting to know in what sense they were "always accessible" when, as is often the case, the trigger is external.

6. The number of strongly corroborated cases of recovered memory is actually much larger than has been acknowledged in popular or academic writings about the subject of recovered memory (see generally, Recovered Memory Project, 2000; Cheit, 1998).

References

Abraham, Carolyn. 1993. "Not Just Part of a Career." *Ottawa Citizen* (December 17): A5.

American Law Institute. 1956. *Model Penal Code and Commentary.* 87.

American Prosecutors Research Institute. 1994. *Legislation Extending or Removing Statutes of Limitations for Offenses Against Children* (Alexandria, VA: National Center for Prosecution of Child Abuse).

Arnold, David. 1992. "Priest Who Left Worcester Still Controversial in Canada." *Boston Globe* (August 6): 29.

Brown, Daniel, Alan W. Sheflin, and Charles Whitfield. 1999. "Recovered Memories: The Current Weight of the Evidence in Science and in the Courts." *Journal of Psychiatry and the Law* 27, no. 1 (Spring): 5–156.

Cheit, Ross E. 1999. "Junk Skepticism and Recovered Memory: A Reply to Piper." *Ethics & Behavior* 9, no. 4: 295–318.

———. 1998. "Consider This, Skeptics of Recovered Memory." *Ethics & Behavior* 8 no. 2: 141–60.

Cheit, Ross E., and Erica Goldschmidt. 1997. "Child Molesters in the Criminal Justice System: A Comprehensive Case-Flow Analysis of the Rhode Island Docket (1985–1993)." *New England Journal on Criminal and Confinement* 23, no. 2 (Summer): 267–301.

Conte, Jon R. 1986. *A Look at Child Sexual Abuse* (Chicago: National Committee for the Prevention of Child Abuse).

Corriea, Robert, and Linda Borg. 1993. "'I'm Sorry,' Porter weeps." *Providence Journal-Bulletin* (December 7): A1.

Ernsdorff, Gary M., and Elizabeth F. Loftus. 1993. "Let Sleeping Memories Lie? Words of Caution About Tolling the Statute of Limitations in Cases of Memory Repression." *Journal of Criminal Law & Criminology* 84, no. 1: 129–74.

Freyd, Jennifer J. 1996. *Betrayal Trauma: The Logic of Forgetting Childhood Sexual Abuse* (Cambridge, MA: Harvard University Press).

Fried, Stephen. 1994. "War of Remembrance." *Philadelphia Magazine* (January): 66–71, 149–57.

———. 1987. "Boy Crazy." *Philadelphia Magazine* (October): 127–32, 178–205.

Gardner, Martin. 1993. "The False Memory Syndrome." *Skeptical Inquirer* (Summer): 370–75.

Gardner, Richard. 1992. *True and False Accusations of Child Sex Abuse* (Cresskill, NJ: Creative Therapeutics).

Gray, Ellen. 1993. *Unequal Justice: The Prosecution of Child Sexual Abuse* (New York: Free Press).

Herman, Judith. 1992. *Trauma and Recovery* (New York: Basic Books).

Hoffman, Richard. 1995. *Half the House* (New York: Harcourt Brace & Co.).

———. 1999. "All One Struggle." Manuscript of Keynote Address to the To Tell the Truth Conference. Rhode Island College, Providence, RI, November 7.

Hu, Winnie. 2000. "Pataki Calls for End to Limit on Prosecuting Rape Cases." *New York Times* (February 10): B4.

Hulick, Doane. 1996a. "Ex-officer Accused of Raping Girl Wants Evidence Suppressed." *Providence Journal-Bulletin* (March 13): 1, B3.

———. 1996b. "Retired Priest, 75, is Charged with Raping Girl in 1965." *Providence Journal-Bulletin* (March 29): 1, B4.

Jones, David A. 1981. *The Law of Criminal Procedure* (Boston: Little, Brown).

Lamb, Sharon. 1996. *The Trouble With Blame* (Cambridge, MA: Harvard University Press).

Loftus, Elizabeth F. 1993. "The Reality of Repressed Memories." *American Psychologist* 48, no. 5 (May): 518–37.

Loftus, Elizabeth F. 1995. "Remembering Dangerously." *Skeptical Inquirer* (March): 19–29.

Loftus, Elizabeth F., Maryanne Garry, and Julie Feldman. 1994. "Forgetting Sexual Trauma: What Does It Mean When 38% Forget?" *Journal of Consulting and Clinical Psychology* 62, no. 6: 1177–81.

McNamara, Mark. 1995. "Fade Away: The Rise and Fall of the Repressed-Memory Theory in the Courtroom." *California Lawyer* 15, no. 3 (March): 36–42.

Minow, Martha. 1999a. "Memory and Hate: Are There Lessons From Around the World?" Manuscript of Gilbane Fund Lecture, Number 1. Brown University, Providence, RI, October 19.

———. 1999b. "Between Nations and Intimates: Can Law Stop the Violence?" Manuscript of Gilbane Fund Lecture, Number 3. Brown University, Providence, RI, November 2.

New York Times. 1993. "A Guilty Plea to Molesting 28 Children as a Priest" (October 5): A22.

Pendergrast, Mark. 1995. *Victims of Memory* (Hinesburg, VT: Upper Access Press).

Prosser, William L. 1971. *The Law of Torts* (St. Paul, MN: West Publishing Co.).

Providence Journal-Bulletin. 1995. "Former Priest Convicted of Sexual Assault." *Providence Journal-Bulletin* (July 12): C1.

Recovered Memory Project. 2001. Ross E. Cheit, ed. *http://www.brown.edu/Departments/Taubman_Center/Recovmem/Archive.html*

Robinson, Paul. 2000. "Justice Can Never Come Too Late." *Washington Post* (May 3): A23.

Salit, Richard. 1995. "2 Former Scout Leaders Face Assault Charges." *Providence Journal-Bulletin* (June 16): A1, 10.

Saltzman, Jonathan. 1994. "Jury Finds Quattrocchi Guilty of Sexual Assault." *Providence Journal-Bulletin* (July 1): C5.

San Francisco Chronicle. 1995. "North Bay Priest's Papers Tell About Molestations" (November 11): A17.

Sheflin, Alan W., and Daniel Brown. 1997. "Repressed Memory or Dissociative Amnesia: What the Science Says." *Journal of Psychiatry and Law* 24, no. 2 (Summer): 143–88.

Turner, Kiban, 1996. "Traumatic Memory" (Unpublished master's paper, Department of Psychology, Duke University, Durham, NC).

Uelman, Gerald F. 1983. "Making Sense Out of the California Criminal Statue of Limitations." *Pacific Law Journal* 15, no. 1 (October): 35–83.

Wall Street Journal. 1993. "A Clear Voice" (October 8): A14.

Williams, Linda Meyer. 1994. "Recall of Childhood Trauma: A Prospective Study of Women's Memories of Child Sexual Abuse." *Journal of Consulting and Clinical Psychology* 62, no. 6: 1167–76.

Williams, Mary R. 2000. "History and Analysis of Delayed Discovery Statutes of

Limitations in Adult Survivor Litigation." *Journal of Aggression, Maltreatment &*
Trauma 3, no. 2: 49–71.

Yapko, Michael. 1994. *Suggestions of Abuse* (New York: Simon & Schuster).

Legal Cases

Commonwealth v. Sher, 1999 Pa. Super. 138 (1999).

Hammer v. Hammer, 142 Wis.2d 257; 418 N.W.2d 23 (Wis.App. 1987)

K.M. v. M.H. (1992) 3 S.C.R. 6 [Canada].

Prudential-LMI Ins. v. Superior Court, 51 Cal.3d 674; 274 Cal.Rptr. 387; 798 P.2d
1230 (Cal. 1990).

Riley V. Presnell, 409 Mass. 239; 565 N.E.2d 780 (Mass. 1991).

Shamloo v. Lifespring, Inc., 713 F.Supp. 14 (D.D.C. 1989).

State v. Quattrocchi, 681 A. 2d 879 (R.I. 1996).

Tyson v. Tyson, 107 Wash.2d 72; 727 P.2d 226 (Wash. 1986).

8

Peace on Earth Begins at Home: Reflections from the Women's Liberation Movement

JUDITH LEWIS HERMAN

How can we stop violence against women? This has been a central question facing the international women's movement in the last three decades. As feminists have sought to name and understand the vast scope of this problem, we have also begun to think about political violence in new ways. Following Minow, I would like to expand on some of the commonalities of violence between nations and between intimates.

First, a point that may seem obvious, but that is all too often overlooked, is that violence works. People often use violence to get what they want. In sexual and domestic life, violence is used worldwide by men to dominate women. In the United States, a recent national survey, conducted by the National Institute of Justice in collaboration with the Communicable Disease Center, reports that 18 percent of women have been victims of rape, and 22 percent have been beaten by an intimate partner (Tjaden & Thoennes, 1998). Most such crimes are never reported to police. Victims fear the consequences of disclosure because, more often than not, the perpetrators are well-respected men, and their crimes are socially condoned. The high prevalence of sexual and domestic violence is by no means unique to this country. Throughout the world, crimes such as wife-beating, rape, rape-murder, honor killings, dowry killings, and witch-burnings serve a political function of intimidation, reminding women of their place (United Nations Population Fund, 2000). These acts of violence, often carried out in a ritualized fashion similar to lynching, are both expressions of a system of male supremacy and a means of perpetuating it (Brownmiller, 1975).

When it comes to communal or national conflict, people also frequently use violence to get what they want. One group of people may want to drive another group out of a disputed territory or kill them and take possession of their land. A recent example would be the campaigns of "ethnic cleansing" in the Balkans. Or one group of people may want to establish tyranny over another in order to benefit from their labor and service. The Apartheid system of South Africa represents an extreme modern example. These crude aims, common to the long history of warfare, have lost none of their popular appeal in the modern world, though they may be cloaked in modern racist, religious, or nationalist rhetoric. They cannot be realized without systematic resort to violence.

Systems of Coercive Control

While violence is necessary to establish and maintain a system of dominance, it is rarely sufficient. A well-established system of coercive control aims to legitimate the power of the perpetrator, so that overt displays of force are rarely required. When dominance achieves legitimacy, the violence upon which it ultimately rests is hidden, minimized, or excused. Violence is also far more effective when combined with other methods of control. As battered women say: it's not just the violence. It is the entire system of coercive control that enables a batterer to control his family, a gangster to control a neighborhood, or a small ruling elite to establish tyranny over an entire nation.

Similar methods of coercive control are practiced worldwide, whether in the vast political prisons of a police state or in the intimate prisons of abusive families (Amnesty International, 1973). The perpetrator seeks to monopolize and control the sources of information, to isolate his victims from any potential social support, and to suppress any signs of autonomy or initiative. Isolation may be carried out by physical seclusion and restraint, or just as effectively by shaming and social degradation. Autonomy and initiative are broken down by intrusive regulation of the patterns of daily life, by capricious enforcement of inconsistent and petty rules, and by interspersing feared punishments with occasional unpredictable rewards. These methods, consistently applied, tend to reinforce the belief that the perpetrator is all-powerful and break down any external signs of resistance.

For some perpetrators, however, outward submission is not enough. They are satisfied with nothing less than total surrender of the will. This is the ultimate fantasy of the totalitarian dictator, the torturer, the pedophile, the sadist (Goodwin, 1993). As long as the victim is able to maintain any degree of dignity or self-respect, the perpetrator's dominance is not complete. Perhaps the most effective way to destroy a victim's self-respect is to force her to betray her own moral principles or her most valued relationships. Once this has happened, the victim may offer no further resistance, because she no longer feels that she deserves to live. Many systems of coercive control develop elaborate degradation rituals to destroy the victim's moral identity and to alienate her from family and community. The sociologist Orlando Patterson describes these rituals as an essential feature of slavery (1982). Degradation rituals are also highly developed in totalitarian systems and in some religious cults, and they are central to the practice of violence in intimate relationships.

We do not yet understand how individual perpetrators, in privacy, manage to reinvent the same coercive methods that are practiced in totalitarian political or religious systems. In many authoritarian, all-male organizations, initiates may be taught to participate in demeaning or frankly violent attacks on women as part of group bonding. For example, research on the prevalence of rape on college campuses has found that assaultive and coercive behavior toward women is fostered in groups such as sports teams and fraternities (Koss, 1994). The pornography industry is another common cultural transmitter of sadistic fantasies and practices. A frank ideology of domination pervades the pornographic media; indeed, some feminist theorists have proposed that the erotization of dominance is the defining characteristic of pornography (MacKinnon & Dworkin, 1997). A considerable body of literature suggests that pornography renders most viewers more callous toward women, and reduces inhibitions among men already disposed to sexual violence (Malamuth & Donnerstein, 1984).

Another important link between private and political violence may also be found in the organization of the commercial sex industry. Prostitution of women and children occurs worldwide. We have little reliable data on the full scope of the sex trade; we do know, however, that it ranks very high in the commerce of the world. The power to buy sex is an accepted male entitlement in many cultures, including our own. We also know that the demand for commercial sex cannot be fulfilled without recourse to violence. Women, even desperately poor women, simply do not volunteer for prostitution in anywhere near sufficient numbers to satisfy the market. This is the case even in countries where prostitution has been decriminalized or legalized. Moreover, a major portion of the sex trade involves children and adolescents, who cannot volunteer, and therefore must be recruited by deception or force. The sex trade, whether on a local, national, or international level, is largely controlled by criminal gangs (Hughes, 2000).

John Keegan, the military historian, calls attention to the durability of so-called "irregular" forces throughout the ages and across cultures (1993). These are cohesive and secretive groups of men, often bound by elaborate symbols and rituals, an ideology of heroic superiority, contempt for civilians—especially women and children—and a glorification of violence. In modern terms they are the gangsters, the secret police, the death squads, the paramilitaries of the world. They are the "made men" who carry out programs of ethnic cleansing and keep dictatorships running. They are also the men who organize the local and global traffic in drugs, guns, and sex. Systematized methods of coercion are part of the working repertoire of local gangsters. In prostitution, these methods must be developed to a high art, since the entire enterprise depends upon the control of women's bodies. Thus the pimp, a familiar figure throughout the world, may be an important intermediary beween the practices of private and political violence.

The sex trade might also be considered an endemic reservoir in which methods of coercive control are maintained and refined, to be called upon in times of war. The enslavement of so-called "comfort women" by the Japanese military during World War II is an example that has only recently been brought to public attention. In this case, an existing criminal enterprise was nationalized and incorporated essentially unchanged into the war-fighting machinery of the state. In the propaganda of the time, this practice was legitimated through the common fiction of the willing victim; the prostituted women were officially called "patriotic volunteers for the Emperor." Their true status was more apparent in the popular epithet "sanitary public toilets." Their social dishonor was so extreme that even fifty years later, in the first lawsuit filed against the Japanese government, only one victim was willing to reveal her name. Kim Hak-soon, a sixty-eight-year-old Korean woman, testified that she decided to come forward only after all of her close relatives were dead, so that her disclosures would not bring shame upon them. The feminists who exposed these atrocities pointed out that while official state sponsorship of prostitution ended with the war, widespread trafficking in Asian women persists to this day, with passive if not active collusion of the authorities (Watanabe, 1994).

Resistance and Intervention

For victims of intimate violence, effective resistance begins with understanding that violence is a means to an end. If the purpose of the violence is to establish dominance, then the strategy of resistance must engage the entire system of coercive control rather than reacting to isolated acts of violence. A new conceptual language is often required to clarify the nature of the problem and to challenge the rationalizations and excuses that legitimate the violent behavior. Battering, stalking, and sexual harassment are terms developed by the women's movement to describe types of calculated and relentless oppression to which women are frequently subjected. In this country it has taken three decades for the feminist movement to effect a significant change in public attitudes toward sexual and domestic violence. In each instance, it has been necessary to reframe public understanding of these crimes, so that they are understood not as episodic, impulsive acts of "passion" but as systematic efforts to keep women in a subordinate state. As awareness of domestic violence has increased, as more services and legal protections have become available, and as social tolerance for domestic violence has declined, it appears that more women are escaping sooner from violent relationships. We are even beginning to see some hopeful signs that in this country the death rate from domestic violence has begun to decline (Fox & Zawitz, 2000).

For individual victims, the path to recovery begins with the ability to name the problem and disclose it to others. As in the case of the so-called "comfort women," victims who speak out often risk public disgrace as well as retaliation by the perpetrator. That is why the organizing strategy of the feminist movement begins with the creation of confidential relationships in small groups of women, where secrets can be shared without shame. The mutual support of the group is a powerful antidote to the fear and isolation imposed by the perpetrator. Once victims feel some sense of belonging, they may find the courage to expose the violence and to challenge its legitimacy.

The next step is the creation of a safety plan. This is a concept developed most fully in the battered women's movement. Establishing safety is a complex project that requires careful attention to each woman's particular circumstances. She must come to a realistic assessment of the risks she faces and develop a strategy for self-protection and economic survival. She must consider whether she can remain in her own home environment, whether temporary flight to shelter or a safe haven may be necessary, and whether and under what circumstances she might seek intervention. These considerations are fraught with danger, because initial signs of resistance are likely to be met with an escalation of violence. There is no one formula for ending the violence. There is considerable evidence, however, that appeasement does not work. Most perpetrators respond only to clear and decisive intervention by persons in a position of authority. This intervention may take the form of a civil protection order, police arrest, or, in the most serious cases, criminal prosecution.

For bystanders who might wish to help stop the violence, several obstacles may present themselves. Minow identifies apathy as the most serious impediment to action, but apathy may be a mask for ignorance, confusion, or fear. Bystanders may fail to recognize a pattern of coercive control and may tend to dismiss incidents of violence as an unfortunate aberration or as a private quarrel for which both parties are equally to blame. The perpetrator's denials and rationalizations are often convincing, especially when buttressed by claims of familial sovereignty. Bystanders are often deterred by the argument that the victim's plight is simply none of their business. It may be also difficult for bystanders to empathize with the victim. Most victims do not behave according to sentimental notions of nobility and innocence. People who have been subjected to coercive control are often profoundly demoralized. Their capacity for initiative and autonomous action may have broken down under the domination of the perpetrator. Their behavior may appear ambivalent or even at times frankly self-destructive. This makes it all too easy to blame them for their own predicament.

Then there is the practical difficulty of confronting perpetrators. Because so much is at stake, most perpetrators are not inclined to give up without a fight. Bystanders who seek to intervene may risk harm to themselves, and the cost of intervention is generally more than anyone wants to pay. Token displays of concern, or even of force, are rarely effective. Establishing safety is a serious undertaking, requiring careful strategy, well-coordinated mobilization of resources, and sustained attention over a prolonged period of time. It is hard to stay engaged without becoming as obsessive as the perpetrators themselves. For all of these reasons, bystanders often fall into a pattern of ineffective intervention. Long periods of denial or appeasement may be punctuated by brief episodes of arbitrary resort to force. This inconsistent behavior may actually worsen the plight of victims and deepen their feelings of isolation and despair.

One of the first studies of police intervention in domestic violence cases demonstrated that a policy of mandatory arrest was the most effective deterrent to further incidents of violence (Sherman & Berk, 1984). I believe that such policies were effective because they were clear, simple, and consistent, and because they forced the police to take domestic violence seriously for the first time. Mandatory arrest policies provided a powerful antidote to ingrained police attitudes of ambivalence or frank sympathy for perpetrators. More recently, many advocates for battered women have argued that such policies are too inflexible, and should be modified to allow greater self-determination for victims (Mills, 1998). Clearly, any intervention that denies power and agency to victims is ultimately self-defeating. Intervention is most likely to be effective when it is based on a strong cooperative alliance between the victim and the intervening third parties.

Analogies in the political realm are legion. The recent history of peace-keeping efforts in the Balkans offers a tragic lexicon of ambivalent and ineffective interventions. For years, bystanders ignored or misinterpreted clear indications of a murderous policy of domination. It was only too easy to rationalize inaction by attributing the violence to "ancient ethnic hatreds," for which all parties were equally to blame, rather than to one group's organized and systematic aggession (Malcolm, 1996). A textbook example of an ineffective "safety plan" would be the establishment of the so-called "safe haven" in the Bosnian city of Srebrenica. In this case, the peacekeepers did not merely fail to deter aggression, but actually facilitated it, both by their own inadequate display of force, and by their efforts to prevent the persecuted group from organizing in its own defense. The tragic result was a massacre in which peacekeeping troops were forced to act as accomplices. This outcome was only too predictable to anyone who has worked for any length of time in the battered women's movement. Belatedly, would-be peacekeeprs discovered the same principles that have proven effective in cases of domestic violence. The violence stopped only when the bystanders finally took a clear and unambiguous stand in defense of the victims and intervened with sufficient force to contain the aggressors.

Recovery and Reconciliation

Once safety has been established, survivors often need assistance to recover from the effects of prolonged and repeated exposure to violence. Fear, bitterness, shame, and self-hatred may persist long after the relationship of coercive control has ended. In order to overcome the legacy of violence, survivors need the opportunity for some kind of reckoning with the past. They need to be able to make sense of their experience to themselves and to tell their stories to others. And they need some form of social acknowledgment of the injustice they have suffered, in order to restore their dignity and repair their sense of connection to a larger community (Herman, 1992).

Then there is the question of what is to be done with the perpetrators. People who have grown accustomed to getting their way by force have little incentive to change. Battered women have learned this the hard way. Many, if not most victims of domestic violence do not initially wish to end the relationship; they simply want the violence to stop. They often hope for reconciliation and are eager for their partners to seek "help."

Batterers, however, rarely think there is anything wrong with their behavior. Even those who genuinely regret the violence generally feel entitled to control their partners, and view violence as a legitimate last resort. Treatment programs for batterers have had limited success in changing these attitudes. Their main effect seems to be on victims rather than on perpetrators. The supervision of a domestic violence treatment program buys battered women some time to get their lives together, so that they are prepared for permanent separation once they realize that their partners are not going to change. For sex offenders, the treatment success rate is even less impressive. Motivation for change is generally low. Most perpetrators deny or minimize their offenses, blame others for their troubles, and seem to lack empathy for their victims. A court mandate is generally needed to enforce even token compliance. At best, long-term treatment offers the kind of close external monitoring that seems to be required if these men are ever to be integrated safely into their communities (Barbaree & Marshall, 1998).

Crimes of violence against women are still, for the most part, crimes of impunity. Most victims do not seek justice in court. Among those who do, a surprising number are not primarily interested in seeing the offender punished. Rather, they want to ensure that the offender will no longer be permitted to abuse other people or to profit from his crimes. In addition, they often want some material restitution for the harm done to them. But beyond these concrete and practical measures, what victims want most is vindication. They want the bystanders, finally, to take a stand. They want public acknowledgment that what the perpetrators did to them was wrong. They want the burden of shame lifted from their shoulders and placed where it belongs.

In the United States, the Victims of Crime Act (1984) introduced a number of reforms designed to make it easier for victims to seek justice. These include first, the possibility of obtaining compensation for the expense of medical or mental health treatment, based on an administrative complaint. This grants victims some recognition of the harm that has been done and supports their efforts to recover, without requiring them to endure the rigors of an adversarial legal process. Because victim compensation funds are drawn from fines on convicted offenders, the award of compensation constitutes an indirect form of social restitution. No compensation can ever fully remedy the harm of violent crime. Victims derive great moral satisfaction, however, from the knowledge that offenders have been compelled to contribute to their recovery.

Additional reforms aimed to make the criminal justice system less intimidating to victims and encourage them to come forward. Courts were staffed for the first time with Victim-Witness Advocates, who could explain the complexities of the legal system, help victims prepare for trial, and accompany victims in court. In cases where the offender was convicted or pled guilty, victims were granted the opportunity to address the court at sentencing, giving what is called a "Victim-Impact Statement." These measures were designed to give the victim a greater voice in the justice system and to restore trust between the victim and her community. Recent studies indicate that such reforms do indeed increase victims' sense of satisfaction with the justice system (Kilpatrick et al., 1998).

In the political arena, countries emerging from war or dictatorship face similar questions of justice and restitution. How can amends be made to victims? How can perpetrators be held accountable? How can victims and perpetrators go on living in the same community? Like victims of intimate violence, victims of political violence need a respectful and open forum for public witnessing and acknowledgment of the wrongs done to them. Granting victims a voice is particularly important where crimes have been committed under the cloak of state legitimacy.

The most highly developed recent example of such a forum on a national level is South Africa's Truth and Reconciliation Commission (TRC). In this unprecedented experiment in national consciousness-raising, testimony was heard from over 20,000 people, and hearings were broadcast daily on radio and television. Like the victims of sexual and domestic violence, the vast majority of the victims of state-sponsored violence who testified before the TRC did not seem interested primarily in punishment of the offenders. Rather, they sought restoration of their own sense of dignity, through public recognition of the injustices they had suffered (Krog, 1998).

Because amnesty for political crimes was contingent on individual confessions, the TRC was also very successful in breaking down the perpetrators' denials. With over 8,000 confessions, the TRC was able to document organized criminal activity at the highest levels of government (Meredith, 1999). These revelations, though they came as no surprise to the black majority, established an uncontested history of massive, state-sponsored human rights violations that discredited the Apartheid system even among many of its white beneficiaries. However, granting amnesty to perpetrators left unresolved the question of accountability. Like the perpetrators of sexual and domestic violence, the vast majority of offenders who filed amnesty applications felt entitled to power and did not regret their crimes. They confessed simply to avoid the risk of prosecution (Gobodo-Madikizela, 1999). Once they acknowledged the facts, they were acquitted of any further responsibility for either apology or restitution to their victims. It is hard to imagine satisfactory social reconciliation under such conditions.

The Victims of Crime Act (VOCA) model for victim compensation, though it was developed for individual crime victims, might also be useful for nations attempting to rebuild in the aftermath of war or dictatorship. This model offers a new way of resolving the vexing question of accountability, by placing the burden of restitution on criminal perpetrators *as a group*. This avoids the twin pitfalls of accountability that is either too specific or too general. Holding individual perpetrators accountable for compensating their victims is too specific. Too many legitimate claims will go uncompensated, simply because the particular torturer, rapist, or murderer cannot be identified or caught. On the other hand, holding an entire society accountable for the crimes of a minority is too general. It is not clear, for instance, that a democratic successor government can justly be required to pay reparations for crimes committed under a previous dictatorship that was detested by a majority of its own subjects. Often, as in the case of South Africa, it is hard to give priority to the claims of victims when an entire country has been plundered and impoverished.

In the VOCA model, the monies for victim compensation are not drawn from general tax revenues, but rather from a trust fund based on fines levied on convicted perpetrators. Thus, the government does not assume direct responsibility for the damages, but it does assume responsibility for bringing perpetrators to justice, collecting fines, and recovering any stolen assets. Symbolic show trials of a few egregious offenders are less important, in this model, than systematic enforcement of the law against endemic criminal behavior. Compensation for any particular victim does not depend on conviction of the particular person who wronged her, but perpetrators as a group are held accountable for making some amends, both to victims and to the community.

The case of the women forced into prostitution by the Japanese army during World War II illustrates the importance of the principle of accountability. Because the Japanese government has so far refused either to apologize or to compensate victims, a group of former "comfort women" have chosen to press their claims in the U.S. courts, arguing that ordinary limits of jurisdiction do not apply in cases of massive human rights violations. This case is a conceptual landmark. In Minow's terms, it extends the boundaries of the rule of law. It challenges both the traditional concepts of sovereignty that have protected state-sponsored violence, and the traditional concepts of privacy that have protected sexual and domestic violence. It also exposes prostitution as a form of organized crime at the intersection of the public and private spheres.

Although private donors have offered compensation to the victims, most have refused to accept the money, even though many are elderly and in need. Clearly, these women understand that money alone is meaningless as a form of restitution. They rightly insist that those responsible for the crimes, individually or as a group, must be the ones to pay damages. It is not the place of bystanders to offer compensation. Bystanders can contribute much more to social healing by joining with victims in their fight to hold perpetrators accountable for their crimes. When victims perceive that the larger society recognizes the legitimacy of their cause, and is willing to take action on their behalf, social reconciliation can begin.

References

Amnesty International. (1973). *Report on torture*. London: Amnesty International Publications.

Barbaree H. E., & Marshall, W. L. (1998). "Treatment of the sexual offender." In R. M. Wettstein, ed., *Treatment of offenders with mental disorders*. New York: Guilford.

Brownmiller, S. (1975). *Against our will: Men, women and rape*. New York: Simon & Schuster.

Fox, J. A., & Zawitz, M. A. (2000). *Homicide trends in the US*. Washington, DC: U.S. Department of Justice, Bureau of Justice Statistics.

Gobodo-Madikizela, P. (1999). Personal communication.

Goodwin, J. M. (1993). "Human vectors of trauma: Illustrations from the Marquis de Sade." In J. M. Goodwin, ed., *Rediscovering childhood trauma: Historical casebook and clinical applications.* Washington, DC: American Psychiatric Press.

Herman, J. L. (1992). *Trauma and recovery.* New York: Basic Books.

Hughes, D. M. (2000). "Men create the demand: Women are the supply." Lecture at Queen Sofia Center, Valencia, Spain (November).

Keegan, J. (1993). *A history of warfare.* New York: Knopf.

Kilpatrick, D. G., Beatty, D., & Howley, S. S. (1998). *The rights of crime victims— Does legal protection make a difference?* Washington, DC: National Institute of Justice Research in Brief (December).

Koss, M. (1994). *No safe haven: Male violence against women at home, at work and in the community.* Washington, DC: American Psychological Association.

Krog, A. (1998). *Country of my skull.* Johannesburg: Random House South Africa.

Malamuth, N., & Donnerstein, E. (1984). *Pornography and sexual aggression.* New York: Academic Press.

Malcolm, N. (1996). *Bosnia: A short history.* New York: New York University Press.

MacKinnon, C. A., & Dworkin, A. (1997). *In harm's way: The pornography civil rights hearings.* Cambridge, MA: Harvard University Press.

Meredith, M. (1999). *Coming to terms: South Africa's search for truth.* New York: Public Affairs.

Mills, L. G. (1998). *The heart of intimate abuse: New interventions in child welfare, criminal justice and health settings.* New York: Springer.

Patterson, O. (1982). *Slavery and social death.* Cambridge, MA: Harvard University Press.

Sherman, L. W., & Berk, R. A. (1984). "The specific deterrent effects of arrest for domestic assault." *American Sociological Review* 49: 261–72.

Tjaden, P. & Thoennes, N. (1998). *Prevalence, incidence and consequences of violence against women: A national survey.* Washington, DC: U.S. Department of Justice NCJ 172837.

United Nations Population Fund. (2000). *Lives together, worlds apart: Men and women in a time of change.* New York: United Nations Population Fund.

Watanabe, K. (1994). "Militarism, colonialism, and the trafficking of women: 'Comfort Women' forced into sexual labor for Japanese soldiers." *Bulletin of Concerned Asian Scholars* 4: 3–16.

9

The Thin Line between Imposition and Consent: A Critique of Birthright Membership Regimes and Their Implications

AYELET SHACHAR

Introduction

Martha Minow's inspiring 1999 Gilbane Fund lectures challenge us to face our own tendencies to exclude, marginalize, oppress, and dehumanize certain of our fellow human beings because of their group identity. Rejecting the tendency to turn a blind eye to these most depressing aspects of cultural, religious, ethnic, and national diversity, Minow's clear and passionate voice challenges us to think creatively about new ways to use law as a means to seek remedies for those who have been harmed, and to prevent, as far as possible, similar recurrences in the future. Minow, in short, encourages us to take responsibility and action for breaking such patterns of hatred. Her Gilbane lectures offer an important and innovative contribution to the recent attempt to develop *restorative* concepts of justice in place of the traditional retributive understandings of law and conflict resolution.[1]

But there is another theme that runs through these lectures. Minow calls for an uncompromising search for responses to mass atrocities that can rebuild trust and accountability in the face of past cruelty. This search implicitly directs her argument to the spaces and means through which intergroup hatred and violence are created and maintained. Minow's lectures describe incidents for which the boundaries that distinguish victims from perpetrators (according to their group membership) are already constituted and clearly marked. What falls beyond the bounds of Minow's excellent discussion is an exploration of how these boundaries are constructed and sustained over time. After all, an individual cannot be targeted because of ethnic, religious, or national affiliations, if there are no preconceived boundaries and procedures for maintaining such identities.

In this comment paper, I therefore wish to step back from the immediate and urgent problems of hatred and violence, and pursue an inquiry into the birthright rules that shape and uphold the demarcation of difference between persons as a result of their group membership.[2] Nowadays it is common to recognize that group-based identities are not biologically inscribed; rather, they are socially constructed and historically constituted—often through law.[3] This understanding serves as the basis of my analysis. However, I want to suggest that this understanding of identity raises as many problems as it resolves. For example, the social construction theory does not explain what precise legal mechanisms are used to define, maintain, and ultimately assign meaning to group membership as the boundary that distinguishes insiders from outsiders.[4] Nor does this theory provide satisfactory answers to inquiries concerning the uneasy relationship between choice and imposition in the construction of identity. In beginning to address these questions, this chapter focuses on the normative problems that are created by the allotment of membership in a religious or national community by virtue of birthright. Specifically, my aim is to disentangle some unexpected connections between the highly charged and topical issues of personal law, group membership, and birthright citizenship.

I pursue this task by schematically presenting and critically evaluating two distinct membership and status-allocating mechanisms: those that automatically designate individuals into specific religious communities (*personal law regimes*); and those that designate individuals into specific national communities (*citizenship-attribution rules*). What follows is my attempt—inspired by the threads that Minow's lectures weave so deftly between family and nation (or the "intimate" and the "collective")—to extend them into a critique of the principle of birthright membership itself.[5]

My argument advances in three major steps. In section one, I describe the use of religious personal law as a means of drawing boundaries and perpetuating "difference" between and among citizens who belong to the same body politic. In section two, I spell out the basic difficulties that are generated by legal procedures that uphold birthright membership, such as those maintained by religious personal law regimes. I demonstrate this by discussing several interconnected problems that may severely limit the right of choice and of exit of individuals who have been ascriptively assigned membership in such communities. Turning from the group level to the state level, in section three I show how many of the problems that are easily visible when the subject of discussion is an "imposed" religious identity, are in fact replicated through the prevalent legal principles for attributing citizenship status in modern political communities: namely, *jus sanguinis* and *jus soli*.[6] Some combination of these legal principles are accepted by virtually all countries in the world as the factors giving an individual automatic status as a full member of a particular political community.[7]

This chapter closes by offering some unexpected and disturbing conclusions about the role of those arenas marked off as "intimate" in the public construction of the collective—not only in minority communities, but also in constituting the citizenry of liberal polities. I conclude by pointing to the deep and uncomfortable similarities (which we often prefer to ignore) between the modern state's continued reliance on birthright principles in the assignment of citizenship, and the much-criticized uses of personal law in maintaining religious group identities.

I. Personal Law Regimes

Both contemporary and historical legal systems have at times permitted different sections of the population to be governed according to the specific ("personal") laws of their respective recognized religious communities, instead of the general ("territorial") laws of the state.[8] The application of such laws is *personal* (i.e., attached to the person), whereas the application of state law is *territorial* (i.e., based on physical presence in a given territorial unit).

Personal law regimes date back to the ancient world. They were also common during the medieval period, flourished on an Empire-wide level in the Ottoman *millet* system, and were widely recognized at the height of the colonial era. In their colonial variants, personal law regimes were often strategically used to help prevent social upheaval in the conquered territories. They created a delicate balance between the introduction of the colonizers' law (usually applied to the regulation of commerce and criminal law) and the preservation of certain pre-existing societal and legal norms (usually applied to the regulation of the conduct of women and the family).[9] One means of achieving this balance, which was particularly favored by the British in their administration of colonies in Asia and Africa, was to grant legal recognition to religious and customary rules that governed "private" relationships (such as marriage, adoption, legitimacy, inheritance, control over matrimonial property), as well as the definition of group membership *per se*.[10] According to this scheme of governance, different ethnic, religious, and tribal communities were recognized as being entitled to a degree of autonomous jurisdiction over matters of personal status and property, as well as membership demarcation, and held exclusive or preferred jurisdiction over these issues.

The allocation of such jurisdiction to different communities *within* a single political community institutionalizes a degree of legal pluralism, and allows cultural diversity to flourish. It diverges from the American constitutional tradition that erects a "high and impregnable wall of separation" between state and church (or law and religion). Such separation, as exercised in the United States, relegates the power of religious communities to the realm of voluntary association that belongs in civil society. Membership in such an association may bear important symbolic and spiritual value for the individual, but it does not subject that individual to the jurisdiction of the church in legal matters governed by the state.

A regime of personal law, on the other hand, elevates the binding authority of recognized religious communities to a plane equivalent or parallel to that of state law. This route to meeting the challenges of diversity generates serious dilemmas concerning the resolution of conflicts that may arise between competing sources of jurisdiction, such as group (or church) and state. Specific complications arise when defining the appropriate limitations that may be imposed upon such semi-autonomous communities, particularly where their traditional practices infringe on basic rights encoded in national constitutions or international conventions.[11] For a host of reasons (which I address in detail elsewhere), such in-group rights violations tend to injure women disproportionately, especially when the group's personal law regime curtails their freedom of choice and control over matters of personal status (such as entry into or exit from marriage), as well as their property entitlement in case of separation, divorce, or death of a spouse.[12]

Yet if personal law regimes are so flawed, gender discriminatory, and problematic (in terms of the complex conflict-of-law problems they generate), is it not reasonable to expect that they will disappear in due course from the law books of countries that still uphold them, especially in the current age of expedited transnational legal borrowing and cross-jurisdictional learning?[13] Theories of modernization, for example, suggest that personal law regimes will eventually disappear, as part of the "development path" of postcolonial societies. Instead of having many traditional sources of regulation, each affecting only a segment of the population (according to religious, ethnic, or racial affiliation), the modern state, so the argument goes, will consolidate exclusive legal authority. To date, however, there is no conclusive evidence to support this prediction. While various postcolonial societies have "rationed" their personal law systems since achieving national sovereignty, they have tended *not* to abandon these systems altogether. Personal law regimes, then, have been too prematurely pronounced creatures of the past.

Moreover, although we are accustomed to state-centered perceptions of law (which themselves rely on the modernist assumption that all persons belonging to a given sovereign unit are ultimately subject to a sole and normatively superior source of dispute resolution, for example, a national "supreme" court), this assumption itself is increasingly proving unrealistic—in Western as well as non-Western parts of the world.[14] With increased global interdependence, most legal activities are already governed by a complex mosaic of regulations deriving from national as well as local, provincial, regional, supranational, and international sources of law.[15] Personal law regimes can thus be viewed as yet another variant of the contemporary scenario in which overlapping sources of authority compete to regulate specific legal relationships. However, I treat them here as a distinct category because, unlike other potentially conflicting laws from within and beyond the state level, personal laws regulate the crucial question of *status*—the allocation of membership entitlement—based on some common group characteristic that is assigned to an individual *at birth*.[16]

Thus, when a child is born in a country where a system of plural personal laws is in effect, the child will automatically be assigned a religious affiliation. From that moment onward, the child will be subjected to the jurisdiction of that community's legal system (in those matters over which the community has gained binding authority over its members). This ascriptive classification of a child into a specific membership community is usually recorded in an official document, for example, a birth certificate or live-birth registry.[17] Personal law regimes that allocate religious (or other) group affiliations at birth are therefore by definition "difference-preserving." Each recognized religious community is, within this system, vested with the legal power to demarcate and police its own membership boundaries by defining which children it accepts as its "own." While state representatives are usually responsible for the process and apparatus of documenting the registration of the child with some state institution, it is the officials of each recognized religious group who determine whether a child is entitled to birthright membership in their respective community (in accordance with each group's recognized personal law and lineage rules).[18]

This "sorting" function has important public ramifications. Whereas one law should apply to all persons equally under the modernist conception, members of different groups are expected to be subject to different rules, according to their birthright membership affiliation under a personal law regime. Imposed group identity ties the child into the fabric of her religious community—often for life. It may also have a dramatic impact on the set of rights, resources, and opportunities that are open to her—especially under conditions of severe intergroup conflict, such as those discussed in Minow's lectures, where assigned membership in a victim's or perpetrator's group may make all the difference to those lives.

II. Problems Generated by Ascriptive Group Membership

In light of this brief exposition of what constitutes personal law regimes, in the following pages I explore the main normative problems that are generated when reliance on an automatic (and in certain cases, irrevocable) assignment of membership at birth—according to the respective communities' personal status and lineage rules—comes to determine which specific (group-based) rules will regulate key events in one's adult life. These problems include: the lack of initial choice and its long-term consequences; the concept of "naturalized" boundaries; the availability (or lack thereof) of avenues for internal change; and the potential for maltreatment of outsiders by group members. I examine each of these categories in turn.

Imposed identity A major objection to any system of personal law is that it automatically imposes a group affiliation upon the individual. When membership is assigned at birth, there is no mechanism for the exercise of initial choice by the individual: she will be treated, registered, and officially counted as a member solely because she is born to a parent who belongs to the community. This legal mechanism for allocating membership not only serves to demarcate the collective's boundaries (and to locate each individual in relation to those boundaries); it also subjects the individual to a set of rules and commitments encoded in the personal status laws of her group.

Still, the lack of initial choice could be considered a mere technicality, if it were easily revocable at a later stage, or if such membership did not carry a host of social meanings and legal obligations. However, in practice, an imposed affiliation often does carry such meanings and obligations. Moreover, leaving one's birthright religious community may prove legally and practically difficult, if not impossible.[19]

This lack of choice makes personal law regimes particularly oppressive. In violent, deeply divided societies, imposed group identity not only locates (and potentially traps) an individual in relation to a particular community. It also marks the individual as a potential victim of intergroup hatred because of the politicized animosity that is attached to group membership. Internal and external pressures may therefore make exit an unrealistic (and perhaps even an undesirable) option for a person born and raised in the midst of such conflicts, since his own sense of identity may already have been tainted by this heritage of hatred and distrust.

Membership and individual freedom An affiliation that is imposed on a person at birth, along with the constitutive experience of membership, can thus have lifelong consequences. No group membership is value-neutral; it affects the opportunities available to many of us, and our basic understanding of the world. This is because ascriptive birthright affiliation in a given community may determine the language we identify as our mother tongue, the culture we recognize as our own, the physical landscape we call "home," and the set of practices, beliefs, and values that are "naturally" intelligible to us (i.e., are part of a "shared vocabulary" that we come to recognize as our own, and that offers a context of choice in which meaning is attributed to different acts and norms).[20]

In other words, assigned membership in a collective is hardly ever simply a formality. Instead, it may significantly "constitute" the self. But does this ascriptive cultural membership inevitably *inhibit* personal freedom? For many years, modernization theory has held exactly that.[21] However, in recent years, several commentators have challenged this assumption (which, in turn, serves as the basis for the prediction that individuals will choose to give up their traditional identities in pursuit of greater autonomy, mobility, and choice).[22] These scholars argue that cultural memberships are crucial for *allowing*—rather than inhibiting—individual freedom, because such memberships ensure that we can make meaningful decisions within cultural narratives that provide the prisms through which we identify experiences as relevant and valuable.

Will Kymlicka, a prominent advocate of this view, explains that "freedom involves making choices among various options, and one's societal culture not only provides these options, but also makes them meaningful to one."[23] Group membership, it is argued, is not an obstacle to be removed. Rather, it is a *precondition* for ensuring that individuals can make meaningful decisions about their lives in a secure context of identity.[24]

But at the same time, it is equally valid to observe that any collective identity or shared vocabulary may also *restrict* our choices.[25] Such membership (with its power to define our horizons) forecloses certain possibilities and alternatives just as it secures and makes others intelligible.[26]

Avenues for internal change and entrenched inequalities   The complex relationship between group membership and individual freedom is even more vulnerable to criticism when birthright rules are part of a tradition that is extremely resistant to internal change. For example, if there are only limited avenues for legitimate revision of the tradition, and if only certain categories of group member are deemed qualified to engage in dialogue about the necessity and feasibility of such revision, then it is hard to understand how the claim can be made that such membership fosters the individual freedom of *all* group members.[27] If anything, it seems more plausible to argue that it does so only selectively, while laying an undue burden on historically vulnerable group members.

Membership at birth by no means confers immunity from certain entrenched patterns of power inequality within the group. Such inequalities may be merely societal (based on wealth, age, social status, and so on), but they may also be *legally* sanctioned in accordance with the group's personal law. Discrimination that comes in the latter form can be difficult to challenge. It often rests on distinct gender, caste, race, or other related patterns of internal exclusion that disadvantage some group members on the grounds of perceived "immutable" characteristics, which presumably justify their maltreatment in private and public life. When such patterns of discrimination and maltreatment are encoded in the group's personal law tradition, then the assignment of membership at birth not only limits individual choice; it also licenses, and in the process perpetuates, intragroup patterns of severe inequality.[28]

In practice, various religious personal law regimes do *not* ensure the same opportunities for all members. Gender-biased rules that govern matters concerning marriage and divorce, for example, often limit the choices and opportunities that are available to women (in comparison to other group members), although in theory, they are presumed to all enjoy the same opportunities within their cultures.[29] This is not to suggest that women do not find value and meaning in their communal member-ship and identity. However, the fact remains that certain group mem-bers, women in particular, are often asked to shoulder a disproportion-ate burden (again, compared to other group members) in preserving the community's distinct *ethos* and *nomos*.[30] Such restrictions may be part and parcel of an effort to demarcate the group's "difference" vis-à-vis other communities.[31] But they may also have a double punitive effect on vulnerable members, exposing them both to the risk of internal discrimi-nation *and* the threat of external targeting due to their group identity.[32] Thus, even where a system of personal law assists in preserving the core tradition of a societal culture (thus allowing some members a secure context of choice), it may impose an unacceptable burden on other, historically marginalized members of that group's population.

The right of exit   So far I have deliberately underplayed the apparently obvious set of solutions to the problem of imposed identity, that is, the host of possible ways to transform a tradition through resistance, dissent, and (ultimately) exit. Arguably, even if one is "born into" a specific com-munity, one can later challenge the basic assumptions of a culture (or its "shared vocabulary"), or fight to revoke or modify certain unfair group norms and practices.[33] In extreme cases, one may sever ties from a birth-right community by revoking one's membership—that is, by using one's right of exit when one is precluded from effectively expressing one's voice within the group, or when loyalty implies subordination.[34]

In practice, however, matters are often more complicated. Certain reli-gious, tribal, racial, ethnic, and national collectives may make legal claims regarding group membership that are solely based on an individ-ual's birthright entitlement to membership—regardless of subsequent decisions (or unilateral "expatriation" actions) taken by the individual herself.[35] For example, not all religious communities recognize acts of membership withdrawal—even if such acts are voluntary and are recog-nized by the state—as automatically terminating one's membership in one's attributed birthright community.[36] Such limitations to the right of exit can have dire consequences. They limit one's freedom of choice and conscience, while at the same time potentially locking the individual into a context of vulnerability due to relations of domination within the group. Under a regime of personal law, then, even if one *attempts* to resist the authority, norms, and ways of life of one's community, one may be un-able to exit that community fully.

"Naturalized" boundaries   Membership is not only hard to terminate; for some, it may also be hard to acquire.[37] Indeed, the very notion of group membership has little meaning if it fails to create some kind of a persistent boundary, border, or distinction between those who are "inside" and those who are "outside" the group. As Jules Coleman and Sarah Harding argue, membership is a valuable public good.[38] Michael Walzer goes further, stating that "[t]he *primary* good we distribute to one another is membership in some human community."[39] Once we think about membership in these terms, it becomes evident that control over the terms of admission to the status of membership is crucial for any community's self-determination.

In this account, birthright membership rules fulfill an important task: they allow each community to demarcate its own boundaries by shaping the circle of persons that it automatically defines as its members, as those who fall under its jurisdiction.[40] Attribution of membership at birth institutionalizes a legal mechanism for "filing" individuals into such jurisdictions. At the same time, membership rules also play a key role in the process of maintaining the community over time, by providing the formal bonds that connect the past to the future and identifying who is automatically considered part of the tradition. Personal law and lineage rules thus demarcate a pool of individuals who are collectively responsible for maintaining the group's values, practices, and distinct way of life. Of course, birthright membership rules cannot by themselves guarantee that all children born to a given community will decide to remain participants as adults in that group. However, when the initial imposition of identity is compounded by the experience of membership (and a limited right of exit), it is not surprising that most religious communities, like nations, ultimately acquire the majority of their members through birth rather than through adult choice.

The power (and danger) of birthright membership rules thus lies in their ability to "naturalize" membership boundaries by attributing them to the accident of birth, and by ascribing legally constituted differences (between groups) to an apparently rational, independent means of defining such boundaries. It is striking that even established liberal polities rely on ascriptive means for the transmission of citizenship through the legal mechanism of birthright entitlement.[41] Citizenship, like assigned group membership, is a passport (literally) to a host of rights and obligations that are attached to that status.[42] Although a web of regional and international conventions now attempt to protect the rights of noncitizens, and some scholars have been quick to declare the arrival of a "postnational" era (where national citizenship rights are replaced by universal human rights protections),[43] the thin line between exclusion and membership can still make a dramatic difference in one's life, for example, in terms of the protection of one's basic dignity, security, and participation rights.[44] Birthright citizenship, then, is not only an instrument of social closure, but also a precondition for the enjoyment of certain rights (and the fulfillment of certain duties) that are directly tied to the status of full membership.

Such attribution of status on the basis of an *unchosen* condition—namely, the accident of birth to certain parents, or birth in a certain territory—clearly represents an exception to the basic tenets of liberal political theory: primarily, the idea that political membership ought to be founded on individual choice and consent.[45] Yet we know that ascriptive membership rules are still practiced and upheld by various religious communities, as well as by the citizenship laws of virtually every country in the world.[46] Any serious attempt to challenge the dominant principle of birthright entitlement must therefore begin by recognizing its immensely powerful hold on our imagination: as a means for the collective community to assert a link back into time immemorial, and forward into an indefinite future.[47]

Maltreatment of outsiders   Intergenerational continuity and exclusivity thus appear to be the hallmarks of any personal law/birthright membership system; a system of personal law (or birthright citizenship rules) must by definition draw explicit lines between "us" and "them." These lines of distinction may be used benignly; for example, to emphasize the unique cultural heritage of the group or the nation. However, they may also be used malevolently; for example, to terrorize people who were born on the "wrong side" of the border. Moreover, we know from the literature on nation-building that an effective way to create a unified collective is by contrasting it with a (real or imagined) outside enemy or threat.[48] Such processes can cause the stigmatization and degradation of specific "others," to the extent that their dehumanization can culminate in the types of dangers and atrocities that Minow's lectures so potently warn us against. Acts of violence that are specifically directed against such targeted nonmember "outsiders" can further contribute to the process of consolidating group power and uniformity, because they overshadow internal inequalities and differences.

Several recent studies have gone as far as to argue that a causal link can be identified between growing divisions within a given community (e.g., caste conflict within the Hindu majority in India in the 1980s), and the rise in intercommunal conflict (in this context, Hindu-Muslim conflict).[49] The persuasive power of this argument must be tested in each specific interethnic, interracial, or interreligious conflict. However, as a theoretical perspective, it certainly adds an important dimension to the challenge that Minow poses: how to break existing cycles of hatred by searching for new responses "that etch a path between vengeance and forgiveness."[50]

In this search for new responses, it is crucial that we understand how collective identities are legally maintained, and how individuals become assigned into membership communities that significantly shape their life prospects. Such a study may help clarify the processes whereby an accident of birth comes to justify membership in one group or another, as well as shedding light on the staying power of ascriptive mechanisms for such attribution of identity. As we have seen, birthright membership rules draw explicit boundaries between groups in ways that are socially and historically constructed (according to each group's specific personal law and lineage rules, and each state's citizenship rules). Since these membership rules rest on the circumstances of birth, it is tempting to essentialize these boundaries and view them as representing some "real" difference between blood and blood, community and community, one human being who "naturally" belongs to the group and her neighbor who is ascriptively precluded from such status because she was born on the other side of the border. It does not require much pessimism to see how these highly charged, boundary-drawing activities can fuel and re-invigorate the ethnic, religious, and national flare-ups of hatred that are at the heart of Minow's inquiry.

Yet if we accept the argument that many features of the legal principle by which individuals are assigned to different communities through the lottery of birth are objectionable, how can we come to terms with the fact that even access to *membership in a state* (presumably the ultimate corrective alternative to identity-group–based balkanization) relies on a very similar mechanism of ascriptive birthright entitlement?

III. State and Birthright Membership

Citizenship, as a modern state concept, refers to the legal status of full membership in a particular political community. It confers upon the individual the protection of her political community, and crowns the citizen as the legitimate representative of that state's distinct cultural, linguistic, and historical narrative.[51]

While based on a principle of internal inclusion (all citizens formally bear equal status of full membership), national citizenship must also erect external borders that exclude noncitizens from the same membership status (and the security that this status provides).[52] According to the ideal type of national citizenship, every person should belong to one and only one state.[53] Rainer Bauböck describes this schematic picture of an orderly world occupied by clearly distinct political membership communities as having "a quality of simplicity and clarity that almost resembles a Mondrian painting. States are marked by different colors and separated from each other by black lines. . . . [This] modern political map marks all places inhabited by people as belonging to mutually exclusive state territories."[54] The legal dichotomy of citizen versus alien underpins this fundamental (and overly rigid) understanding of the landscape of national borders. As in the case of religious communities, the important question is: how, and on the basis of what rules and principles, do people get to be counted as citizens rather than aliens?

A. AUTOMATIC ASSIGNMENT OF MEMBERSHIP: THE PRINCIPLES OF *JUS SOLI* AND *JUS SANGUINIS*

Two legal principles govern the acquisition of citizenship in a state as a matter of right: *jus sanguinis* and *jus soli*. Both, however, rely on the principle of ascriptive birthright.[55] According to the principle of *jus sanguinis*, automatic membership is assigned to a child born to a citizen parent (the "parentage" principle for the transmission of membership). According to the principle of *jus soli*, automatic membership is assigned to a child born in the territory of the state (the "birthplace" principle for the transmission of membership). No country relies exclusively on either one of these principles alone.[56] Instead, they uphold various combinations of *jus soli* and *jus sanguinis* to determine who is a natural-born citizen.[57]

Historically, *jus soli* originated from the medieval concept of loyalty between subject and monarch, as developed in English common law. In 1608, this principle was legally crystallized in the landmark *Calvin's Case*, which elaborated a theory of subjecthood that firmly based this status on ascriptive grounds: namely, that political membership was automatically assigned by the circumstances of one's birth—in this case, birth under the allegiance of a particular sovereign and within his territorial jurisdiction.[58] Such birthright entitlement created a set of mutual and lifelong obligations that were perpetual and inalienable. The sovereign owed the subject physical protection, just governance, and "all the rights and liberties of an Englishman," whereas the subject owed the sovereign complete loyalty, obedience, and service.[59] Neither party could break this bond of allegiance.[60] *Jus sanguinis*, on the other hand, gained full meaning as a modern concept only in the process of nation-building in Europe. *Jus sanguinis* was adopted in postrevolutionary France as an egalitarian alternative to the "hierarchical" *jus soli* principle, which was judged to have been tainted with monarchist history and with concepts of subjecthood rather than citizenship.[61]

What both these principles (*jus soli* and *jus sanguinis*) have in common, however, is the notion that political membership should be attributed *at birth*. The distinction between them refers to the preferred connecting factor—birthplace or parentage—which is given priority in demarcating a respective state's membership boundaries.[62] As Christopher Eisgruber observes, it is tempting to think that a rule that makes birthright citizenship "contingent upon the place of a child's birth is somehow more egalitarian than a rule that would make birthright citizenship contingent upon the legal status of the child's parents."[63] But this distinction, as Eisgruber himself notes, can easily lead us astray. *Both* principles of membership attribution at birth are equally arbitrary: one is based on the accident of geographical borders; the other on the brute luck of descent.[64] Unlike residency, consent, lottery, or need, the acquisition of automatic (birthright) membership in the body politic is arguably the least defensible basis for distributing access to citizenship, because it allocates rights and opportunities according to the morally arbitrary fact of an individual's circumstances of birth.[65] Instead of nullifying or minimizing the natural contingencies of birthplace or parentage, such assignment of citizenship amplifies their significance.

We no longer approve of heredity as a relevant criterion for almost any admission procedure (in the areas of employment or higher education, for example). However, we do accept birthright as the one and only criterion for automatically bestowing political membership on the individual. Even the most progressive countries still ascribe citizenship entitlement to their members by virtue of birth.[66] In the United States, as well as in most other countries, birthright citizenship is the prime avenue for assignment of political membership.[67] The arbitrary circumstances of our birth may thus come to determine crucial aspects of our lives—

aspects we have never chosen, or ever had a chance to affect. For those of us fortunate enough to have been born in Western democracies, citizenship serves, in the words of Joseph Carens, "as a modern equivalent of feudal privilege—an *inherited* status that greatly increases one's life chances."[68]

In a world fraught with severe inequalities across borders and between nations, birthright citizenship inevitably becomes implicated in processes that maintain global injustice. It dooms some children to membership in a polity that fails to provide them with minimal levels of security, food, shelter, health care, basic economic and social infrastructure, or even minimally stable political institutions, while allowing others the bounty and privilege of belonging to stable, rule-of-law, affluent democracies.

How can such injustice stand? Surprisingly, with a few exceptions, the practice of birthright citizenship is hardly ever challenged by contemporary political and legal theorists.[69] What we do find in the literature are several works that criticize the morality of closed borders, as well as a growing body of legal scholarship that argues for the expansion of rights to nonmembers.[70] However, the former arguments speak primarily to the issue of mobility, and the latter focus on participation. Neither directly challenge the connection between birthright and citizenship.[71]

The primary way in which the subject of ascriptive entitlement to political membership arises in policy debates in the United States is through the targeting of those children of illegal immigrants who currently benefit from the Fourteenth Amendment's expansive declaration of the *jus soli* principle, according to which "all persons born . . . in the United States, and subject to the jurisdiction thereof, are citizens of the United States." Several commentators have tried to construe constitutional arguments that *limit* the application of this right to children born in the United States to a citizen or legal immigrant parent.[72] A version of this proposal was formulated into a constitutional amendment in 1995.[73] The amendment failed, but the testimony surrounding it invoked a debate about the historical origins and legal meaning that ought be attributed to the American *jus soli* principle as codified in the Fourteenth Amendment. At about the same time, in neighboring Canada, a similar proposal to amend the *Citizenship Act* was advocated by the Report of the Standing Committee on Citizenship and Immigration, titled *Canadian Citizenship: A Sense of Belonging*. The recommendation suggested that "[c]hildren born in Canada should be Canadian citizens only if one or both of their parents is a permanent resident or Canadian citizen."[74] This proposal (like its American counterpart) never materialized into law.

No side in the American or Canadian debate challenged the legitimacy of the birthright principle per se. Rather, the issue at stake was the *generality* of the application of this principle—whether it should continue to apply to all children born in the territory, or be construed to apply more narrowly, only to children whose parents are legally within the borders, or whose parents are *already* members of the body politic.[75] The former (more generous) application is more just and fair, as it ensures that no one born on American (or Canadian) soil can be excluded from full membership in the political community due to the actions of others over whom they have no control—in this case, the illegal residence of their parents.[76] This is a powerful argument for not excluding one category of persons (i.e., children of illegal immigrants) from the application of a general membership principle. It speaks primarily to the need to establish an *internally inclusive* means of citizenship attribution once a given political community has agreed on some rule for defining membership. However, it does little to justify a specific principle of attribution (here, birthright) over other competing principles (such as need, consent, or residency, for example). Nor does a more generous application of a state's birthright membership rule transform the *externally exclusive* nature of this ascriptive mechanism for assigning political membership.[77] This latter, exclusionary aspect of collective identity accounts for some of the darker alleys of membership, which, in turn, help to maintain the cycles of hatred that Minow insists we break.

B. QUESTIONING THE BIRTHRIGHT TRADITION: LESSONS FROM THE CRITIQUE OF PERSONAL LAW REGIMES

Although the assignment of political membership in a sovereign state according to the principles of birthplace and parentage may seem "natural," there are good reasons for treating this process with deep suspicion, and for subjecting it to the type of critique we identified earlier in relation to the shortcomings of religious personal law regimes. In other words, I wish to draw an (admittedly provocative) analogy between birthright attribution of citizenship and personal law rules of membership, and then take the argument a step further to suggest that citizenship through birthright is susceptible to some of the very same problems that make personal law regimes so unattractive. Personal law regimes, as we have seen, "naturalize" difference through law. On this count, the attribution of citizenship at birth fares no better than personal law rules.[78]

The critical reflections I offer in the following pages intend to strengthen a more permeable conception of groupings and boundaries, as advocated by Minow and others, in lieu of the previous view of group and national boundaries as immutable. Finding cracks in the apparently unbreakable wall of the "blood and soil" notion of membership (with its often destructive impact on intercommunal relations) may prove helpful in steering us toward the ultimate challenge that Minow's Gilbane lectures pose: to build a sustainable future in places where hate and violence once bred unchecked.

Imposed identity   Birthright citizenship, by virtue of its ascriptive nature, limits an individual's initial choice of membership. A child is automatically counted and registered (or not counted and not registered) as a citizen, entirely according to relevant connecting factors of birthplace (*jus soli*) or parentage (*jus sanguinis*). Entitlement to citizenship imposes a set of rights and obligations on the individual, as well as automatic submission to the dominant law of the land (by nature of its territorial jurisdiction), just as imposed religious group membership subjects the individual to the personal law jurisdiction of her respective community.

Membership and individual freedom   Citizenship in a state clearly involves more than simply defining the boundaries of inclusion/exclusion. Such membership usually implies that the native-born citizen will be immersed in a specific societal culture, with its distinct languages, institutions, legal norms, and national symbols.[79] Each country maintains a specific view of its place in the world, and promotes a particular narrative of history.[80] This sense of collective identity is then transmitted from generation to generation. While democratic and pluralistic societies are, in principle, more open to different opinions and diverse readings about what it means to be, for example, "an American," or "a Canadian," or "a German," there are still some core aspects of each collective identity that grow out of the experience of membership in that respective national community.[81] Democratic societies are clearly more likely to respect the argument that individuals can challenge their own community's dominant norms than traditional religious groups. To live up to their promises, however, birthright citizenship rules must also allow the native-born citizen opportunities to question her own continued membership in the political community into which she happens to have been born (I return to this point later in this section).

Avenues for internal change and entrenched inequalities   Unlike the majority of personal law codes of religious communities, the governing norms of democratic political communities are open to change through the political process. With the (late) arrival of the universal franchise in most parts of the world, no formal distinctions between citizens can be made in terms of their capacity and eligibility to vote or to run for office due to their gender, race, tribal membership, national origin, and so on.[82] At least in principle, each person's political voice carries the same weight in terms of shaping the rules that will govern her community. The same can hardly be said for most religious communities, where the transformation of personal law codes is not likely to be achieved by popular vote.[83]

Political avenues for internal change and dissent, which are part and parcel of democratic governance, are thus both more open and inclusive than those of traditional religious communities. This is one arena in which related principles of ascriptive membership have generally led to different long-term consequences (from the perspective of the individual who is assigned membership in such communities). Whereas in a democratic polity all citizens can now ideally expect to have equal rights and an equal share of the political voice, the same benefits are still highly contested in many traditional religious communities.[84]

"Naturalized" boundaries   The power to define who is inside and who is outside the political community is one of the key features of the modern institution of citizenship. In the words of Rogers Brubaker, "Every modern state formally defines its citizenry, publicly identifying a set of persons as its members and residually designating all others as noncitizens, or aliens."[85] Citizenship, then, offers a *bounded* notion of membership. It protects *our* political community and its members, by excluding all others.[86] This privileging of "our" community, argues Louis Michael Seidman, "logically implies a comparatively diminished concern for the welfare of others: by their nature, communities must have boundaries, and the boundaries can have meaning only if some difference [exists] between those situated on either side of them."[87]

Maltreatment of outsiders   National citizenship remains a status to which access is restricted, primarily through birthright: only children born to present members or within the state's territory can enjoy this privilege as a matter of right.[88] Such exclusivity assumes that the principle of birthright justifies differentiating rights and opportunities between insiders and outsiders, to the extent that the public good of membership itself is distributed according to this arguably morally arbitrary criterion. As is the case with religious communities, national collectives often strengthen their own internal cohesiveness by mobilizing hate and fear against targeted groups of outsiders: those who do not qualify as members due to their pedigree.

The ideological weight of the distinction between citizens and foreigners ("us" and "them") can lead to bleak outcomes if it is used to justify the stigmatization and dehumanization of those deemed as "outsiders."[89] The line between the value of community membership (as a social cooperative unit that provides a context of meaning, history, choice, and so forth), and the distrust and alienation that group membership boundaries may nourish, is extremely thin. This, unfortunately, is true for both national and communal memberships. Their shared reliance on ascriptive membership rules (through personal law regimes or citizenship attribution rules) clearly does not assist in reducing the animosity toward nonmembers (i.e., those coded as "different," or (even worse) "unfit" for inclusion in the body politic).

What is often overlooked is the fact that the "citizen-alien" distinction is not made on the basis of some specific quality or deserving status that insiders possess or have acquired (in comparison to "outsiders"); for example, as a result of their compassion, hard work, education, talent, or need. Rather, what maintains this distinction is simply the reliance on the arbitrary power of extant membership rules that constitute birthplace and parentage as "innate" criteria for citizenship.

But with the gradual removal of trade barriers between nations in recent years, is it not plausible to imagine a similar relaxation of rules that distinguish aliens from citizens? To date, the increase in cross-border commercial activity has in fact been accompanied by the exact opposite—the rapid erection of new and more sophisticated barriers to *exclude* nonmembers.[90] As Peter Andreas notes, this increased policing activity is evident, most strikingly, along the United States–Mexico border, and along the external borders of the European Union.[91] These borders, as he observes, "are increasingly protected and monitored, not to deter armies or impose tariffs on trade, but to confront a perceived invasion of 'undesirables,' particularly illegal immigrants."[92]

The right of exit   Finally, let us consider the most powerful answer to my critique of birthright entitlement. Surely individuals are free to leave their political community, are they not? If so, then birthright citizenship creates no obstacle to their individual freedom, nor does it necessarily restrict their choices (at least no more than any other means of attributing membership). If anything, such rules can be understood as enhancing their choices and respecting their webs of relationships with meaningful others. As birthright citizens, people are *ensured* membership in at least one political community—hopefully one in which they can feel at home, secure in its practices and habits of life, and equal to all other members. If they wish, so the argument goes, they may try to improve their lot by moving to another country, say, one that offers better economic or educational opportunities, higher standards of human-rights protection, or greater political stability. And if they stay in their home country, surely we can treat this *inaction* as an indication of their implied consent to their "imposed" birthright affiliation, can we not?

Such an argument might be convincing in a world of open borders, but this is not the world in which we live. While a state cannot hold an individual citizen captive, it is not necessarily obliged to consent to an act of expatriation by an individual. These legal formalities are only part of the problem, however. In order to have a real right of exit, which can be freely exercised at will, there must be a *safe destination*—and no state in the current world system can guarantee its citizens that another state will accept them. Such inclusion (in a new political community) depends solely on the discretion of the receiving polity. States are free in international law to define the circle of their members as they see fit. Because of this freedom, no international authority can force a country to accept individuals who have voluntarily left their own birthright political community. In fact, even if they left their country *involuntarily*, all that international law guarantees them is the right of *nonrefoulement*; that is, a right to *temporary* asylum for those who fall under the definition of "refugee" (according to the 1951 Refugee Convention), for as long as the situation in their home country prevents their safe return to that polity.[93]

Apart from the special case of protected refugees, there are *no* guaranteed rights to remain in any country other than the one to which persons belong as citizens. While citizens are technically free to leave their home country, they must individually find a new political community that will accept them as long-term residents. Some people may have family members in another polity, which might make their search for a new permanent home easier. Others may have to depend on their talent, education, and skill, in the hope that another country will allow them legal entry under a "skilled workers" category (based on their ability to contribute to the receiving country's economy).[94] However, these limited options for emigration are a far cry from an established right of exit—they are simply a tribute to the fact that on the margins, *some* individuals will be able to legally change their birthright membership community.

Perhaps the most telling figure concerning international immigration is reported by the United Nations Population Fund. Of the global population, the proportion of international migrants worldwide has remained steady for the past thirty-five years: they represent *a mere 2 percent* of the total world population.[95] Everyone else, it is safe to assume, has remained members of the political communities into which they were ascribed citizenship by virtue of birth. (Allowance must be made for some margin of error here, given that illegal migration does not generally appear in the host countries' statistics, nor can it be fully accounted for in the United Nations statistics.)

What are we to make of this data? Defenders of the birthright principle might champion it as evidence of the fact that this is indeed a "good" principle—one that seems intuitively natural, administratively convenient, and politically uncontested.[96] Moreover, they might argue that it proves that people prefer not to move and "are inclined to stay where they are unless their life is very difficult there."[97] But given a world of closed borders, how can we ever be certain that people have decided to remain in their native political communities out of *free choice*, rather than because of strict immigration rules that mean that they have no other polity (other than that to which they accidentally belong by birth) that would permanently accept them?

To clarify this last point about the motivation for inaction, let us consider a different scenario. Assume that we have statistical evidence that shows (as it does) that most battered wives do *not* leave their abusive partners, or that, historically, most slaves did *not* attempt to run away from slaveholders. Can we conclude that their *inaction* represents implied consent to their oppression? I think not. It may simply represent their despair, or in the words of Carol Rose, their recognition that there is "no alternative game [for them] to play."[98] Similarly, we cannot assume that people do not leave their home country because of their "love" of their birthplace or birthright community. All that we can safely claim, given the circumstances of bounded political communities protected by guarded national borders, is that we do not know why people stay in their communities of birth. We can speculate, in light of our understanding of analogous situations, that without a secure right of exit, there is no guarantee that birthright membership will not eventually turn into tyranny and oppression.[99]

We have no problem recognizing the possibility of oppression when the object of our critique is switched from national collectives to religious (or other) minority communities. Indeed, in this context, even the most generous defenders of the principle of freedom of association limit the associative right by means of a complementary requirement that individuals have a secured right of exit.[100]

Ironically, a less impeded right of exit is typically offered to persons residing in countries that respect different communities' personal law regimes. In most countries, they can expect to find legitimate refuge from their own community's traditional law (although not from its initial imposition of identity) by turning to a civil court that applies the state's territorial law. "Opting out" in this way is a far-from-ideal solution, as it may lead to severe communal sanctions against those individuals who dare to "betray" their membership collective and its authorized institutions.[101] Achieving justice through "exit" is hardly ever an attractive option. However, it may offer a last-ditch resort when voice and loyalty fail to provide effective remedy or internal change. Surprisingly, given all the attention paid to the injuries that group members may suffer at the hands of their own religious (or other) subnational communities,[102] we tend to ignore the acute problem of *imposed* political membership by modern states themselves—the fact that, as citizens, we have no secured venue of permanent departure from the birthright community into which we happen to have been born under circumstances entirely beyond our control.

To clarify, most democratic polities allow us, their citizens, the formal right to leave our political communities of birth. The problem is that we have no guaranteed *right of entry* into any other sovereign country. Under such circumstances, it is wrong to assume that nonexit or nondissent necessarily implies "acceptance" of the political community into which one belongs ascriptively. Differently put, because the current world system does not allow individuals any guaranteed right of exit from their ascribed political community, it would be misguided to conclude that people remain in their birthright membership communities out of choice: they may have no other alternative *but* to stay. Under such conditions, people may simply learn to accept, and come to identify with, the national identity imposed upon them at birth—not necessarily out of free will, but more likely as a result of the lack of any real alternative.

Conclusion

Inspired by Minow's Gilbane lectures, this chapter has drawn a provocative analogy between personal laws that maintain religious communal identities and citizenship laws that regulate access to political communities. Surprisingly, both systems of membership preservation share a crucial feature—reliance on the morally arbitrary fact of birthright as the relevant connecting factor between the individual and the community, making the "intimate" the basis of an *ascriptive* collective affiliation.

State citizenship rules fare better than personal law regimes when evaluated according to the twin criteria of the possibility for internal change and the problem of entrenched inequalities—at least under circumstances of civil peace. Nevertheless, birthright citizenship rules fail to offer viable answers to many other deep problems that plague personal law membership rules, such as the concept of "naturalized" borders, the potential for maltreatment of outsiders, and the failure to distinguish clearly between choice and imposition of identity.

If the argument pursued here concerning the politicized and essentialized attribution of status based on the mediating procedure of birthright were to be accepted, then a major overhaul of the way in which political membership is assigned to individuals at present would be required. The best place to begin, I suggest, is by questioning the "natural" tie between birthright and citizenship—a practice that is objectionable because of the various constraints it imposes on individuals and the risks it exposes them to—all without providing them a real and viable right of choice or exit. We rage against personal laws that lead to such restrictions. Why should we accept them when they occur on the state level?

Notes

1. For a concise overview of these developments, see Elizabeth Kiss, "Moral Ambition Within and Beyond Political Constraints: Reflections on Restorative Justice," in Robert I. Rotberg and Dennis Thompson, eds., *Truth v. Justice: The Morality of Truth Commissions* (Princeton, NJ: Princeton University Press, 2000), pp. 68–98. See also Jennifer Llewellyn and Robert House, *Restorative Justice: A Conceptual Framework* (Ottawa: Law Commission of Canada, Discussion Paper JL2-6, 1999), at *http://www.lcc.gc.ca/en/forum/rj/paper.html*: "Restorative justice begins from the premise that the most effective response to conflict is to repair

the harm done by the wrongful act. Material and symbolic reparations begin the process of restoration, but restoration means more than receiving compensation. For those harmed, restoration means repairing the actual damage caused by wrongdoing and restoring their sense of control over their lives. . . . The restorative justice approach responds to the immediate conflict and encourages the development of respectful relationships among those who are wrongdoers, those who have suffered harm and members of the community." Ibid., p. 5.

2. Although there are various sociological, political, and psychological factors that shape our conceptions of membership, my goal in this chapter is to appraise the legal procedures that assign individuals into such membership communities in the first place.

3. See, for example, Ian F. Haney López, *White by Law: The Legal Construction of Race* (New York: New York University Press, 1996).

4. The demarcation of membership boundaries does not necessarily lead to violence between groups. Specific factors or events must be present in order to trigger the deterioration of an otherwise legitimate demarcation of collective identity into a means of labeling nonmembers as unworthy of protection and basic human dignity. The exploration of these particular factors is beyond the scope of this chapter.

5. On the relationship between the "intimate" and the "collective," see Gilbane Fund Lecture #3 (November 2, 1999). This connection runs through much of Minow's work. See, for example, "All in the Family & in All Families: Membership, Love and Owing," *West Virginia Law Review* 95 (1992–93): 275–332.

6. Most countries use a combination of these two principles in assigning political membership by virtue of birthright. See infra section III.A.

7. I offer a detailed discussion of these legal principles in "Children of a Lesser State: Sustaining Global Inequality through Birthright Citizenship Laws," in Stephen Macedo and Iris Marion Young, eds., *NOMOS XLIV: Child, Family, and the State* (New York: New York University Press, Forthcoming).

8. Edoardo Vitta, "The Conflict of Personal Laws," *Israel Law Review* 2 (1970): 170. Personal law regimes may also recognize ethnic or tribal groupings; however, this chapter focuses primarily on religious communities.

9. Ibid., p. 182. See also Deniz Kandiyoti, "Identity and its Discontents: Women and the Nation," in Patrick Williams and Laura Chrisman, eds., *Colonial Discourse and Post-Colonial Theory* (New York: Columbia University Press, 1994), pp. 376–91.

10. Personal law regimes generally demarcate membership boundaries in two related ways: first, by developing complex lineage rules that determine, who, by virtue of birth, is eligible to acquire full membership in the group; and second, by defining who can become a group member by way of marriage. For a detailed discussion, see Ayelet Shachar, *Multicultural Jurisdictions: Cultural Differences and Women's Rights* (Cambridge: Cambridge University Press, 2001), chap. 3.

11. Of special interest here is the applicability of the Convention on the Elimination of All Forms of Discrimination Against Women, given the findings that continue to show that the norms encoded in certain communities' religious personal law rules tend to perpetuate women's discrimination and subordination. For such findings, see the collection of essays in Rebecca J. Cook, ed., *Human Rights of Women: National and International Perspectives* (Philadelphia: University of Pennsylvania Press, 1994).

12. I have discussed some of the troubling gender effects of such in-group rights violations in "Group Identity and Women's Rights in Family Law: The Perils of Multicultural Accommodation," *Journal of Political Philosophy* 6 (1998): 285–305; and in "On Citizenship and Multicultural Vulnerability," *Political Theory* 28 (2000): 64–89. For further discussion, see, for example, Celestine I. Nyamu, "How Should Human Rights and Development Respond to Cultural Legitimization of Gender Hierarchy in Developing Countries?" *Harvard International Law Journal* 41 (2000): 381–418.

13. On "borrowing" and cross-jurisdictional learning, see Anne Marie Slaughter, "A Typology of Transjudicial Communication," *University of Richmond Law Review* 29 (1994): 99–137; H. Patrick Glenn, "Persuasive Authority," *McGill Law Journal* 32 (1987): 261–98; Karen Knop, "Here and There: International Law in Domestic Courts," *New York University Journal of International Law and Politics* 32 (2000): 501–35.

14. Such state-centered perceptions of law may take on different variations in practice. For example, some countries are unitary while others are federal, some allow for linguistic diversity while other establish a national language as the official language, and so on.

15. For some of the literature that is burgeoning on this subject, see, for example, Daniele Archibugi, David Held, and Martin Köhler, eds., *Re-imagining Political Community: Studies in Cosmopolitan Democracy* (Stanford, CA: Stanford University Press, 1998); Shachar, *Multicultural Jurisdictions*, supra note 10; Michael J. Trebilcock and Robert Howse, *The Regulation of International Trade*, 2nd ed. (London: Routledge, 1999), pp. 500–22; J.H.H. Weiler, *The Constitution of Europe: "Do the New Clothes Have an Emperor?" and Other Essays of European Integration* (Cambridge: Cambridge University Press, 1999).

16. As mentioned above, this article focuses on personal law regimes that define an individual's religious affiliation. However, personal law regimes can also define tribal membership, or national membership. For further discussion, see infra, section III.

17. Such registration may later appear in one's identity card or other official documents certified by the state. Note that the powers held by group officials must be distinguished from *territorial* birthright membership, which is governed by state authorities.

18. Under systems of multiple personal laws, certain children can be assigned membership in more than one religious community by virtue of birth (for exam-

ple, if the parents belong to different religious communities and neither has forfeited their membership). Yet birthright assignment of membership can also lead to a rare situation in which a child is not assigned membership in any religious community by virtue of birth, since she or he does not qualify as a member according the personal law and lineage rules of her or his respective communities. For example, this may occur if the father of the child is Jewish and the mother is Muslim, because Jewish law follows a matrilineal assignment of membership, whereas Muslim law follows a patrilineal assignment of membership. On the question of "who is a Muslim" in India, see Paras Diwan, *Muslim Law in Modern India*, 4th ed. (Allahabad: Allahabad Law Agency, 1987); similar tensions arise in Israel over the question of "who is a Jew." Importantly, each child will usually be entitled not only to membership in a religious community, but also to membership in a political community (according to the state's territorial law and citizenship rules). Both status assignments occur at birth. According to Israeli law, for example, a child born to an Israeli parent will automatically be entitled to Israeli citizenship, as well as to membership in a recognized (Jewish, Muslim, Druze, Bahai, or Christian) religious community.

19. For example, in Israel, people cannot escape the jurisdiction of an assigned religious community unless they formally convert to another religion. In India, conversion has also been used as a means to "avert" the rules of one community and subject oneself to the rules of another community. This problem is discussed by the Indian Supreme Court in *Sarla Mudgal v. India*, a 1995 case that explored the legal problems associated with conversion to Islam allegedly undertaken in order to practice polygamy.

20. For a detailed discussion, see Will Kymlicka, *Liberalism, Community and Culture* (Oxford, UK: Clarendon Press, 1989), pp. 162–81.

21. The canonical text here is John Locke's *Second Treatise*, which defends a theory that bases the obligation to obey the law on individual consent of members of the relevant society. See Locke, *Two Treatises of Government*, Peter Laslett, ed., 2nd ed. (Cambridge: Cambridge University Press, 1970), pp. 365–67. For a critical account of consent theory in liberal thought, see Don Herzog, *Happy Slaves: A Critique of Consent Theory* (Chicago: University of Chicago Press, 1989).

22. For a critique of this assumption, see Will Kymlicka, "Modernity and National Identity," in Shlomo Ben-Ami, Yoav Peled, and Alberto Spektorowski, eds., *Ethnic Challenges to the Modern Nation State* (New York: St. Martin's Press, 2000), pp. 11–41.

23. Ibid., p. 22.

24. Kymlicka, *Liberalism, Community and Culture*, supra note 20, p. 166.

25. See Yoav Peled and José Brunner, "Culture is Not Enough: A Democratic Critique of Liberal Multiculturalism," in *Ethnic Challenges to the Modern Nation State*, supra note 22, pp. 65–92.

26. Space does not permit discussion of the rather complex causes of this enabling as well as limiting function of a secure context of identity. It is neverthe-

less sufficient to observe that even a relatively open community must privilege certain assumptions, practices, and beliefs as uncontested (i.e., the way "we do things here"), at the expense of other equally plausible understandings of the world.

27. Of course, "outsiders" to a group may also feel that they have some vested interest in changing the membership rules of that group, especially if such rules exclude them from membership. However, these issues fall beyond the scope of this discussion.

28. I address this point at greater length in "The Perils of Multicultural Accommodation," supra note 12.

29. For feminist critiques of this state of affairs, see, for example, Frances Raday, "Israel—The Incorporation of Religious Patriarchy in a Modern State," *International Review of Comparative Public Policy* 4 (1992): 209–25; Amrita Chhachhi, "Forced Identities: The State, Communalism, Fundamentalism and Women in India," in Deniz Kandiyoti, ed., *Women, Islam and the State* (London: Macmillan, 1992), pp. 144–75.

30. For further discussion, see Shachar, *Multicultural Jurisdictions*, supra note 10.

31. As Margaret Lamberts Bendroth observes, in her study of gender and contemporary evangelism in the United States, "[g]ender issues stood at the heart of fundamentalist desire to be different" from the dominant forces in American culture. See Margaret Lamberts Bendroth, *Fundamentalism and Gender: 1875 to the Present* (New Haven, CT: Yale University Press, 1993), pp. 3, 5. This desire (and the heightened regulation it often imposes on women) is by no means unique to evangelical strands of Christianity. We find similar patterns in many other religious communities where rigid interpretation of a group's tradition can lead to sanctioned intragroup violations of women's basic rights. For a detailed discussion, see, for example, Courtney W. Howland, "The Challenge of Religious Fundamentalism to the Liberty and Equality of Women: An Analysis under the United Nations Charter," *Columbia Journal of Transnational Law* 35 (1997): 271–377.

32. Critical race feminists have offered various examples that illustrate this problem. See, for example, Angela P. Harris, "Race and Essentialism in Feminist Legal Theory," *Stanford Law Review* 42 (1990): 581–616.

33. Several scholars have suggested that the most powerful critics are those who have a direct membership stake in the relevant community. Michael Walzer elegantly defends this position in *Interpretation and Social Criticism* (Cambridge, MA: Harvard University Press, 1987).

34. Here I am adapting somewhat freely Albert Hirschman's three categories of "exit," "voice," and "loyalty" to the context of cultural resistance. See Albert O. Hirschman, *Exit, Voice, and Loyalty: Responses to Decline in Firms, Organizations, and States* (Cambridge, MA: Harvard University Press, 1970).

35. To illustrate this point, consider the case of *Mississippi Band of Choctaw Indians v. Holyfield*, 490 U.S. 439 (1988), which raised important issues concern-

ing birthright membership in a Native American community. There, a pregnant woman who was also a tribe member "went to some effort to see that her children were born outside the confines of the Choctaw Indian Reservation." She later voluntarily consented to the adoption of her twin babies by a nontribal family. However, the tribe's representatives objected to the adoption, and challenged the legality of the adoption proceedings. The case eventually reached the U.S. Supreme Court, which held that according to the Indian Child Welfare Act of 1978 (ICWA), the tribe (not the state or the individual) had the authority to determine such proceedings, because the children that were given for adoption were "its" children. The tribe's interests, it was held, could trump the explicit consent of the parents—who had hoped to avoid the tribe's ascriptive membership rules by giving birth to the children outside the territorial jurisdiction of the tribe. I critically evaluate this decision in *Multicultural Jurisdictions*, supra note 10, chap. 5.

36. This can lead to a situation where the same person is simultaneously considered a *nonmember* (according to state law) but is still counted as a *member* (according to their group's personal law). Related problems of "dual status" can also occur when marriage is solemnized according to religious law, but the legal act of divorce is regulated by civil law. In such circumstances, the parties to the civil divorce are free to remarry other partners (according to state law), but may still be considered married according to the rules of their group's personal law regime. For further discussion of the complexities that arise in practice due to the intersection of religious and civil law regimes, see Ayelet Shachar, "The Puzzle of Interlocking Power Hierarchies: Sharing the Pieces of Jurisdictional Authority," *Harvard Civil Rights-Civil Liberties Law Review* 35 (2000): 385–426.

37. Historically, for example, women were not generally able to bestow membership on their husbands. In certain cases, they were even stripped of their own birthright membership upon marrying a foreigner. For a detailed discussion, see Nancy F. Cott, "Marriage and Women's Citizenship in the United States, 1840–1934," *American Historical Review* 103 (1998): 1440–74. Similar patterns of exclusion may occur at the community level as well. For example, several Indian tribes in North America adopted membership rules that deprived women who married men from outside the tribe of the right to transmit tribal membership to their children. Men who married outside the tribe were not subject to the same sanction; their children were considered full members by virtue of birth. See, for example, the controversial case of *Santa Clara Pueblo v. Martinez*, 436 U.S. 49 (1978). In Canada, a federal law (the Indian Act) upheld such gender-discriminatory policies. The relevant provisions of this law were challenged in the case of *Canada (Attorney General) v. Lavell* [1974] S.C.R. 1349, but to no avail. The UN Human Rights Commission criticized the Indian Act in *Lovelace v. Canada* 36 U.N. GOAR Supp. (No. 40) Annex XVII; U.N. Doc. A/36/40 (1981). The gender-discriminatory provisions of the Indian Act were finally overturned through legislation. See *An Act to Amend the Indian Act*, R.S.C. ch. 32 (Supp. I 1985) (Can.).

38. See "Citizenship, the Demands of Justice, and the Moral Relevance of Political Borders," in Warren F. Schwartz, ed., *Justice in Immigration*, (Cambridge: Cambridge University Press, 1995), pp. 18–62.

39. Michael Walzer, *Spheres of Justice: A Defense of Pluralism and Equality* (New York: Basic Books, 1983), p. 31 [emphasis added].

40. I borrow the circle metaphor from William Rogers Brubaker in "Citizenship and Naturalization: Policies and Politics," in William Rogers Brubaker, ed., *Immigration and the Politics of Citizenship in Europe and North America* (Lanham, MD: University Press of America, 1989), pp. 99–125. Alex Aleinikoff also uses this metaphor to refer to different "tiers" of membership. See T. Alexander Aleinikoff, "The Tightening Circle of Membership," *Hastings Constitutional Law Quarterly* 22 (1995): 915–24.

41. To date, even in the European Union, the creation of a European citizenship has not been accompanied by the harmonization of the citizenship laws and traditions of the member states. See Randall Hansen and Patrick Weil, "Introduction: Citizenship, Immigration and Nationality: Towards a Convergence in Europe?" in Randall Hansen and Patrick Weil, eds., *Towards a European Nationality: Citizenship, Immigration and Nationality in the EU* (Hampshire, UK: Palgrave, 2001), pp. 1–23.

42. For example, in most countries, only citizens are guaranteed the franchise, and only they have an inalienable right not to be deported from their national homeland. Military service, meanwhile, is a classic example of an obligation that in most countries only citizens must bear (at times of crisis). The word "citizen," as Linda Kerber observes, still carries "overtones inherited from antiquity and the Renaissance, when the citizen made the continued existence of the city possible by taking up arms on its behalf." See Linda K. Kerber, "A Constitutional Right to be Treated Like . . . Ladies: Women, Civic Obligation, and Military Service," *University of Chicago Law School Roundtable* (1993), p. 104. An exception to this rule is found in the United States, where resident aliens who are not permitted to vote in national elections can be (and in the past have been) drafted. However, relatives of foreign-born soldiers killed during active-duty military service may apply for the granting of posthumous citizenship to the deceased.

43. This argument has been powerfully made by Yasmin Nuhoglu Soyal, *Limits of Citizenship: Migrants and Postnational Membership in Europe* (Chicago: University of Chicago Press, 1994). See also Saskia Sassen, *Losing Control? Sovereignty in an Age of Globalization* (New York: Columbia University Press, 1996), pp. 59–99.

44. The distinction between citizen and noncitizen is still material even in countries that extend fairly expansive rights to long-term residents. In the United States, see Linda S. Bosniak, "Membership, Equality, and the Difference Alienage Makes," *New York University Law Review* 69 (1994): 1047–1149. For a comparative perspective, see Christian Joppke, "The Legal-Domestic Sources of Immi-

grant Rights: The United States, Germany, and the European Union," *Comparative Political Studies* 34 (2001): 339–66.

45. Note, however, that Brubaker suggests that the preservation of such legal mechanisms is functional, and to some degree inevitable, because of the administrative clarity and convenience this ensures. As he puts it: "Birth is an unambiguous event about which states maintain relatively clear administrative records." See Brubaker, supra note 40, p. 101.

46. See Patrick Weil, "Access to Citizenship: A Comparison of Twenty-five Nationality Laws," in Alexander Aleinikoff and Douglas Klusmeyer, eds., *Citizenship Today: Global Perspectives and Practices* (Washington, DC: Brookings Institution Press, 2001), pp. 17–35.

47. For a different notion of "imagined" communities, see Benedict Anderson, *Imagined Communities: Reflections on the Origin and Spread of Nationalism*, rev. ed. (London: Verso, 1991).

48. For a review of the literature recently published on this subject, see James D. Fearon and David D. Laitin, "Violence and the Social Construction of Ethnic Identity," *International Organization* 54 (2000): 845–77.

49. See Ornit Shani, "The Resurgence of 'EthnoHinduism'—A Theoretical Perspective," in *Ethnic Challenges to the Modern Nation State*, supra note 22, pp. 267–93. In her account, "Hindu-Muslim conflict, in India's post-independence phase, derives some of its venom from conflicts between Hindus, in which the threat which Hindu militants claim is posed by 'external' others—the Muslims— is actually the peril of violating the Hindu 'sacred' order from within." Ibid., p. 270. Anthony Marx also shows how interracial conflict was used to unify the previously divided white community after the civil war in the United States. See Anthony W. Marx, *Making Race and Nation: A Comparison of South Africa, the United States, and Brazil* (Cambridge: Cambridge University Press, 1998).

50. Gilbane Fund Lecture #1 (October 19, 1999), p. 7.

51. See Will Kymlicka and Wayne Norman, "Return of the Citizen: A Survey of Recent Work on Citizenship Theory," *Ethics* 104 (1994): 352–81.

52. Rogers Brubaker stresses this point in *Citizenship and Nationhood in France and Germany* (Cambridge, MA: Harvard University Press, 1992), pp. 21–34.

53. In past decades, however, political communities have gradually come to accept the practice of dual or multiple citizenship. See T. Alexander Aleinikoff and Douglas Klusmeyer, "Plural Nationality: Facing the Future in a Migratory World," in T. Alexander Aleinikoff and Douglas Klusmeyer, eds., *Citizenship Today: Global Perspectives and Practices* (Washington, DC: Brookings Institution Press, 2001), pp. 63–88.

54. Rainer Bauböck, "Citizenship and National Identities in the European Union," Harvard Jean Monnet Working Paper (April 1997), p. 1. Baucock contrasts this ideal picture with the real-life complexity that arises from the multiple affiliations that persons may hold, as well as the reality of geographical mobility.

55. Citizenship can also be acquired through immigration and naturalization—but, as such, it is not a matter of right, nor attributed at birth. I briefly discuss these possibilities for membership acquisition below.

56. In Britain, Canada, and the United States, for example, historically the *jus sanguinis* principle operated alongside the *jus soli* principle, and was established by statute (whereas the *jus soli* principle was originally a creation of the common law jurisprudence).

57. See Ann Dummet and Andreas Nicol, *Subject, Citizens, Aliens and Others: Nationality and Immigration Law* (London: Weidenfeld and Nicolson, 1990), p. 7.

58. See Polly J. Price, "Natural Law and Birthright Citizenship in Calvin's Case (1608)," *Yale Journal of Law and the Humanities* 9 (1997): 73–145, esp. p. 83.

59. See Peter H. Schuck and Rogers M. Smith, "Consensual Citizenship," *Chronicles* (1992): 21.

60. In American jurisprudence, the principle of *jus soli* was modified to permit an individual the right to unilaterally terminate her membership in the home community. In other polities, however, the perception of expatriation still echoes the more traditional English common law concept of perpetual allegiance to one's native political community. Under the common law approach, the right of expatriation is neither natural nor inherent in each citizen. Rather, it is an expression of the state's authority to determine who is and who is not a member. Thus, an individual may make a declaration to the effect that he or she desires to renounce her citizenship. Such renunciation, however, will only take effect once consent of the sovereign has been granted.

61. See Dummett and Nicol, *Subjects, Citizens, Aliens, and Others*, supra note 57, pp. 81–82. However, in the late nineteenth century, France adopted the *jus soli* principle, which automatically transforms second- and third-generation immigrants into citizens by virtue of birth within the territory. For a detailed account of the reasons that led to this policy change, see Rogers Brubaker, *Citizenship and Nationhood in France and Germany*, supra note 52, pp. 85–113.

62. To date, there is no governing international principle that can force a country to adopt one or another method of citizenship transmission. Instead, each political community or country is free to chose its own method of assigning citizenship, as a manifestation of its autonomy and sovereignty.

63. See Christopher Eisgruber, "Birthright Citizenship and the Constitution," *New York University Law Review* 72 (1997): 59.

64. Ibid. In theory, one might argue that the *jus sanguinis* birthright rule is more easily justifiable than a *jus soli* rule because it rests on a "relational" understanding of membership (i.e., one that privileges family ties) as opposed to a purely individual-centered vision of membership. This defense of the birthright principle fails, however, to provide us with the tools with which to examine whether such reliance on family and birth in the acquisition of membership indeed increases human dignity, or runs the risk of perpetuating oppressive pat-

terns of reliance on intimate relations in bestowing political membership. For example, there is damning historical evidence that shows how privileging birth (or marriage) as the moment of membership attribution has led to increased regulation and policing of women within various communities. I discuss this latter point in greater detail in "Should Church and State Be Joined at the Altar? Women's Rights and the Multicultural Dilemma," in Will Kymlicka and Wayne Norman, eds., *Citizenship in Diverse Societies* (Oxford: Oxford University Press, 2000), pp. 199–233.

65. John Rawls argues that the effects of natural and social contingencies are "arbitrary from a moral point of view," and must not influence the choice of principles of justice. See John Rawls, *A Theory of Justice* (Cambridge, MA: Harvard University Press, 1971), p. 136. Joseph Carens elaborates and expands on this theme in his discussion of the morality of immigration laws. See Joseph H. Carens, "Aliens and Citizens: The Case for Open Borders," *Review of Politics* 49 (1987): pp. 251–73.

66. It must be acknowledged that different political communities uphold different concepts of what membership in the state entails, in terms of the relationship between the individual and her fellow citizens, as well as between the individual and the state. However, for the purposes of this discussion, the important point is that in spite of these different normative underpinnings of citizenship— whether civic-republican, liberal, ethnocultural, or multicultural—all share the common practice of "reproducing citizens" by birth.

67. The principles of *jus soli* and *jus sanguinis* are often accompanied by procedures of immigration and naturalization, which allow nonmembers to "fill in" what they did not naturally acquire at birth. For example, in the United States today, a mere 10 percent of the population is foreign born. See U.S. Census Bureau, "Foreign-born Population Reaches 25.8 Million" (April 9, 1998) *http:// www.census.gov/Press-Release/cv98-57.html*. For further discussion of the recent wave of immigration to the United States, see Marcelo M. Suárez-Orozco, "Everything You Ever Wanted to Know About Assimilation but Were Afraid to Ask," *Dædalus* 129 (2000): 1–30. In Canada, the principle of birthright membership is established in section 3(1)(a) of the *Citizenship Act*, R.S.C. 1985, c. C-29, which states that anyone born in Canada is considered a Canadian citizen.

68. Joseph H. Carens, "Aliens and Citizens," supra note 65, p. 252 (emphasis added).

69. An exception to this pattern is found in the work of Peter H. Schuck and Rogers M. Smith, *Citizenship Without Consent: Illegal Aliens in the American Polity* (New Haven, CT: Yale University Press, 1986). Schuck and Smith offer a comprehensive argument against the principle of birthright. They recommend instead the adoption of consent-based citizenship rules. However, the rule they propose still privileges birthright (although it effectively nullifies the distinction between *jus soli* and *jus sanguinis* for children born on American soil). Unlike the current membership rules, Schuck and Smith treat birthright solely as a *proxy*

for future political membership, which must later be affirmed by an act of individual consent to such membership.

70. On advocating for the expansion of rights to nonmembers, see, for example, Linda Bosniak, "Universal Citizenship and the Problem of Alienage," *Northwestern Law Review* (forthcoming); Carens, "Aliens and Citizens," supra note 65; Ruth Rubio-Marín, *Immigration as a Democratic Challenge: Citizenship and Inclusion in Germany and the United States* (Cambridge: Cambridge University Press, 2000).

71. I take up this challenge in "Children of a Lesser State," supra note 7.

72. On this controversial proposal, which essentially argues for amending the Fourteenth Amendment, see Schuck and Smith, *Citizenship Without Consent*, supra note 69. Schuck and Smith's book drew heavy criticism, particularly because of their recommendation that the words "subject to the jurisdiction thereof" in the citizenship clause of the Fourteenth Amendment be interpreted as excluding children born to illegal aliens from entitlement to *jus soli* membership in the American polity. For some of these critical responses, see, for example, Joseph H. Carens, "Who Belongs? Theoretical and Legal Questions About Birthright Citizenship in the United States," *University of Toronto Law Journal* 37 (1987): 413–43; David A. Martin, "Membership and Consent: Abstract or Organic?" *Yale Journal of International Law* 11 (1985): 278–96; Gerald L. Newman, "Back to *Dred Scott*," *San Diego Law Review* 24 (1987): 485–99.

73. See H.R.J. Res. 56, 104th Cong. (1995). See also "Societal and Legal Issues Surrounding Children Born in the United States to Illegal Alien Parents: Joint Hearing Before the Subcommittee on Immigration and Claims and the Subcommittee on the Constitutions of the Committee of the Judiciary," 104th Cong., 1st Sess. 32, 1995.

74. See "The Report of the Standing Committee on Citizenship and Immigration," *Canadian Citizenship: A Sense of Belonging* (Ottawa: Canada Communication Group, 1994), p. 17.

75. The proposed constitutional amendment would have permitted the transmission of citizenship by virtue of *jus soli* only for children who have at least one parent who is a citizen or legal resident of the United States.

76. Persuasive defenses of this "responsive" or "democratic" principle of inclusion have been developed by Eisgruber, "Birthright Citizenship," supra note 63, and Rubio-Marín, *Immigration as a Democratic Challenge*, supra note 70.

77. Note that this critique of birthright citizenship is directed here at both "civic" and "ethnic" understandings of the nation. While adopting a different instrument of inclusion, *jus soli* (in most civic nations) and *jus sanguinis* (in most ethnic nations), both types of nations privilege, and actively maintain, *ascriptive* notions of membership. The difference between them may arise in terms of the immigration and naturalization policy they adopt, which may be more exclusionary (if it allows a "right of return" only to those who are already considered

descendants of the nation), or more inclusive (if immigration and naturalization are blind to ethnic, racial, or national origin). Contrary to common belief, not all states that adhere to the "ethnic" concept of nationalism adopt exclusionary immigration and naturalization policies. For further discussion, see Shachar, "Children of a Lesser State," supra note 7.

78. What follows is a concise introduction to this path of inquiry. Note that my critique of birthright membership rules is not intended to challenge the deep attachments that people may feel to their national or communal affiliations, nor do I wish to render judgment on the legitimacy of maintaining such distinct political and cultural units of collective identity. However, my discussion does aim to challenge the existing and largely unquestioned method of acquiring membership within such collectives—whether national or communal—whenever they are based primarily on attribution of status through birthright.

79. See Kymlicka, "Modernity and National Identity," supra note 22, p. 14.

80. See, for example, E. J. Hobsbawm, *Nations and Nationalism since 1870: Programme, Myth, Reality* (Cambridge: Cambridge University Press, 1990).

81. In a report issued by the Canadian Standing Committee on Citizenship and Immigration in 1994, this point was made in the following way: "[I]n our view, the requirement of physical residency in this country is essential to the process of 'Canadianization.' This happens by living here. . . . Residency is an experience, a Canadian experience, for which there can be no substitute." See *Canadian Citizenship: A Sense of Belonging*, supra note 74.

82. The only legal limitation imposed on this general right to vote is the requirement that the voter reach the age of majority and be of full mental capacity, as defined by the relevant polity. Certain other limitations may apply in relation to the right to run for office for selected political posts; for example, the native-born requirement in the case of the president of the United States.

83. Nor are the more traditional elements within such religious groups necessarily committed to providing opportunities to interpret (and possibly revise) sacred texts or established customs to *all* group members, regardless of gender, caste, and so on.

84. There are, however, other (more progressive) interpretations of any religion that may adhere more fully to principles of equality. Historically, in most democratic polities, the acquisition of political voice by women, for example, was connected to the removal of legal barriers to formal equality between citizens, such as the abolition of the infamous "coverture" doctrine. It remains to be seen if similar processes of revoking entrenched inequalities within groups will be followed by increased political access to the processes of transforming the rules governing their communities of faith by women (and other previously excluded sectors of the population).

85. Brubaker, *Citizenship and Nationhood*, supra note 52, p. 21.

86. For a provocative defense of the understanding of citizenship as a concept

of bounded caring, see Louis Michael Seidman, "Fear and Loathing at the Border," in Warren F. Schwartz, ed., *Justice in Immigration* (Cambridge: Cambridge University Press, 1995), pp. 136–46.

87. Ibid., p. 139.

88. A similar pattern is repeated on the supranational level; for example, with the acquisition of EU citizenship open only to those persons who are already defined as citizens of the member states.

89. The targets of violence and mass atrocity may also be "outsiders from within": persons who are cast as less than full members because they belong to specific targeted groups within the body politic. They may be equal citizens according to their passports (as German Jews were in the 1930s), but their vulnerability indicates (and perpetuates) their second-class citizenship status in practice.

90. See, for example, the collection of essays in Brian Barry and Robert E. Goodin, eds., *Free Movement: Ethical Issues in the Transnational Migration of People and Money*, (Philadelphia: Pennsylvania State University Press, 1992).

91. Peter Andreas, "The Escalation of U.S. Immigration Control in the Post-NAFTA Era," *Political Science Quarterly* 113 (1998–1999): 591–615.

92. Ibid., p. 591. Saskia Sassen suggests that we can think about such external borders not only as sites for the regulation of the movement of individuals, but also as a symbolic manifestation of state power per se, in an era when many of the traditional functions of national government power have devolved to other agents (both "above" and "below" the state level). See Sassen, supra note 43. Recent proposals to adjust the status in the United States of illegal migrants from Mexico may, at first glance, seem to challenge this trend. This is a misguided impression, however. While representing a welcome development—in that these proposals suggest that persons who have de facto become members in a society can also enjoy the full benefits (and protections) of citizenship—such adjustment of status reiterates the significance of the "citizen-alien" distinction as the basis for distributing (or withholding) such benefits.

93. Article 1 of the Convention defines a "refugee" as a person who: "owing to a well-founded fear of being persecuted for reasons of race, religion, nationality, membership of a particular social group or political opinion, is outside the country of his nationality and is unable or, owing to such fear, is unwilling to avail himself of the protection of that country; or who, not having a nationality and being outside the country of his former habitual residence as a result of such events, is unable or, owing to such fear, is unwilling to return to it."

94. Skilled workers account for approximately half of the annual intake of immigrants to Canada and to Australia. These figures are far lower for the United States, which relies primarily on family-reunification immigration categories.

95. United Nations Population Fund, *The State of the World Population 1999*, chap. 2, figure 5, at *http://www.unfpa.org/swp/1999/chapter2d.htm*.

96. Brubaker, for example, defends this practice primarily due to its adminis-

trative convenience and the *realpolitik* fact that citizens would have nowhere to go to if they gained no automatic membership on the basis of birthplace or parentage. See Brubaker, "Citizenship and Naturalization," supra note 40; *Citizenship and Nationhood*, supra note 52.

97. See Walzer, *Spheres of Justice*, supra note 39, p. 38.

98. See Carol M. Rose, "Women and Property: Gaining and Losing Ground," *Virginia Law Review* 78 (1992): 453.

99. At the very least, imposed national affiliations, which rest on connecting factors of "blood or soil," severely restrict the access of the vast majority of the world's population to the basic goods of stable government, minimal health care services, submission to the rule of law, and democratic accountability.

100. See, for example, Chandran Kukathas, "Are There Any Cultural Rights?" *Political Theory* 20 (1992): 105–42. Even when such a right of exit is secured, there may still be serious concerns about the *distribution* of access and the *capacity* to exercise this right.

101. Note that the community to which the individual belongs by virtue of birthright may not recognize the validity of the state court's decision in a matter that, according to that community's own norms, must be regulated solely by its personal law rules.

102. I myself have contributed to this body of literature. See supra notes 10 and 36. For other feminist lines of critique, see, for example, Martha Nussbuam, *Sex and Social Justice* (Oxford: Oxford University Press, 1999); Susan Moller Okin, "Feminism and Multiculturalism: Some Tensions," *Ethics* 108 (1998): 661–81; Sawitri Saharso, "Female Autonomy and Cultural Imperative," in Will Kymlicka and Wayne Norman, eds., *Citizenship in Diverse Societies* (Oxford: Oxford University Press, 2000), pp. 224–42.

When Memory Speaks:
Remembrance and Revenge in *Unforgiven**

AUSTIN SARAT

> But he also wondered about himself, that he cannot learn to
> forget but always remains attached to the past: however far and
> fast he runs, the chain runs with him. It is astonishing: the
> moment, here in a wink, gone in a wink, nothing before and
> nothing after, returns nevertheless as a specter to disturb the
> calm of a later moment. Again and again a page loosens in the
> scroll of time, drops out, and flutters away—and suddenly
> flutters back again into a man's lap. Then man says "I
> remember" and envies the animal which immediately forgets
> and sees each moment really die, sink back into deep night
> extinguished forever.
>
> —Friedrich Nietzsche, *The Use and Abuse of History*, 8–9

Introduction

What is the role of memory in vengeance and the violence it entails? What is the relationship among past, present, and future that vengeance creates? How are narrative connections made between those who are injured and those who use violence to reply to such injuries? Do certain kinds of memories sustain vengeance while others diminish it? In the typical revenge story the answers to these questions seem rather straight-forward. Injury, so the story goes, demands redress and where redress is not forthcoming in the near term, injuries should not be forgotten.[1] For those looking for non–vengeance-based conceptions of justice, memory

* Another version of this essay will appear in the *Indiana Law Journal*. For their helpful comments and suggestions, I am grateful to Dedi Felman, Susan Sage Heinzelman, Ian Malcolm, Richard Sherwin, Nancy Rosenblum, and Martha Umphrey.

is one important source of trouble;[2] in the face of unremediated injury, forgiveness, if not forgetfulness, is the answer.[3] For victims, memory is one source of pain; the past constitutes the true victimization.[4] The call of the victim is to rectify the past, to placate memory by silencing the ghosts whose constant call is for vengeance.

In the usual story of revenge, the voice of the victim is an urgent call both to remember and also to obliterate memory, to attend to the past and to make a different recollection. One hope is that a new memory, the memory of a blood-letting punishment, "can be substituted for the shameful memory of the evil deed that one was powerless to prevent."[5] Vengeance expresses "a wish to change the world and right the past, to be seen and counted in a private and ultimately a public conversion of memory, to reassign guilt and to end that unending memory of horror that is, says Aeschylus, 'a relentless anguish gnawing at the heart.'"[6] But not all forms of remembrance speak in the same way to this wish and this anguish. Some ways of remembering bring about change; others do not. Some ways of remembering keep alive horror; others do not. Some ways of remembering fuel vengeful violence; others do not. Some memories are "marketed," associating vengeance with honor, arousing people to engage in vengeful violence by glorifying and/or romanticizing it. Other memories are the product of direct experience with violence in which what is remembered is the face of death itself. In this essay I explore these different kinds of memories and their complex connections to revenge.

Whatever the connection between remembrance and revenge, vengeance's "wish to change the world" and the "relentless anguish" that is revenge have long been the objects of critique in legal and political thought.

> The official anti-vengeance discourse has a long history beginning with the Stoics, taken up and elaborated by medieval churchmen, and later by the architects of state building. Revenge is still a kind of *eminence grise* in the 17th and 18th century classic texts of liberal moral and political philosophy . . . The Other for this particular tradition of philosophy is none other than the ethic of honor and glory, the ethic of revenge.[7]

Modern legality is founded on the belief that revenge must and can be repressed, that legal punishment can be founded on reason, that due process can discipline passion, and that these categories are both knowable and distinct.[8] Aladjem observes that this inclination to make revenge over into a rational principle of justice has roots in democratic theory and in certain suppositions of natural law. It arose in claims about the founding of the state, where it was said that a process of consent converts the laws of nature into those of civil society and that the state acquires its right to punish from consenting individuals who thereby relinquish a natural right to avenge themselves. From the beginning, however, that reasoning presents a paradox: the state is supposed to arise from the inclinations of individuals as they might be found in nature, but it must rescue them from the very same inclinations . . . [A] vengeful "natural man" turns to the state as a place of appeal from the injustices of nature *and* from the excesses of his own revenge.[9]

Or, as Susan Jacoby notes,

Justice is a legitimate concept in the modern code of civilized behavior. Vengeance is not. We prefer to avert our eyes from those who persist in reminding us of the wrongs they have suffered. . . . Such people are disturbers of the peace; we wish they would take their memories away to a church, a cemetery, a psychotherapist's office and allow us to return justice and vengeance to the separate compartments they supposedly occupy in twentieth-century life.[10]

Retribution, with its advertised virtues of measured proportionality, cool detachment, and consistency is contrasted with vengeance—the voice of the other, the primitive, the savage call of unreason, a "wildness" inside the house of law which, by nature, will not succumb to rational forms of justice.[11] Vengeance must be kept at bay, so the argument goes, because it represents an unwarranted concession to an anger and passion that knows no limits.[12] As Augustine put it,

We do not wish to have the sufferings of the servants of God avenged by the infliction of precisely similar injuries in the way of retaliation . . . [O]ur desire is that justice be satisfied . . . [W]ho does not see that a restraint is put upon the boldness of savage violence, and the remedies fitted to produce repentance are not withdrawn, the discipline should be called a benefit rather than a vindictive punishment.[13]

Akin to such "vindictive punishment" is hatred, a defiant and "sinful" unwillingness to forget injuries and forgive those who injure us.[14] Vengeance, in this view, is "crazed, uncontrolled, subjective, individual, admitting no reason, no rule of limitation. . . . Conventional wisdom con-

ceives of vengeance cultures as barely cultured at all, all id and no superego: big dumb brutes looking for excuses to kill."[15]

In their unceasing efforts to overcome id with superego and to construct
a legitimating ideology, modern legal orders substitute the calm calculation of deterrence, the empathetic understanding of rehabilitation, and the
stern, but controlled, discipline of retribution for the emotionalism of
revenge.[16] Justice becomes public and the voice of the victim, or the
vengeful anger of the victim's kin or champion, is merged with the dis-
tanced state bureaucracy which speaks for "the People" against whom all
offenses to the criminal law are said to be directed.[17] As Beccaria states,

> It is sometimes the custom to release a man from the punishment of a
> slight crime when the injured pardons him: an act, indeed, which is in
> accordance with mercy and humanity but contrary to public policy; as
> if a private citizen could by his remission do away with the necessity
> of the example in the same way that he can excuse the reparation due
> for an offense. The right of punishing does not rest with an individual,
> but with the community as a whole, or the sovereign.[18]

The opposition between revenge and retribution is close to the core of
a set of dichotomies that structure the ideology of liberal political
thought generally and liberal legalism in particular.[19] These dichotomies
are centered in the opposition between passion and reason.[20] Despite
many important efforts to suggest the rationality of revenge[21] and to
show its normative content,[22] this opposition still persists in philosophical
treatments of the subject. Thus, for example, Shklar contends that
revenge is "uniquely subjective, not measurable, and probably an un-
quenchable urge of the provoked heart. It is the very opposite of justice,
in every respect, and inherently incompatible with it. . . . Revenge is not
detached, impersonal, proportionate or rule bound."[23]

Not "detached, impersonal, proportionate, or rule bound"—these are
the defining defects of revenge, which are juxtaposed to the "advantages" legal punishment provides, at least in theory. But Shklar herself
admits that vengeance is never effectively and fully purged from a system of justice:

> If effective justice preempts, neutralizes, dilutes, and all but replaces
> revenge, it cannot abolish it, either as an emotion or as an active re-
> sponse available to us, especially in personal relations. For most peo-
> ple retributive justice is justice, but it remains a frustrating substitute
> for revenge, neither eliminating nor satisfying its urging.[24]

Revenge, as Shklar argues, is an urge lurking in the shadows, whose presence, at least in liberal theory, provides one reason for the founding of the modern state, and whose continuing force fuels the apparatus of punishment itself.[25] Connolly suggests that

> Punishment exacts revenge on the past, and the past is not necessarily confined to the past acts of the one punished. . . . Revenge through law offers immediate gratification to the offended. . . . In crime and punishment two contending calls to revenge clash on the streets and in the courts, and each is refueled by the collisions between them.[26]

Revenge can be renamed, but not contained. It can be repressed, but neither denied nor forgotten.

Martha Minow's "Memory and Hate: Are There Lessons From Around the World?" (chapter 1) reminds us of the unforgettable nature of revenge and the role of memory in the constitution of vengeance. Minow suggests that memory, whether the memory of vengeance latent in all legal systems or the memory that calls for revenge, is constructed out of "bits of information selected and arranged in light of prior narratives and current expectations, needs, and beliefs."[27] The experience of unremediated injury does not automatically, and in every case, call for vengeance. And, injuries unremediated do not automatically, and in every case, become the stuff of a vengeance seeking memory. Memories are made and marketed by persons and groups with distinct political agendas. They stoke vengeance because they are encouraged to do so. But memory may be made to play other roles, constraining if not obliterating vengeful impulses. Thus Minow calls on those interested in understanding vengeance and the violence it entails to attend to the complex, paradoxical, frequently contradictory role that memory plays, sometimes fueling a quest for revenge that seems insatiable, sometimes quelling it.

Taking up Minow's call means turning from the disciplined effort to marshal evidence about the "truth" of the past to the slippery terrain on which individuals and groups invent traditions[28] and record partisan versions of the past on the basis of which they seek to construct particular conditions in the present.[29] Pierre Nora writes,

> Memory, is life, borne by living societies founded in its name. It remains in permanent evolution, open to the dialectic of remembering and forgetting, unconscious of its successive deformations, vulnerable to manipulation and appropriation. . . . [H]istory, on the other hand, is

the reconstruction . . . of what is no longer. . . . History, because it is an intellectual and secular production, calls for analysis and criticism. . . . At the heart of history is a critical discourse that is antithetical to . . . memory.[30]

Acts of commemoration are the very stuff of politics;[31] in and through our political processes we decide who or what should be remembered or memorialized and in what ways.[32] As David Thelen argues, "[M]emory, private and individual, as much as collective and cultural is constructed, not reproduced. . . . [T]his construction is not made in isolation but in conversations with others that occur in the contexts of community, broader politics, and social dynamics."[33]

In the present moment, as Nora reminds us, memory is "above all archival. It relies on the materiality of the trace, the immediacy of the recording, the visibility of the image. . . . Even as traditional memory disappears, we feel obliged assiduously to collect remains, testimonies, documents, images, speeches, any visible signs of what has been."[34] Museums, monuments, and the like are today, Nora argues, the locations of memory, the sites to which collective memory is attached. If that is indeed the case, one might ask whether tales of vengeance themselves might be one of what Nora calls "*les lieux de memoire.*"

Here our interest is directed to the temporal dimension of revenge, the way it stands in relation to the past, the present, and the future. Vengeance re-enacts the past, both intentionally and unconsciously, and it is one place where the present speaks to the future through acts of commemoration.[35]

In this essay I want to take up Minow's call to explore the linkage between memory and vengeance through a reading of Clint Eastwood's *Unforgiven*. This 1992 film, itself a classic of the revenge genre, commemorates the film Western,[36] with its story of the triumph of good over evil and of heroic men taming wild territory. But here commemoration is not celebration. *Unforgiven* is a classic in part because it complicates that story.[37] As Miller notes, "It puts in issue and complicates the assumptions of the revenge genre by troubling itself about the fact that the demands of heroism and of being at the center of heroic narrative may put one in a position that compromises perfect justice."[38]

Unforgiven is important because it provides not only reworking of the revenge tale but also a thoughtful reflection on the complex connection of remembrance and revenge. It is a story about storytelling and the consequences of the stories we tell for the lives we lead and the deeds we do. It puts storytelling itself on trial as it explores the way memories are constructed and the way they mold action. It constructs a dichotomy between monumental memory, which glorifies violence, and direct, "realist" memory that restrains it. It praises the latter while condemning the former. In this film, a past of purposeless violence is unforgiven. Injuries unredressed are unforgiven. But doing vengeance violently is also unforgiven. While we are called on to remember unforgivable injury, certain kinds of remembering and certain kinds of action, too, may be unforgivable.

The Voice of Remembrance and the Urge to Revenge: Simple Justice and Heroic Tales

Unforgiven tells the story of William Munny (played by Clint Eastwood).[39] Munny was once one of the West's most ruthless and feared men, but at the opening of the film he has retired from his life of violence and is a middle-aged, widowed father of two, trying without great success to make a go of it as a pig farmer. The drama of the film unfolds when a young cowboy, the Scofield Kid, appears at the farm and asks Munny to join him in his plan to collect a $1,000 reward. The bounty, put up by a group of prostitutes, is an inducement for vengeance. It is offered to anyone who kills two men; one, Quick Mike, a hot-tempered brute, slashed the face of Delilah, a prostitute who laughed when she saw his tiny penis. The other, Davey, was inadvertently involved in the slashing incident. The prostitutes post the reward when the town's sheriff, Little Bill, responds to the slashing by letting the cowboys go on the promise that they will compensate Skinny, the man who owns the saloon where the prostitutes work, for the income he will lose because of the injuries to Delilah. As Miller says about this part of *Unforgiven*, "The slashed woman doesn't figure in Bill's compensatory scheme; he agrees with Skinny in seeing her as property, or at least not sufficiently individualized so as to have a compensable claim in her own right."[40]

The slashed woman plays almost no role in the vengeance tale told in *Unforgiven*. Indeed, Delilah is virtually voiceless. She makes no claim; she asks for no remedy, nor does she seek to enlist others to speak on her behalf. Nonetheless, the call for vengeance is heard. The voice of vengeance speaks through Alice, another prostitute who acts as Delilah's perhaps unwanted champion. As another of the prostitutes asks, "If Delilah doesn't care one way of the other what are we getting all riled up about?" This unanswered question is a question about the structure of

vengeance itself and about who is authorized to speak the memory of
injury.

When memory speaks out seeking vengeance, the vehicle of its articulation may be displaced. It may not be the voice of the victim that counts. Instead, the memory of injury often is marketed by moral entrepreneurs whose cause may not be identical to those on whose behalf they act.[41]

Throughout *Unforgiven* Alice speaks enthusiastically as the voice of vengeance. Immediately after Delilah is slashed, Alice asks, "You gonna hang them, Little Bill?" And, when Bill seems inclined to whip them instead, Alice says, "A whipping? That's all they get after what they done?" Bill eventually settles on a scheme to compensate Skinny. In response, Alice says, "You ain't even gonna whip them? . . . For what they done Skinny gets some ponies and that's it? It ain't fair." Bill answers by asking "Ain't you seen enough blood for one night?"

Here the basic structure of a revenge tale is put in place.[42] An injury is done and the law either does not respond or fails, from the perspective of the victim or those who call on law to remember her injuries, to respond adequately.[43] Yet we are reminded that vengeance does not speak in a precise calculus of pain returned for pain inflicted. Alice seeks death for the man who slashed Delilah's face and for his less culpable companion. Is death proportional to the injury inflicted? Do Mike and Davey both deserve the same punishment?[44]

The contrast between Delilah's silence and Alice's insistent appropriation of her cause—Alice's insistence that Delilah's injury not be forgotten—is marked late in the film when the prostitutes learn that Davey has been shot by Munny and the Scofield Kid. "I didn't think they would really do it," Delilah remarks. By contrast, Alice yells to a crowd of men in the street, "He had it coming for what he done. He had it coming and the other one too."

But what is Alice's agenda? While some suggest that "the women have interests that justify their vengefulness on behalf of Delilah,"[45] *Unforgiven* leaves its viewers to ask why Alice imagines that she can or should speak for Delilah. Is she like the leaders who, as Ignatieff wrote about the war in the Balkans, stirred up war by convincing "neighbors and friends that in reality they had been massacring each other since time immemorial" when history "has no such lesson to teach?"[46] Is her call for vengeance based on a sympathetic identification with Delilah? Or is it perhaps a prudent investment in deterrence? Or perhaps she is taking out her own anger and resentment toward all of those who "ride" her

Alice with Little Bill

Alice revenge

and the other prostitutes "like horses." Whatever her agenda, she uses memory to fuel vengeance; she insists that without revenge the memory of injury cannot be placated.

There are two other figures in the film who use memory to stoke the violence that vengeance requires, but in neither case is it their own memory that they use. The first is the Scofield Kid. It is the Kid who initially enlists Munny as his partner in responding to the prostitutes' call for vengeance and securing the reward. He seeks out Munny because he has heard of Munny's youthful exploits from his Uncle Pete. When the Scofield Kid first arrives, Munny is struggling in the pig pen on his farm. Witnessing this scene the Kid says,

> You don't look like no rootin', tootin', son of a bitchin', cold-blooded assassin, someone that shot Charlie Pepper up in Lake County. . . . You shot Charlie Pepper didn't you? And you are the one who killed William Harper who robbed that train over in Missouri. . . . Uncle Pete says that you were the meanest son of a bitch alive and that if I ever wanted a partner for a killing you were the worst one, on account as you are cold as the snow. You don't have no weak nerve.

The Scofield Kid

Later he asks Will about another incident that his Uncle Pete has told him about, an incident that foretells the film's climatic shootout in Skinny's saloon. "Say Will," the Kid asks, "that business up in Jackson County, that really happen? . . . There was two deputies up close to you. They had you dead to rights. You pulled out your pistol and shot them both to hell. Uncle Pete says he never seen nothing like it."

The Scofield Kid lives in a mythic world, a world of larger-than-life violent men and of victims avenged. He aspires to join that world, to become a heroic instrument of vengeance. He "flees resignation and uses history as a means against resignation."[47] Through Munny he constructs what Nietzsche called "monumental" history.[48] This history provides "knowledge that the great thing existed and was therefore possible and so may be possible again. He is heartened on his way; for his doubt in weaker moments, whether his desire is not for the impossible is struck aside. . . . In most cases, however, no reward beckons him unless it be fame, that is, the expectation of a place of honor in the temple of history."[49]

But the Scofield Kid's is not the voice of someone who has killed, of someone for whom there are real memories of vengeful violence. That the Scofield Kid is young and has difficulty seeing more than fifty yards ahead of him perhaps foretells his fate in a film about a middle-aged killer turned pig farmer. Thus, after his first and only killing, the Kid renounces violence. Giving his gun to Munny he says, "Keep it. I'm never going to use it again. I'm never going to kill no one, no more. I ain't like you Will. . . . I guess I'd rather be blind and ragged than dead." Memory stands as the Kid's tutor, only this time the memory is not monumental. This time it is his own, not Uncle Pete's, the remembrance of the stunned look of a man shot at close range in an outhouse.

W. W. Beauchamp, dime novelist, biographer, and chronicler of the violent exploits of the old West is the Kid's cinematic double in *Unforgiven*. Like the Kid he narrates the memories of others, but unlike him Beauchamp is neither young nor sightless. While the Kid needs something to aid his vision, the film repeatedly calls attention to Beauchamp's glasses. While the Kid is young and brave, Beauchamp is cynical and cowardly. While the Kid is naive, Beauchamp knows what he is about. As Miller observes, "The presence of Beauchamp makes the movie into something more than a revenge story. It also becomes an essay on competing heroic styles and the manner of heroic self-fashioning." His business is to create memory rather than to record history, to glorify violence rather than to take note of its gruesome details.[50] That he has no stomach for the reality of the violence he chronicles is suggested when he loses control of his bladder when guns are drawn on English Bob and himself and when he whines about injuries he did not in fact suffer when, later in the film, he finds someone else's blood on his clothes.

Like the prostitutes who work in Skinny's establishment, the memories that Beauchamp crafts, and Beauchamp himself, are continuously in circulation. They sell sex; he sells myths. In the film we see him passed from English Bob (an English dandy who works for the railroad killing Chinese and speaks with disdain about the absence of a monarchical tradition on the frontier. "It is uncivilized shooting persons of substance," he says) to Little Bill and, after the death of the latter, Beauchamp tries to cozy up to Munny, only to have his advances rejected.

Earlier, when Little Bill reads what Beauchamp has written in a pamphlet about English Bob titled "The Duke of Death," he mocks both the publication and its allegedly heroic subject, pointing out its seemingly exaggerated claims and inflated rhetoric. Beauchamp replies that it is

Little Bill Reading *The Duke of Death*

"generally considered acceptable in the publishing business to take a certain liberty with the cover story" even as he assures Bill that "the events described in the book are taken from the accounts of eyewitnesses." When Bill says that he was an eyewitness, Beauchamps's pretense to accuracy quickly fades.

He is a maker of myths and memories, not a scribe. He makes memories of other people's memories, fashioning the kind of heroic tales that work to sustain a culture of vengeful violence by eliding the grim realities that vengeful violence produces.[51] He corrupts all by turning violence into "fiction, to pretense, and to collusion between the media and the subjects of its attention."[52] And, unlike the Kid, Beauchamp is not repelled by violence. Indeed, in the presence of a good story, he seems not to notice it. Because of his blindness to violence, he never renounces the heroic tale that romanticizes violence. Thus, at the end of the film we see him watching from the shadows as Munny rides out of town and are left to imagine his next liaison in the business of creating the heroic myths that sustain a culture of vengeance.

Scofield Kid and William Munny

Remembering the Dead, Remembering Death: Memory Against Vengeance

Neither Alice nor Beauchamp, as voices of memory, are able, on their own, to work their will in the world. They are both dependent on their ability to enlist others in vengeful violence. Nor can the Scofield Kid's monumental memory sustain vengeance in its confrontation with the stark realities of violence. While each of them is, at least initially, an enthusiast for revenge, one of the agents who is enlisted to do Alice's bidding, Will Munny, hardly shares their enthusiasm. He rejects Alice's seemingly unambiguous belief in the adequation of injury and response, and, unlike the Scofield Kid and Beauchamp he has seen through heroic myths and monumental history. He remembers the dead and death,[53] weighing the call for revenge against its consequences in dreams ended, lives wasted, children left without parents, and rotting corpses.

While he is, as a result, at best ambivalent about vengeance, Munny is unreservedly hostile to the myths and memories that sustain it. This ambivalence and hostility is highlighted in his initial reluctance to join the Scofield Kid, and, later, after he agrees to do so, has come to town, and

William Munny About to Shoot Little Bill

been beaten by Little Bill, all he can muster is "I guess" when Delilah asks whether he is "really going to kill them cowboys." Still later, in a scene played out under a tree reminiscent of the scene that opens the film, after the two cowboys have been killed, the Scofield Kid begins to come to terms with his own memories, his own understanding of what it means to kill. "It don't seem real," he says, "He ain't going to ever breathe again. He's dead. The other one too. All on account of pulling the trigger."

Munny responds, "It's a hell of a thing killing a man. You take away all he's got and all he's ever going to have."

When the Kid tries to reassure himself by recalling the logic of a vengeance fulfilled, saying, "Yeah, well, I guess they had it coming," Munny replies, "We all have it coming, Kid." Whereas vengeance speaks about what people have coming, about injury and its deserved response, in this play on words Munny's emphasis is the fact that death comes to everyone regardless of desert.[54]

Finally, even when Munny himself has something more personal to avenge, namely the unjustified and brutal beating, killing, and disgrace of his friend Ned at the hands of Little Bill, he can muster neither Alice's enthusiasm for vengeance, her confident voice of remembrance, nor the heroic narrative imagination of the Scofield Kid or Beauchamp.[55] Thus in the signature line of the film, just before he kills Little Bill, Munny responds to his plea, "I don't deserve this, to die like this" by again undercutting the logic of revenge. "Deserve," he says, "got nothin' to do with it." Munny's "self-doubts about his life of violence, the fact that no one ever brought him to justice for his past evil deeds, makes him think the delivery of justice [is] purely random, a matter of good or bad luck."[56]

If for Alice memory fuels the desire for vengeance in the victims and/ or their surrogates, and if for the Scofield Kid and Beauchamp memory is fashioned so as to glorify violence, in Munny memory disciplines the vengeful urge, even as it haunts and torments those who would be its agents. His constant awareness and remembrance of the horror of death, of all death, stands between him and enthusiasm for vengeance and it prompts his refusal to remember. As Nietzsche wrote about people like Munny, the past "presses him [Munny] down and bows his shoulders; he travels with a dark invisible burden."[57]

This difference is marked right from the start of the film in a scrolling narrative that runs as we watch a man digging (a grave) beside a lone standing tree. This narrative brands Munny a known thief and murderer, a man "of notoriously vicious and intemperate disposition," even as it eulogistically tells of the death of his wife, Claudia, a comely woman of twenty-nine, who died, so the narrative says, not, as her mother might have expected, at the hand of William Munny, but from smallpox. It is Claudia who, we learn, domesticated and tamed Munny, more successfully it seems than he is able to domesticate and tame the animals on the farm he has been left to tend.

Whereas Little Bill differentiates among the purposes of violence and those who perpetrate it, separating out "tramps, loafers, and bad men" from good men who make mistakes, and justifies his own "lawful" brutality by contrasting it with the violence of "assassins," Claudia memorializes the danger of violence no matter how "noble" the cause to which it is put. This remembrance afflicts Munny, keeping him constantly in touch with what a life of violence does to life itself and with the real world of death. Throughout the film, he engages in dialogue with Claudia even as he speaks to others, seeking to reassure her that when he goes off to do vengeful violence that he is no longer a killer.

Before joining the Scofield Kid, he visits her grave and tells his children that she liked the flowers he brought her. He tells them that their mother will be looking down on them as he rides off to join the Kid

William Munny and Ned

whom he had previously told, "I ain't like that [a violent person] any more
. . . My wife, she cured me of that. Cured me of drink and wickedness." In
addition, Ned says that "if Claudia were alive, you wouldn't be doing this"
(going off to avenge the injured prostitute). Later Munny repeats to Ned
what he had said to the Scofield Kid, "I ain't like that no more. Claudia, she
straightened me out . . . And just cause we're going on a killing, that
doesn't mean I am going back to being the way I was."[58] When Ned and he
discuss sex, Munny says, "The only woman a man like me can get is one
he'd have to pay for. That ain't right, buying flesh. Claudia, God rest her
soul, would never want me doing something like that."

Not only does Munny have the kind of living connection to the dead
that disciplines his violence, but his memories connect him to the grim
realities of death itself. His life exemplifies Nietzsche's argument that
"whoever cannot settle on the threshold of the moment forgetful of the
whole past . . . will never know what happiness is."[59] Perhaps this is why
Munny refuses the invitation to narrate,[60] to tell the Scofield Kid the truth
about his exploits, a truth which is too painful to keep alive. Munny
claims not to remember the violence he did, responding to the Kid's
questions by saying, "I can't remember. I was drunk most of the time."

He denies memory so that he can live. But memory overcomes denial when, three times during the film, Munny does remember, three times he conjures an image of death.

Each of these recollections is shared with Ned, his longtime friend and companion. Each involves a horrible imagining of the fate that may await him. The first occurs when, sitting together in a darkness illuminated only by a campfire, Munny asks, "Ned, you remember that drover I shot through the mouth and his teeth came out the back of his head? I think about him now and again. He didn't do anything to deserve to get shot." The second remembrance is linked to the nightmarish claim that Munny has seen someone who died long ago. Munny again asks Ned about someone that he (Munny) had killed. "You remember Eagle Hendershot? I saw him." "Will," Ned replies, "he's dead." Undeterred, Munny insists, "I saw him, Ned. His head was all broke open; you could see inside of it."

The third vision of death is less a remembering than a premonition brought on by a high fever that Munny experiences after having been beaten within an inch of his life by Little Bill. "I've seen death," Munny announces. "I've seen the angel of death. He's got snakes for eyes. . . . I saw Claudia, too, all covered with worms. I'm scared I'm dying." His remembrance of the dead is joined to his remembrance of death, producing a powerful fear that conditions the way Munny responds to the call for vengeful violence.

In each of these memories/images of death, what Munny sees is not the living survivor, but the corpse left behind. What he remembers is not the legend, but the twisted remains. His memory is anything but monumental, anything but heroic. Munny's memories of the dead and of death are what Nietzsche called "critical."[61] Such memories "bring the past to the bar of judgment, interrogate it remorselessly, and finally condemn it . . . It is not justice that sits in judgment here . . . but only life, the dim, driving force that insatiably desires—itself."[62]

The depth of Munny's hostility to heroic memory and monumental history is shown in his last interactions with its two primary representatives in *Unforgiven*, the Scofield Kid and Beauchamp. By the end of the film, the former, as I have already indicated, has renounced heroic memory and monumental history in the name of life. This renunciation leads Munny to assure him, "You don't worry. I'm not going to kill you. You are the only friend I've got."

Munny's real enemies are those who create the kind of heroic memory and monumental history that fuel violence and vengeance—this is made clear after the climatic shootout in Skinny's. Beauchamp is in the Saloon with Bill and others celebrating the capture of Ned when Munny appears. It is as if Munny has been reborn, or at least the part of the self that Munny previously had so strenuously renounced has reappeared, a self apparently undivided in its embrace of vengeance. Emboldened by whiskey he seeks out Little Bill and Skinny to avenge Ned's killing and the dishonoring of his body (Ned's body has been left in an open casket outside Skinny's saloon. The casket is decorated with a sign that says "This is what happens to assassins around here").

His entrance is visually arresting, he is again the classic gunfighter, nerves of steel, shotgun at the ready. With little fanfare he shoots Skinny. "Sir," Bill shouts, "you are a cowardly son of a bitch. You just shot an unarmed man." "Well," Munny responds, "he should have armed himself if he was going to decorate this saloon with my friend." Bill demands to know whether he is "one William Munny . . . who killed women and children." "That's right," Munny answers, now in the full glow of recollection embracing the self he had previously renounced. "I've killed women and children and about everything that walks or crawls at one time or another. I'm here to kill you Little Bill for what you did to Ned."

Even as he embraces a vengeful violence Munny insists on debunking its heroic pretensions, linking revenge to killing "women," "children," and "everything that walks or crawls." At this point the camera pans to Beauchamps's face with its wide-eyed look, as if the narrator of other's memories will now become an eyewitness to history. What follows is exactly the kind of action out of which Beauchamp makes the stuff of legends, as Munny kills five men singlehandedly. And when Beauchamp crawls out from under a body that has fallen on him he displays no interest in the horror of the carnage around him. Unlike the Scofield Kid, he is truly blind. Unlike Munny, he is connected to neither the dead nor death itself.

Instead, he tries to substitute Munny for English Bob and Little Bill, wanting him to become a character whose heroic persona he can fashion. "Who did you kill first?" he asks. "I was lucky in the order. I've always been lucky when it comes to killing folks," Munny replies, as if debunking his own larger-than-life agency. When Beauchamp, licking his lips, eager for the full story, persists and asks, "Who was next?" Munny answers in a menacing tone, "All I can tell you is who is going to be last." In contrast to his assurance to the Kid, this scene ends with an ill-disguised threat to kill the author, the myth maker, before he can ply his death-doing, violence-inducing trade again.

Beauchamp and William Munny

Vengeance is done
...done

Vengeance is done, but its costs to those who do it are enormous. Vengeance is done, but unheroically, by someone who has long ago abandoned the idea that there can be either honor or glory in the taking of human life, by a man who is drawn to it reluctantly, regretfully, with a full acknowledgment of the way acts of vengeance sanctify but also dishonor those in whose names vengeance is taken as well as those who take revenge. Memory speaks to remind both Munny and the film's viewers that those who wield the violence of vengeance are, like those whose unjust acts call it forth, unforgiven.

Conclusion

Vengeance, I have argued, depends on memory, but not all memory serves vengeance equally. *Unforgiven* tells this story of remembrance and revenge by relying on a humanist narrative in which the memory of direct experience quells vengeance while monumental memory incites it. This narrative suggests that contact with the grim realities of death is part and parcel of a world in which the violence of vengeance can be left behind, or, if not left behind, then at least taken off its pedestal. The dichotomy between the realist, antinarrative posture of its taciturn leading man, and the mythic imagination of the Scofield Kid or the crassly constructed monumental histories of Beauchamp, may be neither as clear nor as determinate in its implications for the politics of revenge as the film makes it out to be.

Despite these deficiencies, *Unforgiven* is an important statement of the ways in which memory speaks and of the complex connections of remembrance and revenge. This film gives testimony to the power and consequences of the stories we tell about violence and vengeance as well as to the power and consequences of the ways we remember. It invites its viewers to take up the task of re-imagining the terms on which we memorialize injury and injustice and asks us to remember that vengeful violence is always poised precariously between this world's call to do justice and the shrug of indifference that may await us in the next.

Notes

Video stills are from *The Unforgiven*, Malpaso Productions/Warner Bros., 1992.

1. See John Kerrigan, *Revenge Tragedy From Aeschylus to Armageddon* (New York: Oxford University Press, 1996).

2. As Martha Minow notes, "To seek a path between vengeance and forgiveness is also to seek a route between too much memory and too much forgetting." See Martha Minow, *Between Vengeance and Forgiveness: Facing History after Genocide and Mass Violence* (Boston: Beacon Press, 1998), p. 118.

3. "Forgiveness," Minow argues, "involves the one who was wronged in renouncing resentment, stepping out of the wave of repeating rage, and welcoming the other into the circle of humanity, reconnection, and even reconciliation." See Martha Minow, "Memory and Hate: Are There Lessons From Around the World?" (chapter 1).

4. "In the last analysis, it is upon the individual and the individual alone that the constraint of memory weighs insistently as well as imperceptibly. The atomization of a general memory into a private one has given the obligation to remember a power of internal coercion . . . [W]hen memory is no longer everywhere, it will not be anywhere unless one takes the responsibility to recapitulate it through individual means." See Pierre Nora, "Between Memory and History: *Les Lieux de Memoire*," *Representations* 26 (1989): 16.

5. Terry Aladjem, "Vengeance & Democratic Justice: American Culture and the Limits of Punishment," unpublished manuscript, 1992, p. 25.

6. Id., p. 26.

7. William Miller, "Clint Eastwood and Equity: The Virtues of Revenge and the Shortcomings of Law in Popular Culture," in Austin Sarat and Thomas Kearns, eds., *Law and the Domains of Culture* (Ann Arbor: University of Michigan Press, 1998), p. 161.

8. See Susan Jacoby, *Wild Justice: The Evolution of Revenge* (New York: Harper & Row, 1983), p. 115. "Insofar as humanly possible . . . , law attempts to remove personal animus from the process of apportioning blame and exacting retribution. It is the removal of personal animus . . . that distinguishes the rule of law from the rule of passion."

9. See Terry Aladjem, "Revenge and Consent," unpublished manuscript, 1990, p. 9.

10. Jacoby, *Wild Justice*, pp. 2–3. Also Francis Bacon, "Of Revenge," in Hugh Dick, ed., *Selected Writings* (New York: Modern Library, 1955).

11. "A society that is unable to convince individuals of its ability to exact atonement for injury is a society that runs a constant risk of having its members resort to the wilder forms of justice." See Jacoby, *Wild Justice*, p. 10.

12. For a discussion of the role of emotion in justice, see Samuel Pillsbury, "Emotional Justice: Moralizing the Passions of Criminal Justice," *Cornell Law Review* 74 (1989): 655. As William Connolly puts it, "Once revenge infiltrates the call to punish, this eminently desirable drive can expand indefinitely." William Connolly, *The Ethos of Pluralization* (Minneapolis: University of Minnesota Press, 1995), pp. 42–43.

13. St. Augustine, *The Writings of St. Augustine* (New York: Fathers of the Church, Inc., 1947), pp. 168–169.

14. See Jeffrie Murphy, "Getting Even: the Role of the Victim," *Social Philosophy and Policy* 7 (1990): 216. Also Jeffrie Murphy and Jean Hampton, *Forgiveness and Mercy* (Cambridge, UK: Cambridge University Press, 1988).

15. See Miller, "Clint Eastwood and Equity," pp. 162 and 165.

16. See Marvin Henberg, *Retribution: Evil for Evil in Ethics, Law, and Literature* (Philadelphia: Temple University Press, 1990). Also, Michael Davis, "Harm and Retribution," in A. John Simmons et al., eds., *Punishment* (Princeton, NJ: Princeton University Press, 1995).

17. Lawrence Becker, "Criminal Attempt and the Theory of the Law of Crimes," *Philosophy & Public Affairs* 3 (1974): 262.

18. Quoted in J. Ferrer, *Crimes and Punishments* (London: Chatto & Windus, 1880), p. 190.

19. See Roberto Unger, *Knowledge and Politics* (New York: Free Press, 1976).

20. See Gary Peller, "Reason and the Mob: the Politics of Representation," *Tikkun* 2 (1987): 28. See also Allan Hutchison, "Identity Crisis: The Politics of Interpretation," *New England Law Review* 26 (1992): 1173.

21. For a particularly interesting example, see Jon Elster, "Norms of Revenge," *Ethics* 100 (1990): 862. Revenge, Elster argues, "can be rational in terms of the selfish, material interests of the agent. If broader motivations—like the concern to uphold one's honor—are allowed, the task of proving the rationality of revenge becomes easier but also less interesting" (p. 872).

22. Jonathan Reider, "The Social Organization of Vengeance," in Donald Black, ed. *Toward a General Theory of Social Control* (New York: Academic

Press, 1984). See also William Miller, *Bloodtaking and Peacemaking: Feud, Law, and Society in Saga Iceland* (Chicago: University of Chicago Press, 1990), chapter 6. In Durkheim's words, "The need for vengeance is better directed today than heretofore. The spirit of foresight which has been aroused no longer leaves the field so free for the blind action of passion. It contains within it certain limits; it is opposed to absurd violence, to unreasonable ravaging." See Emile Durkheim, *The Division of Labor in Society* (New York: Free Press, 1893, 1964), p. 90.

23. Judith Shklar, *The Faces of Injustice* (New Haven: Yale University Press, 1990), p. 93.

24. Id., p. 94.

25. "Revenge is neither something which can be left behind in nature nor is it a transferrable right. Like Locke's state of nature, it always is with us." See Aladjem, "Vengeance & Democratic Justice," p. 36.

26. Connolly, *The Ethos of Pluralization*, p. 48.

27. Minow, "Memory and Hate," chapter 1.

28. Eric Hobsbawm and Terence Ranger, eds., *The Invention of Tradition* (Cambridge, UK: Cambridge University Press, 1983).

29. On the distinction between history and memory, see Jacques LeGoff, *History and Memory*, Steven Rendall and Elizabeth Claman, trans. (New York: Columbia University Press, 1992).

30. Nora, "Between Memory and History," pp. 8–9. But see Davis and Starn, "Rather than insisting on the opposition between memory and history . . . we want to emphasize their interdependence." Natalie Zemon Davis and Randolph Starn, "Introduction," *Representations* 26 (1989): 5. Or, as Burke argues, "Both history and memory are coming to appear increasingly problematic. Remembering the past and writing about it no longer seem like the innocent activities they were once taken to be. Neither memories nor histories seem objective any longer . . . In both cases . . . selection, interpretation and distortion is socially conditioned." See Peter Burke, "History as Social Memory," in Thomas Butler, ed., *Memory: History Culture and the Mind* (Oxford, UK: Blackwell, 1989), pp. 97–98.

31. See John Gillis, ed., *Commemorations: The Politics of National Identity* (Princeton, NJ: Princeton University Press, 1994). Also Nathan Wachtel, "Introduction: Memory and History," *History and Anthropology* 2 (1986): 218; Barry Schwartz, "The Social Control of Commemoration: A Study in Collective Memory," *Social Forces* 61 (1982): 15; and Michael Kammen, *Mystic Chords of Memory: The Transformation of Tradition in American Culture* (New York: Knopf, 1991).

32. Paul Connerton, *How Societies Remember* (Cambridge: Cambridge University Press, 1989), p. 21.

33. David Thelen, "Memory and American History," *Journal of American History* 75 (1989): 1119.

34. Nora, "Between History and Memory," p. 13.

35. Gillis, *Commemorations*

36. M. Yacovar, "Re-membering the Western: Clint Eastwood's 'Unforgiven,'" *Queen's Quarterly* 100 (Spring 1993): 247. See also, L. Engel, "Rewriting Western Myths in Clint Eastwood's New-Old Western," *Western American Literature* 29 (1994): 261.

37. M. W. Blundell, "Western Values, or the People's Homer: 'Unforgiven' as a Reading of the 'Iliad,'" *Poetics Today* 18 (1997), 533.

38. Miller, "Clint Eastwood and Equity," p. 183.

39. For an interesting analysis of the name Will and Munny see Thomas Dumm, "Unworking Death in 'Unforgiven': Law, Ethos, Violence," unpublished manuscript, p. 9.

40. Miller, "Clint Eastwood and Equity," p. 184.

41. Thus legal systems in the United States and Europe have been confronted by stern challenges in the name of victims' rights. See George Fletcher, *With Justice For Some: Victims' Rights in Criminal Trials* (Reading, MA: Addison-Wesley, 1995). See also Lois Forer, *Criminals and Victims* (New York: Norton, 1980). Here and abroad a movement has emerged that seeks to speak for victims. "Hard on the heels of the civil rights movement, the women's liberation movement, and the movement to expand the rights of criminal suspects, the victims' rights movement burst on the scene in the early 1970s and quickly became a potent political force. Part backlash against what it considered the prodefendant romanticism of the 1960s, the victims' rights movement was also a spiritual heir to the '60s ethos. With its suspicion of bureaucratic government and its concern for the disempowered, the victims' rights movement spoke for the 'forgotten' men and women of the criminal justice system." Stephen Schulhofer, "The Trouble with Trials: The Trouble with Us," *Yale Law Journal* 105 (1995): 825. The tendency of criminal justice systems in Western democracies is to displace the victim, to shut the door on those with the greatest interest in seeing justice done. In response, those who speak for victims are demanding that their voices be heard throughout the criminal justice process. David Roland, "Progress in the Victim Reform Movement: No Longer the 'Forgotten Victim,'" *Pepperdine Law Review* 17 (1989): 35. "Historically," Roland argues, "crime victims have been forgotten in the criminal justice system. The system, as it evolved, protected the rights of the accused with zeal, while ignoring the victim's plight."

42. Kerrigan, *Revenge Tragedy From Aeschylus to Armageddon.*

43. Austin Sarat, "Vengeance, Victims, and the Identities of Law," *Social and Legal Studies* 6 (1997): 163.

44. Miller, "Clint Eastwood and Equity," p. 184.

45. Id., p. 185.

46. "Consciousness of ethnic difference . . . only turned into nationalist chauvinism when a discredited Communist elite began manipulating nationalist emotions in order to cling to power." Michael Ignatieff, "The Balkan Tragedy," *New York Review of Books* (May 13, 1993): 3.

47. Friedrich Nietzsche, *The Use and Abuse of History*, Adrian Collins, trans. (Indiannapolis: Bobbs-Merrill, 1949), p. 15.

48. Id.

49. Id.

50. Miller, "Clint Eastwood and Equity," p. 195.

51. C. Plantinga, "Spectacles of Death: Clint Eastwood and Violence in 'Unforgiven,'" *Cinema Journal* 37 (1998): 65.

52. Miller, "Clint Eastwood and Equity," p. 197.

53. For a more complete exploration of this theme, see Dumm, "Unworking Death . . ." Also Plantinga, "Spectacles of Death."

54. As Dumm suggests, this is "a hard truth that may be acknowledged by the killer, a truth that cannot, however, be known." See Dumm, "Unworking Death in 'Unforgiven,'" p. 11.

55. Miller notes what he calls "equivocations on the morality of revenge" even in the shootout in Skinny's saloon, where revenge seems most clearly justified. See "Clint Eastwood and Equity," p. 192.

56. Id., p. 195.

57. Nietzsche, *The Use and Abuse of History*, p. 5.

58. Dumm provides an insightful reading of these denials. See Dumm, "Unworking Death in 'Unforgiven,'" p. 9.

59. Nietzsche, *The Use and Abuse of History*, p. 9.

60. For an analysis of this refusal see Miller, "Clint Eastwood and Equity," p. 197.

61. Nietzsche, *The Use and Abuse of History*, p. 20.

62. Id.

Power, Violence, and Legitimacy: A Reading of Hannah Arendt in an Age of Police Brutality and Humanitarian Intervention

IRIS MARION YOUNG

In the spring of 1999 I was completing a book on democracy. Its arguments assume a basic commitment to democratic values—the rule of law, liberty, equal respect, and a desire to work out disagreement through discussion. Suddenly I was paralyzed in my work. With NATO bombs raining on Yugoslavia, reflection on the essentially nonviolent values of democracy felt irrelevant at best and arrogantly privileged at worst.

While living in Vienna in 1998 I had followed with horror the escalating attacks by Serbian soldiers on both armed and unarmed Albanian Kosovars, which seemed more immediate there than they had in the United States. Thus in the early months of 1999 I had hoped that the negotiations including the United States, Western European countries, Russia, and Yugoslavia would succeed in stopping this violence. When European negotiators delivered their final offer and it was rejected by Yugoslavia, for a few days I swallowed the self-righteous rhetoric of United States and European leaders, and I approved of the NATO war.

When it became clear that the war made the Serbian army more able and willing than before to force the flight of hundreds of thousands of Albanian Kosovars, and that NATO had foreseen these consequences without planning a response to them, I was dumbstruck. When it further appeared that NATO's strategy was to target civilians and cripple the economy of an entire country, I was overcome with shame and rage. Obsessed with this war and the fact that it was being waged by nineteen of the world's democracies, none of which had consulted with their citizens, I felt impelled to think about violence. But where could I turn to help me think? In this moment of rupture I reopened one of the only works of recent political theory that reflects specifically on the theme of violence, Hannah Arendt's essay, *On Violence*.[1]

Arendt there notes that political theorists have rarely reflected on violence as such. While there is a long tradition of theoretical writing on warfare, most of this theorizes about strategy, balance of power, or the meaning of sovereignty violation, rather than reflecting specifically on the meaning and use of violence per se. Forty years later, her observation remains valid. Although the last decades of the twentieth century saw acts of violent horror that mock midcentury pledges of "never again," most contemporary political theorists have neglected systematic reflection on violence in public affairs.[2] Perhaps just as remarkable, in the vast recent literature interpreting and extending Arendt's ideas, there is little focused discussion about her conceptualization of violence and the logic of its relation to other key political concepts.[3]

In this essay I focus on Arendt's small text on violence, which distills and expands some of the insights and positions she developed in other texts, such as *The Origins of Totalitarianism, On Revolution*, and *The Human Condition*.[4] *On Violence* is a dense and suggestive essay. I find its positions confusing and that Arendt does not follow through on an elaboration of some of its important distinctions. Her central and self-consciously counterintuitive claim is that power and violence are opposites. I aim to make sense of this contentious claim, and to explain how it challenges commonly accepted understandings of the relationship between these terms. I shall elaborate Arendt's claim that violence may sometimes be justified, but it cannot be legitimate. Through this reading of Arendt, I will reflect on and evaluate manifestations of official violence that I believe enjoy too much acceptance in contemporary societies: the use of violent means by police, and military intervention that claims to protect human rights. Along with Martha Minow, I will criticize a view of the state and law that takes violence as a necessary and normal tool. Minow argues that the normalized use of violence by states contributes more to fueling cycles of violence than it does to halting them.[5] Arendt's distinction between power and violence offers material for criticizing official violence and for an alternative conceptualization of state power.

Prelude: Clearing Away the Mess

Written at the height of the Vietnam War and in the wake of campus protests all over the world, *On Violence* reveals Arendt as the arrogant conservative many of us wish she were not. Despite her theoretical praise for council democracy, when something like it erupts on campus lawns in her neighborhood, Arendt reacts more like an annoyed professor than a republican citizen. She shares with the student protestors a revulsion of the war in Vietnam; indeed, this is one of her motives for writing the essay. However, she thinks that the logic of the student movements undermines the spirit of the university, especially when students demand to study subjects they deem more "relevant" than the standard curriculum.

Antiwar activists and curriculum reformers, however, apparently are not the people most to be feared. It is the "appearance of the Black Power movement on the campuses" (p. 18) that most disturbs her. Arendt heaps contempt on these students who demand courses in "nonexistent subjects" like women's studies or Black studies, and asserts that this movement has succeeded in forcing universities to admit unqualified students. Arendt thought that universities were going to hell, that student radicals, especially Black student radicals, were responsible for this sorry situation, and that this tragedy was symptomatic of a general loss of public reason.

The interest of Black radicals, she says, is to lower academic standards, and to bring the cries of brute social need to ivied halls, where their din drowns out all deliberation. Influenced by Sartre, Fanon, Mao, Che and other confused and dangerous revolutionaries, the Black student movement celebrates violence, and in so doing it abandons the nobility of the Civil Rights movement. "To expect people, who have not the slightest notion of what the *res publica*, the public thing, is, to behave non-violently and argue rationally in matters of interest is neither realistic nor reasonable" (p. 78). Arendt's attitude toward student radicals and especially toward Black radicals, as expressed in this text, is embarrassing and offensive. As some important recent commentary on Arendt's writing as a public intellectual points out, Arendt had a poor understanding of racism in America and of the movements around her resisting it.[6]

The text has other political flaws. Arendt surely overdraws the distinction between Marx, who, for all his commitment to an idea of progress, never gave up an understanding of praxis, and twentieth-century Marxism, in the persons of Sartre and Fanon, which she regards as naive, dangerous, corrupted, and mechanistic. In this text, as in others, moreover, Arendt insists that the entrance of need onto the public stage of modernity leads to nothing but mischief. Many have argued that she is simply wrong about this, and I agree with them.[7] Arendt's ideas have many such problems and prejudices, but I do not need to repeat the criticisms that others have well made. The core conceptualization of violence and power that I wish to elaborate from Arendt's suggestive reflections, however, can be disentangled from these other concerns and set out on its own. Contemporary politics can learn much from doing so.

Violence as Rational and Instrumental

I find no definition of violence in Arendt's essay. I shall assume that by *violence* we mean acts by human beings that aim physically to cause pain to, wound or kill other human beings, and/or damage or destroy animals and things that hold a significant place in the lives of people. Active threats to wound or kill also fall under a concept of violence.[8] In this essay Arendt reflects not on any and all forms and occasions of violence, but on violence in public affairs, those actions and events where individuals and groups express aggression, hate, disagreement and conflict concerning issues of government and rules, coexistence and exclusion, and the like in violent ways. In this essay Arendt aims to overturn several misconceptions about such political violence. Before dwelling on the most important of those, namely Arendt's claim that violence is confused conceptually with power, I shall briefly review another mistake political theorists make about violence, according to Arendt.

One reason that few philosophers choose to theorize about violence, Arendt suggests, may be that they believe that violence is irrational and unpredictable. According to this understanding, violence is pervasive but senseless. It ruptures routine, and breaks and destroys people and things, but because of its unpredictability and irrationality there is little that theory can say about it. This statement is partly true and partly false. Violence is unpredictable in the same way that action is unpredictable, but it is not usually irrational.

A key characteristic of violence, says Arendt, is its reliance on instruments, the instruments of destruction. Violence is more or less fierce in proportion to the ability of its instruments to inflict damage and destruction on people and things. Not only does violence usually involve the use of instruments, the technical development and number of which magnify destructive effects, but the wounds and killing wrought in acts of violence are usually themselves instrumental. Wanton acts of violence are less common than calculated, deliberate, planned, and carefully executed violent stratagems aimed at specific objectives. In that sense most acts of violence are rational. They are, however, also unpredictable for the same reason that action itself is unpredictable.

In *The Human Condition* (see note 9), Arendt develops her particular concept of action, and distinguishes it from labor and work. Human activity counts as action insofar as it consists in initiative, in bringing something uniquely new into the world. An action is not predetermined from antecedent conditions. Consequently, action is subject to interpretation. The agent has purposes of his or her own construction, which have their place in a narrative of his or her character and plans. Unlike labor or production, for Arendt, action is essentially social because it takes place in relation to others' plans and meanings. For this reason not only is an action unpredictable, a rupture of routine, but so is the reaction of others to an action. Action is an expression of natality, beginning, not only because it ruptures routine, but also because the response of others makes its consequences unpredictable. To the extent that people engage in violence as a means to enact their purposes, violence is also unpredictable, a rupture in the course of events.

Violence appears as the most salient, unpredictable phenomenon in human affairs only because modern theory tries to conceptualize politics within a science that can render its events predictable. Efforts to turn the study of politics into a science, according to Arendt, are as old as Plato. In their modern form, these efforts construct public affairs and the course of history as subject to regularities. Arendt mentions two models of history and politics as in principle predictable: an organic model and a production model. The organic model treats history and social change like biological processes. The seeds of the present are in the past; societies and regimes grow, reach maturity, and eventually decay and die. Under the pens of thinkers such as Nietzsche and Sorel, Arendt suggests, violence becomes as inevitable in history as death is in nature. Violence can even become a positive aspect of politics in this framework, because it prunes away the dead wood and generates new growth.

The production model, on the other hand, imagines political events as under the control of a planner guiding them to their intended end. Many revolutionaries of both right and left act as though politics can realize a social plan. Those who try to reduce politics to bureaucratic administration display a similar image of public affairs as ideally under the control of rational plans and well-honed instruments, which properly trained people can use to bring about predictable consequences. This production model can also give a neutral or positive place to violence in history; to produce something out of raw material it is necessary to do violence to its initial form.

Perhaps noticing the instrumental character of violence accounts for its being inserted into a production model of politics. Both the production model and the organic model of politics and history, however, deny the specificity of human affairs as *action*. They endeavor to dissolve the novelty of human actions into instances of general trends and tendencies. Violence is closer to action than production, insofar as it constitutes a rupture in predictable routines, insofar as it relates subjects to one another, and insofar as the performer cannot predict its consequences because he or she cannot predict how others will react. While violence is connected to the realm of action in these ways, Arendt's main claim in this essay is that violence should be distinguished from power, understood as the capacity for collective action.

Confusion of Violence with Power

Perhaps another reason that political theorists reflect so little on violence as such, Arendt suggests, is that they assume that violence is already subsumed under their subject matter when they theorize about political power. Theorists and political actors typically confuse violence with power. They either take power to be based on the capacity for violence, or they conceptualize violence as an extension of power. Arendt's main task in this essay is to distinguish these two concepts. I shall elaborate the meaning of her distinction, and argue that it has important normative implications.

Political philosophy should be careful to distinguish between several apparently close concepts: power, force, strength, authority, and violence. Force is a strictly physical concept, the energy that moves and resists inertia, what imposes constraints or breaks through them. Strength counts as the ability both to exert and to resist force. A body is strong insofar as it can overcome the resistance of another, or insofar as it resists the force that aims to act upon, move, or transform it. A person is strong just insofar as he or she moves against the resistance of things and persons. Strength is indivisible and resides only in one body. Use of strength to exert force, though, can be magnified through instruments. By acquiring instrumental means of exerting force for the sake of destruction and the threat of destruction, individuals or groups often can induce the compliance of others with their commands or wishes. Violence relies on force and strength, and magnifies them with instruments.

Arendt insists, however, that power is conceptually and practically entirely different from violence. Power consists in collective action. Power is the ability of persons jointly to constitute their manner of living to-

gether, the way they organize their rules and institutions through reciprocal self-understanding of what the rules are and how they foster cooperation. Thus power relies not on bodies and instruments that exert
force, but primarily on speech—the interpretation of meaning, the articulation of new ideas, the dynamics of persuasion, the linking of understanding and action. Power establishes and maintains institutions; that is,
regulated and settled means of cooperating to bring about collective
ends. It has its basis in the consent and support of those who abide by,
live according to, and interpret rules and institutions to bring about new
collective ends. Those who engage in collective action must communicate and cooperate, discuss their problems and jointly make plans. Insofar as successful institutions mobilize the cooperation of a large number
of people in their operations, who understand the meaning and goals of
the institutions, know the rules, and in general endorse their operations,
they embody power.

Power is distinct from strength in that it exists *between* people rather
than in them. Power is a feature of action and interaction insofar as
people understand one another's words and deeds and coordinate with
one another to achieve mutually understood ends. Thus power involves
some kind of agreement, whether in word or action. Those who participate in the collective action that founds and maintains institutions and
the enactment of their ends must know what they are doing and engage
with one another to coordinate their actions.[9]

With these distinctions, Arendt stands opposed to a major tendency in
modern political theory. She holds that the confusion of violence with
power stems from a common understanding of state power as the exercise of sovereign domination. Political power, in this view, is nothing
more than the rule of some over others, the exercise of command and
successful obedience. While Max Weber is hardly alone in this view, his
theory of the state may have exerted the most influence over contemporary thinking. For Weber the state has the monopoly over the legitimate
use of violence. In this paradigm, state and law are founded on the
capacity for violence: the state and its legal system is simply the vehicle
that a hegemonic group creates for itself to further its purposes, maintain
itself in power, and rule over the rest.[10]

Arendt agrees that if in fact political power, or government, means
simply that state officials of whatever sort—kings, lords, presidents, cabi-
net ministers, generals—exercise dominion over the actions of other in a
territory, then power and violence are sensibly associated. There is no
doubt that many rulers have relied on killing or torture and threats to

induce compliance with their wills and goals from subjects, and that they often succeed. "If the essence of power is the effectiveness of command, then there is no greater power than that which grows out of the barrel of a gun" (p. 37).

Arendt argues, however that the success and stability of even despotic regimes over a long term depends on eliciting the voluntary cooperation of at least a large mass of subjects with rules and institutions that enact their living together and their common projects, that is on power understood as collective action. Even government understood as sovereign dominion depends for its success on a regularity of mutually understood, cooperative activities, and in this respect on the consent of those ruled.

Historically, such consent and support were often tied to beliefs in the *authority* of the rulers. Government as sovereignty has rested on the use of violence far less than on belief systems that have anointed certain individuals or groups with the *right* to the service and obedience of others. Ideologies of authority construct the ground of right in values and personages that transcend politics and mundane narrative time. Authoritarian hierarchical systems of government derive their power to a great extent from the commitment of subjects to these beliefs in the transcendent ground of the right to rule.[11] Thus Arendt suggests in *On Violence* that we should also distinguish the concept of authority from power. Authority is the quality of receiving unquestioned recognition and obedience, derived from a transcendent origin from which the ruler's right derives. Power, on the other hand, in the sense of collective action, depends on persuading subjects in the here and now to cooperate.

Modernity erodes authority, according to Arendt; the disenchantment of the world means it becomes more difficult for rulers to succeed in eliciting obedience by appealing to unquestioned transcendent foundations. The egalitarian and democratic impulses of modernity reject belief in the divine right of kings or the superior wisdom of philosopher princes that gives them the right of command. Moderns attempt to install science as a new kind of authority, and efforts to base a political hierarchy on expertism continue to be partially successful. The order of experts is not stable, however, because it rests on no timeless and otherworldly cosmology. Under these circumstances rulers who aim to exercise dominion over subjects must depend even more than before on the collective action of those ruled and their commitment to prevailing institutions and practices.

This fact becomes most apparent if and when people withdraw their consent, when people begin to act collectively toward different ends than those the rulers intend or desire. Rulers are helpless before such a shift in power. If they have the means of violence at their disposal—which usually means depending on the power of organized armies—they can attempt to impose their will on a disobedient public through force. The ruler can bomb neighborhoods, eliminate opponents, and keep a threatening watch over people to limit their ability to communicate and cooperate. Violence and the threat of violence can in this way destroy power, but never create or sustain it. Since power depends on collective action, it rests on the freedom of a plurality of distinct individuals aiming to foster their institutions. The tyrant who rules through violence is relatively impotent. While he may prevent action and resistance, and he may be able to enforce service of his needs and desires, he can accomplish nothing worldly.

Of course, history is cluttered with regimes structured by relations of ruler and subject, and these often rely on the threat of violence to compel obedience to the ruler's will when actions threaten to undermine or resist that will. But such regimes of domination are weak insofar as they must depend on compulsion in this way. They are powerful only if at least a large segment of the people they govern cooperate through consent and collective will, sustaining the institutions in which they live together, express their meanings, and enact their collective goals.

Thus Arendt contrasts power and violence.

> Power and violence are opposites; where one rules absolutely, the other is absent. Violence appears where power is in jeopardy, but left to its own course it ends in power's disappearance. This implies that it is not correct to think of the opposite of violence as nonviolence; to speak of nonviolent power is already redundant. Violence can destroy power; it is ultimately incapable of creating it. (p. 56)[12]

Though violence and power are opposites in this conceptual and phenomenological sense, Arendt says that they often occur together. Although governments often rely on the use and threat of violence, systems of government that rest on command and obedience must also rely on the collective action of subjects—power—for their effectiveness. While movements to resist or overturn such regimes must mobilize mass power of collective organization to succeed, they often use violence, too, to aid their objectives. That epitome of violence, war, is also an example of power. A disciplined army depends on the solidarity of its soldiers, their willingness to work together and protect each other under stress.

Power and violence are opposites, but they often occur together. This sounds contradictory.[13] By interpreting Arendt's distinction between violence and power not only as conceptual, but also as *normative*, we can make sense of this statement. While violence and power *in fact* often occur together, they need not, and they *ought not*, at least not often and not very much. The interpretation of governance that identifies it with sovereign dominion is problematic because it conceives of political power as necessarily oppressive, and living under government as necessarily a denial of freedom. There is another interpretation of government that does not assume the inevitability of a relationship between command and obedience, and the necessary connection with violence these seem to entail. Arendt uses a Greek word for this alternative: *isonomy*. Jeffrey Isaac describes *isonomy* as "a concept of power and law whose essence did not rely on the command-obedience relation and which did not identify power and rule or law and command."[14] *Isonomy* names a process of governance as self-government, where the citizens have equal status and must rely on one another equally for developing collective goals and carrying them out. Insofar as government in this form depends on speech and persuasion, it precludes violence and violence is its opposite. Government ought to be the exercise of power as the expression and result of people coming together, assessing their problems and collective goals, discussing together how to deal with them, and persuading one another to adopt rules and policies, then each self-consciously acting to effect them.

Arendt finds occasional historical bursts of sheer collective action and publicity, when a plurality of people through their mutual understanding and collective promising create a public as the space of the appearance of singular and plural deeds and as the expressions of their freedom. People govern themselves by means of rules they formulate, understand, and trust one another to follow, as a condition of their own cooperative action. They enact collective projects that originate from their public deliberations upon their institutions, problems, and desires. In this fragile space of power there are no rulers to be obeyed, though there are often leaders and great persuaders.

> What makes a man a political being is his faculty of action; it enables him to get together with his peers, to act in concert, and to reach out for goals and enterprises that would never enter his mind, let alone the desires of his heart, had he not been given this gift—to embark on something new. (p. 82)

Such a statement about the meaning of political action—power in Arendt's sense—seems so abstract as to be vacuous. When people act in concert with their peers, what are they *doing?* What are these goals and enterprises that would otherwise never enter their minds, that are original ruptures in the passage of events, that exhibit this mysterious quality of natality? The question becomes even more acute when one takes into account Arendt's insistence that action is wholly distinct from labor and work, distinct from activities of producing what will meet needs and consuming those products, on the one hand, and from the fashioning of those works that not only build social surroundings, and serve as instruments of living and doing, but also stand as lasting monuments to a people and culture, on the other hand. If collective action neither serves the goals of building cathedrals nor producing food, then what are its goals and enterprises?

Some commentators have complained that Arendt's strong distinction between the social and the political is both unacceptably conservative and renders the concept of political power empty. Arendt decries what she perceives as a modern propensity for the public sphere and law increasingly to be dominated by discussion of how to alleviate *social* problems—poverty, unequal distribution of wealth, discrimination, urban blight and development, water and transportation planning, the organization of health care, and so on.[15] This deep distrust of an interest in bringing social issues into the light of public discussion partly explains her antipathy to the Black Power movement.

In the essay we are considering, Arendt's vitriolic remarks about bureaucracy are tied to this insistence that the political should not be tainted by the social. Attention to the social elevates the meeting of needs to the primary purpose of government, purges government of politics, and thereby levels it to the lowest common denominator. Bureaucracy attempts to harness people's energies into a kind of machine in which the administration of things will meet needs. The goal of bureaucracy is to implement rules and procedures that determine routines that workers and clients can follow, rendering themselves fungible, to achieve production, distribution, and service delivery objectives as efficiently as possible. The purpose of bureaucracy, that is to say, is to reduce as much as possible any need for *action* in Arendt's sense.

> In a fully developed bureaucracy there is nobody left with whom one can argue, to whom one can present grievances, on whom the pressures of power can be exerted. Bureaucracy is the form of government in which everybody is deprived of political freedom, of the power to

act; for the rule by Nobody is not no-rule, and where all are equally powerless we have a tyranny without a tyrant. (p. 81)

The bureaucratic principle is the opposite of power and collective action. Whereas people acting collectively are *mindful* of their goals and deliberate about the best means to achieve them, in the logic of bureaucracy the means are related to the ends not through opinion and deliberation, but through regulated routine, where distinct activities are efficiently organized. The whole point of bureaucratic logic is that participants should not have to think about how to achieve coordinated ends. Bureaucracies create hierarchies of command and obedience that are supposed to make the operation of routines more efficient. Just to the extent that people become disempowered, however, the bureaucracy becomes less able to fulfill its role in the administration of things and the meeting of needs. Its parts fail to coordinate; the system becomes irrational, or it becomes corrupt—its command mechanisms come to serve private gain rather than the achievement of collectively agreed-upon ends. Thus even the effective pursuit of public administration depends on power in Arendt's sense—that people act collectively in a self-conscious way that involves deliberation, persuasion, and following through the collective will with implementation.

As I understand Arendt's concepts, the successful achievement of any socially organized ends depends on power. Collective action is awesome and monumental, but difficult to achieve and sustain. Military campaigns, imperial rule of extensive territory, the establishment of an effective health care service, the organization of a mass resistance movement that brings down a dictatorial regime, the conduct of constitutional dialogue over a period of years—these all require and manifest power in Arendt's sense. There seems to me to be no reason to exclude matters having to do with meeting needs, production, and service provision from the scope of activities to which such power can and should be brought to bear. It is not only bureaucratically organized meeting of needs that carries dangers of the dissipation or corruption of power; they all do. Power only exists as long as it is actively sustained by the plural participants in the endeavor who self-consciously coordinate with one another. If they withdraw their commitment or ease their communication, or if acts of violence break up their relationships, only a shell will be left.

Power, and the political, then, I interpret as an *aspect* of any social institution or collective activity, including some of those that enact sovereign dominion or repressive domination. Institutions cannot be effective for long unless they have occasions when participants set their collective goals, discuss what institutions, rules, and practices would best coordinate their actions to achieve those goals, and make commitments to one another to carry out their responsibilities in the system of cooperation.

Power is thus necessary for government, but it is also fragile. People easily and often lose this sense of public promise, and disperse into the impotent privacy of a concern for their own survival or pleasure. To the extent that governing institutions remain, they freeze into routinized bureaucracies, become cronyist semi-private operations, or elicit conformity through terror. The use of violence in public affairs is normatively questionable not only because killing and causing suffering are prima facie wrong. Violence is also morally problematic because its use, especially if routine, widespread, or massive, endangers power. "Violence appears where power is in jeopardy, but left to its own course it ends in power's disappearance" (p. 56). When rulers or those who most benefit from a given order of things find that they or their goals lose popular support, they often try to restore their power through the use of violence. Such actions may well reduce resistance but they do not restore power. Violence not only harms individuals, but it makes their lives difficult to carry on as before. When either rulers or resisters adopt the use of violence as a regular means of trying to elicit the cooperation of others, they tend to produce the opposite effect: flight, retreat into privacy, preemptive strikes, distrust of all by all. The use of violence in politics is problematic, moreover, because its consequences so easily and often escalate beyond the actors' specific intentions. Violent acts tend to produce violent responses that radiate beyond the original acts.

Arendt's concept of power is abstract and incomplete. Although she discusses people's movements and revolutions as well as the activities of governments, her theory tends to ignore structural social relations, and their manner of channeling power to the systematic advantage of some and disadvantage of others. Her conceptual distinction between power and violence, however, which I have interpreted as having normative significance as well, opens important possibilities for rethinking the relations of power and freedom.

Legitimacy and Justification

Thus far in this essay I have reviewed Arendt's discussion of several confusions about violence and politics to which Arendt believes many theorists have been prone: that violence is irrational or inevitable, and, most importantly, that violence is the basis of power. In the following passage she signals another common confusion, which she traces to this confusion of violence and power:

> Power needs no justification, being inherent in the very existence of political communities; what it does need is legitimacy. . . . Power springs up whenever people get together to act in concert, but it derives its legitimacy from the initial getting together rather than from any action that then may follow. Legitimacy, when challenged, bases itself on appeal to the past, while justification relates to an end that lies in the future. Violence can be justifiable, but it never will be legitimate. Its justification loses in plausibility the farther its intended end recedes into the future. (p. 52)

Like so much else in this text, Arendt's claims here are provocative and suggestive, but she does not elaborate them further. In this section I will try to follow through on this distinction between legitimacy and justification. Making sense of these claims is key for the arguments about official violence that I will make in the next section. Power does not need justification, but does require legitimacy; violence calls for justification, but it can never be legitimate. What does this mean?

Both legitimacy and justification are concepts of moral reasoning. Both concern ways of giving reasons for an action or structure. In the passage quoted, Arendt offers only one hint about the difference in these forms of giving an account: legitimation appeals to the past, while justification appeals to the future in relation to the act.

To find more texts that will help unlock this mystery, one can turn to *On Revolution*. There Arendt draws a connection between power, in the sense of original collective action, and the activity of founding new institutions, which can preserve that power and give it embodiment in law.

> Power comes into being only if and when men join themselves together for the purpose of action, and it will disappear when, for whatever reason, they disperse and desert one another. Hence, binding and promising, combining and covenanting are the means by which power is kept in existence. . . . Just as promises and agreements deal with the future and provide stability in the ocean of future uncertainty where the unpredictable may break in from all sides, so the constituting, founding, and world-building capacities of men concern always not so much ourselves and our own time on earth as our "successor" and "posterities."[16]

Power consists in collective action, people coming together and supporting one another to do deeds and accomplish goals the likes of which "would never enter his mind, let alone the desires of his heart, had he not been given this gift" (OV, p. 82). Power is often fleeting, however; it springs out of relations between people who accomplish something, and then dissipates. For power to be a force in politics, it needs to be institutionalized, and this is what foundings accomplish. In founding a constitution, the empowered collective gives itself relative permanence, a permanence guaranteed through covenants. In the moment of founding, participants in a public mutually promise to abide by principles that guide institutions, to organize and give their energy to the implementation of the institutions, and to be loyal to the institutions and to one another through them. The mutuality of promise making is important for Arendt. She cites the spirit of American revolutionaries who, she says, found legitimate power only in the reciprocity and mutuality of promises made between equals, as distinct from the spurious power of kings and aristocrats, which was not founded on mutual promising.

Arguments that government actions, policies, laws, or representatives are legitimate, then, are backward looking because they refer to founding promises. To say that these leaders or policies are legitimate is to make the argument that they are in conformity with, a present embodiment of, the principles and promises that institutionalize the public's power. Making such an argument, I suggest, requires more than the recital of a history or the citation of founding documents. An argument for the legitimacy of present officials, actions, or laws, I suggest, involves a *renewal* of the power that came into play in the original process, which itself reaffirms the promises, a new commitment of the collective's participants to one another in terms of mutuality and reciprocity. To argue that a government or policy or action is legitimate in these ways does not itself imply that they are just, right, or good. To the extent that institutionalizing power involves *mutual* promising, however, there is an implicit commitment to the justice or rightness of principles to guide future action, at least as concerning relations with one another.

With this notion of legitimation we notice another important difference between Weber and Arendt. Despite his identification of the state with sovereign dominion that rests on monopoly over the means of violence, Weber agrees with Arendt that the naked imposition of domination by continual force and violence is an unsteady basis for ruling. State power is most stable, according to Weber, when it carries legitimacy. Weber's concept of legitimacy, however, is positivistic: rulers have legitimacy just insofar as their subjects accept some rationalization of their ruling position. This could be a religious story about their divine right, or it could be a story about their aristocratic natures, or about how their greater intelligence or skill make them suited for leadership. Or it could be a story about how people have agreed to establish a constitution. As I understand Weber, the content of the story does not matter as much as that it functions to elicit consent from subjects.[17]

In the passage I quoted from *On Revolution*, Arendt distinguishes mutual promise and covenant that give power legitimacy from simple consent. I take it that consent is only the absence of opposition and resistance, a willingness on the part of subjects to go along with the rules and decrees, and such consent usually has some basis in belief. Each subject consents alone, however, in relation to the state. Covenants to which accounts of the legitimacy of political officials and actions appeal, on the other hand, are public, indeed they are the effects and institutionalizations of publics that emerge from collective action.

As I understand Arendt's distinction, justification is a less complex affair than legitimation. First, only an action whose moral value is *in question* requires justification. This is why Arendt says that power needs no justification. The default position for power is that it is valuable; acting in concert enables a unique and wonderful kind of freedom that human beings experience in no other way. The default position for violence, on the other hand, is that it is a disvalue. Violence destroys, and it is not very violent unless it destroys valuable things—human lives or things meaningful to human lives and action.

Thus any act of violence calls for justification, an account of why it is morally acceptable. When Arendt claims that such an account is always forward looking, she refers to the instrumental character of violence. A justification of violence can only appeal to the good it brings about, its consequences. Justification of violence cannot be retrospective in the ways that are arguments about legitimacy, because violence is always a rupture that severs the continuity of the present with the past. Arendt claims that the plausibility of a justification for violence declines the further its intended good consequence recedes into the future.

Arendt does not offer criteria for what justifies violence in politics. A thorough account would require more space than I have in this essay. The argument I will make next about official violence, however, presupposes some understanding of the limits of the justification of violence. I will assume that most acts of violence cannot be morally justified; they are in the service of wrongful efforts on the part of some people to dominate and coerce others into doing what they want, or to remove the resistance of others. A narrow range of violent actions may be justified, however, according to such considerations as the following: whether they are likely to prevent serious harm, under circumstances where other preventive measures are not available; and whether they are constrained in their consequences, that is, do not have harmful consequences that reach beyond their immediate effect, whether intended or unintended. Few real-world acts of violence satisfy these conditions, I suggest, especially in the context of politics and public affairs.

There is a final aspect to the distinction between the legitimate exercise of power and the justification of violence that I interpret from Arendt's hints. Whereas arguments about the legitimacy of one act or policy can often appeal to previous arguments about legitimacy, arguments justifying violence cannot appeal as such to precedent. As I said above, there is a kind of default character to legitimacy that justifications of violence do not share. If it can be shown that a government is legitimate, then the presumption follows that its acts and policies are legitimate. The legitimacy of one law or policy helps reinforce the legitimacy of others. This is appropriate if legitimacy corresponds to a web of institutionalized power expressing the mutual commitments of a public. Because any act of violence is a rupture that endangers that potential or actual commitment and mutuality, however, each act of violence must be justified on its own, on a case-by-case basis, not by appeal to similar acts from the past, but by argument about its particular unique circumstances and consequences. While there may be very general moral principles and criteria that can be used in such arguments, no institution or authority can produce a set of rules that morally legitimate acts of violence in advance.

Official Violence

I will now apply this interpretation of the opposition of power and violence to a particular class of violent acts: those perpetrated by agents of the state as a means to achieve their mission of law enforcement. In "Between Nations and Between Intimates," Martha Minow suggests that government's "uses of violence—in response to crime, disorder, homeless people, and international affairs—also contributes to a pervasive message that violence is acceptable, necessary, and even admirable."[18] She argues that if we wish to prevent violence in spaces as different as living rooms and open fields, we must question the widespread assumption that states ought to use violence to achieve their legitimate ends. I think that Arendt's distinction between violence and power, along with my elaboration of her distinction between legitimacy and justification, can help in this project.

The two differing interpretations of state power that I have reviewed—the Weberian and the Arendtian—yield two radically different understandings of official violence. A Weberian interpretation finds the threat and use of violence to be an essential and normal component of the actions of legitimate state officials in carrying out their duties. The critical view of violence that I find in Arendt, on the other hand, along with her theory of power as collective action, imply that official violence is always questionable, and thus requires justification. Official violence often fails this justificatory test.

I examine official violence in two forms: police violence in domestic law enforcement and the use of military force by one or more states against another state or states with the aim of responding to violations of human rights or the threat of such violations. A Weberian interpretation of state power or sovereignty, I argue, has difficulty making sense of a concept of police brutality; Arendt's theory offers the conceptual means to do so. International "police actions" that claim to enforce international human rights law, or so-called humanitarian intervention, can be theorized on analogy with domestic law enforcement criteria. If one accepts Arendt's distinction between violence and power, I shall argue, then acts of so-called humanitarian intervention become questionable.

POLICE BRUTALITY

Arendt herself thematizes police brutality in her essay. She embeds her impassioned criticism of this mode of official violence in an arrogant interpretation of the student radicalism and Black community activism. Recall that she heaps contempt on students who demand courses in "non-existent subjects" like women's studies or Black studies, and asserts that these movements have succeeded in forcing universities to admit unqualified students by threatening violence.

Given these deep prejudices against student radicalism, it is especially interesting that she reserves the worst condemnation for official violence—for the impotent bigness of the United States and the Soviet Union amassing their weapons of mass destruction, and for the police who respond to protestors with gas, batons, and guns. Police brutality against essentially nonviolent demonstrators is responsible for radicalizing the student movement. Violent and massive police attacks on protestors at the Democratic National Convention in Chicago in 1968 were a sign of the utter impotence of both the Chicago city administration, its police force, and the members of the ruling establishment of the country. When officials have lost power—that is, when they no longer have the support and cooperation of masses of people—they rarely resist the temptation to substitute violence for power. Almost inevitably, however, the resort to violence further undermines power, and violence becomes a senseless and irrational end in itself.

In one of her appendices Arendt hypothesizes that police brutality is linked to police inefficiency. To the extent that the police force is unable to prevent crimes or solve those already committed, they resort to acts of naked violence against people in the streets. Whether or not her claimed correlations are correct, she expresses a judgment few juries in the United States today share: it is not the prerogative of police officers to brutalize citizens when attempting to perform their duties. Arendt worries about a Black racism that responds with violent rage to "ill-designed integration policies whose consequences their authors can easily escape" (p. 77). She seems to fear a ragged horde rising up from the privacy of its poverty to obliterate what little is left of a civilized public sphere. She judges more horrible, however, the prospect of a white racist backlash in which "the climate of opinion in the country might deteriorate to the point where a majority of its citizens would be willing to pay the price of the invisible terror of a police state for law and order in the streets" (p. 77). Such words make an eerie echo in this age where prison-building is a growth industry, sweeping homeless people from the streets with fire hoses has become common, and the number of executions has quadrupled in ten years.

In the late 1990s the U.S. Justice Department, not exactly a promoter of nonviolence and quiet reason in law enforcement, nevertheless found that some of the routine behavior of police departments in cities like Pittsburgh was so egregious in its violation of the rights of citizens that it ordered and supervised changes. In Chicago, front-page headlines reported at least a dozen questionable police shootings of citizens in the year 2000. Other citizen complaints are too numerous to report; local protests against policy brutality are nearly as regular as church services, but I sense little outrage among most of my neighbors. The streets of Cincinnati recently erupted with anger at what many African Americans perceived as systematic police abuse. In November 1999 in Seattle, we saw a police riot reminiscent of the Chicago of 1968 that Arendt condemns, but this was mild compared to the actions of police in Genoa in

April 2001. Today, it seems to me, perhaps even more than at the time Arendt wrote these words, we have "a kind of police backlash, quite brutal and highly visible." This is something that political philosophers do not generally discuss.

On those rare occasions when police are put on trial for their acts of violence against citizens, juries usually absolve them of guilt. Even in cases where unarmed people have been shot dead by several police officers, the police and their advocates have been able to convince juries that their actions fall within their proper line of duty and that their role gives them discretion to use violence when they interpret a situation as requiring it to do their job. Arendt is probably right to suggest that one explanation for why such police violence is so little questioned is that many people believe that it will be used primarily to contain a minority that does not include them. I suggest that an additional explanation for a relatively widespread willingness to condone or excuse official violence results from the ideology of state power that understands it as founded in violence.

The idea that the state is nothing but monopoly on the legitimate use of violence slides easily for many people into the idea that the use of violence by legitimate agents of a legitimate state is itself legitimate. By this account, since the power of the state is ultimately grounded in control over the means of violence, the use of violence by agents of the state is simply an extension and expression of their power. It matters for this account that the state is legitimate, that it brings about and enforces a rule of law, that its agents obtain their offices through proper procedures, and so on. Given a legitimate state whose officials are trying to enforce the law, however, many people think that the maintenance of such "law and order" requires a "show of force." Some might go further: law enforcement officials and other state agents ought to display their willingness to employ the means of violence in order to ensure obedience to the law, and they are most convincing in this display if they actually use violence on a regular basis.

Such an understanding of state power does have a concept of the abuse of power by police. When police use their power in ways that promote their personal gain, when they are corrupt or themselves criminal, they grossly abuse their power. A conception of state power that sees it as grounded in or inherently connected to violence, however, has great difficulty forming a concept of police brutality under circumstances when police believe they are properly doing their job. As long as the official is acting "in the line of duty" and claims that the violent acts are normal or necessary, it seems that many people find them morally acceptable.

As I have discussed above, according to the alternative conceptualization suggested by Arendt, the power of states consists in ways they institutionalize the ability for collective action. State institutions can organize decision making and executive bodies that mobilize to solve collective problems and then the energy to solve them. They actualize this potential only to the extent that people work in them with one another to bring about those results through consciously coordinated action. When state institutions fail to create and implement solutions to collective problems or enact collective visions, which is often, they lack power, and no amount of violence will compensate for that lack. Indeed, the use of violence against those who fail to join the effort is more likely to weaken the ability of the collective to act than to enhance it.

This does not mean that powerful state institutions cannot and should not sometimes force people to abide by its laws and regulations and contribute to its collective goals. *Coercion* is an inevitable and proper aspect of legal regulation. The sovereigntist view of state power, however, too quickly equates coercion with the threat of violence. I do not have the space to develop a full argument for the claim here, but I suggest that successful coercion is usually more a result of power than of violence. Where there are settled laws and regulations whose objectives are clear and widely accepted, and which were legislated by means of legitimate procedures, then those who attempt to violate or circumvent the laws suffer various forms of sanction, shaming, and punishment often without any violence at all being brought to bear. Some people who would otherwise not do what these laws require are motivated to obey them because they fear these consequences, but this is not the same as saying that they are motivated by the threat of violence.

Arendt's account of power and violence suggests that the use of official violence is always deeply problematic and always calls for specific justification. It can never be regarded as normal and legitimate, because it cannot appeal to founding first principles that authorize it, and because each act of violence endangers the trust and security on which collective power rests. Some acts of official violence may be justified, but these can only be decided case by case, according to restrictive criteria like those I outlined above: their scope is limited, their effects immediate and contained, and the harm they prevent worse than the one they inflict. Insofar as coercive regulation may rely on the use of physical restraint and force to subdue resisters, it may sometimes be justified. There ought to be the strongest presumption against the infliction of injury, however, let alone killing. My observation of contemporary police practices in the United States today, as well as many other places, leads me to conclude that many police officers as well as citizens consider such acts a normal and acceptable extension of state power. Every specific act of official violence, however, needs as much justification as acts of violence committed by others, and nothing can legitimate them in advance.

Martha Minow is right to worry that the state's embrace of violence in such systems as police training for assaulting, shooting. and brutalizing suspects may contribute to a general societal approval of violence. She points to a few cities in the United States that have embraced community policing as an alternative model by which to structure the entire practice of policing, where "the use of state power does not model the violence it is intended to prevent."[19] Community policing is a decades-old concept in the United States, of course; its concepts and practices in most cities, however, are confined only to a few neighborhoods or programs, alongside and in the context of more general models of policing that rely on threat and use of violence as normal. This balance should at least be reversed, with threats of violence infrequent and contained within a context of organized citizen cooperation and watchfulness.

SO-CALLED HUMANITARIAN INTERVENTION

The last two decades have seen swift support for the conviction that human rights principles should override the claim by states that sovereignty gives them the absolute right to regulate what goes on in their territories in whatever way they choose. There is increasing support in the world for the principle that, especially when there are serious and extensive violations of human rights by a state, or when a state is unable to protect its citizens from massive violence, outside agents not only have a right but a duty to intervene to try to protect lives and well-being. I endorse this general direction of international law that limits state sovereignty for the sake of promoting human rights. Nevertheless, I find disturbing that some international actors appear to assume that such commitments to human rights themselves legitimate the decision by some states to make war on others. Arendt's distinctions between power and violence, and particularly her argument that violence may sometimes be justified but never legitimate, are useful, I suggest, for reflecting on moral issues of so-called humanitarian intervention. I shall argue that these issues about the morally appropriate use of violence parallel those concerning domestic police action.

The judgment has become widespread that the sovereignty of states that seriously violate human rights can be overridden by outsiders who seek to prevent or sanction such violation. International law concerning human rights requires transparency and enforcement, and only state institutions have the powers these requirements imply. In the absence of global state institutions today, single states or coalitions of states recently have taken it upon themselves to act as global police, invading other states or bombing them from above, they claim for the purposes of enforcing human rights. The assumption seems to be strong that it is morally permissible and may be morally required for states to engage in military action against states that violate human rights.

A relatively new development in this evolving human rights regime consists in efforts to legitimate such interventions. Especially in the last decade, some of the world's strongest military powers and alliances have engaged in nondefensive military actions for which they have first sought and claimed to have received legal or quasi-legal authorization. Western powers sought and received the approval of the UN Security Council before they launched their war against Iraq. While the NATO war against Yugoslavia did not have the authorization of the United Nations, NATO claimed that it was legitimate because of the process of discussion and decision making that took place among the leaders of its nineteen members, as well as among a few states outside the alliance. In such processes, world military forces attempt to legitimate their actions when they appeal to international principles they claim have or ought to have the force of law, and when they can point to procedures of international discussion and decision making that they claim authorize their actions. The opinion seems to be taking hold among powerful international leaders and many in the general public, moreover, that the use of violence against "rogue" states is acceptable and normal, and needs little or no justification beyond a consensus that the state is a law breaker.

If Arendt's account of violence and power is right, however, such immediate and massive resort to violence as a tool of international law enforcement may be a sign of impotence more than power. I believe that this evolving situation where some states and perhaps also the United Nations speak and act as though they were legitimate agents empowered to do what they judge necessary to enforce the law may be at least as dangerous to peace and international stability as is international anarchy. There appears to be little international imagination for alternative methods of motivating or compelling compliance with human rights norms, and almost no international will to install competent institutions that could enact more settled discussion and cooperation among peoples of the world. When war, indeed devastating war, is almost the first resort of international police powers, and when states engage in what they believe is righteous violence, it opens gulfs of distrust.

In Arendt's account, the use of violence in international relations can be no more legitimate than in domestic life. While international violence, like domestic violence, may sometimes be justified, there too justification must be in terms of its consequences and not by appeal to any supposedly authorizing covenants or principles. Especially when air war and the use of indiscriminate weapons such as land mines are the preferred military means, the claim that such violence is justified is usually difficult to sustain in Arendt's terms: the destruction is too massive, the consequences too long term and unpredictable, too many lives are risked and lost, especially those of civilians. In this era when weapons of mass destruction continue to proliferate, their use against a state on one occasion stimulates their defensive accumulation by others. At the beginning of her essay, Arendt declares that these frightful instruments of war have rendered such action irrational. "The technical development of implements of violence has now reached the point where no political goal could conceivably correspond to their destructive potential or justify their actual use in armed conflict. Hence, warfare—from time immemorial the final merciless arbiter in international disputes—has lost much of its effectiveness and nearly all its glamour" (p. 3).

So I will return to my beginning, the NATO war against Yugoslavia. There are significant similarities between this war and incidents of police brutality. NATO claimed that its actions were aimed at stopping the perpetration of crimes by a rogue state. That state had committed crimes against humanity, and NATO claimed to be acting as a legal agent for humanity itself, rather than acting to further its on specific treaty interests or the specific interests of its member nations. NATO officials spoke and acted as if this police-for-the-world role authorized it to use any and all military force in whatever way and for as long as necessary to achieve its objective, the military defeat of Yugoslavia and the capitulation of its president to the terms NATO set for the return of the Kosovar Albanians and the establishment of a government in which they would exercise self-government.

The Independent International Commission on Kosovo, of which Martha Minow was a member, concluded in its report that the NATO war was not legal, because it did not have UN authorization. The Commission argues, however, that the war was legitimate. Given the harms coming to Albanian Kosovars, the fact that NATO is multinational, had procedures for deliberation, and had the capacity for military intervention, the Commission agrees with the claim that NATO in this case was acting for humanity in response to a humanitarian crisis. One of its major recommendations for the future of international relations is that institutions and procedures be put in place that can put the legal authorization of humanitarian wars on a firmer footing.[20]

I have argued above that it is a mistake to think that the fact that the state authorizes police to enforce the law itself licenses police to be violent. Use of violent means by police must be independently justified not by appeal to prior authorization, but by showing that the consequences of the violent acts will prevent more harm than they produce. The same holds, I contend, for international relations. I hope that the world is moving toward a condition where there are stronger transnational institutions with the ability legally to authorize multinational and global organizations to police the behavior of states toward the people within their territories as well as toward other states. It is dangerous to assume, however, that stronger institutions of international law themselves can and should authorize the use of violence. Just as in the domestic case, violence must be justified by arguing that it is the only means available to do good, that it does more good than harm, and that it is effective without having undesirable long-term consequences. By such reasoning, I submit that the NATO war was not justified.

Despite its conclusion that the war was legitimate, the Independent Commission also offers much evidence that the war did not achieve its objectives of saving the lives and society of the Albanian Kosovars, and that, in general, it wreaked more destruction than it prevented. Before March 1999, Serbian forces had employed terror to drive many Albanians in Kosovo away from their homes, but after European protection monitors were pulled out in advance of the NATO bombing campaign, the forced removal and killing of civilians by Serb forces hugely increased. While the report lays first responsibility for the death and suffering inflicted on the removed Kosovars at the feet of the leaders of the Republic of Yugoslavia, they find nevertheless that the NATO campaign aided and abetted the "ethnic cleansing" operation. Not only did the Western "humanitarian" war contribute to suffering on a mass scale, but neither the NATO states nor the United States were at all prepared to respond to the masses of people flooding over burdened border states.

After the war, most of the refugees returned to Kosovo, but it is hard to say that they went home. The bombing had virtually destroyed the country. Around 120,000 houses in Kosovo were destroyed or damaged by the war, and 250 schools needed repair. Roads were in ruins, bridges destroyed, telephone lines down, and there was no electricity. Thousands of unexploded cluster bombs lay in fields and alleys, and are still killing people. Both the uranium dioxide released into the atmosphere by some of the shells and the toxic leaks caused by some of the bombs have made Kosovo an environmental disaster area.

The war not only destroyed economic and environmental infrastructure, but institutions as well. At war's end, there was no functioning health care system, judiciary, or banking system. To the extent that any local governments remained, most were unable to police the streets or perform even the most basic municipal services.

The moral calculation of the consequences of the NATO war must count harm to Serbs as well as to Albanians. Because NATO was unable seriously to weaken the Serbian military with its air war, it took the war to the cities of the north, where endangering civilians was unavoidable; about 500 civilians were killed in Serbia, and at least 820 wounded by NATO sorties. Many more suffered as a result of the virtual elimination of electricity, telecommunications, and industrial capacity of the country.

The war's aftermath so far does not give hope that its long-term consequences are positive. The forces occupying Kosovo under the official mandate of the United Nations could not prevent the killing of hundreds of Serbs from Kosovo, and the expulsion of most of the rest. Since June 1999 Albanian Kosovars have not exercised the self-government they desire, but have effectively been ruled by an international organization. Ethnic conflict and distrust in the region have not abated and are probably worse as a consequence of the war.[21]

Based on the account of violence that I have derived from Arendt, war cannot be legitimated, as NATO tried to do, but it may perhaps be justified. Such justification comes only by appeal to consequences, I have argued, and those consequences must take all persons affected equally into account. Despite its allegedly noble purposes, then, I think we must conclude that the NATO war was wrong. Theorists, political leaders, and citizens should be careful not to confuse violence with power, whether exercised by legitimate agents of the state or international law. In an age of brutality, we should be very suspicious of the use of violence, and do far more to build institutions that organize the power of collective action without violence.

Notes

1. Hannah Arendt, *On Violence* (New York: Harcourt Brace and Company, 1969).

2. There are a few exceptions. See Ted Honderich, *Violence for Equality* (London: Routledge, 1989), and Sergio Cotta, *Why Violence* (University of Florida Press, 1985).

3. John McGowan does focus specifically on the concept of violence in Arendt. See McGowan, "Must Politics be Violent? Arendt's Utopian Vision," in Craig Calhoun and John McGowan, eds., *Hannah Arendt and the Meaning of Politics* (Minneapolis: University of Minnesota Press, 1997), pp. 263–96.

4. I am grateful to the following people for comments on an earlier version of this essay that saved me from much wrong-headedness: David Alexander, Bat-Ami Bar On, Leah Bradshaw, Michael Geyer, Bonnie Honig, Jeffrey Isaac, Patchen Markell, Martin Matustik, Nancy Rosenblum, William Scheuerman, and Dana Villa.

5. Martha Minow, "Between Nations and Between Intimates: Can Law Stop the Violence?," esp. this volume.

6. See Robert Bernasconi, "The Double Face of the Political and the Social: Hannah Arendt and America's Racial Divisions," *Research in Phenomenology* XXVI (1996): 3–24; Anne Norton, "Heart of Darkness: Africa and African Americans in the Writings of Hannah Arendt," in Bonnie Honig, ed., *Feminist Interpretations of Hannah Arendt* (University Park: Pennsylvania State University Press, 1995), pp. 247–62.

7. The best critique of Arendt's idea of the social and its separation from the political is Hanna Pitkin's. See Pitkin, *The Attack of the Blob* (Berkeley: University of California Press, 1999).

8. For the purposes of this essay, I am limiting discussion to physical forms of violence; their incidence is frequent and horrible enough to call urgently for inquiry. I recognize that there may well be phenomena of psychological violence, various ways that people are able to destroy the spirit of other persons without doing them bodily damage. Indeed, some of Arendt's other writings have rich veins to mine for such a concept of psychological violence. Because nonphysical forms of violence present more serious conceptual problems, and because the phenomenon Arendt seems most concerned with in this essay is violence that involves bringing physical pain to, wounding, or killing human beings, I limit my discussion here to that form.

9. Arendt, *The Human Condition* (Chicago: University of Chicago Press, 1958), esp. chapter 28.

10. Max Weber, "Politics as a Vocation," in H. H. Gerth and C. Wright Mills, *From Max Weber* (New York: Oxford University Press, 1946), pp. 77–78; Jurgen Habermas contrasts Weber's instrumental and positivistic view of state power with Arendt's view, which he interprets as more normative and based in commu-

nication. See Habermas, "Hannah Arendt on the Concept of Power," in *Philosophical-Political Profiles* (Cambridge, MA: MIT Press, 1983), pp. 171–88.

11. See Arendt, "What is Authority?" in *Between Past and Future* (New York: Viking Press, 1968), pp. 91–142.

12. Compare Leah Bradshaw, "Political Authority and Violence," paper presented at the Canadian Political Science Association meetings, Quebec City, August 2000.

13. Nancy C. M. Hartsock suggests that in fact Arendt does undermine her concept of power by saying that power and violence often occur together. See Hartsock, *Money, Sex and Power* (New York: Longman, 1983), pp. 220–21.

14. Jeffrey Isaac, *Arendt, Camus and Modern Rebellion* (New Haven: Yale University Press, 1992), p. 149.

15. See Pitkin, *The Attack of the Blob.*

16. Arendt, *On Revolution* (New York: Viking Press, 1965), p. 175.

17. Max Weber, "Politics as a Vocation," pp. 79–81; "The Social Psychology of World Religions," in Gerth and Mills, *From Max Weber*, p. 294.

18. "Between Nations and Between Intimates: Can Law Stop the Violence?," p. 67.

19. "Between Nations and Between Intimates," p. 70.

20. Independent International Commission on Kosovo, *Kosovo Report: Conflict, International Response, Lessons Learned* (Oxford: Oxford University Press, 2000), esp. chapters 6 and 10.

21. Information about the conduct of the war and its aftermath drawn from the *Kosovo Report*, chapters 3, 4, and 10.

Ross E. Cheit is Associate Professor of Political Science and Public Policy at Brown University. He is currently working on a book about the law and politics of child sexual abuse cases in the United States. **Carey Jaros** graduated from Brown University in 2000 with a B.A. in Law and Public Policy. She is currently an Associate Consultant at Bain & Company in Boston.

Marc Galanter is the John and Rylla Bosshard Professor of Law and South Asian Studies at the University of Wisconsin, Madison, and Centennial Professor at the London School of Economics and Political Science. He has written extensively on litigation, lawyers, and legal culture in the United States, India, and the United Kingdom.

Fredrick C. Harris is Associate Professor of Political Science and Director of the Center for the Study of African-American Politics at the University of Rochester. He is the author of *Something Within: Religion in African-American Politics*, which won the V. O. Key Award for Best Book in Southern Politics and the Distinguished Book Award from the Society for the Scientific Study of Religion.

Judith Lewis Herman, M.D., is Clinical Professor of Psychiatry at Harvard Medical School and Director of Training at the Victims of Violence Program at Cambridge (MA) Hospital. Dr. Herman is the author of two award-winning books: *Father-Daughter Incest* and *Trauma and Recovery*. She has lectured widely on the subject of sexual and domestic violence.

Frederick M. Lawrence is Law Alumni Scholar and Professor of Law at the Boston University School of Law. He has published articles concerning bias-motivated violence, federal criminal civil rights laws, and freedom of speech, and is the author of *Punishing Hate: Bias Crimes Under American Law*. He was awarded an Inns of Court Fellowship in 1996 at the Institute for Advanced Legal Studies in London and a Ford Foundation Grant in 1998 and 1999 for the study of racially motivated crimes under British law. Prior to joining the Boston University faculty, Professor Lawrence was an Assistant U.S. Attorney for the Southern District of New York, and was Chief of the Civil Rights Unit of that office from 1986 to 1988.

Martha Minow has taught at Harvard Law School since 1981. Her books include *Making All the Difference: Inclusion, Exclusion, and American Law; Not Only for Myself: Identity, Politics and Law;* and *Between Vengeance and Forgiveness: Facing History After Genocide and Mass Violence.* She has served on the Independent International Commission on Kosovo, established by Sweden, and she is an adviser to Facing History and Ourselves, a nonprofit organization devoted to training teachers and developing curricular materials to help young people resist violence and intergroup oppression.

Nancy L. Rosenblum is Professor of Government at Harvard University. She is the author most recently of *Membership and Morals: The Personal Uses of Pluralism in America,* editor of *Obligations of Citizenship and Demands of Faith: Religious Accommodation in Pluralist Democracies,* and co-editor with Robert C. Post of *Civil Society and Government.*

Austin Sarat is William Nelson Cromwell Professor of Jurisprudence and Political Science at Amherst College and director of the college's program in Law, Jurisprudence, and Social Thought. He is author and editor of many books, most recently *When the State Kills: Capital Punishment and the American Condition* and the edited collections *Pain, Death, and the Law* and (with Thomas R. Kearns) *Law and Human Rights: Concepts, Contests, Contingencies.*

Ayelet Shachar is Assistant Professor of Law in the Faculty of Law, University of Toronto. She has written extensively on issues of group rights and gender equality as well as citizenship theory and immigration law. She is the author of *Multicultural Jurisdictions: Cultural Differences and Women's Rights.*

Eric K. Yamamoto is a Professor of Law at the William S. Richardson School of Law at the University of Hawaii, Manoa. For 2001–2002 he held the Haywood Burns Civil Rights Chair at the CUNY Law School in New York. Professor Yamamoto is a noted human rights lawyer.

Iris Marion Young is a Professor of Political Science at the University of Chicago. She is the author of *Justice and the Politics of Difference* and most recently *Inclusion and Democracy.*